Vera Sokolova

CULTURAL POLITICS OF ETHNICITY

Discourses on Roma in Communist Czechoslovakia

ibidem-Verlag
Stuttgart

Bibliografische Information der Deutschen Nationalbibliothek
Die Deutsche Nationalbibliothek verzeichnet diese Publikation in der Deutschen Nationalbibliografie; detaillierte bibliografische Daten sind im Internet über http://dnb.d-nb.de abrufbar.

Bibliographic information published by the Deutsche Nationalbibliothek
Die Deutsche Nationalbibliothek lists this publication in the Deutsche Nationalbibliografie; detailed bibliographic data are available in the Internet at http://dnb.d-nb.de.

Cover picture: Bill Thompson, III

∞

Gedruckt auf alterungsbeständigem, säurefreien Papier
Printed on acid-free paper

ISSN: 1614-3515

ISBN-10: 3-89821-864-3
ISBN-13: 978-3-89821-864-1

Printed in Germany

Contents

Acknowledgements

In researching and writing this book I benefited from the support and help of many people and institutions. First and foremost, I would like to acknowledge and thank for the institutional, financial and intellectual support my graduate Alma matter, the University of Washington in Seattle, especially the departments of history and anthropology, where this research project began. Professor Uta G. Poiger, her work, energy and support, have for many years been the driving inspirational force guiding my own intellectual and academic development, for which I would like to take this opportunity to deeply thank. Professor James R. Felak never let me get away with an argument or thought without a fierce battle, forcing me to always think through the furthest implications of my suggestions and conclusions. These exercises, which I loved and hated at the same time, have left a deep impact on my ability to critically scrutinize texts of others as well as my own arguments. Many of my friends and colleagues both at the University of Washington and elsewhere have participated in reading and discussing various aspects of this book. In particular, I would like to thank for friendship, support and intellectual inspiration over many years to Kari Tupper, Kate Brown, Jitka Malečková, Rob Mitchell, Teri Balkenende, Paulina Bren, Robert Self, Ali Igmen, Katherine David-Fox, Norman Wacker, Mirek Vodrážka, Gabriela Vorlová, Hanka Bartošová, Bridget Alexander, Heidi Strupp, Marie Noe, Miroslav Noe, Jana Štěpánová, and Nicole Borůvka.

The research for this project and writing of this book could not have been carried out without the generous financial support of many fellowships and grants, which I held over the years from the University of Washington (Aldon Duanne Bell Award in Women's History, Chester Fritz Fellowship, Rondeau Evans Fellowship); Association of Women in Slavic Studies; Social Science Research Council; Wodroow Wilson International Center for Scholars in Washington, D.C.; the Ford Foundation; Open Society Fund; the New School for Social Research in New York; Center for Advanced Holocaust

Studies USHMM in Washington, D.C.; and the School of Humanities of Charles University in Prague.

After my return to Prague, my work and intellectual interests grew in new exciting directions, especially thanks to the working environment of the budding department of gender studies at the School of humanities of Charles University in Prague. This milieu has opened new research questions and theoretical intersections in front of me, which have been reflected in the pages of this book. In particular, I would like to thank my friends and colleagues Kateřina Kolářová, Petr Pavlík, Hana Havelková, Blanka Knotková-Čapková, and Zuzana Kiczková, who have provided tremendous help and support in the past several years, as I was trying to finish this project. Also, many of my students have brought meaning to my work, have challenged my thinking, and have provided inspiration to my research and writing. I would like to thank them all.

On a personal level, I would like to thank especially my mom and my brother, who have always supported me in everything and anything I have done. Last, but certainly not least, my deepest thanks and love go to Michael L. Smith, my life partner and companion, who has contributed a lion's share to everything I do. Without his presence, support, intellect, patience and wisdom this project could not have been completed.

To end with, I would like to thank very much dr. Andreas Umland and ***ibidem***-Verlag for their interest in my work. As well, the anonymous reviewer provided insightful and useful commentary, which I believe has significantly improved the final version of this book. Of course, all responsibility for the arguments, assertions and conclusions on the following pages is purely my own.

Introduction

This book maps out the history of the linguistic and social practices directed at the Roma during the communist period and explains how contemporary Czech society has come to understand the Romani population in terms of inherited social, medical and juridical ideas.[1] Rather than focusing on the Roma as the object of analysis, I problematize assumed notions of "Gypsiness" and "Czechness" in mainstream society by highlighting the role of a number of different socialist discourses in constructing images of the Roma as socially deviant and abnormal. By uncovering the lines of continuity in the intersections of ethnic discrimination, social deviance and citizenship from the 1950s to the collapse of communism, this book comes to terms with a variety of questions that have not been so far adequately addressed in the literature. What under-

1 This book uses several terms to refer to the Roma: Roma, Romani, Romany, Gypsy, and gypsy. The usage of these terms makes an effort to be historically and conceptually consistent. When referring to arguments I am making, when I discuss the present context and when I use or point to the present self-identification of the Roma, I use the term "Roma." "Romani" indicates a modifier referring to, for example, Romani population, Romani parenting, Romani behavior, etc. Following the main linguistic trend, I use "Romany" to designate the standardized Romani language. When discussing primary documents, the work strictly adheres to the terminology used in the sources, thus predominantly using the term "Gypsy" or "gypsy," depending on whether the documents themselves use a capital or lower "g." However, since the main arguments of the book relate to the discursive production and perception of "Gypsiness," the term "gypsy" is also used in all contexts when I am trying to demonstrate "gypsy" as a constructed concept. When commenting on rhetoric used in documents, I leave the term as it is. When I refer to Roma as *perceived* as "Gypsies," I use parentheses to indicate the constructedness of the term. A detailed discussion of my conceptual and theoretical understanding of the construction and "reality" of "Gypsiness" and Romani culture in chapter one makes it clear that I do not consider "Roma" to be some authentic, primordial identity that would signify the "real" essence as opposed to their constructedness as "Gypsies." Rather, I see both concepts as constructed. The crucial aspect of my distinctive usage of these two terms is the context in which they are constructed and used, how they are politicized and what significations they carry in public discourses. Since "Roma" has been primarily used by people who either identify themselves as such or for various reasons claim to speak on their behalf, while "Gypsy" historically bears the connotations of speaking about the "Other" from the superior position of the "Self", in the general narrative of the book I maintain this distinction.

lying assumptions informed the socialist regime's understanding of "Gypsiness," and how did these conceptions relate to notions of citizenship, equality and normality? How and why did the meaning of the terms "Gypsies" and "Roma" become imbued in popular discourse with perceived unhealthiness and social deviance? And finally, what implications does this historical process of translating the perceived lifestyles and culture of the Roma into non-ethnic frames of reference have for understanding racism[2] and ethnic sensibilities in the country today?

Two historical examples can illustrate the fundamental questions this book will address. First, in 1958, the communist regime passed a law prohibiting nomadism. Nomads were defined as people who "wander from place to place, even if they are permanently registered in some village, and avoid honest work or support themselves through dishonest activity."[3] Second, in 1972, the Ministries of Health of both federal republics of Czechoslovakia issued a Sterilization Decree designed to prevent the involuntary and ill-informed sterilization of all Czechoslovak citizens by outlining strict requirements an applicant had to fulfill in order to be granted permission to undergo the procedure.[4]

These two laws, passed almost fifteen years apart, had three important traits in common. First, they both claimed to be "protective" laws. Second, nowhere in either law was there a mention of race or ethnicity. And third, both laws were used to target the Roma, denying them basic civil and human

---

2 This book uses a specific definition of the concept of "racism," which is not connected primarily to the usage of the term as derived from physical anthropology. This argument posits that 'racism' is useful only when used and applied in connection with the concept of race and the ensuing fixation on "typical" racial traits. In this sense, this usage describes the racist attitudes of the late 19th and first half of the 20th centuries, referring to the physical mergers on the background of the idea of evolution. The concept of "racism" that this book is using adheres to the argument that racism consists in intentional practices and policies and unintended processes or consequences of attitudes towards the ethnic 'other'. Thus, this book argues, it is not necessary to possess a concept of 'race' in order to describe and analyze prejudices and discrimination towards other peoples.

3 "Law About Permanent Settlement of Nomadic Persons" (*Zákon o trvalém usídlení kočujících osob*) č. 74/1958 Sb. Ustava ČSSR.

4 "Decree on Sterilization, Bulletin of the Ministry of Health of the Czech and Slovak Socialist Republic" (*Věstník Ministerstva Zdravotnictví České a Slovenské socialistické republiky,*) Part 1-2, Volume XX, February 29, 1972.

rights. In compliance with the first law, Czechoslovak nomadic Roma, who constituted less than ten percent of the overall Romani population of Czechoslovakia, were suddenly and forcibly settled. Through the same law, many of the settled Roma were deliberately categorized as "nomadic" or "half-nomadic" based of their alleged "deviant" lifestyle or behavior, and had their names placed on a registry, which made them vulnerable to constant surveillance, harassment and discrimination. As a result of the second law, Romani women were sterilized at an astonishingly higher rate than non-Romani women and forced into sterilization either through threats by social workers or through state-promoted financial incentives.

The application of these two laws, arguably the most extreme examples of repressive policies used against the Roma, raises urgent questions about the politics of ethnicity in Communist Czechoslovakia: How and why were these ethnicity-neutral and "protective" laws translated into practice as punitive laws that distinguished the Roma by ethnicity? Why did Czechoslovak doctors, lawyers, educators and social scientists read these laws as a license to enact a policy of Romani assimilation? How and by whom were the boundaries between "Gypsies," "Czechs" and "Slovaks" drawn and what consequences did these definitions have?

This book explores the "Gypsy question" (*cikánská otázka*) in communist Czechoslovakia and examines what state policies toward the Roma tell us about citizenship and the relationship of state and society under Czechoslovak communism. It illustrates how the Czechoslovak state treated the Roma as a problem, indeed an obstacle to progress, and how it inconspicuously tried to assimilate them out of existence.[5] However, many laws and policies that in practice targeted the Roma, denying them basic civil and human rights, were in theory ethnicity-neutral, treating the "objects" of the policies as "socially backward or pathological" elements. Though there were occasional references to Romani distinctiveness as cultural difference, gradually

[5] There is, of course, a fundamental difference between the end of the existence of the Roma per se and the end of their existence as a distinct ethnicity or culture separate from the Czechs and Slovaks. Despite the disturbing practice of encouraged and forced sterilization of Romani women, discussed in detail in chapter six, the main process of "disappearance" of "Gypsies" happened in the discursive realms of demographic statistics and scientific studies, based on the Roma's ability and willingness to conform to the mainstream behavioral and social norms.

"Gypsy" came to be defined primarily in terms of social deviance. The book traces this process of the discursive production of knowledge *about* the Roma under communism, investigating how and why this rhetoric of deviance replaced the rhetoric of ethnicity as the fundamental framework of state policies dealing with the Roma.

The dismissal of Romani ethnic difference as mere social deviance allowed the non-Romani majority to collectively deal with its anxiety about "Gypsies" without explicitly referring to their ethnicity. Though a more general study of the perception of the Roma by Czechoslovak society at large would be valuable, my work focuses on the political and broadly social arena where state bureaucrats and local political officials used the rhetoric of deviance to specifically target, subordinate and assimilate the Romani population. Focusing on the discrepancies between written laws and policies (that were ethnicity neutral and promoted as "protective") and their implementation (which resulted in punitive practices directly targeting the Roma), this book seeks to expose the intricate relationships between official beliefs, institutional policies and popular consciousness under the communist regime. For it was these relationships that informed each other and together created the mechanisms of social control that enabled the discrimination of Czechoslovak Roma to flourish under the guise of social welfare.

It is impossible to blame exclusively the "regime," "Roma" or "people" for the discrimination, because there was no main agent or perpetrator that masterfully carried out a plan of coercion and assimilation. Instead, the peculiar shape of discrimination against the Roma was made possible and framed by popular discourses about health, socialization and normality that were reinforced by official communist ideology. Because such discourses were key instruments of power and social control under communism, the following chapters have a strong Foucauldian undertone. At the same time, human agency does matter. For one, the Roma were not passive recipients of their fate. They found means to engage the production of categories and policies, largely aimed at their subordination, in ways that benefited them. For example, at least some Romani women used sterilization, available to them thanks to discriminatory attitudes of Czechoslovak doctors and social workers much more readily than to non-Romani women, as a defense tool against their own unwanted pregnancies. The Gypsy-Roma Union, even though established as an assimilative institution which was designed to reeducate the Roma into "Czechs" and "Slovaks" and gradually strip them of their own culture, never gave up the struggle of articulating a distinct Romani ethnicity in the face of its continual dismissal. And the profound Romani segregation, both in housing and in the educational system, which was a living contradiction of the official rhetoric of inclusion and equality, throughout the years of the communist regime played a role in providing a sense of cohesion and group consciousness among the Roma, based on which they were able to start building their political identity after 1989.

Perhaps even more importantly, by focusing on local bureaucrats and officials who implemented official policies and projected popular discourses into their evaluations, my work argues that discriminatory policies were in practice a direct outcome of the activities and judgments of local actors who used popular conceptions of "Gypsies" as their frames of reference. Without these local actors, the sometimes well-intended and egalitarian welfare policies of the regime would not have been implemented in such blatantly discriminatory ways. Focusing on the construction of "Gypsy" as a label of social deviance, this work disrupts the comfortable assumption that Roma were easily identifiable subjects whose history can be non-problematically separated from the history of "Czechs" and "Slovaks."

The discursive shift of replacing the ethnic and cultural content of the term "Gypsy" with ideas from social pathology (for the purposes of assimilation) was accompanied by a redefinition of "Gypsy culture" and Romani collective values with allegations of their filthy lifestyle, incompetent parenthood, unhealthy reproduction, unnatural sexuality, etc. The articulation of the cultural difference of the Roma depended largely on the binary opposition of "normal," meaning Czech or Slovak, and "deviant" or "backward," meaning "Gypsy". The perception of social difference was integral to articulating ethnic difference without using the rhetoric of ethnicity.[6] As a result of these negative and pejorative projections, many Roma tried to escape stigmatization by dis-

6 For a similar argument in a different context, see an insightful article by Eric D. Weitz, "Racial Politics without the Concept of Race: Reevaluating Soviet Ethnic and National Purges," *Slavic Review*, 61:1 (Spring 2002):1-29.

tancing themselves from these notions of "Gypsiness," which in turn facilitated a social erosion of a potential unified Romani ethnic and cultural identity.[7]

As sociologist Jan Průcha argued, the communist past has produced a certain paradox. Current generations of Czechs (and Slovaks), aged 30 to 60, grew up in an artificially homogenous society, where various kinds of diversity – racial, ethnic, cultural or sexual – were presented as matters distant in time and place. Despite its overbearing ideological component, social education under communism was based on ideas of humanism and equality that instilled in many Czechs and Slovaks the belief that racism is something wrong, detestable and foreign.[8] At the same time, in the aftermath of the Second World War people very rarely encountered difference and diversity, and when they did, they were generally taught to understand such differences as social pathologies. The paradox is that while classical "scientific racism" or explicit racial discrimination were virtually absent in the official public sphere under communism, today's nationalism, xenophobia and implicit racism have in fact deep historical roots in communist society. In the recent study, Průcha aptly expressed the essence of the problem when he argued that "for millions of Czech the only standard of humanity is 'decency' (*slušnost*) – behavior appropriate to generally accepted norms. At the same time, since childhood we are taught that there exists only one decency. To dehumanize the 'indecent' ones then is very easy."[9]

---

7 However, this is not to argue that there otherwise certainly would have been a unified Romani ethnic and cultural identity. Even today, Romani unity is mostly regional, often based around clan/family affiliations, with a fair amount of inter-familial rivalry and clash. Rather, this was to point out that the circumstances of the pejorative and negative projections effectively prevented any possibility of even working on a positive and unified Romani identity.

8 Jan Průcha, *Multikulturní výchova: Teorie, praxe, výzkum*. (Praha: nakladatelství ISV, 2001). For a valuable treatment of contemporary Czech ethnic tolerance (or the lack thereof) toward the Roma from the Western perspective, see especially Rick Fawn, "Czech Attitudes Towards the Roma: 'Expecting More of Havel's Country'?" *Europe-Asia Studies*, 53:8 (2001): 1193-1219. Fawn also argues that there is a paradox between the derogatory and often discriminatory treatment of the Roma on the one hand and "the ethos of liberalism and tolerance accorded to Czech society by many of its own citizens, intellectual and law makers, and especially by its admirers and supporters abroad" on the other hand. (p. 1193).

9 Průcha, 11.

In fact, decency – or what I have been calling normality – was used by the communist regime as a mechanism of social control (often in the guise of social welfare), and applied to perceived patterns of Romani behavior, such as their educational habits, sexual habits, forms of public congregation, and so on. However, most authors writing on the Czech Roma, and East European Roma in general, have fairly positive assessments of the communist machinery of social welfare and praise the efforts and intentions of the regime to enhance the economic conditions and possibilities of the Roma. These authors acknowledge that discrimination and repression were taking place, but attribute these shortcomings to the structural impossibilities of communism and resulting inadequacy of the system.[10]

On the one hand, these authors praise communist bureaucrats for their egalitarian values and just intentions, regardless of the final outcome of state policies toward the Roma. On the other hand, they see the assimilative policies toward the Roma as a necessary side effect of the communist ideology and the paternalistic efforts of the regime in general. In many ways, these authors identify "intentions" in a context-free way. What is not adequately addressed in their analyses is an examination of how even "the best of intentions" were inscribed within an institutional and discursive context that transformed intended policy goals from the start, and with the help of local officials "from below," led to discriminatory policy outcomes quite opposite from what one can purport those intentions might have been.[11]

Another group of scholars, analyzing the high degree of racial discrimination and ethnic violence in Eastern Europe after 1989, argue (or at least assume) that these are relatively new phenomena that emerged as an effect of the democratic and economic transitions after the collapse of commu-

---

[10] Among these authors belong, for example, Zoltan Barany, David Crowe, Tomáš Grulich, Vladimír Šedivý, or Viktor Mároši (all discussed and cited later) or the edited volume by Will Guy, ed., *Between Past and Future: The Roma of Central and Eastern Europe* (Hatfield: University of Hertfordshire Press, 2002).

[11] A notable exception to this trend is a recent excellent and quite critical study of the institutional treatment of the Roma in the Czech lands during the communist regime by Czech historian from Ostrava University Nina Pavelčíková, *Romové v českých zemích v letech 1945-1989.* SEŠITY Úřadu dokumentace a vyšetřování zločinů komunismu č. 12 (Praha: ÚDV, 2004).

nism.[12] As a number of political analysts have theorized, economic "shock therapy" could lead to social backlashes against reformist ideas in the name of nationalism or protectionism.[13] The successive shocks on Czech and Slovak society after 1989 – democratization, immigration, globalization, market reforms, and insecurity in a new world – are all seen as determinants of xenophobia and intolerance toward minorities.[14] As a correlate to this view, the communist regime is seen as largely a-xenophobic and neutral on the question of race. According to sociologist Pavel Říčan, "the Roma were accepted quite well [...] Racist aversion against them – if it existed at all – was low."[15]

While not disparaging the significance of post-communist political and economic shocks, my work emphasizes the historical continuities between contemporary xenophobia and the strategies the communist regime used to deal with the "Gypsy question." Rather than seeing democratization and post-communist shocks as historical ruptures that produced xenophobia from within themselves, my work argues that these events simply facilitated the explicit manifestation of xenophobia, while the origins and underlying motivations for xenophobic and racist behavior were rooted in the kinds of political practices and popular discourses this book will narrate.[16] The communist re-

---

[12] The proponents of this view include, for example, Eric Hockenos, *Free to Hate: the Rise of the Right in Post-Communist Eastern Europe* (New York: Routledge, 1993); Timothy Garton Ash, *History of the Present: essays, scetches and dispatches from Europe in the 1990s* (London: Penguin, 1999); also by the same author: *Magic Lantern: the Revolution of 1989 witnessed in Warsaw, Budapest, Berlin and Prague* (New York: Vintage, 1993); *The Uses of Adversity* (Cambridge: Penguin, 1989); or Paul Polansky and Marcus Pape (discussed and cited later.)

[13] For example, Adam Przeworski, *Democracy and the Market: Political and Economic Reforms in Eastern Europe and Latin America* (Cambridge: Cambridge University Press, 1991).

[14] Renata Salecl, "How to Identify with the Suffering Other" and Gyorgy Csepeli, "The Role of Fear in Ethnic and National Conflicts in Eastern Europe", both in *Grappling with Democracy: Deliberations on Post-Communist Societies, 1990-1995*, ed. Elzbieta Matynia (Prague: SLON, 1996).

[15] Pavel Říčan, *S Romy žít budeme – jde o to jak*. (Praha: Portál, 1998), 25.

[16] Other authors, who have argued in similar ways, include Toby F. Sonneman, "Old Hatreds in the New Europe: Roma After the Revolutions," *Tikkun*, 7:11 (1992):52 or Rodolfo Stavenhagen, *Old and New Racism in Europe. New Expressions of Racism: Growing Areas of Conflict in Europe* (International Alert, ed., SIM Special No. 7. Utrecht: Netherlands, Institute of Human Rights, 1987).

gime's obliviousness to issues of ethnicity and racial discrimination was embedded in the post-WWII self-perception of Czechoslovakia as a country of ethnically homogenous society of Czechs and Slovaks. This belief, which was in direct contrast with the relatively progressive attitudes towards ethnic minorities during the interwar First republic, enabled the communist state to approach the Roma not as an ethnic group, but rather as a socially deviant and backward segment of the population that ultimately led, I suggest, to the visible radicalization of xenophobia and ethnic tensions in Czechoslovakia after the collapse of communism in 1989.

However, this is not to argue that the xenophobic, ethno-centric tendencies in communist Czechoslovakia, which this book explores and narrates, are somehow specific only to Czechoslovakia, Eastern Europe or Czechs and Slovaks. Parallel legislative and social examples of the processes of linguistic labeling toward the Roma are readily available also in Western Europe, in countries such as Germany, Austria or the United Kingdom. Mechanisms of social control, aimed at diverse minorities and social groups are also not reserved only for undemocratic and totalitarian regimes but are an integral part of functioning democracies as well, as is discussed in detail in Chapter one.[17]

Structure of the Book

Chapter One introduces the theoretical and conceptual framework of the work and contextualizes this study within the relevant, mostly anthropological and historical, scholarship. The chapter is divided into four sections. The first section discusses the limits and benefits of different concepts of culture and applies those debates to my attempt to define "Gypsiness" in constructivist

[17] The discursive processes, which this book describes, can be perhaps better labeled as a form of tribalism, or ethnic nationalism, as analyzed and put forward especially in the works of Ernest Gellner and Benedict Anderson. I am grateful for this argument and observation to the anonymous reviewer for *ibidem*-Verlag, who commented on my manuscript. See, Ernest Gellner, *Nations and Nationalism* (Ithaca: Cornell University Press, 1983); Benedict Anderson, *Imagined Communities: Reflections on the Origin and Spread of Nationalism* (New York: Verso, 2006); Peter F. Sugar and Ivo John Lederer, eds. *Nationalism in Eastern Europe* (Seattle, London: University of Washington Press, 1994, 3rd ed.).

terms. I also discuss the problems of writing a history of a "culture" and explain the strategies I will use in relation to this issue. The second section of the chapter is devoted to a discussion of discourse analysis, which reflects the influence on this study of Foucauldian concepts of decentralized power and discourse as a mechanism of social organization and control. The third section takes the totalitarian thesis as its starting point. Cold war histories of East European communist regimes often envisage these regimes as artificial, monolithic leviathans that controlled and hegemonically ruled over a mass of relatively passive people. By critiquing this thesis as well as institutionalist conceptions of power, I open up a conceptual space to articulate an alternative conception of power based on the domination of certain types of discourses in politics and society. I then compare the politics of race in the United States with the politics of ethnicity in the "Gypsy question" in Czechoslovakia to argue that despite differences in regime type both countries exercised similar forms of power to marginalize a significant segment of the population. Finally, in the fourth section I discuss the politics of gender in communist Czechoslovakia and explain how the discourse of "normalcy" was used to subjugate Romani women in quite different ways than Romani men.

Chapter Two introduces the context of the immediate post-WWII situation, where my narrative of Czechoslovak strategies to the "Gypsy question" begins. The chapter analyzes how the Roma came to be regarded as a "foreign" and "filthy" element in society and interprets these stereotypes as part of an exclusionary and xenophobic process of nation-building, manifested in the widely-supported expulsion of ethnic Germans and Hungarians from Czechoslovakia. Inherited policies toward Gypsies from the interwar period, such as Law 111/1927 on "wandering gypsies," played a significant role in infusing cultural norms into the Roma legislation of the first two postwar decades. The chapter traces the continuities of these norms and analyzes how they became integrated with communist ideology in the 1950s – particularly with regard to the anti-nomadic law of 1958 – to create a composite notion of "Gypsy asociality." The product of this and other laws in the 1950s and 1960s, I suggest, was the evolution of a new type of discriminatory cultural politics of ethnicity grounded in official perceptions about how Romani social behavior failed to correspond to socialist norms of decency.

Chapter Three examines the presence of the "Gypsy myth" and stereotypes in Czechoslovak popular discourses. It discusses the world of imagery, fact, and fiction about "Gypsies" that created the frameworks for interpretations and implementation of policies that legitimized Roma's assimilation and discrimination in terms of elevation backward, inferior and dangerous people. The chapter shows that stereotypical images of "Gypsies" were not only available to the Czechoslovak population during the post-WWII era, but that they were being used and reproduced in the production of Czechoslovak fiction, entertainment and academic writing about the Roma throughout the communist period, providing a "sense-making space"[18] for scientific studies allegedly proving Roma's mental inferiority, tendency to sexual promiscuity and propensity to criminality.

The following three chapters delve directly to the heart of the communist assimilative efforts from three substantially different angles. Building on the foundational analysis developed in the first part of the book, they focus on different political and social arenas where Czechoslovak society's recognition of Romani identity only in terms of demeaning, asocial expectations was particularly paramount. These chapters comprise the major case studies of the book and focus on how official socialist rhetoric was translated into practice by political actors at the local level, producing significant discrepancies between official policies, their implementation, and their concrete effects on Romani lives.

Chapter Four discusses the life and death of the only political body that the Roma were allowed to create during the communist period. The Union of Gypsies-Roma (*Svaz Cikánů-Romů*) was created in the hopeful atmosphere of the second half of the 1960s, leading up to the Prague Spring in 1968. The circumstances of the establishment and dissolution of the Union reveal that the regime actively sought to suppress Romani attempts at articulating Romani ethnic identity and thus to fill the category of "Gypsy" with positive valuations. The regime permitted the establishment of the Union only in exchange for its function as a primary organ of assimilating the Roma. The records of the activities of the Union disclose that on several occasions the Union lead-

[18] This concept is borrowed from Kathleen Stewart's analysis of production and existence of culture and identity in Appalachia and explained in detail in Chapter one.

ers sought official recognition for Roma as an ethnic national minority. This struggle for recognition resulted in a number of different power tactics by the Party, such as cutting the Union's budget and ultimately dissolving it for "failing its integrative function."

Chapter Five discusses education as the primary site of the socialization of Gypsies into proper "socialist citizens." It first examines the "Gypsy question" in the world of the social sciences, following the shift in the Czechoslovak social policy in the early 1970s that facilitated the rise of anthropological, psychological and criminal studies of "Gypsies," thus gradually transforming the "Gypsy question" into a discourse of social deviance. Educational texts also romanticized Roma as "wandering gypsies," were both fascinated and repulsed by their "wildness," "filthiness" and "primitiveness," and employed the colonial rhetoric that Czechoslovak society was "civilizing the savage." These sentiments unconsciously reveal how fanciful yet harmful images of Roma as the "Other" became a significant way in which Czechoslovak society attempted to deal with Romani difference without having to recognize the Roma as a distinctive ethnic group. Further, the chapter discusses the inextricable link of "Gypsy" parenting and family environment with social pathology, showing how these notions led to discrimination against Romani children in the educational system. The ways in which both Roma and non-Roma were educated about issues of difference, normalcy and pathology go far to explain the presence of xenophobia in society at large and its resurgence after the end of the Cold War.

Chapter Six is concerned with the disquieting practice of sterilizing Romani women, analyzing its circumstances and consequences. It traces the shift in Czechoslovak population policy toward emphasizing "quality rather than quantity" in the early 1970s and the gradual conversion of these concerns into a discourse of social deviance and sexuality. This shift in focus allowed the Czechoslovak state to define respectable citizenship in terms of "proper" gender relations and restricted definitions of "proper" parenthood to the nuclear family, excluding the Roma from meaningful membership in the national community without explicitly referring to their ethnicity. "Gypsy" sexuality and parenthood during the communist period were defined explicitly in terms of primitiveness, unhealthiness, and ignorance, while "Czechoslovak" sexuality and parenthood were defined in terms of civilization, healthiness, rationality, and progress.

This juxtaposition of "normalcy" and "deviance," which supplanted ethnic difference, enabled Czechoslovak (non-Romani) society to deal collectively with its anxiety about "Gypsies" without comprehending the ethnic and racial dimensions of those encounters. From the testimonies of sterilized Romani women as well as from the documents written by local medical doctors and social workers, it is clear, for example, that much of the initiative to pressure Romani women to undergo sterilization came from these local health practitioners. The doctors, shielding themselves with the rhetoric of population policy, insisted they were solving a socio-economic problem. Yet, at the same time, by urging Romani women to undergo sterilization they clearly interfered with Roma's reproductive rights and reintroduced biological difference into the organization of Czechoslovak society.

Finally, the *Conclusions* provide a conceptual ending to the book by bringing the preceding chapters together in a discussion of current patterns of explicit and implicit ethnic intolerance and xenophobia that were built up through the communist period. It discusses the consequences of the policies and rhetoric used under communism on the ethnic sensibilities and tolerance of Czechoslovak society after the collapse of the communist regime. The popular rhetoric used after 1989 to describe the Roma reveals how much current racist and xenophobic attitudes are embedded in the history of Czechoslovak society's attempts to deal with the "Gypsy question."

I Theoretical and Conceptual Frameworks

According to various demographic studies, at the beginning of the 1970s the Romani population in Czechoslovakia numbered approximately 300,000 people, constituting about two and half percent of the overall Czechoslovak population.[19] The demographers conducting the 1969 census cheerfully announced that these numbers positively reflected the government's efforts at assimilation:

> . . . in 1968 the population of Gypsies *naturally* increased by 5,905, but the absolute difference since the previous study showed an increase by only 2,474 Gypsies, which means that more than 3,400 Gypsies were *released* from the new study [...] This fact demonstrates a satisfactory speed of Gypsy integration with the rest of the population.[20] (emphasis mine).

Clearly, being a "Gypsy" in communist Czechoslovakia was not a fixed identity. Acquiring the label Gypsy in the official census of the socialist regime was by no means based solely on one's ethnic origins, but was rather a culturally constructed category that served changing political objectives. On the one hand, the Roma were considered "citizens of Gypsy origin," a phrase that, at least on the surface, indicated a recognition of the distinctive ethnic roots of the Romani population. On the other hand, all throughout the communist period the Roma were denied the status of being a national ethnic minority.

While scientific studies, as well as the media, consistently operated on the assumption that one was born, rather than became, a "Gypsy," the official position of the regime was that one could in fact fully "shed" one's Gypsiness through successful assimilation. Those Roma deemed to be fully integrated

---

19 Karel Kára, "Cikáni v ČSSR a jejich společenská integrace," *Sociologický časopis*, 12:2 (1977): 366-379; Květa Kalibová, *Demografické a geodemografické charakteristiky romské populace v České republice* (Praha: Univerzita Karlova, 1995); and, by the same author, *Sources on Information on the demographic situation of the Roma/Gypsies in Europe*. (The European Council, Feasibility Study, 1997).

20 Vladimír Srb and Olga Vomáčková, "Cikáni v ČSSR v roce 1968," *Demografie*, 11:3 (1969): 221-239; 221.

into the majority society were no longer counted during demographic studies as Gypsies. In other words, the number of "Gypsies" fluctuated not because the Roma were physically leaving or disappearing, but because they could be defined into and out of existence by the whims of those in power, depending on the Roma's willingness and ability to conform to accepted ideological and social norms.[21]

The questions of how exactly this difference was measured, by whom, and what categories and tools were used that informed these surveying methods, are missing from the communist works discussing the politics of the "Gypsy question." It is important to note that very sporadically socialist monographs on the Roma include historiographical information and meaningful footnotes, which would provide evidence for the authors' conclusions. Rather, the works often state simply "research 1962," which one assumes was supposed to self-evidently satisfy all potential inquiries into the validity of the questions asked and the legitimacy of the methods used. How well many of the Roma were "cured" of their "Gypsiness" by the end of communism was demonstrated in the 1991 census (the first post-communist census to recognize "Roma" as a nationality) when only 114,116 Roma in Czechoslovakia officially declared themselves as Roma. The official statistics compiled by Regional Committees (*Národní výbory*) in 1989 claimed that Czechoslovakia had 399,654 Gypsies. In 1990, on the other hand, the representatives of newly established Romani organizations estimated the number of Roma to be approximately 800,000.[22]

The malleability of Romani identity, from the point of view of official definitions, popular perceptions and Romani self-affiliations, makes it very problematic to historically trace "Roma" as a homogenous (even if internally structured) group. Writing a linear history of the Roma or mapping out Czechoslovak ethnic discrimination by assuming a stable Romani subject is a theoretically futile and analytically unproductive effort. Instead, this work tries to point out the necessity of producing a multi-layered analysis sensitive to the processes according to which "Gypsies" and "non-Gypsies" could coexist

---

21 For a detailed discussion on *how* "Gypsiness" was determined see Chapter five.

22 Milena Hübschmannová, *Šaj Pes Dovakeras: Můžeme se domluvit* (Olomouc: Univerzita Palackého, 1993), 26.

and were constantly being defined and redefined by different actors across the political spectrum.

This chapter discusses the theoretical and conceptual frameworks of the book. It is divided into four sections: the first explores the viability and limits of the concept of culture as a tool of understanding difference in communist societies. The second section explains the significance of using a discourse analysis as one of the main analytical approaches for this study. The third part of the chapter focuses on the political frames of hegemony and marginalization and the mechanisms that perpetuate these systems of domination in various political contexts. Finally, the fourth section discusses the intrinsically gendered dimension of Romani marginalization and discrimination and positions this history in the context of the relevant gender scholarship.

I.1 The Problem of Writing Romani Culture

One recent night in Prague, a friend and I were discussing a report on the evening news in which young Romani people from various regions of the Czech Republic complained about the futility of trying to find employment in the country. My friend passionately tried to explain to me why he would never employ a Rom if he had to choose between comparable Romani and non-Romani applicants. He insisted his point of view was not racist:

> It's not about racism. It's about culture. There are cultural differences that you just can't get around. I share a culture with Czechs, but there are obvious cultural gaps between Roma and myself. It's not racial discrimination, it's only a cultural preference.[23]

His argument left me deeply disturbed, but I knew that I had heard arguments like this countless times before. It was yet another instance when "culture"

[23] Zdeněk Salzmann used a very similar example in his afterword to a recent book on new ethnography in East Central Europe when he argued that "the typical comment by the Czechs is said to be: 'I'm not a racist, but I don't like the Gypsies.'" Zdeněk Salzmann, "Afterword", in *Changes in the Heart of Europe: Recent Ethnographies of Czechs, Slovaks, Roma and Sorbs*, Timothy McCajor Hall and Rosie Read, eds. (Stuttgart: *ibidem*-Verlag, 2006): 341.

provided a cheap shelter for ignoring the historical marginalization of a people and was given the explanatory power to justify the exclusionary practices of cultural membership. Furthermore, there was another troubling aspect of my friend's use of "culture," one that concerned the communist regime's strategy for dealing with ethnic difference: that the concept of "culture" became a mechanism for translating characteristics affiliated with a particular ethnic group into seemingly ethnic-neutral rhetoric of social deviance and "asocial behavior."

This section theorizes the hidden face of "culture" in communist Czechoslovakia. It first provides a brief overview of the evolution of the concept of culture in anthropological writing, a detour, which I believe is necessary for a meaningful discussion of the limits of the concept of culture and how it relates to this book. Secondly, these theories of culture are applied to the Romani studies literature in order to problematize the sharp boundaries between Romani and non-Romani culture in that literature. I then briefly discuss my own use of the concept of culture as a *subject of discourse*, which, at least in communist Czechoslovakia, was appropriated as a political tool for marginalizing the Romani population on the basis of their perceived asocial characteristics.

"Culture" is one of those words that travel with biblical elasticity from one context to the next. Constantly changing shape like an amoeba, culture often comes to rescue those needing a safe verbal refuge for both simple ideas and complex arguments. The positive aspects of culture are easy to recount and celebrate. The concept of culture can be, above all, an important tool for the political and social emancipation of marginalized groups. However, not all dimensions of the culture concept are positive. While celebrating and building on the positive aspects of culture, there are great dangers in defining the boundaries of a particular culture too neatly and dogmatically. Culture is a living process, not a product that can be packed in a box and displayed in a museum. Moreover, "culture" has to be always situated in the context of individual and collective power and access to power.

"Culture" emerged historically in 19th-century Western social sciences as a strategic tool in understanding the self and the other. The first, elite definition considered culture the highest attainment of a people. Behind this definition was the idea that culture was a privilege, something one had or did not have. This definition made an explicit distinction between high and low culture; there was nothing relative about it.[24] Culture, like the concept of dignity, then came across as an universal standard of value and became a critical area that needed to be protected, cultivated and passed on to the masses in order to civilize them. A second, philosophical definition adopted a much broader vision of culture as that which defines humanity as other than pure nature. This definition applied the idea of culture as a form of refinement, an area of intervention designed to cultivate and nurture the values of humanity. This intervention of the superior was seen as a noble enterprise, transmitting values that were seen as universal to peoples who were thought to live in the "state of nature." Even though remarkably different, these two definitions appeared historically at the same time and worked together to promote ideas of European expansion and domination.

At the beginning of the 20th century, as a response to these highbrow notions, British anthropologist E. B. Tylor defined culture as a total way of life of a people.[25] Tylor's idea of culture as "the complex whole," also used by Franz Boas and Marcel Mauss, tried to communicate that culture was a possession of everyone, not a thing of the privileged few. This concept pointed to the totality of social life and attempted to define culture as the overarching structure that organizes all its parts and activities. This definition quickly became a cornerstone of modern social sciences and rapidly evolved into a critique of Western superiority and domination, arguing for the equality of all cultures. In other words, anthropologists and ethnographers, while studying the social structure of tribal cultures, discovered that all cultures are similar in their ability to create a total way of life and are equal in their capacity to produce complexity and a comprehensive social structure, which was then used as a way to justify the equal worth of all cultures.[26]

---

[24] This notion of culture was bound up with class hierarchies. See, for example, Charles Taylor, *Sources of the Self: the Making of the Modern Identity* (Cambridge, MA: Harvard University Press, 1989).

[25] Sir Edward Burnett Tylor, *Primitive Culture* (New York: Harper, 1958).

[26] Franz Boas, *Anthropology and Modern Life* (New York: Norton, 1928); Edward Sapir, *Culture: Genuine and Spurious* (Berlin, New York: Mouton de Gruyter, 1999; first published in 1924); Marcel Mauss, *The Gift: Forms and Functions of Exchange in Archaic Societies* (New York: Norton, 1967); Margaret Mead, *Coming of Age in Samoa: A Psy-*

Building on Tylor's understanding of culture, Ruth Benedict used her account of Zuni culture to argue against the idea that "Western" culture represents the pinnacle of humanity.[27] She pointed out that tribal societies represented a kind of "golden age" of civilization and possessed virtues and qualities that the West has since lost. Although she had the benevolent intention of portraying non-Western cultures as having alternative systems of values, she also portrayed those cultures as totalities. Based on her *gestalt* approach to culture, Benedict argued that we cannot understand the parts of a culture before the culture is perceived and grasped first as a totality. There is, however, a paradox in Benedict's theory. On the one hand, she assumes that all cultures are similar in their ability to create a total way of life, believing that we have to take a leap of faith and assume this complexity before we begin to analyze it. On the other hand, she also implicitly argues that Native American cultures exist on a simpler scale than Western cultures, and so we can totalize, and therefore understand and analyze, these cultures in a way that we cannot do for Western ones. This inherent judgment and evaluation of cultures as being simple or complex resulted from Benedict's failure to reflect upon, on the one hand, the power relationship and distance between her own dominant background and position as an observer and, on the other hand, the Zuni culture she studied.[28]

One of the first anthropologists to take seriously the relationship between the anthropologist, his or her context and the ethnographic field he or she studies was Clifford Geertz. Geertz looked at culture not as a totalized whole, but as an ever-changing web of significations that people use to get on in the world. He suggested that "culture" cannot be explained by objective causes (as, for example, Marvin Harris tried to do in his interpretation of ritual cannibalism as a result of protein deficiency[29]) because it is not itself "objective" like nature, but inter-subjective, bound up with what people consider meaningful in their encounter with others and things in the world. The implica-

---

chological Study of Primitive Youth for Western Civilization (New York: Morrow Quill Paperbacks, 1973).

27 Ruth Benedict, *Patterns of Culture* (New York: Houghton Mifflin Co., 1934).

28 *Ibid.*, especially chapter one.

29 Marvin Harris, *Cultural Materialism: the Struggle for a Science of Culture* (New York: Random House, 1979).

tion of this view for studying other societies is that scholars have to in some sense "participate" in the society in order to get a "local knowledge" of what are or are not meaningful human expressions in that society. Writing culture, according to this view, involves a dialogical relationship between a scholar and society according to which cultural expressions reveal themselves depending on how the scholar immerses him or herself in them.[30]

Roy Wagner's study of "cargo cults" picked up this approach, which Wagner expanded into an argument about culture as a *process*, a dialectical relationship between invention and convention.[31] Wagner argued that our very realities upon which we base our behavior, actions, institutions and theories are the results of human invention and its conventional interpretation. He asserted that implicit in Western anthropology is the idea of salvaging "cultures" for archival purposes. This salvaging idea gave anthropology tremendous sense of urgency to preserve and record the richness and diversity of human possibility before various cultures fall prey to the forces of modernization. Wagner criticized the earlier constructions of culture based on the collection of finite and peculiar characteristics, poignantly calling these collections "museum assemblages," that resulted in over-determined systems of otherness that one studied and reproduced.[32]

Wagner's work represents a break in anthropology's understanding of the concept of culture that ushered in reflexive anthropology, which dissolves the hard boundaries between subjects and anthropologists, and tackled the notion of difference from new angles. Kathleen Stewart, for example, argued that since things are so "black and white" in America, it is not surprising that African-American culture has become a "talisman" of cultural difference in the

---

[30] Clifford Geertz, "Thick Description", in *Interpretation of Cultures* (New York: Basic Books, 1973); and *Local Knowledge: Further Essays in Interpretive Anthropology* (New York: Basic Books, 1983).

[31] Roy Wagner, *The Invention of Culture* (Chicago: University of Chicago Press, 1981).

[32] Wagner, 27. For insightful elaborations of these arguments see, for example, Jean-Paul Dumont, *The Headman and I: Ambiguity and Ambivalence in the Fieldwork Experience* (Austin: University of Texas Press, 1978); Michael Taussig, *Mimesis and Alterity: A Particular History of the Senses* (New York: Routledge, 1993); Timothy Mitchell, *Colonizing Egypt* (Berkeley: University of California Press, 1988); or the documentary movie *Trobriand Cricket: an Ingenious Response to Colonialism*, dir. Jerry W. Leach (Berkeley: University of California Media Center, 1975).

United States.[33] Instead, Stewart tried to find the "other" America *within* the American self. The challenge for Stewart was how to present cultural difference in a way that will make a difference. Unlike Lila Abu-Lughod, who argued for salvaging the concept of culture for the purposes of political mobilization of marginalized groups,[34] Stewart was willing to completely abandon culture and find it in latencies, excesses and gaps. Her work sought out a more discursive concept of culture, one based on the tradition of fieldwork-based writing that attempts to find "culture" in stories people in Appalachia tell, as well as in the pauses, silences and spaces that surround those stories. She argued that often more important than *what* people tell is *how* they tell it and what they decide *not* to tell, for culture exists in the *act* of speaking, which is socially determined and results in collective "sense-making." Stewart concluded by suggesting that culture can be evoked and developed only through "multi-layered narratives" of the poetics in the everyday existence of things.[35]

However, culture is not just about what is or is not signified through the act of speech. It is also bound up with relations of power that predominate both within societies and between them. Abu-Lughod argued that culture is an "essential tool for making other" and hence "cultural difference" is not a reality but a relationship of power and dominance. *Defining* a people as a totalized culture can be a form of domination because it enables one group to label, and thus make "real," behaviors and experiences in ways that the defined group might reject or not identify with. Both Abu-Lughod and Arjun Appadurai, for whom culture represents a "tool of incarceration," argue that the concept's emphasis on essential difference has some legitimacy, but that the differences that matter are not taxonomic in nature, but ones bound up with

---

33 Kathleen Stewart, *A Space on the Side of the Road* (Chapel Hill: University of North Carolina Press, 1998).

34 Lila Abu-Lughod, "Writing Against Culture," in *Recapturing Anthropology*, Richard Fox, ed. (Santa Fe: School of American Research Press, 1991). Abu-Lughod first proposed these ideas in her *Veiled Sentiments: Honor and Poetry in Bedouin Society* (Berkeley: University of California Press, 1986) and further developed them in *Remaking Woman: Feminism and Modernity in the Middle East* (Princeton: Princeton University Press, 1998).

35 Stewart, 35.

domination and subordination.[36] In an era when cultures are being "deterritorialized" through migration, diaspora and economic and social mobility, anthropology must pay attention to the plurality of identities and power structures both within and between people.

One thing the anthropological debate on the concept of culture suggests is that the more dominant societies (like the Czechs and Slovaks) seek to define a group's culture (such as the Roma), the easier it is to exclude it, attack it, or marginalize it. Defining an ethnic group or a culture often rests on fictionalized narratives of cohesiveness based on a list of attributes that supposedly all members of the given group share. As the next section shows, this resonates with the ways in which European societies have historically interpreted Romani culture. The misperceptions and mythologies about Romani cultural traits are not merely demeaning, but are a part of these societies' repertoire of power that has served to further marginalize the Roma within Czechoslovakia and Europe at large.

Early scholarship on the Roma has shared some of the problematic trends of anthropology's attempt to record cultural experience and identity in definite terms. Because of the Romani history of migration and diaspora, Romani studies were first closely affiliated with linguistic anthropology. In the early 1970s, Roma scholars attempted to define Romani identity and pin down the precise place of the Roma's origin through the study of their beliefs, customs and linguistic etymology in relation to those phenomena in the regions through which they passed.[37] The idea behind these scholarly endeav-

---

36 Arjun Appadurai, "Global Ethnoscapes", in Fox, ed., *Recapturing Anthropology*. This concept is demonstrated by Abu-Lughod's attention to "halfies" and Appadurai's "hyphenated Americans." Also, James Clifford brilliantly explored these processes in his study of the "Identity in a Mashpee", in *The Predicament of Culture* (Cambridge, MA: Harvard University Press, 1988).

37 Lal Chaman, *Gypsies: Forgotten Children of India* (Delhi: Ministry of Information and Broadcasting, 1962); Jan Kochanowski, "The Origins of the Gypsies," *Roma*, 1:1 (1974): 25-28; Anirudh Joshi, "The Etymology of the Word 'Gajo'," *Roma*, 1:1 (1974): 47-49; A. P Sharma, "Distinct Identity of ROMA," *Roma*, 2:2 (1976): 5-7; Grattan Puxon, *ROM: Europe's Gypsies* (London: Minority Rights Group, 1975); W. R. Rishi, *Roma: The Panjabi Emigrants in Europe, Central and Middle Asia, the USSR, and the Americas* (Patiala: Punjabi University, 1976). Also, Werner Cohn, *The Gypsies* (Reading, Mass: Addison-Wesley Pub. Co., 1973) or Emílie Horváthová, "K otázke etnokultúrného vývoja a etnickej klasifikácie Cigánov," *Slovenský Národopis*, 22:1 (1974): 3-14.

ors was that if one could identify the place and time of the Roma's origin, one could give a coherent and fixed identity to them and explain cultural differences between Roma in terms of differences in the states through which they passed. Although most scholars nowadays agree that the Roma originally came from the Punjab region of Northern India (a claim mainly based on and supported by etymological evidence), Ian Hancock, one of the most recognized American Roma scholars, has cautiously warned against attempts of trying to trace "[Romani] biological descent to India," despite the "emotional significance" of such a step.[38]

The Roma are not a cohesive and homogenous nation or culture living in one territory. In fact, not all "Gypsies" share in the same culture and "Gypsy historical experience" has not been confined to ethnic Roma only. The nomadic aspect of their historical experience both created the link that stereotyped all Roma as one group and at the same time prevented the development of a unified Romani identity prior to the Holocaust. Many Roma were travellers, many were sedentary, but all were forced at one point or another to resort to nomadism by often ruthless policies of the state.[39] Comparing Ro-

---

38 Ian Hancock, "Standardization and Ethnic Defence in Emergent Non-Literate Societies: The Gypsy and Caribbean Cases" in *Language, Blacks and Gypsies: Languages without a Written Tradition and Their Role in Education*, eds. Thomas Acton and Morgan Dalphinis (London: Whiting & Birch, 2000), 9-23. Hancock recognizes the importance of a definite homeland for the supporters of the Romani nationalist movement but argues that while the linguistic evidence points to India as the Romani ancestral homeland, it would be misleading to think that Romani origins can be located firmly and only in India or that all Roma today can trace their origins to that region. On the other side of the debate, in a recent article Radu Ioviță and Theodore Schurr have argued, based on "available biological anthropological data for Roma origins and population history (from molecular genetic and clinical studies) ... that Gypsy populations share common biological origin, a reality that should not be ignored." Radu P. Ioviță and Theodore G. Schurr, "Reconstructing the Origins and Migrations of Diasporic Populations: The Case of the European Gypsies." *American Anthropologist*, New Series 106:2 (2004): 267-281.

39 For most recent treatment of the interconnection between travelling and exclusion see Angus Bancroft, *Roma and Gypsy: Travellers in Europe: Modernity, Race, Space and Exclusion* (Aldershot and Burlington, VT: Ashgate Publishing, 2005). See also, Alain Reyniers, *Gypsy Population and their Movements within Central and Eastern Europe* (Paris: OECD, 1995); Angus Fraser, *The Gypsies* (Oxford: Blackwell Press, 1995); Bartoloměj Daniel, *Dějiny Romů* (Brno: Univerzita Jana Evangelisty Purkyně, 1993). Martin Block, *Gypsies, their life and their customs* (New York: AMS Press, 1987); Lech Mróz, *Geneza Cygánow a ich kultúry* (Oswiecim: Biblioteczka Cyganologii Polskiej, 1993).

mani historical experience to the West Indians of the Caribbean societies, Hancock has argued that Romani nomadism and diaspora from India, and later on from Eastern Europe, has been a response to centuries of Romani enslavement by various political regimes.[40] Despite the often uniform popular conception of Roma as travellers, forced migration was a part of an interdependent dialectic of nomadism with government oppression, and has resulted in centuries of co-existence built on hatred and antagonism. Because of their gradual territorial migration and their perceived unwillingness to assimilate, the Roma, with their "anachronistic style of life," were often seen by both regimes and writers as "physically threatening and ideologically disruptive."[41]

The linguistic approach of early Romani studies often assumed quite rigid boundaries between Roma and non-Roma. Scholars adhering to this approach tended to disregard people who considered themselves half Roma, one-quarter Roma, or one-eighth Roma, "Roma" who do not speak Romany or "non-Roma" who do, or people who are familiar with Romani cultural traditions and others who are not. Rather than challenging a European popular imagination that tends to see Romani culture as a total way of life and labels it in order to marginalize it, these early studies inadvertently affirmed those notions by de-politicizing Romani identity and by affirming the popular belief that Roma were "other" and therefore did not have their "true" home in Europe.

Not surprisingly, hardly any books were written *by* the Roma themselves until World War II.[42] Rare exceptions to this trend were autobiographical accounts of Roma and Gypsies who usually only retroactively wrote about their lives and experiences.[43] However, the Roma's lack of a written history

---

40 Ian Hancock, "Standardization," 10.

41 Jean Pierre Liegeois, *Gypsies: An Illustrated History* (London: Al Saqi Books, 1985), 13. Also see, Eva Davidová, "K vymezení a specifice současného cikánského problému v Československu," *Sociologický časopis*, 6:1 (1970): 29-41.

42 See for example David Crowe. *A History of the Gypsies of Eastern Europe and Russia*. (New York: St. Martin's Press, 1995); David Crowe and John Kolsti, eds. *The Gypsies of Eastern Europe*. (Armonk, New York: M. E. Sharpe, 1991); or Jean Pierre Liegeois, *Roma, Gypsies, Travellers*. (Strasbourg: Council of Europe Press, 1994).

43 Among these belong especially autobiographies of Betsy Whyte, *The Yellow on the Broom* (Edinburgh: Chambers Press, 1979); Dora Yates, *My Gypsy Days: Recollections of a Romany Rawnie* (London: Phoenix House, 1953); Jan Yoors, *The Gypsies* (New York: Touchstone Book, 1983); Marta Adler, *My Life with the Gypsies* (London:

has not prevented the proliferation of fictional accounts *about* them that reveled in stereotyped images of the Roma both as romanticized wanderers, eternal nomads, exotic dancers, passionate lovers, fascinating fortune tellers and magical healers, and as damned thieves, social parasites, plunderers, mythical children stealers and disseminators of disease and bad luck.[44]

Early academic literature on the Roma reflected their absence in historical discourse. Romani participation in history was not measured by their achievements or integration, but rather by their spatial movement throughout the world. Because the Roma have not been, as an autonomous nation or culture, a part of Western historical writing based on the Western belief in historical progress through time (even though they technically occupied "Western" space), they have naturally represented the "Other" for the Western world.[45] All nations and cultures that count themselves to be a part of the

---

Souvenir Press, 1960); Silvester Boswell, *The Book of Boswell: an Autobiography of a Gypsy* (London: Gollancz, 1970); Gipsy Petulengro, *A Romany Life* (New York: Funk & Wagnalls company, 1936); Konrad Berkovici, *The Story of the Gypsies* (London: Jonathan Cape, 1929).

44 For review of the images of Gypsies in Western literature see, Katie Trumpener, "The Time of the Gypsies": A 'People Without History' in the Narratives of the West," *Critical Inquiry*, 18:4 (1992): 843-884; Ian Hancock, "Non-Gypsy Attitudes toward Rom: The Gypsy Stereotype," *Roma*, 9:1 (1985): 50-65; by the same author, "The Function of the Gypsy Myth," *Roma*, 12:3 (1987): 35-44; Thomas Acton, "Ethnic Stereotypes: who are the true Gypsies?", in ed. Thomas Acton, *Current Changes amongst British Gypsies and their Place in International Patterns of Development* (Oxford: Oxford University Press, 1971); James Kenedi, "Why Is the Gypsy the Scapegoat and Not the Jew?" *East European Reporter*, 2:1 (1986): 11-14; "Non-Gypsy Attitudes toward Rom: The Gypsy Stereotype," *Roma*, 9:1 (1985): 50-65. Most notorious examples of stereotyped literary treatments of the Roma include D.H. Lawrence's, *The Virgin and the Gipsy* (New York: A.A. Knopf, 1930); Alexander Pushkin's, *The Gypsies* (1824); Victor Hugo's *The Hunchback of Notre Dame*; or Prosper Meriméé's, *Carmen* (London: George Routledge & sons, 1877), which became world-famous especially thanks to its transformation into opera by George Bizet in 1875). See also Jeremy Sandford, *Gypsies* (London: Secker & Warburg, 1973).

45 For similar argument in the case of the Mongols see Kevin Stewart's *The Deep Dark Heart of Asia: Mongols in Western Consciousness* (Lewiston, NY: The Edwin Mellen Press, 1997). One of the most insightful theoretical discussions of the relationship between nomadism and state structure is Gilles Deleuze's and Felix Guartari's essay "1227: Treatise On Nomadology – The War Machine", in *A Thousand Plateau: Capitalism and Schizophrenia* (Minneapolis: University of Minnesota Press, 1987), 351-423. For a discussion on anthropological conceptions of time and progress see, for exam-

Western philosophical tradition measure their historical change and continuity by time. To the contrary, the history of the Roma in these accounts is not based on what they have achieved, but on where they have gone.[46] This difference has influenced the nature of academic scholarship on the Roma in two ways. First, Romani history has been traditionally recorded only as an additional dimension of other countries' histories, treating the Roma perpetually both as a foreign element and as a homogenous group whose history can be recorded separately from the history of the majority.[47] Second, the Romani ostracism has resulted in early scholarship based on victimology, heightened by the Romani experience during the Holocaust.

Arguably, it was the Holocaust that fully drew the Roma into Western historical discourse as historical subjects. According to the Nazi ideologues, like Jews, the Roma were guilty of the simple crime of existence. Whether nomadic or sedentary, during WWII the Roma were hunted by the servants and prisoners of the ideology of racial purity.[48] Paradoxically, becoming racial

---

ple, Johannes Fabian, *Time and The Other: How Anthropology Makes Its Object* (New York: Columbia University Press, 1983).

46 One of the most interesting accounts articulating this point is Tony Gatlif's artistically beautiful documentary *Latcho Drom* (*Safe Journey*), which traces in parallel the historical journey of the Roma from their homeland in India in 4 B.C. into Western Europe in the 20th century. As the movie unravels the geographical journey westward, so progresses the time, creating a controversial account of poverty and primitiveness as a mark of the Orient and progress and modernity as the Western phenomenon. (New York: New York Video, 1996).

47 Some of the early influential socio-anthropological accounts of the presence of the Roma in various countries and societies include Judith Okely's discussion of Gypsies in Britain, *The Traveller-Gypsies* (Cambridge University Press, 1983); Anne Sutherland's analysis of the Roma in the United States, *Gypsies: The Hidden Americans* (London: Tavistock Pulishers, 1975); Jean-Paul Clebert's account of Romani experience in Western Europe, *The Gypsies* (Baltimore: Penguin Books, 1963); or Marlene Sway's look at the American Northwest, *Familiar Strangers: Gypsy Life in America* (Urbana: University of Illinois Press, 1988).

48 For comprehensive accounts of the *Pořajmos*, the Romani Holocaust, in English see Guenter Lewy, *The Nazi Persecution of the Gypsies* (Oxford: Oxford University Press, 2001). For excellent account in German, see Michael Zimmermann, *Verfolgt, vertrieben, vernichtet: Die Nationalsozialistische Vernichtungspolitik gegen Sinti und Roma* (Essen: Klartext Verlag, 1989). See also, Toby Sonneman, *Shared Sorows: A Gypsy Family Remembers the Holocaust* (Hatfield: University of Hertfordshire Press, 2002); Gabrielle Tyrnauer, "The Fate of the Gypsies during the Holocaust." (Washington: U.S. Holocaust Memorial Council Special Report, 1985); Michael Burleigh and Wolfgang Wippermann, *The Racial State. Germany 1933-1945* (Cambridge: University Press,

subjects and victims in their own right also marks the beginning of recording of Roma history as a legitimate subject. Not surprisingly, this scholarship has been heavily influenced by the Roma's historical experience as victims. The majority of early Roma's own historical accounts have centered on their experience during the Holocaust and their persecution by various ruling elites and state governments, for which Hancock coined the phrase "pariah syndrome."[49] Even when advocating the status of the Roma as a national ethnic minority in the late 1960s, the president of the Union of Gypsies-Roma in Czechoslovakia, Miroslav Holomek, chose not to emphasize the historical achievements of the nation (as has been the tradition in most nationalistic discourses at the time), but rather Roma's "ability to stick together in the face of constant hostility and define their identity in opposition to other groups."[50]

Following the intellectual and theoretical developments in the fields of anthropology, history and sociology since the late 1970s, Romani studies of the last two decades have moved away from the prime emphasis on documenting persecution and tracing Romani origins to producing more complex and conceptually sophisticated works.[51] Especially the concept of identity has come under scrutiny, as ever more scholars argued for problematization of

---

1991); Henry Huttenbach, "The Romani Porajmos: The Nazi Genocide of Europe's Gypsies", *Nationalities Papers*, 19:3 (1991): 373-94. For the Holocaust of East European and Czechoslovak Roma see, especially, Hübschmannová, Milena, ed. *Po Židoch cigáni – svědectví Romů ze Slovenska, 1939-1945* (Praha: Triáda, 2005); Ctibor Nečas, *Romové v Československu v letech 1938-1945* (Brno: Masarykova Univerzita, 1996); Vlasta Kladivová, Konečná *stanice Auschwitz-Birkenau* (Olomouc: Univerzita Palackého, 1994); Dušan Holý and Ctibor Nečas, *Žalující píseň* (Olomouc: Univerzita Palackého, 1995); David Crowe, *A History of the Gypsies of Eastern Europe and Russia*; by the same author and John Kolsti, eds., *The Gypsies of Eastern Europe.*

49 Ian Hancock, *The Pariah Syndrome: An Account of Gypsy Slavery and Persecution* (Ann Harbor: Karoma Publishers, 1987); other Romani Holocaust narratives include: Donald Kenrick, *The Destiny of Europe's Gypsies*. (New York: Basic Books, 1973) and together with Grattan Puxon. *Gypsies Under the Swastika* (Hatfield: Gypsy Research Centre, University of Hertfordshire Press, 1995);

50 Miroslav Holomek, "Současné problémy Cikánů v ČSSR a jejich řešení", *Demografie*, 11:3 (1969): 203.

51 For a comprehensive overview of most important contemporary works in Romani Studies and useful categorization of historical and theoretical conceptualizations of Roma/Gypsy identity see Peter Vermeersch, *The Romani Movement: Minority Politics And Ethnic Mobilization in Contemporary Central Europe* (Oxford and New York: Berghahn Books, 2006): 13-28.

stable categories, showing the plularity, multilayered nature and constructedness of (Roma) identities depending on socio-historical and political contexts. Also, as the field of Romani studies has broadened and matured as an academic discipline, these self-reflexive and (what might previously have been seen as) dissenting works and voices have found their proper place within the field's productive debates.[52]

Anthropological and ethnographic studies of the Roma also took their cue from the self-reflexive approaches of anthropologists such as Michael Taussig or Anna Lowenhaupt Tsing, who argued that even though the self-positioning of the author can open up space for crafting new forms of cultural analysis, it does not represent the authentic voice of excluded minorities. Tsing argued that it would be a mistake to de-intellectualize anthropological literature by taking it as a recording of the essential experiences of the other. According to her, the goal of the new ethnography should be to open up new possibilities for thinking and writing, in which anyone can participate.[53]

The recent scholarly accounts of the Roma, in Eastern Europe and elsewhere, have moved precisely in that direction. They are either producing new complex anthropological case studies of Romani culture, based on oral history and interactive ethnography, describing the Romani struggles for cultural subjectivity and "cultivation, celebration, and reinvention of cultural difference and diversity"[54] or they are following Romani political mobilization and

---

52 This trend can be best documented in the recent works of Adrian Marsh and Elin Strand, eds., *Gypsies and the Problem of Identities: Contextual, Constructed and Contested* (Istanbul: Swedish Research Institute and I. B. Tauris, 2006); David Mayall, *History of Gypsy Identities, 1500-2000: From Egipcyans and Moon-Men to the Ethnic Romany* (New York: Routledge, 2004) or Brian Belton, *Gypsy and Traveller Ethnicity: The Social Generation of an Ethnic Phenomenon* (New York: Routledge, 2005) and by the same author, *Questioning Gypsy Identity: Ethnic Narratives in Britain and America* (Lanham, MD: AltaMira Press, 2005). A promising reading also suggests the forthcoming book by Kalwant Bhopal and Martin Myers, *Insiders, Outsiders and Others: Gypsies and Identity* (Hatfield: University of Hertfordshire Press, 2008).

53 Anna Lowenhaupt Tsing, I*n the Realm of the Diamond Queen: Marginality in an out-of-the-way Place* (Princeton: Princeton University Press, 1993); See also, Michael Taussig, *Shamanism, Colonialism, and the Wild Man: a Study in Terror and Healing* (Chicago: University of Chicago Press, 1987).

54 Michael Stewart, *The Time of the Gypsies* (Boulder: Westview Press, 1997), 4. Other recent, stimulating ethnographic or cultural accounts include, for example, Ian Hancock, *We Are the Romani People* (Hatfield: University of Hertfordshire Press, 2002);

participation, setting the Roma's national struggle within the context of the political science scholarship on European integration, but always using Roma's own voices to tell the narrative.[55]

In conclusion, because "culture" is an abstract concept, attempting to draw a border around it can have detrimental effects. Especially with perpetually disadvantaged groups like the Roma, there is always a danger of pointing to the results of historical discrimination and marginalization and labeling it as "culture." Under the banner of culture, poverty is perceived as a "cultural lifestyle" and unemployment considered a "cultural choice." People are fixed in positions and situations that presumably reflect their cultural identity, but often only represent their strategy for survival.[56]

Because the concept of culture is often a part of the repertoire of power that societies have used to marginalize the Roma, this book does not assume a particular Romani culture or identity, but rather looks at "culture" as one of the discursive strategies Czechoslovak society has used in order to discriminate. "Culture" in my usage resembles that of Kathleen Stewart and Abu-Lughod. I construe culture as a subject or theme of discourse, which is therefore not a latent phenomenon in the world but something that exists in the ac-

---

Thomas Acton and Gary Mundy, eds., *Romani Culture and Gypsy Identity* (Hatfield: University of Hertfordshire Press, 1997); Mattijs van de Port, *Gypsies, Wars and Other Instances of the Wild* (Amsterdam: Amsterdam University Press, 1998) or Isabel Fonseca, *Bury Me Standing* (New York: Vintage Books, 1995).

55 For studies in Romani political emancipation and nationalism see, for example, Zoltan D. Barany, *The East European Gypsies: Regime Change, Marginality, and Ethnopolitics* (Cambridge: Cambridge University Press, 2002); and by the same author, "Living on the Edge: The East European Roma in Postcommunist Politics and Societies," *Slavic Review*, 53:2 (1994): 321-344; Alain Reyniers, *Gypsy Population and their Movements within Central and Eastern Europe* (Paris: OECD, 1995). From classic studies, see especially, Thomas Acton, *Gypsy Politics and Social Change: The Development of Ethnic Ideology and Pressure Politics Among British Gypsies from Victorian Reformism to Romani Nationalism* (London and Boston: Routledge, 1974); by the same author and Claire Palley, et. al. *Coexistence in Some Plural European Societies* (London: Minority Rights Group Report, 1972, 1986); Ian Hancock, "Some Contemporary Aspects of Gypsies and Gypsy Nationalism," *Roma*, 2:1 (1975): 46-55; Nicolae Gheorghe, "The Roma-Gypsy Ethnicity in Eastern Europe", *Social Research*, 58:4 (Winter 1991): 829-44.

56 Another place where this debate on culture has been salient is the U.S. discourse on poverty. See for example, Adolph Reed Jr., "The 'Underclass' as Myth and Symbol: The Poverty of Discourse about Poverty," in his *Stirrings in the Jug: Black Politics in the Post-Segregation Era* (Minneapolis: University of Minnesota Press, 1999), 179-196.

tive acts of speaking, understanding and interpreting. According to this view, cultural discourses lead to collective "sense-making;" they are varieties of ways in which groups talk about themselves and others in order to impose their own order on the world. Following Abu-Lughod, this book writes "against culture" by identifying and challenging the ways Czechoslovak society has used culture to produce rigid boundaries between themselves and the Roma as well as to impose detrimental and demeaning notions of "Gypsy" identity on the Roma. By bringing both of these notions together – that is, by seeing culture as an aspect of discourse and as a form of power – this work seeks to expose forms of discrimination that, as my friend's argument pointed out, are everywhere present today but rarely openly acknowledged.

I.2 Discursive Frames of Social Control

It should be clear from the preceding considerations that a history of a "culture" or a group that assumes essential differences between that culture and others could be used to justify discrimination. "Cultural" differences between Roma and non-Roma could be taken to be the reason for why Roma are thought to value education less, have more promiscuous sexual behavior, are less "clean," and so on. The politics of Romani studies, despite its best intentions of trying to champion Romani emancipation in a variety of different ways, have also produced a set of knowledge claims that have tended to affirm, rather than reject, the politics of difference in the host society. This is because, like the disciplines of anthropology and history, Romani studies produces knowledge claims about a field of inquiry that both projects, as well as reflects, the background societies in which the discipline has its roots.[57]

Rather than participate in the political-intellectual project of interpreting the identities and differences of Roma and non-Roma in communist Czechoslovakia, I argue that an analysis of the official and popular discourses that were used to produce a particular understanding of the Roma as deviant or abnormal can more critically expose the pathways of Romani marginalization

[57] Joan Wallach Scott, *Gender and the Politics of History* (New York: Columbia University Press, 1988).

to the present. By focusing on discourse as a site of political contestation and power, I reject theories of totalitarianism that locate communist power more or less solely within the coercive political institutions of the party-state. Such theories not only problematically treat power as something "above" society and alien to it, but also ignore the role of language in legitimating political practices and in producing truth claims about who the Roma are and how they do or do not integrate within the larger Czechoslovak society.

This book is largely based on critical discourse analysis of the collected primary data, which is by definition mainly interpretive and qualitative, but exposes important systems and mechanisms of marginalization and oppression, enacted through language construction and usage.[58] Using discourse analysis as my main interpretive lens to the cultural politics of ethnicity in the "Gypsy question" serves several related purposes: first, for understanding how political power and social domination is secured in a socialist society; second, for understanding the history of the construction of identity and difference between the Roma and Czechoslovak society; and third, for understanding how official or popular perceptions of the Roma are legitimated. Since the book explores the ways in which Czechoslovak official and popular discourses have constructed the individual and collective subject of the "Gypsy," it points to ideological associations and power dynamics of the discourse, which are often oppressive and exclusionary, but stay invisible or implicit between the lines of the readily-available contents, and thus tend to remain overlooked and under-analyzed dimensions of both texts and contexts.

First, according to Václav Havel's famous analysis of power in "The Power of the Powerless," communist societies are best understood as "post-totalitarian" states in which power is exercised not through coercive force, but

---

[58] For discussions of discourse analysis, see especially, Norman Fairclough, "Critical discourse analysis as a method in social scientific research" (121-138); Siegfried Jäger, "Discourse and knowledge: theoretical and methodological aspects of a critical discourse and dispositive analysis" (31-62) and Teun A. van Dijk, "Multidisciplinary CDA: a plea for diversity" (95-120). All in *Methods of Critical Discourse Analysis,* Ruth Wodak and Michael Meyer, eds. (London: Sage Publications, 2001); See also, Norman Fairclough, *Analyzing Discourse: Textual Analysis for Social Research* (New York: Routledge, 2003); Nelson Phillips and Cynthia Hardy, *Discourse Analysis: Investigating Processes of Social Construction* (London: Sage Publications, 2002) or for a good application of the method, Roman Kuhar, *Media Representations of Homosexuality: An Analysis of the Print Media in Slovenia, 1970-2000* (Ljublana: Mirovni inštitut, 2003).

through the diffusion of ideological discourse in society. Ideology, in Havel's view, links the political system to individuals by creating a linguistic arena where the political system self-referentially legitimates itself through the discourse of socialism. While the political system claims to be humanist, egalitarian and socially just, the "truth" of such a system is that it "serves people only to the extent necessary that people serve it."[59] Because ideology serves the interests of the state rather than being an interpretation of reality, ideology produces "a world of appearances, a mere ritual, a formalized language deprived of semantic content with reality and transformed into a system of ritual signs that replace reality with pseudo-reality."[60] Without accepting Havel's assumption that we can know what is "real" and "true" outside of ideological frameworks, I appropriate his notion that ideology is not a set of ideas standing above society, but is a discursive field containing ideas that are internalized and projected by people in order for them to negotiate their lives in accordance with "official" norms.

If ideology is discursive and "post-totalitarian" power is present when ideology is internalized, then the power to define *how* or *if* the Roma fit or do not fit into Czechoslovak society should also be located in discourse. The different chapters of this book show this to be the case in two different ways. On the one hand, in chapters three and five I argue that romanticized, criminalized and racially-charged notions of the Roma have been a mainstay in Czechoslovak "popular discourse" – perceptions that can be found in cartoons, magazines, movies and so on. Talk about these "popular" notions of the Roma have a long history dating back to the 19th century and earlier, and therefore defy the easy periodization used by many historians. On the other hand, under the conditions of communism "popular discourse" inevitably intersects with the "official discourse" of the state and party organs and academic and scientific literature. In "official" speeches, state actors make ideologically correct but empirically vacuous claims about the Roma as leading improper socialist lives, as being unintegrative, as asocial, and so on. How popular and official discourses intersect is one of the key themes of this book,

---

59 Václav Havel, "The Power of the Powerless," in *Open Letters* (London: Faber and Faber, 1991), 135.

60 *Ibid.*, 138.

because it is precisely at the intersection of these discourses that racially charged popular notions of the Roma become translated into officially sanctioned notions of their social deviance.

In sum, Romani marginalization in communist Czechoslovakia took place largely within the space of language. This does not mean that real Romani women and men did not experience discrimination or the world "outside" discourse is somehow unreal or unimportant for Romani history, but rather that it is through discourse that the Roma have been defined, ridiculed, and forced to undergo sterilization and other punitive practices.[61] However, the millions of Czechs and Slovaks who were familiar with the popular and official conceptions of the Roma would hardly have thought that such discourses could have been such a strong tool of subordination. This is because these discourses were hegemonic: they had the power to establish the obvious or common sense understandings of the Roma that are taken for granted as "true" and which go without saying.[62] Unlike democratic societies where marginalized groups can appropriate language in order to contest the hegemonic power of popular beliefs and official prescriptions, in communist Czechoslovakia such a discursive arena was never officially sanctioned, and except for the years when the Union of Gypsies-Roma was at its peak, the Romani population had few avenues of communication to talk back.

Second, discourse was also the space where the identities of Roma and non-Roma were constructed and played out. As Joan Scott argued in a very different context, "identities and experiences are variable phenomena ... discursively organized in particular contexts and configurations."[63] Who counted as a "Gypsy" in the eyes of the state had very little to do with one's putatively "real" ethnicity but rather depended on how one was situated within

---

61 See also Joanna Richardson, *The Gypsy Debate: Can Discourse Control?* (Exeter and Charlottesville, VA: Imprint Press, 2006). Like I do in this book, Richardson, in a discussion of the treatment of the Roma in Great Britain, also argues that "discourse can be used as a tool to control those who refuse to conform to societal norms" and adds that while "discourse can be controlling ... it is perhaps more the actions that discriminatory discourse can lead to that are the real mechanisms of control. (p. 1-2).

62 This conception of hegemony resembles that of Gramsci. Antonio Gramsci, *Selections from the Prison Notebooks of Antonio Gramsci* (New York: International Publishers, 1972).

63 Scott, *Gender and the Politics of History*, 5.

officially sanctioned categories of the proper and improper, normal and deviant, and integrated and unintegrated. Such categories created an identity of "Gypsiness" regardless of how people may have seen themselves.

In the 1969 census, referred to at the beginning of the chapter, state commissioners went door to door to tabulate people's nationality through a perceived social status, marking "C" (for *Cikán* - Gypsy) on the form regardless of how people may have identified themselves. In that case, who counted as a "Gypsy" was largely a function of interpretation of the official discourses on socialization and integration that the commissioner internalized as an agent of the state. It follows from this that when studying the marginalization of the Roma one cannot take for granted some primordial or prediscursive notion of who is or is not a Rom, because the identities at issue are the ones discursively produced. Instead, one must study the historically specific practices through which such descriptions of the Roma were circulated, became salient, and became forced onto people as the official interpretation of their own lives and history.

Third, discourse is not only a locus of power or a site of the production of identities, but it is also the means for legitimating state policies that subordinated the Roma. As Foucault pointed out, the Western discourse on sexual repression legitimated various institutions that mediated how people should interpret themselves;[64] in a similar vein, the discourse on social normalcy and deviance legitimated a wide range of state policies aimed at correcting such deviant behavior, regardless of whether the Roma were enunciated as the official target of those policies. Further, legitimating discourses made sense out of state policies by placing them within the framework of official ideology and beliefs, whether such policies were about sending problematic children into remedial schools or sterilizing certain types of women. Because official discourse had this legitimizing function, the ways in which popular conceptions of the Roma entered into the implementation of state policies were easily masked. That is, popular perceptions of the Roma, while never officially

---

64 Michel Foucault, *The History of Sexuality: An Introduction* (New York: Vintage Books, 1985). Other works by Foucault that this book most significantly draws from include: *Discipline and Punish: The Birth of the Prison* (New York: Vintage, 1979); *The Order of Things: An Archeology of the Human Sciences* (London: Tavistock, 1970); and *Birth of the Clinic: An Archeology of Medical Perception* (New York: Vintage, 1973).

sanctioned, entered into political practices through the actions of the local officials who carried them out. These practices in turn became a part of the acceptable and "correct" application of the law by receiving the legitimating stamp of the state apparatus.

In sum, I seek to sidestep the problems of narrating a "history of the Roma" by instead positioning identity claims about the Roma as themes within the discursive field of communist power. Official discourse was the arena where ideologically correct conceptions of the Roma were defined, but also where institutionalized practices were enunciated and carried out. Popular discourse was the parallel arena where racially charged notions of Romani/non-Romani difference were circulated, but not repressed, because ethnic or racial categories were rarely discussed in public spaces. This focus on discourse, however, does not mean that power was "autonomous" or that agency does not matter. On the contrary, it was precisely local political officials who, by using their own authority to interpret the ethnically neutral policies from above, were the conduits for translating the terms of popular discourse into officially sanctioned political practices.

I.3 Political Location of Power

In her reflections on the role of individual responsibility for sustaining communist power structures, Hungarian philosopher Éva Ancsel pointed out that there is no such thing as collective guilt just as there is no such thing as collective responsibility. She argued that blaming the harmful effects of the previous regime "on the system" was a simple, but inadequate interpretation of history because "in reality everyone played their part in maintaining this system."[65] Her argument was a direct response to one of the most pervasive paradigms of historical writing on Eastern Europe during the Cold War: the idea that East European communist regimes were monolithic leviathans controlling and ruling a mass of relatively passive people. As Czech historian Ka-

65 Éva Ancsel, interview with Barbara Einhorn, Budapest, May 26, 1990. Cited in Barbara Einhorn, *Cinderella Goes to Market: Citizenship, Gender and Women's Movements in East Central Europe* (London, New York: Verso, 1993), 5. (Havel makes the same point in his "Power of the Powerless").

rel Kaplan argued in 1987, the communist regime in Czechoslovakia was Janus-faced: its "formal façade" of allegedly "democratic" party institutions covered up the "the real structure of the party ... that results from its power mission, from its exercise of absolute control over society, from its efforts to resolve all social problems and direct every movement in society by means of its resolutions and instructions."[66]

Such conceptions of communist regimes as having "absolute control over society," though largely discredited today, have still had a lasting and pervasive effect on how historians of Eastern Europe conceive of "power" under communism. By challenging some of these assumptions, as well as by drawing comparisons between race relations in the United States and in communist Czechoslovakia, this section will propose an alternative conception of social and political power in Czechoslovakia that can better express the processes by which the Roma were marginalized, defined, and discriminated against.

The "totalitarian thesis" of East European communism could be summarized in the following way:[67] With the Russian Revolution, Soviet history became determined by the totalitarian political dynamics of the Communist Party. Over time, party leaders solidified political power through centralized bureaucratic organization, police surveillance, ideological orthodoxy, disciplined leadership and party control over all social positions of prominence. Stalin perfected these mechanisms of power and asserted absolute control over society through mass terror, purges, the secret police and an ever more totalized party apparatus. According to the totalitarian point of view, Stalin

---

66 Karel Kaplan, *The Communist Party in Power: A Profile of Party Politics in Czechoslovakia* (Boulder and London: Westview Press, 1987), xiii. By the "façade" Kaplan meant the structure of the party in a "system of tens", meaning that the ratio of party members to the total population is 1:10, a regional apparatchik oversees ten basic organizations, a region is made up of ten districts, the country is formed by ten regions, and so on, suggesting democratic rule, when in fact such a system is most suitable for effective control and surveillance. See also, Barbara Jancar, *Czechoslovakia and the Absolute Monopoly of Power: A Study of Political Power in a Communist System* (New York: Praeger Publishers, 1971).

67 No one particular author may accept all of this conception; it is simply meant as an illustration of a typical, "totalitarian" conception of communism's main aspects, which can be found in many different historical works. For a more sustained discussion of the thesis, see Stephen F. Cohen, *Rethinking the Soviet Experience* (Oxford: Oxford University Press, 1985).

could be easily compared to Hitler, because they were both masters of using the state to terrorize their respective societies through total control of all main aspects of life.[68] Stalinist zealotry subsided after his death in 1953, but the apparatus of the party-state remained more or less intact and became installed, to different degrees, in the countries of the Eastern Bloc. Up to 1989, the Czechoslovak party-state continued to exert absolute control of a passive, "privatized" Czechoslovak society by punishing dissenters, pacifying people through consumer goods, deploying constant surveillance, preventing access to education for ideologically unfit subjects, and using party membership as the access to social mobility.

There is no need to rehearse all of the criticisms of this conception here, but a few of them are noteworthy. First, the totalitarian consensus ignored forms of popular resistance that were quite common in many communist societies, such as political subversion through folk music, literature and historical symbols.[69] Second, the consensus conceived of the nomenklatura and other political actors as automatons of the party-state, not as agents with their own ideas, intentions and sources of power. Third, East European history was conceived as primarily political, with cultural, social, religious and gender history allegedly determined by the political dynamics "from above." And fourth, but perhaps most importantly, the totalitarian thesis presupposed the normative claim that communism was inherently evil, coercive and violent, a claim that no doubt sprung in part from the fact that Slavic Studies as a discipline became highly politicized as a result of its financial and ideological dependency on the U.S. Cold War foreign policy.[70]

---

68 For a critical appraisal of this argument and relevant literature, see for example Ian Kershaw, "Totalitarianism Revisited: Nazism and Stalinism in Comparative Perspective," in Ian Kershaw, ed., *The Nazi Dictatorship: Problems and Perspectives of Interpretation* (London, Baltimore: Edward Arnold, 1985 and 2000).

69 For example, see Jan Kubik, *The Power of Symbols Against the Symbols of Power: The Rise of Solidarity and the Fall of State Socialism in Poland* (University Park: The Pennsylvania State University Press, 1994).

70 Stephen White, "Political Science as Ideology: The Study of Soviet Politics" in *Political Questions*, ed. B. Chapman and A. Potter (Manchester, 1975) and Alexander Dallin, "Bias and Blunders in American Studies on the USSR", *Slavic Review* (September 1973). For other insightful critiques of the totalitarian thesis see, for example, Mary Fulbrook, *The Anatomy of a Dictatorship: Inside the GDR, 1949-1989* (New York: Oxford University Press, 1995); by the same author *Citizenship, Nationalism and Migration in*

Even if many scholars do not accept the totalitarian thesis, it still has entered into the general way that power under communism has been conceived -- as intrinsically based in the political institutions of the party-state. Whether or not such power was totalized, many East European scholars talk as if in communist countries the only source of power with any impact was institutional. Yet an overly institutionalized conception of power can easily ignore other possible historical narratives and explanations of life at the time.

For example, in a recent, well-researched and argued account of the history of the Roma in Eastern Europe, Zoltan Barany set out to investigate the story of Roma's historical oppression in the region, emphasizing the plight of the Roma in the aftermath of the collapse of communism.[71] Barany compared four different types of political regimes that ruled in seven different countries of Eastern Europe in the past four hundred years – imperial, authoritarian (meaning interwar and Nazi), socialist and the newly emerging democratic regimes – in order to analyze what effect different regimes have had on marginalization and discrimination of the Roma. Barany conceded that there were significant differences in the treatment of the Roma by individual East European countries and that "conservative Czechoslovakia enacted a more and more repressive approach to ethnic minorities as time went on."[72] Despite this admission, however, Barany concluded that state socialist regimes were the most successful in providing the Roma with equal rights. His argument was partially based on the assertion of Czech historians Tomáš Grulich and Tomáš Haišman that the putatively "enlightened" policies of assimilation – such as educational, housing, hygiene and health programs – were not repressive.[73] This argument found resonance with Barany's belief that socialist regimes most fully achieved "equal rights of the Roma."[74]

Europe (New York: Routledge, 1996); Svetlana Boym, *Common Places: Mythologies of Everyday Life In Russia* (Cambridge, MA: Harvard University Press, 1994); or Yuri Slezkine, "The USSR as a Communal Apartment, of How a Socialist State Promoted Ethnic Particularism," *Slavic Review*, 53:2 (Summer 1994): 414-52.

71 Zoltan Barany, *The East European Gypsies: Regime Change, Marginality, and Ethnopolitics* (cited earlier).

72 *Ibid.*, 38.

73 Tomáš Grulich and Tomáš Haišman, "Institucionální zájem o cikánské obyvatelstvo v Československu v letech 1945-1958," *Český lid*, 73:2 (1986): 72-85.

74 Barany, 44.

Barany reached the conclusion that the Czechoslovak state was not repressive toward the Roma because his analysis was based mainly on the explicit *content* of policy. That is, Barany took the letter of the law at face value, assuming that the egalitarian wording of assimilationist policies more or less reflected the benevolence of the regime to promote Romani welfare. He also surmised that the content of policy was what was ultimately implemented – that the party-state apparatus was a homogenous and coherent entity in which all power emanated from above – and therefore did not pay enough attention to whether or not policies in their application were repressive or not.

This book challenges these assumptions in several different ways. First, I focus on the discursive face of power rather than its overt, institutional form. Institutional conceptions of power, like the totalitarian thesis itself, ignore how laws, ideas and norms actually affect people in their everyday existence. They also ignore the role of "societal attitudes" in influencing how doctors, educators and other low-level state actors treated Romani citizens in everyday contexts. A discursive conception of power, on the other hand, can bring the roles of societal attitudes, official rhetoric, cultural norms and other factors to bear on the marginalization of Roma in the country. As Foucault argued on numerous occasions, "power relations are rooted deep in the social nexus, not reconstituted 'above' society as a supplementary structure whose radical effacement one could perhaps dream of."[75]

Such a thesis applies just as well to capitalist societies as socialist ones: in each case, locating power involves looking at the concrete ways one group is objectified, defined and subordinated. Official laws may be one, but certainly not the only, site where such power was exercised. In fact, low level officials constituted a very important "nexus" in Czechoslovakia because they were participants or purveyors of two different discourses – popular discourses about the Roma *from below* and official discourses on the "Gypsy question" *from above* – and they thus had the potential of inflicting double harm on the Roma by translating one discourse into the other.[76]

---

[75] Michel Foucault, "The Subject and Power," cited in Hubert Dreyfus and Paul Rabinow, *Michel Foucault: Beyond Structuralism and Hermeneutics* (Chicago: University of Chicago Press, 1983): p. 222.

[76] An extension of this argument brings an interesting question about potential radicalization of such rhetoric in regions with higher concentrations of Romani population. Even

Second, policies written in the legal code of the regime are never the same as policies as they affect real people. This is because, even if local officials are ordered to follow directives from above, they still have the *discursive freedom* to interpret and apply laws according to the popular prejudices and stereotypes that inform their attitudes and behavior. This does not mean that local officials were free to do what they wanted or that they were not monitored by their superiors. Rather, it means that such officials, simply as interpretive beings, could have applied policies in ways that more directly related to popular consciousness and culture than according to the ideological straightjacket of the letter of the law. According to this view, local actors have agency and are embedded in social and cultural networks that shape their behavior – precisely the types of "state-society" relations that the totalitarian thesis rejects from the start.[77]

Third, "marginalization" by definition requires agents who marginalize. Institutionalist conceptions of power create sharp conceptual divisions between state and society and have the potential to remove society from positions of responsibility for the harmful legacies of communism. On the other hand, theories of power rooted too much in social structures or overarching discourses lose sight of how people internalize ideas and exercise power in practice.[78] Between these conceptions, my work identifies teachers, writers, medical doctors and other low level state actors as having the power to marginalize because of their capacity to translate ethnically demeaning conceptions of the Roma into ideologically sound and punitively lawful practices.

---

though this book does not have enough data to argue in this way, the following chapters show that some of the most racist rhetoric and initiative on the part of local actors did come from such regions, for example Ostrava or Eastern Slovakia.

77 For an insightful discussion of discourse and agency in context, see also Pierre Bourdieu's concept of "habitus", in *Language & Symbolic Power* (Cambridge, MA: Harvard University Press, 1991).

78 Some interpreters believe that Foucault makes this mistake. According to Axel Honneth, for example, Foucault maintained a "systems-theoretic" position that all social interaction is essentially permeated by relations of subordination and domination. To the contrary, I think that Foucault never fully maintained a systems-theoretic conception of power. In the *History of Sexuality* and the essay "The Subject and Power," Foucault formulated a conception of subversive politics in which individuals interrupt "systems" of power while creating "new modes of subjectivities." For a critique of the systems-theoretic view, see Axel Honneth, *The Critique of Power* (Cambridge: MIT Press, 1991); chapters 5 and 6.

Lastly, one of the most important forms of power not grasped by institutionalist approaches to history has been the social regulation of normalcy. In communist societies, in the supposed absence of socio-economic differences as signifiers of status, official discourse repressed class-based notions of difference, even though these societies had real class hierarchies of their own (such as between the nomenklatura and the majority population). Without these class signifiers, social differences between people were sometimes cast in terms of "decency" or normality. To be "decent" or normal was a key element of social citizenship. In order to be able to participate in the advantages offered by universal socialist citizenship, individuals and groups were expected to behave in "normal" and "proper" ways.

The concept of "decency" or normality was regulated by both society and the state. On the one hand, it was one of the notions that kept the hegemony of the ruling class functioning; on the other hand, it was also an important way Czechoslovak society differentiated itself from the "indecent" Romani minority.[79] Digressions from the prescribed social normalcy were squarely defined in terms of deviance. A part of the communist enterprise was purifying these differences, whether social or ethnic.[80] In Czechoslovakia, these trends toward homogeneity were heightened by practices enacted even prior to the accession of the communist party to power, such as the expulsion of ethnic Germans and Hungarians after WWII. As stated already earlier, and as discussed in detail in Chapter two, the post-WWII retributive anti-German homogenizing actions, which set the stage and created mental justification for continued communist attempts of ethnic purification, were in contrast to the policy of relative tolerance and ethnic coexistence proclaimed and practiced during the Czechoslovak interwar First Republic.

---

[79] Průcha, *Multikulturní výchova.*

[80] This, of course, was not the case only in Czechoslovakia but in other countries with communist rule as well. See, for example, an excellent account by Kate Brown, *A Biography of No Place: From Ethnic Borderland to Soviet Heartland* (Cambridge, MA: Harvard University Press, 2005); Anastazia Karakasidou, *Fields of Wheat, Hills of Blood: Passages to Nationhood in Greek Macedonia, 1870-1990* (Chicago: University of Chicago Press, 1997); Yuri Slezkine, *Arctic Mirrors: Russia and the Small Peoples of the North* (Ithaca: Cornell University Pres, 1993); Roman Szporluk, *National Identity and Ethnicity in Russia and the New States of Eurasia* (Armonk: M.E. Sharpe Press, 1994); or extensive collection of essays *Cultures and Nations of Central East Europe: Essays in Honor of Roman Szporluk* (Cambridge, MA: Harvard University Press, 2000).

These reflections on power and marginality have shown that the types of discursive power that were exercised under communism are not entirely alien to democratic states. Although democracies are in principle premised on rights and freedoms and authoritarian countries on coercion, these simple axioms do not express how power is exercised through the politics of race, class and gender in each type of country. Studies that applied theories of race to analyses of poverty, welfare systems and urban geography provide stimulating points of comparison to Romani discrimination in Czechoslovakia. Despite the many differences between the histories of such countries, for example Czechoslovakia and the United States, the politics of race in the United States can shed light on the politics of the "Gypsy question" in Czechoslovakia. In particular, in both countries the mechanisms of social control of racial difference are surprisingly similar in their rhetoric, strategies, and, most importantly, in their ability to translate the regulation of cultural/racial differences into the regulation of social deviance.[81]

Take, for example, the "culture of poverty" debate and the emergence of the idea of a "black underclass" in the 1980s and 1990s. The new discourse on poverty that emerged in the American media and public debate was linked to the rightward drift of social welfare toward embracing neoliberalism. Rather than seeing inner-city black poverty as arising from urban deindustrialization or disinvestments in African-American neighborhoods, journalists, scholars and policy experts began to claim that the cause of poor people's plight was not economic conditions, but their own cultural and behavioral characteristics. For example, Ken Auletta made this discursive shift in *The Underclass* by linking "poverty" with "asocial behavior."[82] To him, it is behavioral characteristics that cause poverty, not the other way around. Members of the underclass are set apart by "their 'deviant' or antisocial behavior, by their bad habits, not just their poverty."[83] Further, such "deviant" behavior

81 For studies on race and poverty relevant to this book see, especially: Adolph Reed, Jr., *Stirrings in the Jug*; Dorothy Roberts, *Killing the Black Body: Race, Reproduction, and the Meaning of Liberty* (New York: Vintage, 1999); Patricia Hill Collins, *Black Feminist Thought: Knowledge, Consciousness, and the Politics of Empowerment* (Boston: Unwin Hyman, 1990); and Michael Dawson, "A Black Counterpublic?: Economic Earthquakes, Racial Agenda(s), and Black Politics", *Public Culture,* 7 (1994), 195-223.

82 Ken Auletta, *The Underclass* (New York: Random House, 1982).

83 *Ibid*, 27-28.

does not arise from just anywhere. Because the "underclass" is constructed as black, it was thought to be caused by the particular characteristics of black ghetto culture: crime, drug abuse, lack of values, teenage pregnancy and, above all, "fatherless" households. Once the discursive link between poverty and behavior was established, it was only a small step to link behavior with culture, and culture with race and gender.[84]

As Adolph Reed Jr. summarized, "the underclass carries with it images of drug-crazed, lawless black and Hispanic men and their baby-factory mothers and sisters. According to him [Auletta], the companion image is the so-called 'cycle of poverty,' which focuses on women's living and reproductive practices as the transmission belt that drives the cycle. That focus permeates discussion of the underclass, and those who rely on it avoid confronting its antifeminist premises by running together female-headed households, out-of-wedlock birth, and teenage pregnancy into a single mantra."[85]

This politics of poverty in the United States is remarkably similar to the communist "reading" of "Gypsy" social pathology. In each case, the locus of power was not in particular laws or institutions, but in ideologically charged discursive shifts that convinced people to see the conditions of minorities as being caused by their own "deviant" behavior or criminality. In both the "democratic" United States and "totalitarian" Czechoslovakia, associations be-

---

[84] However, it is important to acknowledge that the link between poverty, culture and race is far more complex. As, for example, Kathleen Stewart's work on Appalachian "poor white trash" has shown, poor whites in America are in some instances even more likely to be blamed for their poverty than are poor blacks, whose racial discrimination tends to be (at least partially) recognized as a substantial and "objective" cause of their plight.

[85] Reed Jr., "The Underclass as Myth and Symbol," 191. See also, Patricia Williams, *Seeing a Colour-Blind Future* (New York: Noonday Press, 1998); also by the same author see an excellent analysis of American hate speech and stereotypical encoding of public figures in *The Rooster's Egg* (Cambridge, MA: Harvard University Press, 1995); For a very insightful and useful discussion of shifting strategies of institutional racism see: Patricia Hill Collins, *Fighting Words: Black Women and the Search for Justice* (Minneapolis: University of Minnesota Press, 1998), especially chapter one "The More Things Change, The More They Stay The Same: Afro-American Women and the New Politics of Containment," in which Collins, through her concept of "inclusionary exclusion," developes a notion of black woman as an "outsider from within," who is no longer excluded through legal prohibition of access to public space. Her containment in the center of the public eye through racist stereotypes functions as a new, smarter way to keep her from any meaningful acquisition of power.

tween poverty and "asocial behavior" and "pathology" were based on the tautological idea that the lifestyles of minorities caused their deviant behavior but also that deviant behavior caused them to have such unruly or unintegrative lifestyles. Such links served the purpose of avoiding the recognition of the existence of racial or ethnic inequality in society. In the United States, the discourse on the culture of poverty ignored the economic causes of inequality at the heart of American liberalism. In Czechoslovakia, the discourse on Romani deviance sought to explain the Roma's failure to integrate into mainstream society in terms of their own behavior and therefore disguised the racial nature of the policies that were thrust at them.

The United States and Czechoslovakia also shared discourses that linked race with criminality. Studies by Mike Davis and Thomas Sugrue, for example, exposed the links between structural racism and spatial organization.[86] To Davis, the retreat of the white privileged class from the devalued inner city into the privileged space of private suburbia results in "spatial apartheid" and produces its own forms of criminality. Moreover, in pointing out the racist dimensions of legal punishments for criminal behavior, Davis provided convincing evidence that what determines prison sentences is not the crime itself, but the interpretation of the crime based on the "reading" of the criminal.[87] In both the United States and Czechoslovakia, conceptions of race determined criminality, regardless of the attempts of official discourse to disguise such links.

In fact, the criminalization of the Roma has a long history, and is one of the factors behind the "culture" of Romani migration. In the 18th and 19th centuries, the Roma in the Czech lands were subjugated by the Habsburgs through corporal punishments and policies forbidding them from settling.[88] During the interwar period, Czechoslovakia enacted repressive laws requiring Gypsies to carry identification cards and prohibited them from entering spa

---

86 Mike Davis, *City of Quartz: Excavating the Future in Los Angeles* (New York: Vintage, 1992); Thomas Sugrue, *The Origins of The Urban Crisis: Race and Inequality in Postwar Detroit* (Princeton: Princeton University Press, 1996).

87 Davis, 230 and 288.

88 Robert Kann and Zdenek David, *The Peoples of the Eastern Habsburg Lands, 1526-1918* (Seattle: University of Washington Press, 1984); Crowe, *A History of the Gypsies of Eastern Europe and Russia*.

towns and resorts.[89] The separate Slovak State and the Protectorate of Bohemia and Moravia during WWII created forced labor camps for the Roma and the Czechs readily sent the Roma to the Nazi gas chambers.[90] Under communism, the subjugation of the Roma yet again changed its discursive face, this time under the guise of the rhetoric of social welfare. In sum, assumptions about race and ethnicity have been the driving forces behind political attempts to criminalize the Roma. Because socialist ideology did not recognize the legitimacy of ethnic difference, criminality became linked with "objective" social characteristics compatible both with official ideology and with the popular sentiments that have mythologized the Roma long before the ascendancy of communism.

I.4 Gendered Frames

To borrow the definition of Sandra Harding, gender is a lens through which the power dynamics and processes of social change in any society are illuminated.[91] Moreover, gender politics is not only one of the most effective tools of social control and organization. It is also one of the primary ways in which one internalizes social discourse. Official discussions of gypsy deviance pointed to gendered explanations for their failure to assimilate, such as their dysfunctional families, backward reproductive and demographic patterns, unnatural sexual behavior, and incompetent parenting. As with the racist dimensions of communist social policy, the gendered aspects of these policies have not been yet adequately discussed in scholarship. The supposed deviance of

---

89 Vladimír Gecelovský, "Právne normy týkajúce sa Rómov a ich aplikácia v Gemeri (1918-1938)", in *Neznámi Rómovia: Zo života a kultúry Cigánov-Rómov na Slovensku*, ed. Arne Mann (Bratislava: Ister Science Press, 1992), 79-90.

90 Nečas, *Českoslovenští Romové v letech 1938-1945*; Hübschmannová, ed., *Po Židoch cigáni*; Marcus Pape, *A nikdo vám nebude věřit: Dokument o koncentračním táboře Lety u Písku* (Praha: G+G, 1997); Paul Polansky, "Czech Government's Cover-up of a Roma Death Camp," paper presented to the Human Dimension Seminar on Roma in the CSCE Region, Warsaw, 1994 (unpublished, now available on-line).

91 Sandra Harding, *The Science Question in Feminism* (Ithaca: Cornell University Press, 1986); these notions are further developed and applied to comparative contexts in Harding's *Is Science Multicultural? Postcolonialisms, Feminisms, and Epistemologies* (Bloomington: Indiana University Press, 1998).

Romani men and women threatened not only socialist progress, but also the gender order of Czechoslovak society as a whole. The repression of gypsy difference under the label of dysfunctionality, deviance and abnormality functioned at the same time as a way to reinforce normalized notions of sexual, reproductive, parenting and gender behavior of all Czechoslovak citizens.

Czechoslovak women (meaning non-Romani) were also controlled by the state's attention to "Gypsy" sexual, reproductive and parental behavior because this gender discourse produced a narrow range of proper gendered behavior for Czech and Slovak women to follow. Frequent comparisons to "Gypsy behavior" in terms of stereotyped, derogatory, and caricatured value judgments, such as "don't behave like a gypsy," "don't have as many children as a gypsy," "don't be as terrible a parent as a gypsy," "don't let your children run around like gypsies," and "don't be (sexually) loose like a gypsy" created injunctions that disciplined the Czechoslovak population to conform to strict sexual and gender norms.[92] Significantly, these remarks were not gender neutral but overwhelmingly related to the female body and woman's behavior, thus primarily disciplining and taming Czech and Slovak women.[93]

Thus far, scholarship on gender in Eastern Europe has strongly concentrated on women, both as subjects of research and an analytical category.[94]

---

[92] Among the stereotypical comments made about Romani gender behavior also appear positive statements, such as "she loves her child like a Gypsy" or "her lover is passionate like a Gypsy." However, as will be seen in Chapter three, the departing point of these metaphors was often perhaps well meant, but used romanticized and demeaning notion of the Roma as a "noble savage." Moreover, in lieu of the official communist policy of denying Romani culture, most literary works revealing Romani traditional values, customs, proverbs, fairy tales and legends from which to piece together a complex picture of the richness of Romani heritage became available only after 1989. See, for example, *Moudrá slova starých Romů*; *Bijav* (*Svatba*); or *Romské pohádky*.

[93] See a special issue of *Romano Džaniben: časopis romistických studií*, III:1-2 (1996), devoted to the issues of women and the politics of gender in Romani culture and Czech Romani communities; see also Hübschmannová, *Šaj Pes Dovakeras*.

[94] It is important to mention that so far, most books and collected volumes concerned with women and gender in Eastern and Central Europe have focused on the transition period and post-communism. There are still very few works on gender and women *during* the communist period. See, for example, the following classic and seminal collections of articles on women and gender in Eastern Europe: *Women, State and Party in Eastern Europe,* eds. Sharon Wolchik and Alfred Meyer (Durham: Duke University Press, 1985) and *Gender Politics and Post-Communism: Reflections from Eastern Europe and the Former Soviet Union,* eds. Nannette Funk and Magda Mueller (New York:

One of the first accounts attempting to evaluate the advantages and shortcomings of state socialism for women, was Hilda Scott's 1974 study *Does Socialism Liberate Women?*[95] As the title suggests, the driving question of this work was whether state structures and the possibilities offered by state socialism provide (mostly economic) conditions for gender equality.

Barbara Einhorn's work about a decade later also focused on "the woman question," exploring women's movements and women's ability to participate in "active citizenship."[96] Einhorn pointed out the ways in which gender inequality was rendered invisible by state socialism – such as the double burden of conceiving of women as "workers" and "mothers" without also placing the same social responsibility on men to be both "workers" and "fathers" – that led to the creation of a gender-blind society. However, her book exposes the second-class citizenship of East European women without providing an equal discussion of how the same practices affected men and relations between women and men. Moreover, she also treated the population of Eastern Europe in a homogenous manner by creating a strong binary of "women" and "men," thus assuming that all men and all women shared in the same (or very

---

Routledge, 1993). For other important studies see also special monothematic issues on women and gender in Eastern Europe of the following journals: *Transitions*, 5:1 (January 1998): "Talking about Women and Men"; *Women's History Review,* 5:4 (1996): "Special Issue: Women in Central and Eastern Europe"; *Hypatia: A Journal of Feminist Philosophy,* 8:4 (Fall 1993): "Special Cluster on Eastern European Feminism"; *Czech Sociological Review*, 7:2 (Fall 1999): "Thematic Issue: The Position of Czech Women in the Society of the 1990s in the Spectrum of Research".

95 Hilda Scott, *Does Socialism Liberate Women? Experiences from Eastern Europe* (Boston: Bacon Press, 1974).

96 Barbara Einhorn, *Cinderella Goes to Market*, p. 5 and chapter 1, "The Woman Question." Einhorn's discussion of citizenship centers around ideas of famous Central European dissidents, Adam Michnik, Georgy Konrad and Vaclav Havel, who all proposed morally acceptable alternatives to Communist citizenship by arguing for politics from below, such as "active self-ogranization" (Michnik), "antipolitics" (Konrad) or "living in truth" (Havel). Based on these notions of active participation and subversion, Einhorn sees citizenship as "not simply formal voting rights... [but] rather it implies active agency and the assertion of full individual autonomy." 3. For further discussions of civil society and citizenship in East Central Europe see, especially, Václav Havel et al., The *Power of the* Powerless; Adam Michnik, *Letters from Prison and Other Essays* (Palo Alto: University of California Press, 1986); Georgy Konrad, *Antipolitics: An Essay* (London: Quartet, 1984).

similar) conditions and experiences. More recent research has shown that this assumption was far from reality.[97]

Other studies successfully shifted the attention from "woman" and her political emancipation to examining the ways in which East European communist regimes used gendered practices to promote the goals of nationalistic ideologies. For example, Gail Kligman's study of the politics of reproduction in Ceaucescu's Romania demonstrated how policies and laws enacted in the name of national progress and growth were deeply gendered.[98] Kligman's study not only exposed the violence of prohibiting abortion and contraception in order to promote national reproduction but also analyzed the role of gender and politics of reproduction on mechanisms of social control. Like my own work, Kligman did not locate the locus of power in policies, laws and court

---

97 Susan Gal and Gail Kligman, *The Politics of Gender after Socialism: a comparative-historical essay* (Princeton: Princeton University Press, 2000) and by the same authors an edited volume *Reproducing Gender: Politics, Publics and Everyday Life After Socialism* (Princeton: Princeton University Press, 2000); Lynne Haney, *Inventing the Needy: Gender and the Politics of Welfare in Hungary* (Berkeley: University of California Press, 2002); Hana Havelková, ed., *Existuje středoevropský model manželství a rodiny? Sborník z mezinárodního sympozia.* (Praha: Divadelní ústav, 1995); S. Bridger, ed., *Women and Political Change: Perpectives from Eastern and Central Europe* (London: Macmillan, 1999). For a recent insightful collection of essays considering gender and women in East Central Europe from comparative perspective see, Sharon Wolchik a J. Jaquette, eds., *Women and Democracy in Latin America and Central and Eastern Europe* (Baltimore: Johns Hopkins University Press, 1998). For studies on most recent problems facing women in Eastern Europe see, *Women 2000: An Investigation into the Status of Women's Rights in Central and South-Eastern Europe and the Newly Independent States.* (International Helsinki Federation for Human Rights, 2000); Insightful articles analyzing gender stratification in Czechoslovakia and the Czech Republic inlude: Hana Havelková, "Abstract Citizenship? Women and Power in the Czech Republic", *Social Politics: International Studies in Gender, State and Society*, 3:2-3 (Summer/Fall 1996): 243-260; by the same author, "Women in and after a 'classless' society", in Christine Zmroczek and Pat Mahony, eds., *Women and Social Class – International Feminist Perspectives* (London: Taylor and Francis Group, 1999), 69-84; Jiřina Šmejkalová, "Gender as an Analytical Category of Post-Communist Studies", in G. Jahnert, J. Gohrisch, D. Hahn, H. M. Nickel, I. Peinl a K. Schafgen, eds., *Gender in Transition in Eastern and Central Europe Proceedings*. Berlin: Trafo Verlag, 2001); and Angie Argent, "Post-Communism and 'Women's Experience'?", in *Feminist Approaches to Social Movements, Communist and Power*, Robin Teske and Mary Ann Tetreault, eds. (Columbus: University of South Carolina Press, 2000).

98 Gail Kligman, *The Politics of Duplicity: Controlling Reproduction in Ceaucescu's Romania* (Berkeley: University of California Press, 1998).

documents, but in the agency of doctors, nurses, and husbands in controlling women's reproduction.

Kligman's strategy of looking at communist welfare state systems through the lens of the abusive politics of reproduction is very useful in considering the treatment of the "Gypsy question" in Czechoslovakia. However, Kligman herself did not pay attention to how the politics of ethnicity related to the politics of reproduction and sexuality in order to examine whether Romani women were encouraged or discouraged to have children "in the name of the nation." This is particularly surprising given that her study focused on Romania, which not only has one of the largest Romani populations in Eastern Europe, but is also known as one of the most hostile countries toward the Roma due to its violent pogroms after 1989.[99]

Traditionally, gender and race have not been used as analytical tools for interpreting socialist medicine and population politics in Eastern Europe.[100] Besides Kligman, there were a few other notable efforts to demonstrate that inclusion of gender analysis shifts significantly the picture of socialist medical sciences, which traditional accounts tend to give. Alena Heitlinger, for example, provided very comprehensive and insightful discussions of socialist welfare systems, gendered medical practices and population politics in Eastern Europe, showing how these institutions rested on the woman as the locus of reproduction and family, and arguing that the rhetoric of gender equality under communism was indeed largely an illusion.[101] On the other hand, Heitlin-

---

99 For treatment of the Roma in Romania see, for example, Nicolae Gheorghe, "Ethnic Minorities in Romania under Socialism," *East European Quarterly,* 7:4 (January 1974): 435-58; Zoltan Barany, "Roma: Grim Realities in Eastern Europe," *Transitions,* 1:4 (March 1995): 3-8; Fonseca, *Bury Me Standing*; Helsinki Human Rights Watch, *Destroying Ethnic Identity: The Gypsies of Romania* (New York: Human Rights Watch, 1991).

100 For classic studies of the politics of reproduction in Eastern Europe see, for example, John Besemeres, *Socialist Population Policy: The Political Implications of Demographic Trends in the USSR and Eastern Europe* (New York: M.E. Sharpe, 1980); Henry David and Robert McIntyre, *Reproductive Behavior: Central and Eastern European Experience* (New York: Springer Publ. Co., 1981); Richard Weinerman, *Social Medicine in Eastern Europe: The Organization of Health Services and the Education of Medical Personnel in Czechoslovakia, Hungary and Poland* (Cambridge, MA: Harvard University Press, 1969).

101 Alena Heitlinger, *Reproduction, Medicine and the Socialist State* (London: MacMillan Press, 1987); *Women and State Socialism: Sex Inequality in the Soviet Union and*

ger matter-of-factly dismissed attention paid to sterilization under communism as irrelevant and meaningless, because this practice was, according to her, "statistically insignificant."[102]

Similarly, Tracy Smith's essay on unexamined institutional racism of state medical services has been instrumental in contextualizing the apprehensions of Romani women to participate in state-provided health care.[103] While others readily read these anxieties of Romani women as a dimension of their "cultural difference" or "preferences,"[104] Smith argued that Romani women's reluctance to submit to "scientific authorities" has to be read as a logical, collectively felt consequence of the Romani historical experience of the Holocaust and other tragedies. However, Smith did not explore the theoretical implications of her argument for considering the intersections of gender and race as a meaningful conceptual framework for the study of the historical marginalization of the Roma. On the other hand, both Michael Stewart and Isabel Fonseca use gender as an analytical tool to expose the gender inequalities and domestic and sexual abuses in Romani families that are often treated as distinctive traits or values of Romani culture, but neither of them use the concept to investigate how gender and race were used in official discourses to marginalize the Roma.[105]

American scholarship of the politics of gender, sexuality and reproduction, on the other hand, has demonstrated that race and ethnicity as analytic

---

Czechoslovakia (Montreal: McGill-Queen's University Press, 1979); and "Passage to Motherhood: Personal and Social Management of Reproduction in Czechoslovakia in the 1980s", in *Women, State, and Party in Eastern Europe,* eds. Sharon Wolchik and Alfred Meyer.

102 Heitlinger, *Reproduction, Medicine and the Socialist State*, 77.

103 Tracy Smith, "Racist Encounters: Romani 'Gypsy' Women and Mainstream Health Services," *The European Journal of Women's Studies*, 4 (1997): 183-196.

104 These arguments about gypsy cultural particularism in the context of institutional services include, for example, Judith Okely, "Gypsy Women: Models in Conflict," in *Perceiving Women*, ed. Shirley Ardener (New York: John Wiley & Sons, 1975); or Carol Silverman, "Pollution and Power: Gypsy Women in America" and Ruth Andersen, "Women of Kalderas", both in *The American Kalderas: Gypsies in the New World*, ed. Matt Salo (Centenary College: Gypsy Lore Society, North American Chapter Publications, No. 1, 1981).

105 Isabel Fonseca, *Bury Me Standing*, especially 40-53, 80-82, 130-32; Michael Stewart, *The Time of the Gypsies*, especially chapters 4 ("We Are All Brothers Here") and 12 (The Shame of the Body).

categories are integral to analyses of gender.[106] Kimberlé Crenshaw coined the term "intersectionality" to describe the inherent interactions and mutual influence gender and race play in constructing social reality and shaping the experience of historical subjects.[107] Since this book is premised on the notion that identities can never be assumed because they are discursively produced, Crenshaw's argument about the constant negotiations of gender, race and sexuality can serve as a useful conceptual lens for studying the "Gypsy question" in Czechoslovakia.

In addition, the literature on comparative eugenics and the politics of reproduction provides convincing empirical evidence for the necessity of treating reproductive politics and sexuality in the context of complex racial, ethnic and nationalistic politics.[108] Dorothy Roberts has argued that "reproductive freedom is a matter of social justice not individual choice" and pointed out that American reproductive politics has been inextricably and inevitably tied with racial politics because black reproduction has been treated as a form

---

[106] One of the most insightful and comprehensive theoretical treatments of this topic is Valerie Smith's *Not Just Race, Not Just Gender: Black Feminist Readings* (New York and London: Routledge, 1998). For other studies most relevant to this book see also, Patricia Hill Collins, *Fighting Words* and a collection of essays *Lure and Loathing: Essays on Race, Identity, and the Ambivalence of Assimilation*, ed. Gerald Early (New York: Penguin, 1993).

[107] Kimberlé Crenshaw, "Demarginalizing the Intersection of Race and Sex: A Black Feminist Critique of Antidiscrimination Doctrine, Feminist Theory and Antiracist Politics," *The University of Chicago Legal Forum* (1989): 139-67.

[108] See for example, Daniel Kevles, *In the Name of Eugenics: Genetics and the Uses of Human Heredity* (New York: Alfred Knopf, 1985); Nancy Stepan, *The Hour of Eugenics: Race, Gender, and Nation in Latin America* (Ithaca: Cornell University Press, 1991); Roger Pearson, *Shockley on Eugenics and Race: The Application of Science to the Solution of Human Problems* (Washington, D.C.: Scott-Townsend Publishers, 1992); Cornelie Usborne, *The Politics of the Body in Weimar Germany: Women's Reproductive Rights and Duties* (Ann Arbor: The University of Michigan Press, 1992); Betsy Hartman, *Reproductive Rights and Wrongs: The Global Politics of Population Control* (Boston: South End Press, 1995); Phillip Reilly, *The Surgical Solution: A History of Involuntary Sterilization in the United States* (Baltimore: Johns Hopkins University Press, 1991); Allan Chase, *The Legacy of Malthus: The Social Costs of the New Scientific Racism* (Urbana: University of Illinois Press, 1980); Robert Weisbord, *Genocide? Birth Control and the Black American* (Westport: Greenwood and Two Continents, 1975).

of degeneracy or social pathology.[109] Similarly, in her study of single pregnancy and motherhood in America, Rickie Solinger exposed the production of myths about black deviant sexual behavior and parenting as consequences of the nexus of racism and sexism inherent in American social and political discourse.[110] Such approaches to the politics of reproduction provide a useful entry point for analyzing the construction of Gypsy deviance and stereotypes of Romani reproduction under Czechoslovak communism.

Obviously, there were dimensions of the "Gypsy question," such as reproductive politics, sterilization practice or discourse on parenting and education, where gender played a more significant role than in others, primarily because in those contexts the politics of race and gender were either directly exercised on female bodies or affected Romani women in profoundly different ways than Romani men. Nonetheless, despite the fact that in several chapters of this book attention to gender is of primary importance, "gender" does not form any separate section but rather permeates the entire work.

The positioning of gender constituted the final part in the presentation of conceptual frameworks and analytical tools that this book is using. The following chapter turns its attention back to postwar Czechoslovakia, where the historical narrative of the "Gypsy question" begins.

---

[109] Dorothy Roberts, *Killing the Black Body: Race, Reproduction and the Meaning of Liberty* (New York: Vintage, 1999), 6-7. For similar arguments see, also, Kathleen Brown, *Good Wives, Nasty Wenches & Anxious Patriarchs: Gender, Race, and Power in Colonial Virginia* (Chapel Hill: University of North Carolina Press, 1996).

[110] Rickie Solinger, *Wake Up Little Susie: Single Pregnancy and Race Before Roe v. Wade* (New York: Routledge, 1992).

II Reframing Injustice: Towards New Politics of Ethnicity

Most of the Czech and Moravian Roma never made it back from the Czech-run labor camps in the Protectorate of Bohemia and Moravia and the Nazi concentration camps in Poland and Germany. Barely six hundred of them returned.[111] By the beginning of the 1950s, however, the number of "Gypsies" in Czechoslovakia swelled up to over 109,000 (16, 752 in the Czech lands, 84,400 in Slovakia)[112] and the "Gypsy question" had become one of the most troubling political, ideological and social issues the communist government faced. In order to understand this development it is necessary to set the "Gypsy question" in the context of ethnic sentiments and the nationality policies Czechoslovakia was pursuing immediately after the Second World War. These circumstances provided crucial conditions for the creation of the societal attitudes toward the Roma that were to mark the entire communist period. Some scholars argue that the decimation of the Czech and Moravian Roma during *Pořajmos*, the Romani Holocaust, represents a break in the historical continuity of the coexistence of the Romani and non-Romani populations in the Czech lands and Slovakia and forms one of the unique aspects of Romani history in Czechoslovakia.[113] This discontinuity was one of the reasons

---

[111] Nečas, *Českoslovenští Romové*, 13-15; Holý and Nečas, *Žalující píseň*; Jana Kramářová a kol. *(Ne)bolí: Vzpomínky Romů na válku a život po válce* (Praha: Člověk v tísni, 2005), an oral history project, which resulted in a book of interviews. The situation in Slovakia was quite different. Most Slovak Roma survived WWII and after the war was resettled into Bohemia and Moravia. For an excellent treatment of the Slovak Roma experience during WWII see especially Milena Hübschmannová, ed. *Po Židoch cigáni* (cited ealier). This book, which has almost 900 pages, is a combination of oral history and historical analysis. More than 60 survivors participated in the seven-year project. See also, Ingrid Vagačová and Martin Fotta, eds. *Rómovia a druhá svetová vojna – čítanka* (Bratislava: Nadácia Milana Šimečku, 2006).

[112] Statistics of the Ministry of Interior as cited in Kalibová, 99.

[113] For example, Jana Machačová, "K výzkumu romského etnika", *Slezský sborník*, 91/3 (1993), 172-177; Ctibor Nečas, *Nemůžeme zapomenout – Našti Bisteras* (Olomouc: Univerzita Palackého Press, 1994).

that enabled Czechoslovak society to perceive the Roma after WWII as a new, foreign element, allowing a sense of alienation and superiority.

This chapter examines the development of institutional policies and societal attitudes toward the Roma in the immediate postwar period, which set the context for later developments. While the majority of historical accounts dealing with the immediate Czechoslovak post-WWII period are devoted either to discussions of how the Communists were able to grab the monopoly of power so easily or to the controversy over the expulsion of the Sudeten Germans from the Czech borderlands, the following chapter shifts the attention to this period in a different direction.[114] It examines official documents and media dealing with issues of social rebuilding, progress and health in order to understand the context, interaction and interrelation between societal sentiments toward the Roma and official answers directed at them.

The chapter is divided into three parts that thematically and chronologically mark the fundamental transformations in the official rhetoric and societal attitudes toward the Roma in the first postwar decade, which participated in the forming of the emerging politics of ethnicity in the country. The first section covers the pre-Communist years of 1945-1948, which were characterized by major demographic shifts of the Romani population, a large degree of social and institutional flux, the absence of a centralized policy on the "Gypsy

---

[114] Despite this traditional trend, there are new insightful and valuable works, broadening the scope of study and complicating the picture. See especially, Eagle Glassheim, "National Mythologies and Ethnic Cleansing: The Expulsion of Czechoslovak Germans in 1945." *Central European History*, 33:4 (2000): 463-486; Benjamin Frommer, *National Cleansing: Retribution against Nazi Collaborators in Postwar Czechoslovakia* (Cambridge: Cambridge University Press, 2005); Bradley Abrams, *The Struggle for the Soul of the Nation: Czech Culture and the Rise of Communism* (Lanham, MD: Rowman & Littlefield Publishers, Inc., 2005) and John Connelly's analysis of the postwar ideological indoctrination of the university systems in Eastern Europe, *Captive University: The Sovietization of East German, Czechoslovak and Polish Higher Education, 1945-1956* (Chapel Hill: University of North Carolina Press, 2000). For older works, see, for example, Karel Kaplan, *The Short March: The Communist Takeover in Czechoslovakia, 1945-1948* (New York: St. Martin's Press, 1987); Timothy Butcher, *The Sudeten German Question and Czechoslovak-German Relations since 1989* (London: Royal United Services Institute for Defense Studies, 1996); Radomír Luža, *The Transfer of the Sudeten Germans: A Study of Czech-German Relations, 1933-1962* (New York: New York University Press, 1964); Karel Lisický, *Problém česko-slovenský a problém česko-německý* (London: Blackwell, 1954).

question," a significant degree of regional and local autonomy, and independent media. Institutionally, the foundation of popular sentiment toward the Roma at this time was prewar "Gypsy legislation" that enacted repressive policies and initiated a concerted effort to either restrict the movement of "Gypsies" or push them beyond the national borders.[115] The textual and contextual analysis of the documents indicates that the initial grappling with the "Gypsy question" was by no means thought-out and united. It was rather chaotic and confused, allowing for outbursts of negative sentiments from the media and cementing a notion that the Roma were a foreign, undesired and dangerous element threatening the peaceful and progressive future of Czechoslovakia.

The second part begins with the political transition of the "Victorious February" of 1948, when the Communist Party assumed power over the country, and covers roughly the first half of the 1950s. During this period the government attempted to centralize its policy toward the Roma and started to articulate arguments for the later replacement of its repressive apparatus with an "educational" one. This shift of strategy of political control ended in the issuance of the decree "Adjustment of Conditions of Persons of Gypsy Origin" in March 1952.[116] The decree was a product of collaborative efforts by the ministries of interior, social care, "enlightenment" and information (*osvěty a informací*), and some other central offices. In a most revealing twist of official rhetoric at this time, this decree did not simply focus on the Roma themselves, but predominantly on the attitudes and behavior of authorities and the rest of the society toward the Roma. The proclaimed goals and rhetoric of the decree reveals how much state authorities became aware of the discrepancy between denying ethnicity to the Roma yet treating them as a separate group.

The last section of the chapter covers the late 1950s, which were characterized by the passing of a fundamentally important anti-nomadic law and subsequent coercive assimilative efforts to physically tame the Roma. The adoption of the law in 1958, representing the culmination of a decade-long effort to physically subjugate the Roma, can be regarded as a major landmark

115 Grulich and Haišman, "Institucionální zájem", 72-85.

116 *Sbírka oběžníků pro Krajské národní výbory* (KNV), roč. IV, 1952, č. 13, poř. č. 140, March 5, 1952.

in the development of the "Gypsy question," as it provided a significant first step in the self-delusive belief of communist officials that "Gypsies" can be herded, contained, silenced and, as an ethnic identity, assimilated out of existence.

II.1 Gypsies as a "Foreign Element"

Like any other country coming out of the rubble of the war, Czechoslovakia after WWII was dealing with a number of difficult and complex issues that were competing for priority in both financial and personnel terms. The full-blown victory of the communist ideology and the change of the democratic regime into a socialist one in February 1948 were still almost three years away. The leadership of the country was negotiating the difficult situation of having had two political representations in exile during the war. On the one hand, there was the official government headed by the prewar president Edward Beneš that during the war had found its exile in London and from there kept pursuing Czechoslovak international diplomacy as well as organized a few major underground resistance activities in the Nazi occupied Protectorate Bohemia and Moravia. On the other hand, there was the unofficial communist leadership that had established its headquarters in Moscow and directed most of the popular resistance and national uprisings during the last two years of the war in both the Protectorate and the Slovak State that separated from Czechoslovakia immediately before the war in 1939 and during the war pursued a pro-Nazi politics.[117] As a consequence of the successful domestic anti-Nazi resistance activities during the war, the communist leadership had

---

[117] For comprehensive analyses of interwar Czechoslovakia and its political scene see James Felak, *At the Price of the Republic: Hlinka's Slovak People's Party, 1929-1938* (Pittsburgh: University of Pittsburgh Press, 1994) or, by the same author, "Slovak Considerations of the Slovak Question: the Ludak, Agrarian, Socialist and Communist views in interwar Czechoslovakia," in *The Czech and Slovak Experience*, ed. J. Morison (New York: St. Martin's Press, 1992). For an insightful study covering the entire existence of Czechoslovakia see, for example, Carol S. Leff, *National Conflict in Czechoslovakia: the making and remaking of a state, 1918-1987* (Princeton: Princeton University Press, 1988); for Slovak-Czech relations, see Jan Měchýř, *Slovensko v Československu: Slovensko-české vztahy 1918-1991* (Praha: Práce, 1991).

greater popular support than the returned London government, a reality confirmed by the win of the Communists in the 1946 elections, when the Party had the strongest showing.[118]

Perhaps understandably, the post-WWII atmosphere was extremely nationalistic. Less than twenty years earlier, during the interwar First Republic, Czechoslovakia espoused a more or less moderate and tolerant approach to ethnic coexistence and demonstrated an awareness of its minorities and sensitivity to ethnic discrimination; sentiments, which emerged directly as a result of long Austro-Hungarian rule. The first Czechoslovak president Tomáš Garrigue Masaryk even explicitly argued that:

> The task of the Czechoslovak Government is to make the minorities feel themselves at home in Czechoslovakia. They must not think of themselves as minorities. Czechoslovakia must become their state, as it is the state of the Czechs and Slovaks. The term "Czechoslovaks" must denote not only the Czechs and Slovaks, but all the inhabitants of the Republic. There is only one way to achieve this end: the way of tolerance and of cooperation.[119]

Unfortunately, World War II changed all that. Already during the war the Beneš-led government in exile had worked on its vision of renewal for postwar Czechoslovakia as a nation state of Czechs and Slovaks – a policy that it vigorously pursued on international and domestic fronts after the war as well. Sobered by the experience from the interwar period and the consequences of the Munich agreement the Czechoslovak representation saw in such an arrangement the only guarantee of the future existence, stability and security of the small country.[120] One of the central components of this nationalist strategy was the government's decision to eliminate undesirable national minorities

---

[118] Kaplan, *The Short March*, 23. Close relations with the Soviet Union was also the core component of Czechoslovak foreign policy, which was built on the central belief that since the West could not be counted on due to the Munich experience, Czechoslovakia needed another strong ally as a reliable protection against Germany.

[119] Cited from Aleš Brož, "Minority Rights in the Czechoslovak State," *Foreign Affairs*, Oct. 1927: 160. I am grateful for this quote to the anonymous reviewer of *ibidem*-Verlag, who commented on my manuscript and suggested I include it.

[120] See, for example, Hugh Ragsdale, *The Soviets, the Munich Crisis, and the Coming of World War II* (Cambridge: Cambridge University Press, 2004); F.G. Campbell, *Confrontation in Central Europe: Weimar Germany and Czechoslovakia* (Chicago: Chicago University Press, 1975).

that were perceived as threatening and destructive to its efforts to build a secure Czechoslovak state.[121] The declarations of the Potsdam Conference in 1945 created favorable conditions for the government's intention to handle problems of ethnicity and nationalism through the expulsion of German and Hungarian national minorities from the Czechoslovak territory.[122]

Recognizing Czechoslovak grievances about the need to appropriately and justly respond to the cruelties that the Nazi regime and its collaborators had inflicted on the Czech and Slovak people, the Allies agreed with Beneš' government that it could "humanely transfer" (which was read and enacted as "ethnically cleanse") Germans from the country.[123] In 1946 and 1947, more than two and a half million ethnic Germans were forcefully and violently expelled from the Czechoslovak borderlands.[124] While these events are visible and well documented episodes of postwar Czechoslovak history, there has been little discussion of the significance of this as a context and prelude for future Czech-Romani relations.

---

[121] Chad Bryant, "Either German or Czech: Fixing Nationality in Bohemia and Moravia, 1939-1946," *Slavic Review*, 61:4 (Winter, 2002): 683-706.

[122] Norman Naimark, *Fires of Hatred: Ethnic Cleansing in Twentieth-Century Europe* (Cambridge, MA: Harvard University Press, 2002), especially Chapter 4, "The Expulsion of the Germans from Poland and Czechoslovakia" (108-138); George Klein and Milan Reban, eds., *The Politics of Ethnicity in Eastern Europe* (Boulder, CO: Eastern European Monographs No.93, 1981); Jaroslav Krejčí and Vítězslav Velimski, *Ethnic and Political Nations in Europe* (New York: St. Martin's Press, 1984). However, the expulsion of Hungarians was never completed. There are several possible explanations for that. For one, the Magyar deportation never received the same degree of support from the Great Powers as the expulsion of Germans did. Two, the Czechs, who dominated the newly reconstituted Czechoslovakia, placed their priority on settling the German question in the Czech borderlands and did not see the Hungarian issue in Slovakia as equally pressing. And three, Germany certainly presented a much greater threat and reason for vengeance to Czechoslovakia than Hungary did.

[123] In this regard, Naimark asserts that "the Polish and Czech cases [of ethnic cleansing] are interesting because they reverse the moral lenses through which we view ethnic cleansing." He also argues that these cases are "instructive in the sense that ethnic cleansing was conceived and carried out by democratic regimes." *Fires of Hatred*, 14.

[124] Naimark argues that "the worst of the ethnic cleansing had already taken place ... by August 1945." *Fires of Hatred*, 15. See also, Ladislav Holý, *The Little Czech and the Great Czech Nation: national identity and the post-communist social transformation* (Cambridge: Cambridge University Press, 1996), 79, 97-99, and 123-24; or Luža, *The Transfer of Sudeten Germans*, chapter one.

I propose that these strategic responses to ethnic problems after 1945 in fact played a crucial role in the way Czechoslovak society subsequently approached and dealt with the Roma. The fact that the international situation after WWII permitted the Czechoslovak government to solve such complex ethnic issues – and allowed for ethnic purification of its citizens' social networks – through such disturbing measures enabled people to believe that an ethnically homogenous state was desirable, just, and internationally acceptable. Furthermore, the ability of the government to eliminate the "Czech-German question" in this way created the illusion that ethnic conflict can be successfully solved through administrative means.

The expulsion of Germans from the Czech lands and Hungarians from southern Slovakia (which never succeeded in reaching similar proportions) created conditions for resettlement policies and programs. The government made significant efforts to compensate population declines through re-emigration and resettlement policies. In the still very chaotic immediate post-war conditions, the government exchanged or attempted to exchange parts of populations with the Soviet Union and Hungary and strived to motivate ethnic Czechs and Slovaks living abroad to return to the country to man the borderlands.[125]

The heightened spirit of post-WWII nationalist rhetoric in official documents and media divided the world into a "Slavic" and a "non-Slavic" one, favoring the "Slavs" in all respects, especially in terms of land acquisition. The presidential decree of June 21, 1945 spoke directly of "confiscation and speedy redistribution of agricultural property of Germans, Hungarians, as well as traitors and enemies of the Czech and Slovak nations."[126] According to paragraph 7, land and agricultural property could be allotted only to persons of "Slavic nationality." If there were not enough land candidates of Slavic origin in a certain area, the land would remain in the hands of the National Property Fund. A month later, Beneš issued another decree that expanded

[125] Helena Nosková et al., *Vývoj národnostní a etnické struktury československé společnosti v letech 1945-1950* (Praha: Ústav soudobých dějin, edice Studijní materiály, 1999), 5-7.

[126] *Dekret prezidenta republiky ze dne 21. června 1945 "O konfiskaci a urychleném rozdělení zemědělského majetku Němců, Maďarů, jakož i zrádců a nepřátel českého a slovenského národa."* Státní ústřední archív (SÚAR) Praha.

the language of the document to directly talk about "settling the land of Germans, Hungarians and other state enemies by Czech, Slovak and other Slavic farmers."[127] The ethnically charged nature of these policies and discourses implicitly created conditions for treating the Roma as "other," "non-Slavic" and strange elements that should be separated from the rest of society.

The Košice Governmental Program (*Košický vládní program*), the first official program for reconstructing the political, economic and societal foundations of the country, proclaimed as one of its binding principles the "prohibition of any discrimination of citizens of Czechoslovakia for racial or religious reasons."[128] In other words, insofar as Roma were not categorized as war criminals or Nazi collaborators, they should be treated like any other citizens of the country. Anna Jurová, a Slovak historian of the Roma, argues that as individuals Roma had the same chances and opportunities to be full-fledged members in society like anybody else. She claims that "they had the opportunity as citizens to integrate into society and employment" and argues that "they were prevented from integrating only as a specific ethnic group with certain rights and interests." According to her, it was the problem of the Roma community itself that it "did not represent any collective subject with its own representation, which would be able to fight for the interests of its ethnic group."[129] In a startling twist of argument, Jurová comes quite close to blaming the Roma themselves for their inability to mobilize and achieve political representation, therefore causing their own discrimination and marginalization.

---

[127] *Dekret prezidenta republiky ze dne 20. července 1945 "O osídlení zemědělské půdy Němců, Maďarů a jiných nepřátel státu českými, slovenskými a jinými slovanskými zemědělci,"* §2. (SÚAR Praha).

[128] *Košický vládní program*, § 3. (Národní knihovna v Praze.) In the context of the time, references about "racial discrimination" were essentially proclamations about racial equality of Jews. The state was quite openly willing to discriminate against Germans and Hungarians on ethnic grounds and, in similar spirit, denunciations of racism almost exclusively meant German abuses against Jews. While there is no direct evidence, it is highly unlikely that the state consciously considered the Roma when making these declarations.

[129] Anna Jurová, *Vývoj romskej problematiky na Slovensku po roku 1945.* (Bratislava: Goldpress Publishers, 1993), 26.

However, documents make it clear that the Roma did not have the same opportunities as "ordinary citizens." Not only were they exempt from the agricultural property laws by virtue of not being of "Slavic" origin, they were also actively prevented from resettling Czech industrial regions. Interestingly, on the one hand, the country was very sensitive to its nationality policies, which prevented all non-Slavic persons from acquiring land. On the other hand, the mobilization of unskilled labor for quarry work in the borderland regions of Northern Bohemia actively recruited people in Slovakia, including Hungarians (who were, as non-Slavs, ineligible to acquire property) but directly excluding the Roma. The Slovak Board of Commissioners issued a binding decree for the Slovak Settlement Office, which stated that "on December 3 [1945] the recruitment of 250 Hungarian workers – breadwinners in Southern Slovakia – had begun." The strict requirements of the decree specified that the "breadwinners" could not be over 50 years of age and they could resettle with their family members only on a limited scale (only three family members per one breadwinner). However, the decree also stipulated that the recruitment should not include "asocial elements," adding explicitly "gypsies" in parentheses for clarification.[130]

This attitude demonstrates that as a group, the Roma were considered "asocial" and thus were not supposed to receive any employment, surprisingly not even in the physically demanding and dangerous quarries, where there was a permanent shortage of manpower. This parenthetic remark is significant for a couple of reasons. Firstly, it seems to indicate that the issue in question was not so much preventing the Roma from acquiring unhealthy jobs, which the rest of the population was minimally interested in, as it was preventing them "infiltrating" a new territory, previously not settled by them, with their families. Secondly, it clearly demonstrates that policies dealing with resettlement, national questions and issues concerning the Roma in particular were by no means unified and that the human factor on the local level stepped into the process of implementation and interpretation from the very beginning.

---

130 SNA Bratislava, fond Úradu predsednictva sboru poverenikov 1945-1960, č. kr. 4, č. sp. II-1. As some documents of complaints of the Hungarians reveal, some of these workers were resettled forcibly against their will.

World War II wiped out the Romani population of the Czech lands in such a way that it made some scholars argue that "in the first months [of the postwar period] the so-called gypsy question seemed to be completely solved."[131] This assertion is supported by a finding of the Czech historian Helena Nosková, who claims that "there is no mention of 'gypsies' at all in the Czech governmental archives for the year 1945."[132] One of the reasons why the Roma did not constitute a separate "problem" for the authorities immediately after the war is the fact that they could be (and were) included in the general battle against "asocial elements" and/or the battle against "foreigners." The wording of the 1927 "Law on Wandering Gypsies" (*Zákon o potulných cikánech*) directly legitimized this kind of treatment. Paragraph 9 of the law "forbids residence in Czechoslovakia to all foreign wandering gypsies who cannot identify themselves with a special residence permit issued by the Ministry of Interior."[133] Based on this legislation, effective until 1950, all state authorities had the power to prevent any persons deemed as "wandering

---

[131] Ctibor Nečas, *Nad osudem českých a slovenských cikánů* (Brno: ÚJEP Press, 1981), 34. According to the 1930 census, there were only 2,974 Roma in interwar Czechoslovakia (from which only 227 were in the Czech lands). However, this number is, according to several demographers and historians concerned with the interwar period, including Nečas, extremely underrated for two reasons. One, it refers only to Roma as a nationality and two, it contains only settled Roma, who spoke Romany. The census defined nationality as a "tribal affiliation whose outer expression is mother tongue." Thus all Roma on the move and those who spoke Czech or Slovak or those who would not designate themselves as Roma would not be included in this census. Cited in Květa Kalibová, "Romové z pohledu statistiky a demografie." In *Romové v České republice, 1945-1998: sešity pro sociální politiku* (Praha: Socioklub, 1999), 91-114. The Czechoslovak Central Criminal Bureau, for example, issued by WWII 36,696 of so-called "nomadic ID cards" to "all nomadic gypsies" living in Czechoslovakia during the interwar period. *Zpráva kriminální ústředny z r. 1948*, E/2 III/6. Cited in Zdeňka Jamnická-Šmerglová, *Dějiny našich cikánů* (Praha: Orbis, 1955), 65. And Gypsy census conducted in the territory of the Protectorate of Bohemia and Moravia in January 1940 counted 6,540 settled Gypsies in the Protectorate alone and indicated that another 500 Gypsies, who were imprisoned at the time (plus an "unspecified number of Gypsies . . . hiding in the woods"), were not even taken into the count. Cited in Josef Mareš, "Vývoj cikánské otázky v Protektorátu Čechy a Morava," *Věstník Úřadu četnické policie*, April 1940, 280-281. (SÚAR Praha, Fond Generálního velitelství četnictva, i.č. 117, čj. 850 k. 63.)

[132] Helena Nosková. "Češi, Slováci a Romové po II. světové válce", *Romano Džaniben*, VII:3 (2000): 58-63.

[133] "Zákon ze dne 14. července 1927 o potulných cikánech." Cited in Jamnická-Šmerglová, 67.

gypsies" from entering into or settling in their regions and expel them beyond the borders of their districts. Under the term "gypsy" were lumped a wide array of people who had nothing in common with the Roma, but were deemed threatening to the society for a variety of reasons. Designating all vagrants as "gypsies" certainly did not contribute to clarifying the term nor did it help the population to distinguish between the Roma and social troublemakers. To the contrary, one can argue that it did much to cement the notion that "gypsies" are an inherent threat to the society's safety and prosperity.

However, there was at least one initiative directly speaking about the Roma. In a shocking statement, immediately following the end of WWII in December 1945, the Prague Regional National Committee[134] (*Zemský národní výbor*) called for the "abolition of gypsy wandering, beggary and theft, as well as securing the proper upbringing of gypsy children." It also asked for "immediately and unconditionally renewing the regulation of the gypsy population, issuing a strict prohibition on nomadism and the free movement of gypsies in the Czech lands, and prohibiting their entrance to Prague, Czech spa towns and some other cities."[135] This document demonstrates that from very early on a language of social deviancy was used to speak about the Roma in order to designate the group as a whole.

This rhetoric nearly resembles the treatment of Sinti and Roma in Nazi Germany when they were systematically prohibited from entering spa resorts and some towns.[136] It is astonishing that this language was used in such an open and outspoken form more than half a year after the Košice Governmental Program announced the end of any discrimination based on race and ethnicity. It also reveals what seemed to be most threatening about the presence of the Roma: the perception of their different lifestyle and values that made

---

134 National Committees were hierarchically set up institutions of regional autonomy that represented the communist version of delegation of responsibility and authority to regional and local rule.

135 SÚAR Praha. Fond Zemského úřadu, č. kr. 855, č. sp. III-8, 1946-1948.

136 For discussions whether Sinti and Roma under the Nazi regime were discriminated from the beginning on a social or racial grounds, see, for example, Henry Friedlander, *The Origins of Nazi Genocide: From Euthanasia to the Final Solution* (Chapell Hill: University of North Carolina Press, 1995), 252; Burleigh and Wippermann, *The Racial State*; Jeremy Noakes. "Life in the Third Reich: Social Outcasts in Nazi Germany," *History Today*, 17:35 (1985), 15-19; Huttenbach, "The Romani Porajmos," 31-33.

them uncontrollable and untamable by conventional means. The combination of accusations of criminal behavior, such as theft and beggary, on the one hand, and different cultural values, such as nomadism and family beliefs, on the other hand, into one unified desire to eliminate Romani difference reveals that the seeds for interchanging social and ethic categories were a part of Czechoslovak social discourse immediately after the war and helped solidify both official and unofficial attitudes toward the Roma.

Even though Haišman argues that in the first years after the war "the official documents were somewhat vague about their attitude toward the Roma,"[137] there are reports that prove that even the highest authorities engaged in rhetoric about the Roma demonstrating hostility and disgust at the very least. Although these reports do not represent official policy in the sense of being enacted legislation, as officially expressed opinions of state authorities about the Roma they offer a glimpse into the subjective sentiments, which entered into the semantic processes that ascribed "asocial" categories to the Roma population. For example, a Deputy Committee of the Ministry of Interior, the highest state institution in the area of domestic security, complained that policies in the forced labor camps opened after the war in Slovakia were "too lenient." In these camps, "most dangerous individuals" were detained for periods of time in order to help to rebuild the country. The authorities complained that such measures, imprisoning people for only limited time, were not adequate because "even after gypsies are released" from the camps "the asocial persons do not stop being dangerous for the society. Besides that what is becoming impossible to deal with is all the baggage (*balast* in Slovak) – old people, women, children, diseases, criminality, the overbearing birth rate."[138] The formulation of this complaint equates the Roma with "overbearing" social problems that characterize them as a group.

---

[137] Tomáš Haišman, "Snahy centrálních orgánů státní správy o řešení tzv. cikánské otázky v českých zemích v letech 1945 až 1947 ve světle tisku," *Český lid*, 76:1 (1989): 4-11; 7. Haišman is not alone in this view. The leniency and vagueness of official documents is supported also by Kaplan, *O cenzuře v Československu v letech 1945-1956* (Praha: Ústav soudobých dějin, 1994). However, both authors speak of the leniency and opacity in relation to later strict censorship, thus their arguments must be taken comparatively and not at face value.

[138] SNA Bratislava, Fond Povereníctva informácií a osvety, 1945-1952, č. sp. 8500/46, č. kr. 43.

Based on these frustrations, the Committee formulated a proposal submitted to the Ministry of Interior that requested that "children younger than 18 should be taken away from nomadic gypsies for social, health and moral/ethical (*mravní*) reasons."[139] Further, the Committee recommended that "professional prostitutes be placed in reformatory institutions."[140] Perhaps because the proposal was rejected and thus never materialized, it has not been discussed in the academic literature on the institutional treatment of the Roma. However, given the official self-delusion about the alleged absence of racist sentiments in Czechoslovakia, such documents carry crucial importance in suggesting the latent discriminatory dimensions of the enacted state policies.

Equally revealing are some of the openly hostile sentiments and attitudes expressed in the Czech and Slovak press. One article, entitled "How gypsies 'take care' of livestock: a strange farmer's cooperative," discusses the high rate of dying livestock in a Czech village. When police came to investigate the case, they found that in the cooperative "there are 25 gypsies employed under the leadership of a Slovak master. ... The animals are dying of thirst, hunger and cold (gypsies do not leave their dwellings in the freezing weather, they even out of pure malice knocked out windows of the sties.)"[141]

In May 1945 the Communist daily *Rudé právo* reported that the "attempt of the Košice labor office to get gypsies to work was successful." This attempt involved a "draft" of the Roma into forced labor camps in Eastern Slovakia. The paper reported that through this step the Slovak authorities were solving "the question of integrating gypsies into the work process." Apparently, "the authorities were finding out which gypsies work, who wants to work and who avoids work (50 gypsies) – those were subsequently taken to the labor camps." In its attempt to appear objective, the newspaper informed its readers that "the purpose of labor camps is to force all malingerers, parasites and freeloaders (among whom most gypsies belong) to work."[142]

Similarly, another Slovak daily reported that the resettlement of local Roma into a former German village Kunešov ordered by the Regional Na-

139 *Ibid.*
140 *Ibid.*
141 *Rudé právo*, September 10, 1945, 3.
142 *Rudé právo*, May 17, 1945, 1.

tional Committee in Kremnica was greeted very positively by both the Roma and the rest of the population who "appreciated that Gypsies, who until now were only a nuisance, can now by appropriate measures become a creative and useful element [of society]."[143] While it is not clear whether the journalists actually asked the residents for their views or simply expressed their own opinions about the situation, it seems that there were commonly shared negative attitudes toward the existence and presence of the Roma.

These kinds of accounts reveal that the media and state officials did not see the Roma necessarily in racial or ethnic terms. However, the ethnic and social categories were symbolically and mutually translatable, not mutually exclusive. The depersonalization of the Roma as an "element" (*živel*, *element*) was undoubtedly a reflection of contemporary attitudes of Roma as dangerous, abstract and uncontrollable. The use of biological metaphors in these documents provoked images of the Roma as a virus spreading through the society or as a people "spreading infectious diseases" to the rest of the population. The use of such metaphors helped produce a generalized fear for the health of the nation that we will later encounter in the rhetoric of the 1970s and 1980s in discussions concerning the unnatural and unhealthy reproduction of Roma.

Several scholarly works argue that immediately after the end of the war "not only the number of gypsies in Slovakia grew, but with them criminality also rose and the safety of the rest of the population was jeopardized."[144] Thus there was an "acute need to start solving the gypsy question as a social problem".[145] Likewise, Jurová argues that

> the gypsy question arose in Slovakia with great urgency for solution as an exceptionally serious social problem of the backward population, elevated by the sharp growth of Romani population, but also as a problem of general safety, as the necessity to eliminate their wandering and growing criminality."[146]

---

143 *Východoslovenská Pravda*, 1945/21, 2.

144 Olga Šrajerová. "K rešeniu romskej otázky na Slovensku po roku 1945," *Slezský sborník*, 91:3 (1993): 178-189.

145 Emília Horváthová, *Cigáni na Slovensku* (Bratislava: Vydavatelstvo Slovenskej Akademie vied, 1964), 3.

146 Jurová. *Vývoj romskej problematiky na Slovensku po roku 1945*, 18.

There is no indication anywhere in the documents why exactly the Roma were a threat to the public safety. The authors refer to "general stealing, swindling, and begging by gypsy families" which was allegedly "frustrating and hard to take for the rest of the society."[147] More than anything else, these seem to be simply recorded sentiments shared by the population, authorities and the press at the time, indicating a rather troublesome tendency in Czechoslovak academic literature to perpetuate unsupported stereotypes of the Roma. Some Roma undoubtedly engaged in the behavior described above, but to conclude from that that the Roma (and especially their "growing number") are a "threat to the general safety" of the population is quite a leap that goes far in exposing how societal prejudices get disseminated and survive, even through scholarship.[148]

What is apparent from the documents covering the late 1940s and the 1950s is that there was a general panic about the Roma, especially in Slovakia. However, the documents give no clear evidence why exactly the Roma were deemed so dangerous. Most often, the sources refer to the Roma's wandering, evading work, asocial behavior, and low level of living. Arguably, what was most threatening were not the Roma themselves but what they represented. Their nomadic behavior, which antithetically ran against the idea of the modern state itself, seemed to unconsciously inspire fear, confusion, anger and envy of their ability to transgress boundaries, both territorial and social, without guilt or much thought.

The media served as the primary access point for Czechoslovak citizens to understand social problems and as such both fed off of widespread resentment of the Roma, while also disseminating the idea of Roma citizens as foreigners. One weekly, for example, reported that:

> Into to the borderland area recently crowded so many gypsies from Hungary, Romania, Ruthenia, Greece, Germany, Austria and other countries that it

[147] Jurová, 25.

[148] It is important to note, however, that this is a classic scapegoat syndrome not reserved only for the Roma. When even a small proportion of a phenotypically disctinct and easily identifiable group engages in problematic social behavior, this leads to the perpetuation and entrenchment of negative stereotypes in feedback cycle of animosity. Were the Roma replaced by another easily identifiable group, the same situation would probably emerge.

> caused a general upheaval because everywhere gypsies just steal, rob, and do other mischief – plus they are spreading various contagious, especially sexually transmitted diseases. Perhaps eighty percent of gypsies have some venereal disease as formal examinations have showed. Besides that they have lice, smell and are dirty. Now, when they bummed and loafed around in the borderlands, when they stole enough for themselves – and now when there is danger they might need to work at the hop-farms or help at the harvest – gangs of gypsies leave the borderlands where they idled and roam to the interior, which will make the farmers there really happy! A gypsy will not work, he wants to wander, steal and live his own life. Gypsies are a terrible advertisement for us. Foreign tourists take pictures of the gypsy gangs, their camps and wagons – soon we will be known abroad as the nation of gypsies (*národ cikánů*). It's really about time the superior authorities wake up and clip the wings of these migratory birds.[149]

This account illustrates how discourses of xenophobia, racial discrimination, social superiority and gender obliviousness fed each other so that each form of difference could be easily identified with the others. The article begins by reinforcing the idea that "Gypsies" are not Czechs by categorizing them as a "foreign element," which serves as the basis for their social license and the reason for their inadequate hygiene and uncontrollable "unhealthiness."

It is not known how exactly the mark of eighty percent of gypsies infected with STDs was established. By reading Roma's "unhealthiness" through their transmission of STDs, the article implicitly affirms the cultural imagination of both Romani men and women as over-sexualized subjects who have the power to spread diseases to the respectable rest of the society. The definition of a "Gypsy" as a negative and socially and morally incompatible subject is then made absolute by claiming the authors know exactly what the Gypsies "want" and what they will and will not do. The article goes on to arouse fears of national shame by warning that foreign tourists, who do not recognize Gypsies as foreigners would identify their behavior with Czech and Slovak culture, a possibility so grave it justifies a call for the intervention of state authorities to eliminate the problem by repressive means.

---

149 "Cikánské radosti českého lidu," *Národní osvobození*, August 8, 1947, 1. There are no statistics available for the immediate postwar period, but it seems reasonable to suspect that the article exaggerated the number of Roma appearing in the borderlands in order to create a sense of urgency and panic.

While unabashedly hostile and outrageous in its caricature of Roma, the article's analysis links up to the popular mythology of Gypsies in a way that ordinary citizens would have easily found accurate and indisputable. By speaking of the Roma as a "terrible advertisement for *us*" and warning that "*we* will be recognized as the nation of gypsies" (emphasis mine), the author(s) exemplify the role of the media in propagating the idea that Czechs need to take matters into their hands, and reeducate, enlighten, repress, or get rid of the Roma (who are not a part of "them"). While hardly unique in the communist period, this type of writing about the Roma – blending nationalism, paternalism and social Darwinism – became increasingly entrenched in the popular imagination, perpetuating the same kinds of sentiments and affirming the idea of Roma as mute objects in need of correction and erasure.

Other dailies and articles also distinguished between "our" or "domestic" gypsies (who, some of the papers claimed, were "no longer a problem" because they had become "proper people") and "foreign" or "strange" gypsies, against whom the state authorities should act with utmost strictness.[150] However, Grulich and Haišman argue that their intensive research of the demographic data from a 1947 provisional survey of the Roma population in the Czech lands shows that the entire issue of "foreign gypsies" was mostly a fabrication by state authorities, who registered most Roma already living in the Czech lands or coming directly from Slovakia as "Gypsies without Czechoslovak state citizenship", thus inflating the number of "foreign" Roma and spreading the myth of a "Gypsy invasion" of Czechoslovakia from all possible directions.[151]

For the first time, there also appeared accusations that the Slovaks intentionally used the postwar chaos to get rid of their Romani population at the expense of the Czechs.[152] While there seems to be no evidence to confidently support or reject this assertion, previously cited documents show that even though the Slovaks professed equally hostile sentiments against the Roma as the Czechs (and thus giving credence to this view) the same sentiments also

---

150 "Cikánská otázka", *Národní osvobození*, September 30, 1947, 3; *Hraničářské slovo*, June 21, 1947, 3; "Toulání po pohraničí a cikánské krádeže už snad ustanou," *Svobodné slovo*, October 29, 1947, 1.

151 Grulich and Haišman, "Institucionální zájem," 82.

152 Haišman, "Snahy centrálních orgánů," 7.

precluded them from recruiting the Roma for resettlement to the Czech lands on charges they were "asocial."

Other articles peppering the Czech and Slovak dailies during the post-war period in the late 1940s worried about "the acute question of the mobility of gypsies in the Czech lands," "adjustments to the residence of gypsies in Czech lands," or "prevention of gypsy vagrancy" as well as the need to "preclude future unruly transfers of gypsies from Slovakia to the Czech lands."[153] Some newspapers even gained access to proposed solutions to the immediate gypsy problems and informed the public about the government's intentions to create "well-run camps" for the Roma. For example, *Lidová demokracie* reported on the extensive influx of "foreign gypsies" who had "insuppressible wandering in their blood" and who "spread infectious diseases." The paper went on to describe the state administration's proposal to create a three-level system of camps for the Roma. In the camps of the first level "gypsies w[ould] be sorted according to their qualities." In the second tier camps would be placed those "whom it is possible to reeducate" and who are willing to take on "useful trade." The third level camps would be for "undisciplinable" gypsies who would be "shipped beyond the borders as soon as possible."[154]

This policy proposal was suggested by a conference session of representatives of several ministries and was officially supported by the Ministry of Social Care. It was later formulated into a government proposal for dealing with the Roma.[155] There is no evidence that this proposal circulated among the public in any other way than through the media, as it was never implemented. The government rejected it in April 1947 for "tinges of racial discrimi-

[153] For example, *Mladá fronta*, *Svobodné noviny*, *Právo lidu*, *Práce*. These papers belonged among the most widely circulated and read not only in the immediate postwar period but throughout the communist period as a whole.

[154] "Co dělat s cikány? – Budou zřízeny tři druhy táborů pro cikány," *Lidová demokracie*, September 18, 1946. However, it is not at all clear what kind of action either the authors or the governmental proposal itself had exactly in mind when referring to "shipping gypsies beyond the borders." Clearly, a simple expulsion of the Roma into neighboring countries without any sound international plan about their immigration and settlement would be either impossible or result in international crisis.

[155] SÚAR Praha. Fond Předsednictva vlády (ÚPV), č. kr. 1163, č. sp. 1424/b/2, 1946.

nation."[156] Along with other policy proposals this document reveals the initial, spontaneous attempts of various officials at solving the "Gypsy question" in ways consistent with the general attitudes toward dealing with undesirable ethnic minorities after the war: detain them, ship them away.

Importantly, the argumentation on which this proposal's rejection was based also indicates the presence of official fears of accusation of racism while trying to solve the "Gypsy question." These anxieties prove that even though the state increasingly denied the ethnic and racial dimension of the Romani issue, it was well aware of it. The proposal demonstrates, above all, that from the very onset of the postwar period neither the state authorities nor the population in general had any intention of incorporating cultural or social diversity into the Czechoslovak society. It is partially understandable, as diversity was seen by many as one of the causes of the destruction of the First Republic and WWII. However, as we shall see later, these negative images of the Roma in the press saturated the everyday public discourse, which later facilitated the continual marginalization of the Roma through discriminatory interpretations of state policies by lower level officials in the good belief of doing "social justice" and promoting the "health of the nation."

Surprisingly, even after the forced labor camp proposal was definitively rejected in the Czech lands, similar initiatives still found their way into policy making in Slovakia. There was, however, a significant difference in these initiatives, one that directly relates to the arguments proposed in this study. Complaining about the frustrating situation in Eastern Slovakia, where the "Gypsy question" was especially acute due to the high concentration of the Roma in this region and the large number of their village dwellings, the regional bureau of the Ministry of Interior in July 1949 proposed the establishment of an office of "gypsy officers" (*cikánští referenti*), whose job would be to "explain to the population that the socialist regime makes no racial distinctions among citizens" but that it only "strives to elevate the gypsy population to the proper standard of living." The officers also had a "duty to induce (*přimět*) gypsies to productive work." Those Romani men and women (here

156 Tomáš Haišman, "Romové v Československu v letech 1945-1967: vývoj institucionálního zájmu a jeho dopady". In *Romové v České republice, 1945-1998: sešity pro sociální politiku*. (Praha: Socioklub, 1999), 137-183.

the documents actually used the designations for both sexes, which is extremely rare in any materials referring to population or a group as a whole) who "despite warning and instructions will not enter into the workforce will be recommended to the forced labor camps." However, the labor camps had a much larger purpose. The officers were also instructed to report to the camps those "gypsies, who suffer from any kind of contagious disease" because in the camps they will be able to obtain "proper medical care." The proposal ended by stipulating that the "gypsy officers" should "prevent gypsy wandering, and bar them from making a living by beggary, idleness, black marketeering, prostitution and other criminal activity."[157]

Like in the Czech lands, in September 1949 the Slovak Ministry of the Interior rejected this proposal as "politically unsuitable because of its tinge of racial discrimination" and issued instead a "Measure against asocial persons in Slovakia," which almost without change retained the content of the previous document, but, for the first time, was fully stripped of the designation "Gypsy" and talked only about "travellers," "wanderers" and "asocial persons," putting repeating emphasis on the "effectiveness of re-educational methods" (meaning detainment in the forced labor camps) for controlling and assimilating these "asocials."[158] By retaining the content of the policy and simply renaming the people in question, the state authorities consciously conflated ethnic categories with categories of social deviance into a collapsed definition of a "gypsy." Over time, this strategic shift in political rhetoric became inscribed into other categories of normalcy, and in fact it remains one of the primary sources of explanation for why in the post-communist period racist versus non-racist ascriptions are so difficult for individuals to distinguish.

II.2 On the Road to Socialism

After the "Victorious February" of 1948, when the Communist Party assumed control over the political system, the repressive discriminatory practices enacted toward the Roma were becoming increasingly a direct contradiction to

---

157 SNA Bratislava, Fond Povereníctva vnútra – Obežníky (PV-O), č. kr. 230/71-1-BK/6, č. sp. 51.

158 *Ibid.*

the proclaimed rhetoric of social and racial equality and the building of a communist society. As the example from Slovakia reveals, the Party was aware of this discrepancy and sought out a new vocabulary and way of addressing its intentions and means. By basing their new approach to the "Gypsy question" on the Marxist notion of class, the goal of state policies became the "gradual liberation of gypsies from the consequences of retardation as a legacy of the capitalist regime..." The cultural reeducation of the Gypsy population intended to quickly ensure that gypsies

> become proper citizens of our homeland, who will understand that only hard work toward the development of socialism will provide them with the security of an increased standard of living and hence a happy future without wrongfulness, poverty and hunger.[159]

In other words, such wording blended calls for unconditional assimilation with the right to a secure life. Not surprisingly, the continual reiteration of this rhetoric throughout a number of different socialist policies gave regional and local officials, who were interpreting and implementing these policies clear signals that the mutual goal of all branches of the state apparatus was to bring the Roma to "proper citizenship" – in other words share the same standards and values – by any means deemed just, moral and socialist.

Until this time, the only piece of legislation that was devoted to the Roma – and directly named them – was Law No. 117 from 1927 that together with amendments from 1928 formed the government policy restricting the movement and basic civil rights of the Roma. Paragraphs 4 and 5 of this law on "wandering gypsies" stipulated that "every traveling gypsy older than 14 years of age" was issued a mandatory identification card with personal data, a personal description and fingerprints that he or she had to carry all the time and "present to police officials on demand."[160] As discussed earlier, there were over 35 thousand of these "nomadic IDs" issued in interwar Czechoslovakia, a number that invites questions about the process of defining "Gypsies."

---

[159] SÚAR Praha. Fond MPS, č. kr. 400, č. sp. 2123 - *Sbírka oběžníků pro Krajské národní výbory* (KNV), roč. IV, 1952, č. 13, poř. č. 140, March 5, 1952.

[160] *Zpráva kriminální ústředny z r. 1948*, E/2 III/6. Cited in Jamnická-Šmerglová, 65.

How "cursory" this number truly might be is evident from the following note written in 1947 by the Central Criminal Office in Prague to justify its decision to exempt a Roma named only as J.H. from being issued a "gypsy license" and thus freeing him from constant surveillance and the obligation to report of his whereabouts and activities regularly to the police:

> Because this case concerns a mulatto (*míšenec*) of gypsy blood [who married a Czech woman and has three children with her], who is permanently settled and employed in agriculture for more than ten years, the Central Criminal Office recommends exemption [of this individual] from the [gypsy] register.[161]

This example plainly demonstrates how confused and intertwined the categories of "social behavior" and "ethnicity" were, not only among the population in general, but on the level of policy enactment as well. Clearly, in order to be classified as a Gypsy – and hence to be marginalized and discriminated against as such – one's social behavior and choice of lifestyle were often more important than ethnic origin.

Toward the end of 1948 the board of commissioners of the Ministry of Interior issued a decree that stated that forcing "Gypsy IDs" and "nomad licenses" simply on to anybody the authorities decided was "unconstitutional, expensive, harmful and futile." According to the decree, "by creating the general duty to work the 'nomad licenses' became relics of the past and the obligation to carry a citizen's ID was enough for the protection of public interests."[162] The rhetoric that Gypsy IDs were unconstitutional and expensive strongly conflates social and ethnic issues by implicitly acknowledging the Roma as a "problematic element" within "Czechoslovak" society. Moreover, this rhetoric also exposes that what was really at stake was the "protection of public interests" and not the protection of the human and civil rights of the Roma.

Paragraph 150, part 2 of the criminal code 88 from 1950 finally abolished the existence of the 1927 law about gypsy wandering for its "tinge (*příchuť*) of racial discrimination incompatible with our constitution and the

---

[161] SÚAR Praha. Fond Zemského úřadu (ZÚ), č. kr. 855, č. sp. III-8, 1946-1948.

[162] SNA Bratislava, fond Policajné riaditelstvo v Bratislave 1920-1945 (1950), č. kr. 31, č. sp. 8/133.

popular democratic regime."[163] This step was not followed by any new measure or legislative amendment that would address the "Gypsy question" as a specific issue or "gypsies" as a specific group. Any problems or concerns associated with the Roma were, apparently, to be solved purely by administrative means. What this legal step meant in practice was that for the first time in Czechoslovak history the Roma were, at least theoretically, equalized in their citizenship rights with the rest of the Czechoslovak society. From 1950 on, there was no legal measure that would set the Roma apart from the population as a specific group of people who are in need of special (in both negative and positive terms) treatment. In Slovakia, the state authorities even expressed the opinion that "it is not necessary to solve the gypsy problem by any specific means; it will solve itself through industrialization."[164]

In December 1950, the Ministry of Labor (*Ministerstvo pracovních sil*) and the Ministry of Social Care published an extensive study called "A Report on the Life of Gypsies in Czechoslovakia."[165] The most interesting aspect of this document lies not in the fact that the authorities claimed that

> work transforms gypsies in truly miraculous ways . . . and [that] gypsies willingly and quickly adjust to reliable work, take on trades, participate in socialist competitions and become Stakhanovites, members and functionaries of the Party and the Labor Union (ROH).[166]

That was, of course, a part of the predictable ideological rhetoric, which the Party used in order to argue that "we are successfully tackling the gypsy question, which no previous regime was able to solve." In a striking revelation, the state authorities admitted in the document that the Roma's

> adjustment to our way of life and their fusion with the rest of the population depends on: a) what kind of relationship the other coworkers [at a given worksite] have toward gypsies, b) what their [the Roma's] housing situation is, and c) what attitude toward them the public has.[167]

[163] SÚAR, Praha. Fond Úřadu předsednictva vlády (ÚPV), č. kr. 1163, č. sp. 1424/b/2, 1946-1951.

[164] Cited in Jurová, *Vývoj romskej problematiky na Slovensku po roku 1945*, 29.

[165] SÚAR, Praha. *Zpráva o životě cikánů v ČSR*. Fond Ministerstva pracovních sil (MPS), č. kr. 47, č. sp. 100-1950.

[166] *Ibid.*

[167] *Ibid.*

In other words, the highest state authorities acknowledged already in 1950 that one of the most important aspects of integrating the Roma into the population as equal citizens was changing the attitude of the majority at both official and popular levels. It is clear that the Party was quite aware that official documents, laws and decrees could not solve the "Gypsy question" by themselves but further required the right attitudes of the society to help reinforce socialist norms in practice.

During the 1950 Employment survey of the Romani population, the state authorities encountered the refusal of some Roma to identify themselves as Gypsies. The survey workers indicated that this refusal came from the "more advanced workers of this minority."[168] This remark is significant for several reasons. From the official point of view at the time, it can be seen as evidence that Roma were being successfully integrated into socialist society. Their refusal to be identified as "Gypsy" can be read as an affirmative identification with "Czech" or "Slovak" identity. On the other hand, it is possible to consider this as one of the first documented cases of Roma themselves protesting and pointing out their discriminatory treatment. By refusing to identify with the category "Gypsy" they demonstrated that it is socially and economically harming to be identified in such a way, thus confirming that the term "Gypsy" did indeed carry negative connotations in the eyes of both the Romani and non-Romani populations.

The way in which Roma were discussed and treated created impossible conditions for building any positive self-identity as well as prevented any positive transformation in the categories through which Roma and non-Roma referred and thought about each other. In such circumstances, it was inevitable that the Roma would develop a conscious detachment from their own community that would continue to post-communist times, culminating in the low levels of self-designations of the term "Roma" in the censuses of 1991 and 2001, respectively.[169]

---

[168] SÚAR Praha, fond Ministerstvo vnitra – Dodatky (MV-D) 1918-1961, č.kr. 1282, č.sp. I/1-882/1, I/1-4521/17, I/1-4521/15, I/1-4521/4, I/1-4521/21, I/1-4521/19.

[169] In 1991 only 114,116 Roma (out of an expected three to five hundred thousand) declared Romani as their nationality. In 2001, less than 30,000 Roma identified themselves by the Romani nationality. Figures in *Výsledky sčítání osob, bytů a domácností za rok 2001: zpráva českého statistického úřadu* (Praha: ČSÚ, 2002).

In March 1952, the Czechoslovak government issued a decree entitled "Adjustment of the conditions of persons of gypsy origin," a joint effort of the Ministries of Interior, Social Work, Enlightenment and Information and some other central offices. The decree stressed the importance of assisting the Romani population and ordered all levels of the state administration to observe the principle of legality and equality. The state administration was supposed to ensure that "National Committees keep the same principles of socialist lawfulness toward the gypsies as they do toward all other citizens, because the laws and decrees of our people's democratic republic are equally binding for all citizens regardless of their nationality or race."[170] Clearly, the state recognized the Roma as a group to whom the principles of ethnicity and race are related, a position that it gradually started to deny.

The decree created an eight-point program for the reeducation of the Roma, which among other goals stated that the organs of state administration should constantly promote activities among the entire population and "in the spirit of Stalinist nationality politics educate [the people] toward a new attitude concerning nationality issues and the liquidation of remnants of racial discrimination." To achieve this, National Committees were supposed to "ensure that the state administration does not discriminate against the gypsy population in public life ... as well as ensure that they [the Roma] are not exposed to any mistreatment because of their origins while visiting theaters, movies, restaurants and shops." It also indicated that more attention should be paid to the school attendance of Romani children so that they can "influence and act upon their parents and other adult gypsies." [171]

Party authorities, such as the organizations of the National Front, the Union of the Communist Youth, the Labor Union and others were supposed to ensure that "incorrect procedures of the state [did] not support a nomadic lifestyle among the gypsies." National Councils were entrusted with the task of "instructing gypsy families of how to use apartments properly, including health related topics, especially from the point of view of realizing what kinds of advantage proper living brings." While solving these individual cases, offi-

[170] Praha. Fond MPS, č. kr. 400, č. sp. 2123 - *Sbírka oběžníků pro Krajské národní výbory* (KNV), roč. IV, 1952, č. 13, poř. č. 140, March 5, 1952.

[171] *Ibid.*

cials were supposed to treat the Roma in such a way "that it is apparent that they are citizens whom the bourgeois regime did not give a chance to become useful and proper members of human civilization, but whom we all today want to help to do so."[172]

By evoking nationalist politics and the need to eradicate racial discrimination, while arguing that "Gypsies" just needed to learn how to live more decently, the entire decree walks a fine line between recognizing Romani ethnic specificity and denying it at the same time, reducing it to mere social backwardness caused by previous (non-communist) regimes. The last statement in particular blatantly claims that the Roma are inferior human beings. The authorities on the one hand professed their desire to liquidate any remnants of racial and ethnic prejudice from the society, but on the other hand demonstrated their utter inability to even produce a rhetoric that would comply with such a noble intention. The wording of official documents from their very onset placed the Roma in a subordinate position. Since, according to official rhetoric, the Roma were not proper members not only of socialist society but of "human civilization" as such, it set an extremely paternalistic, missionary undertone of "civilizing" and "assistance." This widespread attitude served to justify and legitimize the interpretation and implementation of ethnically neutral policies into discriminatory practices that we will encounter in the following chapters.

To reiterate, the point of this book is not to assign blame for the discrimination of the Roma under Communism to the regime or to defend its well-meant effort but rather to understand how it was possible that ethnically neutral policies came to be interpreted in ethnically punitive ways that directly discriminated the Romani population. There is no question that major state policies and documents relating to the Romani population were progressively becoming less and less problematic as pieces of legislation. As policies created outside of popular discourses and sentiments against the Roma in the society, these documents might testify to the innocence and genuine attempt of the regime to "help the Roma." Through a contextual analysis, on the other hand, one can expose the problematic interrelation and dependence of the policies on the attitudes and actions of the society.

---

172 *Ibid.*

In September 1954, the Central Secretariat of the Communist Party devoted one of its meetings to discussing the state of the "Gypsy question." The results of this discussion were formulated in a report that was supposed to be binding for "communists engaged in solving the so-called gypsy question." The Secretariat ordained that it was necessary to "incessantly create such conditions so that gypsies can truly become equal citizens of Czechoslovak Socialist Republic with all rights and obligations." It further mandated that "decisive and inevitable for the further reeducation of gypsies is their permanent work and sedentary living." It was also necessary, according to the Party, "to liquidate gypsy camps and ghettoes in order to get rid of all sources of gypsy isolation." The Roma were supposed to be encouraged to continue their "traditional artistic creativity under the condition that gypsy ensembles would not exclusively perform gypsy programs but would incorporate Czech, Slovak, Soviet and other progressive works into their performances." Lastly, society was also supposed "to struggle to improve the cultural level of gypsies," a plea, which did not include their own cultural heritage, as one might think, but rather implied "the carrying out necessary hygienic and epidemiologic procedures" and "the instruction of Czech and Slovak languages to gypsies, which opens to them wider opportunities . . . to discover a world of cultural wealth."[173]

The state was trying to develop a centralized policy that would systematically address all aspects of what was perceived as the "gypsy problem." However, the power to implement all these initiatives in the mid 1950s rested with regional, and county and local authorities, a fact, which was deeply resented by the local populations, who often felt it was not their own responsibility to deal with these "foreign" problems. The archival correspondence between National Committees, Ministries, and Party Organs are full of complaints from the "Czech" population about the behavior, activities, or simply the presence of the Roma. Analyzing these complaints, Jurová argued that "the rest of the population shunned [the Roma] and rejected them not be-

[173] SÚAR Praha., Fond Ministerstva sociální péče, č. kr. 01-0053-0076/1956, výpis ze zprávy předložené a schválené sekretariátem ÚV KSČ, Sept. 15, 1954.

cause of racial or ethnic reasons but for deficits in their basic hygiene and behavior."[174]

One must wonder to what degree complaints about robberies, theft, vandalism, or simply economic problems that made reference to "Gypsy" activities were actually caused by the Roma and to what degree such behavior was simply associated *with* the Roma. Often one finds in the archives circumstantial "proofs" of gypsy criminality such as "gypsies migrated through here yesterday," "I saw gypsies around," or mentions of "nomadic gangs of gypsies."[175] While such complaints do not amount to proofs for their allegations, they do indicate the degree to which people were willing to associate the presence of Roma with criminal behavior.

The temporary relief of censorship in 1956, following Khrushchev's rise to power in the Soviet Union and the Kremlin's official denouncement of Stalinism, which eased for a while the political climate in all Eastern European satellites, became immediately visible in the press reporting on the Roma. Various accounts suddenly referred to the Roma as a "scourge, who do not work but only beg,"[176] complained about "gypsy violence and stealing,"[177] that they "create problems for the countryside,"[178] and even reported that "a good gypsy is an exception to the rule."[179] In an attempt to put a moralistic spin on the issue, reproaching the Roma for "plundering the country," one daily exclaimed that "some citizens of gypsy origin perhaps do not realize how many of us shed blood and sacrificed their lives for the sake of equality so that we all can live and build a new better world in peace and without fear."[180]

Another article, for example, reported about a public administrator in Slovakia, who, while officially delivering speeches condemning racism in the United States, allegedly referred to the Roma unofficially as "social lepers."[181] These comments in 1956 demonstrate that the fact that such sentiments disappeared from the media and official documents after 1948 does not neces-

[174] Jurová. *Vývoj romskej problematiky na Slovensku po roku 1945*, 113.
[175] SÚAR Praha. Fond MPS, č. kr. 01-0053-0076/1956.
[176] *Večerník*, July 10, 1956.
[177] *Smena*, February 8, 1957.
[178] *Zemědělské noviny*, June 18, 1956.
[179] *Večerník*, December 4, 1956.
[180] *Práca*, December 20, 1956.
[181] *Smena*, May 3, 1957.

sarily mean they also disappeared from popular discourse in general. By making taboo an open display of racial and ethnic prejudice in order not to negate the official ideology of equality, the regime did succeed in eradicating racist slur from official rhetoric and social discourse. However, as this tiny window into public sentiments appearing in the press seems to suggest, racial prejudice and ethnic hostility were surviving under the lid of censorship quite undisturbed and continued to inform the societal attitude toward the Roma.

II.3 The Anti-nomadic Legislation and the Process of Implementation

By 1958, the central organs of the Party came to the conclusion that "all existing measures are failing because of the constant movement of the majority of the gypsy population."[182] After its convention in April, the Central Secretariat concluded that

> it is no longer possible that in a society building socialism such a large part of the population lives according to backward forms of life, which reflects huge hangovers from former social formations, even from primitive periods [...] Their high level of illiteracy and low cultural levels are one of the numerous inheritances from capitalism that so far prevents a large percentage of these citizens of ours from engagement in productive work. Centuries-long oppression and persecution by exploitative ruling classes has left deep scars in the character of gypsies living in our country. In our people's democratic regime they can for the very first time live as free people, but only with grave difficulties are they getting rid of these deficiencies [...] Despite all positive results that have been achieved so far, the general level of gypsies is very low.[183]

While this resolution still uses the designation "gypsy" for describing the Roma, it unconditionally reduces all specificities of Romani culture into a heritage of backwardness in need of correction. It is also noteworthy that this backwardness is attributed not so much to Romani culture itself. Rather it is used as a way to ideologically condemn capitalism and praise socialist regimes as true democracies.

A small group of Romani intellectuals and advocates, especially scholars and academics, argued on a few occasions that the situation of the Roma

[182] SÚAR Praha. Fond MPS, č. kr. 519, č. sp. 2020-1957.
[183] *Modrý bulletin ÚV KSČ*, April 30, 1958. (SÚAR Praha).

should be dealt with as a "nationality question" and that it is necessary to work at awaking Romani national consciousness because the main cause of the disinterest of the Roma in social integration was the blatant ignorance and refusal of the majority population to recognize their culture.[184] However, the regime was not at all ready to engage the "Gypsy question" on such terms and immediately rejected any proposals for Romani political identity or self-representation. According to Karel Holomek, the current chairman of the Union of Czech and Moravian Roma and the son of the chairman of the Union of Gypsies-Roma during the late 1960s, "Romani elite did not have any other choice than to retreat into the background and wait."[185]

Pro-regime scholars, however, immediately hurried to explain that trying to see the "Gypsy question" in nationalist terms is a profoundly mistaken position. According to ideologue Jaroslav Sus, the "national question is a special case of the social question" and the "Gypsy question" can be thus solved only by "social and cultural assimilation, a fusion with a more advanced cultural environment."[186] In other words, a "nation" must achieve a certain level of culture and be civilized enough in order to have the right to call itself a nation. The "Gypsy question," argued Jamnická-Šmerglová, was

> a contradiction between the high level of culture and production of a socialist society on the one hand and an extremely low societal level of the gypsy population [on the other hand] . . . that can be solved only through a conscious politics of assimilation; that means creating conditions for the moving gypsies into higher social and cultural levels and for completely merging them with its social structure and cultural standards.[187]

---

[184] These arguments were formulated for example at Roma conventions in Bardejov and Bratislava, in Slovakia, in 1957 that hosted Roma and their supporters from the whole country. Davidová, *Romano drom*, 192.

[185] Holomek, 300. Holomek argues that the Romani intellectual class, which was a product of the communist regime's effort to find a group of Roma, who on the one hand would consciously distance themselves from their "gypsiness," but on the other help as "citizens of gypsy origin" to assimilate the rest of Romani community from within, existed already in the 1950s, but the time for Romani activism was not ripe yet. (See Chapter four for discussion of the Union of Gypsies-Roma in 1968-73.)

[186] Jaroslav Sus, *Cikánská otázka v ČSSR* (Praha: Nakladatelsví politické literatury, 1961), 9-11.

[187] Jamnická-Šmerglová, 25.

"Cultural differences between Czechoslovak and gypsy populations," as was explained by the central organs of the Party based on scholarly findings, "rest on the deficiencies in their [gypsies'] employment, health, education, housing and hygiene."[188] In other words, the specificities of Romani culture were articulated strictly in negative terms – as aspects of social backwardness and criminality. Romani culture was defined in terms of anti-state activity, which could therefore be dealt with by means of "correction" through assimilation. New committees designed and created by the Central Secretariat of the Communist Party to carry out the "integration" project, which resided in local, county and regional National Committees, were called quite revealingly "Committees for the care and reeducation (*převýchova*) of the gypsy population,"[189] indicating that assistance and assimilation are inextricably linked together.

In the spirit of this attitude, various ministries and central organs issued their own statements and reports immediately prior to the ratification of the anti-nomadic law in October 1958. For example, the Central Labor Union (*Ústřední rada odborů*) concurred with the official governmental take on the issue by stating that the goal of all divisions of the state is to "get rid of the backwardness and the incorrect way of life of citizens of gypsy origin in socialist Czechoslovakia, to increase their standard of living and to reeducate them into being dignified citizens of our socialist society."[190] The resolution of the Secretariat of the Labor Union ordered all central committees of the Labor Union in the regions to guarantee the integration of the gypsy population into work relations, especially by the following means: "a) the distribution [of gypsies] among other workers as individuals or small groups, b) the organization of free qualification courses, and c) increased attention to their social, health and housing conditions." The regional and local committees of the Labor Union were entrusted with the task of "creating in their worksites a comradely environment, organizing mentorships of experienced workers, who will watch

---

[188] Ústřední všeodborový archív (ÚVA) Praha. Fond Předsednictva Ústřední rady odborů, č. sp. 46/292, (1958).

[189] *Ibid.*

[190] ÚVA Praha, Fond předsednictva ústřední rady odborů, č. sp. 46/323 – *Zpráva o plnění usnesení ÚRO*, June 5, 1958.

over gypsies, offering gypsies help with their qualifications and imparting on them the importance of work hours and long-term work."[191]

Finally, in October 1958, the National Assembly ratified law 74/1958 of the Czechoslovak Constitution "On the permanent settlement of wandering persons" (*O trvalém usídlení kočujících osob*). While the majority of documents leading up to this milestone legislation make it clear that the main concern and purpose of this law was to solve the "Gypsy question," the law implicitly denies it. The people whom this law concerned were officially referred to as a "mobile section of Czechoslovak society."[192] Nowhere in the law or its supporting materials was there a single mention of the term "Gypsy."

Besides its substantive content, criticized by other scholars as well, I additionally argue that what makes this law a major landmark in the discourse about the Roma under communism is precisely the fact that it is the first document concerning the Roma that does not mention them by name.[193] Such an omission, central to the main arguments of this book, is not innocent or irrelevant, but a part of a concerted strategy of dealing with the Roma. This "elimination of naming" points to a problematic transformation of the ethnic discourse in Czechoslovakia during the communist regime into a discourse of social deviancy and sexuality that ultimately would lead to the radicalization of ethnic violence in the post-1989 period. Moreover, it shows that the definition of "Gypsy" is indeed at the heart of the history of the Roma in Czechoslovakia that complicates any attempt at telling a linear and comprehensive story of "Czechoslovak Roma." While other scholars have not been able to explain the omission of the term "Gypsy" from the law and limit their discussions to cursory criticism of the content,[194] clearly the answer lies in the fact that men-

---

191 *Ibid.*

192 *Zákon č. 74/1958 Sb.*, "O trvalém usídlení kočujících osob". November 11, 1958. (SÚAR Praha).

193 For example, Barany argues that the law was "discriminatory" to the Gypsies, but pays no attention to the fact that they are not mentioned in the law by name. Likewise Grulich and Haišman analyze in their article the law quite closely, but again without addressing this absence.

194 Such as, for example, Willy Guy, "Ways of Looking at Roms: The Case of Czechoslovakia," in *Gypsies, Tinkers, and Other Travellers*, ed. Farnham Rehfisch (London: Academic Press, 1975), 222; William McCagg, "Gypsy Policy in Socialist Hungary and Czechoslovakia, 1945-1989," *Nationalities Papers*, (1991): 313-336; David Kostelancik,

tioning the Roma directly would imply an incompatible violation of the official socialist rhetoric of human and civil rights.[195] By choosing the terms "nomads," "half-nomads," "free loafers," and "parasites" the law made every effort to make it clear that it spoke strictly about those people, who, in the law's eyes, in fact did take advantage of or disturb the functioning of the society.

Like other major legislation enacted in Czechoslovakia under communism, the law cannot be directly criticized on charges of ethnic or racial discrimination against the Roma. In fact, the law itself cannot be accused of explicit racism because it does not make use of ethnic or racial rhetoric at all. Ironically, the "cleanliness" of the official rhetoric is also the main source of evidence for scholars, who argue for the good intentions of the regime, despite its shortcomings and outcomes, and point to the regime's concern for the welfare and socioeconomic improvement of the Roma.[196] Good intentions aside, it is important to analyze the law in the context of the entire discourse on the "Gypsy question" prior to and after its issuance in order to understand why and how such legislation in fact *functions* as a discriminatory measure.[197] As it is impossible to assess the implications of legislation solely on the basis of its rhetoric, one must also consider the contexts, in which it is embedded in order to understand the range of interpretations and associations the law had in its concrete implementation at local levels.

The title of the law spoke of the "permanent settlement of nomadic and half-nomadic persons." The wording of the law, however, went far beyond the simple prohibition of nomadism. First and foremost, choosing to include both "nomadic" and "half-nomadic" persons into the law created the possibility of applying the law not only to those Roma, who made their living on the road, such as traveling comedians, repairmen, blacksmiths, and so on, but also to

---

"The Gypsies of Czechoslovakia: Political and Ideological Considerations in the Development Policy," *Studies in Comparative Communism*, 22:4 (1989): 307-321.

195 An exhaustive research of secondary literature on the Czechoslovak Roma indicates that so far no author has attempted to analyze the semantics of the law.

196 See for example, William McCagg, "Gypsy Policy in Socialist Hungary and Czechoslovakia", 329; or Willy Guy, "Attempt of Socialist Czechoslovakia to Assimilate its Gypsy Population" (Ph.D. Thesis, Bristol University, 1977).

197 As already discussed in Chapter one, Joanna Richardson provides precisely such an analysis of the controlling and regulatory aspects of discourse in the context of Romani legislation in Britain, in her excellent recent account *The Gypsy Debate: Can Discourse Control?*.

all Roma traveling back and forth from work in the Czech lands and their families in Slovakia or vice versa. It even explicitly encouraged such reading of the text by stating in §2 that "a person leading a nomadic way of life is one who, in groups or individually, wanders from place to place . . . even though he may be registered in some community as its permanent resident." Since most Roma worked as unskilled labor in menial jobs, such employment required frequent and unpredictable mobility. The law opened avenues for arbitrary harassment of Roma at the hands of both the authorities and the general population.[198]

The law relegated the Romani population into a subordinate status of childhood and otherness – to the level of objects, rather than subjects – who needed to be constantly watched after, educated and cared for. Moreover, the settlement of "the nomadic population" was only the first step in a long-term policy of assimilation. Nowhere in the text of the law was it explained how the state authorities are going to recognize and distinguish members of the former "mobile element" once they are settled. Yet it specified and spelled out ways of dealing "with these persons" for years and decades to come, including quite strict punishment for defiance: §3 stipulated that those who "persist in maintaining a nomadic way of life . . . shall be punished by deprivation of liberty from six months to three years."[199]

With the prohibition of nomadism the law inflated the definition of "nomad" by including all who "avoid work" or "work dishonestly." According to the definitions of the directives accompanying the law, "the term nomadism does not concern only the most typical cases of mobility by the use of horse carts but also other and much more common ways of travel such as by train, cars, tractors, or walking."[200] The term "avoiding honest work" was defined as "any conduct whose purpose is to gain ways of support without any endeavor, meaning without work . . . or by such actions or form of conduct that is in conflict with the law or the moral attitudes of our society."[201] Finally, the term "making living by dishonest means" referred to "the most typical and unques-

---

[198] Davidová, *Romano Drom*; Kostelančik, "The Gypsies of Czechoslovakia: Political and Ideological Considerations in the Development of Policy."

[199] *Zákon č. 74/1958 Sb.*, čj. NV/1-0586/58., §2, §3. Ústava ČSSR.

[200] *Ibid.*

[201] *Zákon č. 74/1958 Sb.*, čj. NV/1-0586/58., §2, §3. Ústava ČSSR.

tionable cases of making a living by criminal offences such as prostitution, pimping, hazardous activities, or palm reading ..."[202] Clearly, the definitions of all these terms left ample space for interpretive discretion on the part of local authorities. It also indicates the gendered dimension of the issue, which later proved crucial for judging the "proper parenthood abilities" of the Roma and their "respectable citizenship."

Anna Jurová argues that the law was a "logical and inevitable consequence of piled-up and unsolved problems from the 1950s when social, health, housing and other problems of the Roma accumulated [as if] in a magic circle."[203] Besides the polemical indication that all problems of the "Gypsy question" rested with the Roma, by arguing that the law was "logical and inevitable" Jurová implicitly suggests that it was indeed the social consequences of travelling that made an anti-nomadic law necessary. However, according to statistics and demographic studies, nomadic Roma constituted less than one tenth of all Roma residing in Czechoslovakia in the 1950s, numbering at fewer than 15,000.[204] Moreover, this small group belonged to a very specific group of so-called Olach (or Vlach) Roma, who mostly kept to themselves and did not intermingle with other Roma or non-Roma.

On several cold nights at the beginning of February 1959, members of local police units in all districts of Czechoslovakia enacted a registry count in order to place "all wandering persons" under control. The process of the event might be better described as a raid rather than a demographic census. The brutality and carelessness, with which local and regional authorities enforced the law was only retrospectively recorded through oral history projects and eyewitness accounts. One Romani woman, a little girl at the time, recalled that:

---

202 *Ibid.*

203 Jurová, *Vývoj romskej problematiky na Slovensku po roku 1945*, 58.

204 See for example, Milena Hübschmannová, "Co je tzv. cikánská otázka," *Sociologický časopis*, 6/2 (1970): 105-20; or Říčan, *S Romy žít budeme – jde o to jak*, 27.

> They came at night. It was cold. They woke everybody up. Adults and children. And started to count everybody. They took horses, our biggest friends and helpers. And cut wheels off the wagon – calling us black gobs.[205]

Recorded memories of Roma, many of whom were children at the time, bear witness to the verbal and physical harshness that took place during that census. Wherever the Roma happened to be that particular night, that village or city inherited them into its care as their domicile and was required to provide them with housing, work, schooling, and necessary medical care.[206] Needless to say, such a demand created a lot of hostility and resentment on the part of the non-Roma population that was required to suddenly, immediately – and enthusiastically – take care of the Roma that happened to be within its boundaries that night.

At the end of the raid, the count listed 46,500 people.[207] Clearly, more than 30,000 Roma, who did not belong to the purely nomadic Olachs, fell victim to the deliberate redefining and stretching of the relevant categories of "nomads" in the hands of local bureaucrats. As much as the official rhetoric was concerned with "nomadic persons," who were supposed to be the greatest threat to the safety and progress of the society, practice showed that the main point of the law was to equip state authorities with means and legitimacy to control, tame and assimilate the Roma in a way the regime desired. Especially the category of "half-nomadic" persons makes it evident that "nomadism" was not the only criterion for indicating subjects' belonging to this category; other characteristics, mostly socio-cultural, such as commute to work or large family gatherings, were used as well to classify persons as "nomads" and make them eligible for treatment under the auspices of this law.

---

205 Cited from an oral history project conducted in Southern Bohemia in mid 1990s by the students of Romani studies at Charles University in Prague. In Davidová, *Romano Drom,* 201.

206 *Zákon 74/1958 Sb.*, MV čj. NV/1-0586/58.

207 Statistics cited in Alena Šubrtová, *Z dějin ceskoslovenského sčítání obyvatelstva* (Prague: Acta Universitas Carolinae, 1980); Květa Kalibová, "Romové z pohledu statistiky a demografie", in *Romové v České republice* (Praha: Socioklub, 1999), 91-114; and Ctibor Nečas, *Historický kalendář: Dějiny českých Romů v datech* (Olomouc: Univerzita Palackého Press, 1997), 81.

Jurová admits that the law represented a "discriminatory practice by the totalitarian regime violating basic rights of freedom of abidance and movement." In one breath she claims, however, that "despite that it created conditions for gradual settlement of the Roma, their stabilization in individual locations – something West European Roma, affected by discrimination against settlement in a desired location and acquisition of citizenship, still call for today."[208] In this curious twist of turning a repressive policy into a positive deed based on a comparative strategy of pointing out similarly discriminatory practices (only in a reversed way) enacted against the Roma in Western Europe, Jurová essentially comes down on the side of all those who in the end praise the communist regime for its treatment of the Roma. Czechoslovak Roma, needless to say, could not settle in a "desired location" and their citizenship rights were severely violated in profoundly deeper and different ways than those of the rest of the Czechoslovak population under the communist regime.

While "nomads" were prohibited from retaining their preferred lifestyle under the threat of prison and other sanctions, all organs of the state institutions were ordered by the same legislation to "provide multilateral help to persons leading a nomadic life so that they can start a sedentary life." An integral component of the anti-nomadic law was an order for all segments of the state structure to "relentlessly use educational means in order to achieve that they [the 'formerly nomadic persons'] become proper working citizens."[209]

The executive obligation and power of these measures rested in the hands of regional and local administrations. Reports written about carrying out the policies by regional organizations of the Labor Union expose the ethnic connections that the law took such pains to hide. A report submitted from the Central Board of the Labor Union to the Central Committee of the Party, summarizing the regional situations, notes with satisfaction that "in many regions there were a lot of opportunities created for the *formerly nomadic citizens*" only to complain on the very same page a few paragraphs later that "the law 74/1958 is most severely violated especially in building construction and agriculture [fields] where local factories hire *gypsies* from the registry only

208 Jurová, *Vývoj romskej problematiky na Slovensku po roku 1945*, 59.
209 *Zákon 74/1958 Sb.*, MV čj. NV/1-0586/58.

for seasonal work [and] after the season they fire them, leave them to their fate or ship them to Slovakia."[210] Such guileless criticism of local practice reveals that state officials did not perceive the double rhetoric as problematic, suggesting that administrators on all levels were able to decipher without much thought the subterranean ethnic foundation of the surface social coding.

Commenting on the institutional approach toward the Roma in the 1950s and following the anti-nomadic law, Grulich and Haišman argue that during certain phases of the state efforts to solve the gypsy question "the actual conditions of the reality required adopting legal measures that differentiated gypsies from other citizenry, such as prohibition of nomadism and special cataloguing projects that demarcated gypsy population from the rest of the population."[211] Since the category of ethnic difference (conflated in communist ideology with the category of national minority) was not available as a tool of conceptualizing Romani difference, it was gradually translated into categories of social deviance. Adopting legal measures as ways of "differentiating" and "demarcating" Czechoslovak population into two groups created conditions for treating the "Gypsy question" on binary scales of legal-illegal, proper-improper, normal-deviant. The axis of normalcy and deviance was not created arbitrarily but by political demands to identify and "correct" those who did not fit in the picture of a universal socialist citizen. Since this translative practice rested with local and regional administrations, sentiments that informed popular understanding of the Roma continued to play a major role.

Through adopting a punitive legislation that did not refer to the Roma by name but in reality directly targeted Roma the regime emptied and purified the category of "Gypsy" from any positive aspects of difference. Any digression from social norm became illegal behavior, or improper at best, one that the regime aimed to either punish or correct. In the words of a prominent Gypsy ideologue of the time, "surpassing the backwardness of the gypsies will allow us to succeed in clearing away their difference as an ethnic group and finally create conditions for their ultimate merging with the rest of the

---

[210] ÚVA Praha, Fond Předsednictva ústřední rady odborů, č. sp. 40/292. (Emphasis mine.)

[211] Grulich and Haišman, 81.

population."[212] Clearly, eliminating ethnic difference was not only perceived as a positive process but also as a realizable one. The feasibility of such a proposition rested precisely on the transformation of ethnic difference into social backwardness and deviance, a process which started with the ambiguous rhetoric of the anti-nomadic law.

For the first several years after the issuance of the law, various documents and media used both "formerly nomadic persons" (who were, according to the materials, the real threat to the society, created economic problems, carried diseases, refused to integrate and cooperate, tolerated unacceptable values, such as prostitution, promiscuity, alcoholism, dirt, and so on) and "citizens of gypsy origin" (who were simply victimized inheritors of the inability of previous regimes to eradicate the causes of their backwardness). The rhetoric pretended to distinguish their usage in order to accentuate differences in punitive versus educational measures. In fact, however, the official discourse gradually confused and conflated them to such a degree that in 1965 the Central Committee of the Communist Party was able to create the "Governmental Committee for the Questions of Gypsy Population" and officially exclaim that its purpose was to supervise the "reeducation of gypsy population into proper and valuable members of the society" and "successfully finish the systematic dispersal of gypsy population."[213]

The main purpose of this chapter was to examine the discursive atmosphere of the immediate postwar period in order to lay out the context, in which subsequent policies and laws towards the Roma were created, interpreted and implemented. After the initial period of confusion, the state authorities started to consciously cleanse their rhetoric of mentions of ethnicity and gradually began to redefine their discourse of the "Gypsy question" in terms of social deviance. The media helped to saturate the popular consciousness with negative images of the Roma that were not tied specifically to the communist regime.

The chapter also argued that WWII and the communist takeover in 1948 represents a fundamental break in the history of the Roma in Czecho-

[212] Sus, *Cikánská otázka v ČSSR*, 25.
[213] Usnesení vlády ČSSR č. 502/1958 Sb, z 15. 6. a 13. 10. 1965. (SÚAR Praha.)

slovakia and thus a break in the paradigmatic ways authorities and non-Romani citizens treated and interacted with the Romani population. Once again, the main impetus for these discursive shifts can be located in the aftermath of the genocide of Czech and Moravian Roma during the Pořajmos and the subsequent resettlement of Slovak Roma into the Czech lands. During the initial and crucial stages of this resettlement, governmental and state authorities did nothing to promote the recognition of these people, who legitimately and historically resided on the territory of Czechoslovakia, as Czechoslovak citizens. In fact, this absence of an official discourse of recognition helped cement popular views of the Roma as outsiders and foreigners, who incite fear and are prone to violence. The emergence of the twin rhetoric of foreignness on the one hand and rhetoric of criminal and asocial behavior on the other produced a discursive interface through which the ethnic inferiority of the Roma could be affirmed at the same time that the Roma were officially talked about solely in the language of social deviance.

However, the attitudes and perceptions of gypsy deviance articulated in the postwar period were not born out of thin air. The following chapter is going to demonstrate that the postwar discursive space was not a neutral vacuum, in which ideas and notions about the Roma were created from scratch but that the imaginary space of collective sense-making was already saturated with images and stereotypes that permeated Czech and Slovak popular consciousness at least since the mid 19th century.

III Culture as a "Tool of Incarceration"

Assigning a certain type of culture to a people can be, as Arjun Appadurai aptly termed it, a "tool of incarceration" because it gives those in power to define others means to create symbolic representations through which people make sense of the world. Whether in literature, music, art or speech, language is a fundamental tool that social actors use for exercising power over others. Language involves power not only because it turns others into objects but also because it helps to create the reality of who the *others* are and how they relate to *us*. As Pierre Bourdieu argued, "it is in the constitutions of groups that the effectiveness of representations is most apparent, and particularly in the words, slogans and theories which help to create the social order by imposing principles of di-vision."[214] According to Bourdieu, everyday myths and stereotypes of others gain coherence through linguistic acts and become naturalized and recognized as basic truths, taking on "almost magical power which enables one to obtain the equivalent of what is obtained through force."[215]

This chapter analyzes the ways popular culture in Czechoslovak society prior to the state socialism used linguistic practices to construct lasting and harmful images of Gypsies and links these images to the postwar developments in both popular and academic imagery surrounding the "Gypsy question." In three separate parts, the chapter reveals a line of continuity of these discursive practices, moving from the 19th century literature through the academic writing on Romani history in the 1960s to popular regime satires of the late 1980s. Widely read and circulated popular poetry, fiction, myths and songs created a world of images that depicted the Roma as a-historical people, whose sense of time and space had defied the forces of European modernization. Fictionalized images of the Roma in Czech and Slovak popular imagination both romanticized and demonized them as wandering souls,

[214] Bourdieu, *Language & Symbolic Power*, 129-130.
[215] *Ibid.*, p. 170.

primitive minds, passionate and promiscuous lovers, great narrators, musicians and dancers, and thieves and deceivers.

In this sense, the images of Gypsies that were a part of postwar Czechoslovak popular culture did not radically differ from the images that one would find in other European countries. This is because, I argue, specific descriptions and images of gypsies were often tied to the general belief that the Roma rejected the Western imperative to modernize – to order one's life according to modern modes of production, family and social organization, and the political geography of states and nations. As Katie Trumpener argued, European literature imagined the Roma as the antithesis of European identity: "outside of historical record and historical time, outside of Western law, the Western nation state, and Western economic orders, outside of writing and discursivity itself."[216]

This does not mean that the specific conditions and context of Czech and Slovak society is irrelevant for the production and circulation of gypsy myths. Because language is bound up with local structures of power, images of Gypsies can enter into those power structures to marginalize the Roma not only in words, but in discriminatory policies and exclusionary practices as well. Therefore, the purpose of this chapter is not only to narrate the "Gypsy myth" in Czechoslovak popular discourse from the 19th century through the socialist period but also to argue that popular conceptions of Gypsies created cultural frameworks for interpreting and implementing socialist policies, which legitimized Romani assimilation and discrimination under the guise of socializing a backward, inferior and dangerous people. This chapter thus creates a conceptual framework also for subsequent chapters, which discuss other concrete examples and ways popular discourses were translated into educational, medical, and other punitive practices exercised by agents of the socialist regime.

[216] Trumpener, "The Time of the Gypsies," 860.

III.1 Genealogy of the Gypsy Myth

Romanticized and demonized images of "gypsies," both as individuals and as a group, have been an integral aspect of the Western literary tradition, representing the Roma as a visual spectacle of everything "other" from Western order and progress.[217] Yet this spectacle split into two related but contrary images. On the one hand, writers who have sought to uphold Western principles of "law and order" have seen in the gypsy personality the quintessential criminal. As an Italian professor of psychiatry and criminal anthropology argued in 1918, Gypsies are "a living example of a whole race of criminals, and have all the passions and all the vices of criminals."[218] On the other hand, romanticized and exotic notions of gypsies have become so pervasive that the 1956 edition of the *Encyclopedia Britannica* described "Gypsy" in the following way:

> The mental age of an average adult Gypsy is thought to be about that of a child of ten. Gypsies have never accomplished anything of great significance in writing, painting, musical composition, science or social organization. Quarrelsome, quick to anger or laughter, they are unthinkingly, but not deliberately cruel. Loving bright colors, they are ostentatious and boastful, but lack bravery. They have little idea of time, proportion or measurement, and are superstitious about childbirth, fertility, food and sickness. Their tribal customs sometimes have the force of law. Believing the charms and curses, they admit the falsity of their fortune-telling. They betray little shame, curiosity, surprise or grief, and show no solidarity.[219]

These two different paradigms of the Gypsy myth in the Western imagination were in fact dimensions of the same general perspective. In each case, Gyp-

---

[217] Besides Trumpener and Hancock, for a theoretical treatment of images and stereotypes of the "Other" in Western historical and literary discourse see, especially, Sander Gilman, *Difference and Pathology: Stereotypes of Sexuality, Race and Madness* (Ithaca: Cornell University Press, 1985). Gilman developed a convincing comparative critique of the images of a "wandering Jew" and a "primitive sexualized Black" as necessary components of modern Western identity making. For an insightful analysis of "otherness" of nomads see, Kevin Stewart, *The Deep Dark Heart of Asia*, in which he unraveled a pursuasive argument about the inability of the West to incorporate into its consciousness subjects that defy (and deny) state structures and progress of modernity.

[218] Cesare Lombroso, *Crime: Its Causes and Remedies* (Boston: Little, Brown &Co., The Modern Criminal Science Series, 1918), 40.

[219] *Encyclopedia Britannica* (Cambridge: Cambridge University Press, 1956).

sies were imagined as living in a state of nature prior to history and political order. The paradigm of Gypsy criminality naturalized Gypsy culture, depicting the Roma like people in a Hobbesian "state of war," unable to conform their behavior to abstract laws because of their natural dispositions to stealing, tricking and looting others.[220] The paradigm of the romantic gypsy, on the other hand, imagined them as living like Rousseauvian "noble savages" unbound by the artificial, contractual conditions of modern life.[221] Since both of these views had the common trait of *naturalizing Romani culture* – that is, seeing culture as constituted by brute predispositions, not as a manifestation of transmitted traditions and social interaction – they both played equally into the hands of a socialist regime driven by the quest of achieving social justice through socialization and normalization.[222]

The myth that Gypsies have lived in a state of nature also coincided with the perception of Gypsies as wandering nomads, as a people whose carefree, indeed mysterious, travels were unbound to any structure or law.[223] The myth of nomadism ignored the fact that over the course of the last five hundred years not all Roma were nomadic. Many of them were sedentary and those who did migrate often did so not out of their own free will, but due to perpetual persecution by rulers and states, preventing them to settle or forcing them to conduct commerce elsewhere. One could speculate endlessly what the origins of these myths were. Regardless of their causes, fictionalized accounts of Gypsies espouse their inherent wanderlust, from which all of their other cultural traits stem. According to Hancock, exotic myths of the Gypsy nomad are so ingrained in Western discourses about the Roma, that neither fiction nor academic studies of Romani culture can discuss Roma without making references to their nomadism. He argues that "like Eskimos without

---

220 Thomas Hobbes, *Leviathan* (Cambridge: Hackett Publishing Company, Inc. 1994).

221 Jean-Jacques Rousseau, *A Discourse on Inequality* (New York: Penguin Classics, 1984).

222 For a variety of romanticed images and accounts of the Roma in Western discourse, see footnotes 44 and 45 in Chapter one.

223 For an analysis of the nomadic phenomenon see, besides Stuart and Deleuze and Guartari, also the literary treatment of the issue by Bruce Chatwin, *Anatomy of Restlessness: Uncollected Writings, 1969-1989* (New York: Viking Press, 1996): part III, "The Nomadic Alternative – Letter to Tom Maschler; The Nomadic Alternative; and It's a nomad *nomad* world."

igloos or Indians without teepees, Gypsies without wagons cheat [the anthropologists] of something." While larger societies were able to "progress from horse and cart to automobile, 'exotic' minorities are seen to be losing something of their identity if they do, too."[224]

As a part of the repertoire of the literary and artistic world, the romanticized and demonized Gypsy entered into the popular culture of the Czechoslovak post-WWII population as a figure thematized in songs and art, a character in interwar cinematography and literature, and a protagonist or villain in ideologically acceptable books. As early as 1821, the Czech priest and educator Antonín Jaroslav Puchmajer compiled a book called *A Grammar Book of the Gypsy Language and Thievish Jargon*, which introduced the term "gypsy" into Czech literary consciousness for the first time and which immediately equated Gypsy life with criminality.[225] Gypsy characters then appeared in the writings of many of the major literary personalities of the Czech and Slovak national revival movements in the mid and late nineteenth century. Jindřich Šimon Baar, for example, wrote of the gypsies as a mysterious group "able to do magic" and "command water and fire."[226] Karel Hynek Mácha, Jan Neruda, Vítězslav Hálek, Božena Němcová and Adolf Heyduk in their writings, and Antonín Dvořák and Bedřich Smetana in music, all celebrated Gypsy freedom, their carefree lifestyles and their close proximity to nature.[227] "Their life is full of bliss that must be difficult to renounce. ... Isn't it a thousand times better to sleep in the grass, under the acacia tree, with only the starlit sky above their heads...," marveled Němcová, otherwise noted for her realistic and unsentimental portrayals of the harsh life of Czech, Slovak and Hungarian peasants.[228] It is not clear how much or how little first-hand experience with Roma these authors actually had and to what degree their work

224 Hancock, "Myth," 42.

225 Antonín Jaroslav Puchmajer, *Mluvnice cikánského jazyka a zlodějské hantýrky* (Praha, 1821).

226 Jindřich Šimon Baar, *Český lid* (Praha: J. Otto, 1886).

227 Vítězslav Hálek, *Pohádky z naší vesnice* (Praha: Mladá fronta, 1956); Karel Hynek Mácha, *Básně KHM* (Praha: J. Otto, 1897); Božena Němcová, *Sebrané spisy B.N., svazek X.* (Praha: J. Laichter, 1911); Adolf Heyduk, *Cikánské melodie a jiné písně* (Praha: SNKHLU, 1955).

228 Božena Němcová, *Listy II*, "Dopis Sofii Podlipské, 24. června, 1853" (Praha: Československý spisovatel, 1952), 30-31.

was influenced and inspired by the rampant escapism and romanticism of the era. Many of the Czech authors had close literary ties and were aware of the romantic movements in other places in Europe. There, Alexander Pushkin, Lord Byron, Prosper Meriméé, and later Victor Hugo, just to mention a few, all famously described nomadic Gypsies in their tales.[229] However, regardless of their origin, the romantic images of thieving and traveling Gypsies, who live, as Neruda put it, "under the spell of Gypsy music" and "without obligation to society or any other people,"[230] entered through the works of Czech and Slovak authors into Czech and Slovak popular consciousness and became integral to popular counter-narratives of progress and modernity.

Among the plethora of stereotypical Gypsy images in the Czech literature of the 19th century, one case deserves particular attention. The text in question is a short poem called "The Gypsy Whistle," originally published in 1839 in a collection of patriotic poems *Echoes of Czech Songs* by the famous Czech linguist František Ladislav Čelakovský.[231] What makes this particular poem unique is that, during the communist period, it was the only literary work mentioning "Gypsy" or "Roma" in any of the Czech elementary, middle or high school textbooks (it was included in a compilation of Czech literature for 7th-grade students.)

After conducting an exhaustive search of elementary and secondary level textbooks in the Czechoslovak educational system between 1960 and 1984, I was surprised to discover that this was the only textbook that recognized the presence of the Roma in Czechoslovak society.[232] That is, besides this case all of the other history, geography, literature, civic education, psy-

---

229 Victor Hugo, *The Hunchback of Notre Dame* (New York: The Modern Library, 1941); Alexander Pushkin, *Tsygany* (Moskva: Gosudartvenoe izdavatelstvo detskoi literatury, 1949); Prosper Meriméé, *Carmen* (London: George Routledge & sons, 1877).

230 Jan Neruda, *Knihy básní* (Praha: Orbis, 1951), 555. For a comprehensive treatment of gypsy images in Czech literature, see a very insightful and well-researched B.A. thesis of Veronika Kamenická, "Obraz Romů v české literatuře" (Praha: Pedagogická fakulta Univerzity Karlovy, 1999).

231 František Ladislav Čelakovský, *Ohlasy písní českých* (Praha, 1839).

232 Archive of the State Pedagogical Library of Jan Ámos Komenský in Prague. (Due to lack of archive space and funding, the textbooks are in poor condition, and are stored on dirty shelves without appropriate protection. Except for a limited card catalogue, no organized inventory of this particular archive has been carried out.)

chology and other textbooks failed to recognize the existence of the Roma, in either a positive or negative light.

Memories of Roma adults of their school days during the communist times, recorded in an oral history project carried out in mid 1990s by students of Romani studies at Charles University in Prague led by Milena Hübschmannová, confirmed these findings. "In school they never taught us anything about the Roma. Not about history, not about culture. The only thing was that sometimes the teacher told a Czech child: 'Go wash, you're dirty like a gypsy.'"[233] Romani journalist and poet Jan Horváth shared similar memories: "At school I didn't learn absolutely anything about Romani history. And about our culture neither. They just wanted to make Czechs out of us. I heard all the time: 'don't talk gypsy! Don't speak that slang of yours!'"[234] One of Horváth's most bitter memories was that "at school children constantly cussed us 'gypsies.' They couldn't have had that from their own heads. They must have heard it at home from parents."[235]

A locksmith from Slovakia noted that "about Romani history [I] never learned anything. It was never mentioned. About our culture they only said that we are uncivilized (*nekulturní*)."[236] "When the kids called me 'gypsy' I beat them up... but about Romani history I never heard a word, I don't remember that," reminisced Štefan Holub.[237] Štefan Mika revealed that "until [he] was six, I was the happiest child in the world [...] Then I went to school and for the first time I experienced what it feels like to be ostracized (*odstrčený*)." Mika remembers that he could not understand what the problems of non-Romani children with him were. "I came crying to my dad telling

---

233 Memory of Jan Cína, who started to attend school in 1965. In Hübschmannová, *Šaj Pes Dovakeras*, 87. Cína also remembered that he was most embarrassed at school when he had to change into shorts for P.E. class, because "girls were there. In our house, chastity was a priority and I never saw my mother or father in their underwear." (*Ibid.*, 86.)

234 Memory of Jan Horváth, who attended elementary school in the first half of the 1970s. In Hübschmannová, *Šaj Pes Dovakeras*, 88.

235 *Ibid.*, 87.

236 Memory of Ladislav Žolták, born in 1966 in Spišská Nová Ves in Slovakia. In Hübschmannová, *Šaj Pes Dovakeras*, 89.

237 Besides his name, Holub did not provide any autobiographical information so it is not possible to indicate where and when he went to school. In Hübschmannová, *Šaj Pes Dovakeras*, 88-89.

him they call me 'gypsy'. I had no idea what that was! But I knew it was bad..."[238] Likewise, textbooks for the "remedial" or "special schools" (discussed in chapter five), which in the 1970s schooled almost eighty percent of all Czechoslovak Romani children, did not mention the Roma or provide Romani models for the schoolchildren. Therefore, not only did Romani children lack effective Romani role models upon which to build a sense of ethnic identity, but all Czechoslovak children were educated in a way that denied Romani existence, even in the world of fiction. School, of course, is not the only source for encountering role models but it is one of the most significant ones – arguably even more so in a communist society, which denies freedom of speech and exercises surveillance and centralization of ideas expressed in the public realm.

The "Gypsy" poem, mentioned earlier as the only reference to the existence of the Roma in Czechoslovak textbooks, is a story told by orphans, whose father died and left them his a whistle as the only possession he had. The children reminisced about their father, nostalgically recollecting that

> He could drink, he could play,
> He worked lightly but slept hard,
> And he knew how to shop for nice things
> With five fingers only.
> *Our daddy took very little care of us*,
> But he had an amazing whistle...
> When he whistled, all *cockroaches* (*šváby*) ran away from the house.
> When he whistled in the village, in the town,
> All *German rats* were on the road,
> They had to roam, dance as he whistled,
> And finally [they had to] jump into the local lake.[239]

The text portrays the "Gypsy" father as a drunk musician, lazy worker, thief and bad parent, all images that were reinforced in the communist discourse of

[238] Memory of Štefan Mika, born in 1961, who attended school in Eastern Bohemia. In Hübschmannová, *Šaj Pes Dovakeras*, 89-93.

[239] František Ladislav Čelakovský, "Cikánova píšťalka", in *Čítanka pro 7. třídu* (Praha: Státní pedagogické nakladatelství, 1978), 221. (Emphasis mine.) It is quite likely that the "cockroaches" in the poem are not an innocent neutral remark, but that they, too, refer to the Germans. The original Czech term is "šváb" or "Schwab," which historically has been a pejorative term for Germans in Central Europe. To "shop with five fingers" (*kupovat za pět prstů*) is a common Czech phrase for shoplifting.

the "Gypsy question." The context of this poem's inclusion in communist educational discourse is also important, because elementary, middle and high school "readers" (*čítanky*) during the communist period were all designed and ideologically approved by the Ministry of Education. Moreover, as a selection in a communist textbook of the Normalization period, this poem is significant not only for its portrayal of the Roma, but also for its reference to the Germans as "rats."[240]

In the first half of the 20th century no substantial literary work with significant gypsy theme was produced, even though Gypsy characters peppered novels by well-known authors. Jaroslav Hašek, the author of *The Good Soldier Švejk*, believed by many scholars to have brilliantly carved out the Czech "national character," developed an archetype of a Gypsy thief that came and went through many of his writings.[241] With his characteristic sarcasm, Hašek narrated, for example, "The Gypsy Feast," a story about a Gypsy pig thief, who always denied his crimes, and even when they were proven he managed to talk his way out of them by arguing they always simply somehow "happen to him." In another story called "The End of a Monkey," Hašek described the death of an old circus monkey that traveling Gypsy comedians mourned with a tragic pathos all day, only to happily eat it for dinner that evening.[242] Even though these stories were intended to be comical, they reinforced the myth that the Roma are inherently unethical, changing their values and opinions from one moment to the next. Moreover, the reference to eating a monkey, an animal generally held in affection for its human-like qualities, further enhanced the perpection of Gypsies as primitive savages.

In music, Czech composer Leos Janáček's classical chamber composition *Diary of a Disappeared* explored the sexual relations between a Moravian

---

240 On a treatment of Czech stereotypes of Germans see the classic study of Vladimír Macura, *Znamení zrodu: České obrození jako kulturní typ* (Praha: Československý spisovatel, 1983), esp. pages 140-148.

241 For a comprehensive discussion of the significance of the Švejk character for the development of the Czech national character and nation building, see, for example, Ladislav Holy, *The Little Czech and the Great Czech Nation*, esp. pages 72-73 and 127-130.

242 Jaroslav Hašek, *Črty, povídky a humoresky z cest* (Praha: SNKHLU, 1955), 121. The work constains the stories "Cikáni o hodech" (*The Gypsy Feast*); "Případ cikána Lešky" (*The Case of a Gypsy Leška*); and "Konec opice" (*The End of a Monkey*).

village boy and his "beautiful, passionate" gypsy lover Zefka, "whose color frightens [him]." The young boy Janíček nonetheless became seduced by Zefka's passion, "falling under her spell" and running away from home with her to the deep mountain forests "where fate calls him, where Zefka waits for him with his son in her arms."[243] Zefka, of course, did not exemplify a typical "feminine" and submissive lover, but a wild, uncontrollable woman possessing magical powers over reason. Janíček inevitably fell into the Gypsy world "without senses" but with a full imagination and raw passion, accepting the myth that he had to join gypsy society because a Gypsy woman with such powers and passions could not possibly be able to integrate into his.

The writer Karel Čapek, one of the most renowned and beloved interwar Czech authors, also explored the world of passion and sexuality between a "black girl" and a boy. The novel, *Ordinary Life*, is written as a series of memories of the protagonist's life. One section of the book is devoted to a short-lived relationship between the narrator and a small, apparently Gypsy, girl. The "little black girl, with black hair and dark as a black cat" is described as an exotic element that brought into the quiet and mundane life of the then eight-year-old boy his first sensual experience.[244] While the girl is in all mentions in the book identified by the modifier "black," the boy is never identified by his color, thus promoting the implicit understanding of "whiteness" as a non-racialized identity.[245]

The girl, who also has no name, belonged to a company of "those strange people," who came to build railroad tracks near the narrator's town. The narrator tells us that they, the (white) children from the town, had "strict orders not to go there because weird people live there, whom one cannot trust." These people lived in "plank shacks, between which hanged ragged,

---

[243] Leoš Janáček, *Zápisník zmizelého* (Praha: Hudební matice Umělecké besedy, 1949), 32.

[244] Karel Čapek, *Obyčejný život* (Praha: Fr. Borový, 1935); Section V., 35-42.

[245] For a theorerical discussion of the phenomenon of whiteness as a non-racialized identity see, for example, Vron Ware, "Moments of Danger: Race, Danger, and Memories of Empire," *History and Theory*, 31:4 (1992): 112-144. Ware argues that "society dominated by ideologies of white supremacy often considers 'white' as normal and therefore people who fall into this category see themselves without racialized identity."(118). With almost all of its population being "white," Czechoslovakia would certainly belong to this category. But as Ware's argument suggests, racial concepts position all members of a society, albeit in different ways.

torn clothes." The narrator soon meets a "small, scruffy, black girl" whose language "nobody can understand" but who is "irresistibly ... magical." As much as the boy himself, his parents are enchanted with the girl as well:

> "Look, what eyes that child has!," my father called at my mother. She [the girl] had huge, black eyes with enormously long eyelashes. "She is so beautiful," gasped my mother out in wonder.[246]

The boy is drawn to the little black girl in a strong passionate relationship, which he himself does not understand. They spend the whole summer together, not understanding each other's language, playing together without words and exploring the world of childhood mysteries and urges. The boy does not dare to tell his parents about the relationship, keeping his strictly forbidden trips "to the other side" of the river, where the little black girl lives in a plank shack, "stinky as a dog kennel," as his secret.[247] Suddenly, one day the whole railroad company leaves because one of the men "kills the group foreman in a fight" and is led away in cuffs by the police, "his child running after him." The boy is confused and upset and his neighbor, not understanding his sadness, tells him: "Ah, who knows, which one of them did it! Those people are at every moment in a different place."[248] The boy never sees the little black girl again and the narrative goes on, without ever coming back to this relationship and experience.

What is significant in this novel is that the Gypsies in the story are by no means major or important characters. Their presence is almost accidental and anecdotal. They are simply coloring the picture with a tinge of exoticism, exhilliration, mystery and danger. On the one hand, Čapek describes an irresistible gypsy beauty and innocence, represented by the small black girl. On the other hand, he paints the Gypsies as common-sensical strangers, dark, "half-naked," impossible to understand, dangerous, nomadic, with criminal propensity, which gradates into a murder. In a few suggestive strokes on mere seven small pages, Čapek mixes exactly the combination of romantic

[246] Čapek, 36.
[247] *Ibid.*, 39.
[248] *Ibid.*, 41-42.

adoration and mysterious demonization, which is described in theoretical literature dealing with the gypsy myth.

However, it was not only the world of literature that provided Gypsy myths for the Czechoslovak population. During the interwar period, a number of black and white movies were filmed at the state Barrandov Studios of Prague, which ran in a popular Sunday afternoon series called "Movies for Eyewitnesses" (*Filmy pro pamětníky*) during the communist period. A number of these films depicted ragged "gypsy" characters accompanied by wagons and horses, who were portrayed either in negative terms as thieves and menaces tormenting the region or in romantic terms as charming, passionate, but irresponsible and unstable lovers, which reinforced the image of Gypsies as an exotic "other" belonging to different era and always creating a cause for commotion. These images of Gypsies in film are particularly significant in providing visual representations and stereotypes to accompany literary renderings of Gypsies as thieves, enabling the Czechoslovak population to identify Gypsies according to dress and behavior and to associate their cultural characteristics with their economic position as jobless thieves unable to participate in the means of production of the greater society.[249]

III.2 Roma Images in Popular Culture

These romanticized images of "the wandering Gypsy," a common literary figure of the 19th and early 20th centuries, changed sharply in the course of the next several decades. The "Gypsy anti-hero" reemerged in the communist period as an asocial, negative character, defined either by his tragic inability to assimilate into Czechoslovak society, ending in death or incarceration, or by his happy embrace of communist ideology, resulting in his full assimilation and the dissolution of his "Gypsiness." With time, however, negative portrayals of Gypsies as unable to assimilate were censored from both literature and

[249] For the history of prewar Czechoslovak film and development of the interwar movie industry see, Luboš Bartošek, *Náš film: kapitoly z dějin, 1896-1945* (Praha: Mladá fronta, 1985). Predictably, there is not a single mention about the usage of "Gypsy Myth" in Czechoslovak cinematography in the book.

film, producing another Gypsy myth, one based on the socialist ideal of Gypsies shedding their "backward" social characteristics to successfully assimilate into socialist conceptions of work, family and society.[250]

The few cinematographic works to include Romani characters built on the popular myths of what Gypsies are like focus solely on the supposed ability of communist ideology to magically transform Gypsies "for the better" by giving them access to the advantages of living in a socialist society. Communist films all affirmed that voluntary submission to the ideological and social values of the regime is the only solution to the problem of alleviating the "conditions" of Gypsy "backwardness."[251] A very interesting exception to the ideological trend of cinematographic depiction of the successful transformation of the "backward" Gypsies to socialist citizens is a 1969 film *Larks on a String* (*Skřivánci na niti*) by Oscar-winning director Jiří Menzel.[252] This movie critically reveals the harsh reality of forced labor camps in the 1950s for the "politically unrealiable" (intellectuals, priests, entrepreneurs) and those, who were sentenced for attempted emigration to the West. Besides unfolding a love story of the main character through surrounding context of demagogy, despair, resentment, resistance and resignation, it also depicts an unfulfilled love and marriage dreams of one of the camp guards, who marries a Gypsy girl. The movie is quite interesting in its frank acknowledgement of the lack of understanding and total cultural miscommunication between the Roma and non-Roma characters and in its complex approach to the treatment of the "Gypsy question" – it provides an open critique of the failure of the socialist project of "civilizing" and paternalizing education of the Roma on the one hand, but at the same time participates in cementing the "gypsy myths" of

---

[250] See, for example, Ludvík Aškenazy, "Gabore, Gabore," in *Etudy dětské a nedětské* (Praha: Československý spisovatel, 1963); Božena Benešová, *Don Pablo, Don Pedro a Věra Lukášová* (Praha: SNKLU, 1962); Jan Sekera, *Děti z hliněné vesnice* (Praha: Československý spisovatel, 1952).

[251] For historical treatment of the ideological censorship and criticism of the general nature of cinematographic works during communism see a collection of essays published by the Czech national film archive *Umlčený film: kapitoly z bojů o lidskou tvář československého filmu* (Praha: Národní filmový archív, 1993).

[252] *Skřivánci na niti*, dir. Jiří Menzel, ČSSR, 1969 (Bontonfilm).

backwardness and nomadic longing for freedom and nature on the other hand.[253]

In one of the rawest episodes of the movie, which gradates through the film until a full exposure at the very end, an older communist official regularly comes checking the proper observance of hygienic rules to a Gypsy house. When coming, he always washes with a cloth faces of little dirty Roma children running with a laughter around, announcing that "hygiene is the building bloc of the future" and then asks if the "bathtub is ready," sending the grandma to guard in front of the house. Throughout the movie this scene repeates four times. The last time, however, the scene continues to reveal the true meaning of the "ready bathtub" – it is filled with a naked young Roma girl, who awates to be personally, and of course alone, "washed" by the communist official. Without extra words or unnecessary didactic point, the movie offers a silent but extremely powerful critique of the often problematic ways, through which the socialist project of civilizing the Roma under communism was enacted. This scene can be read not only as a personal failure of one official but also as a metaphor for abuse, inextricably accompanying the assimilation process.[254]

Gradually, "gypsy" characters made their way into the increasingly more daring and subversive columns of the state-sanctioned satirical and humor weekly *Dikobraz* (*Porcupine*). *Dikobraz* was loved and widely read for its ability to make mockery of the regime and its ideology while being subjected to official censorship. The regular appearance and the broad dissemination of *Dikobraz* were instrumental in producing an atmosphere of double-talk and double-meaning that characterized Czechoslovak communism of the 1980s.[255] By mid 1980s, careful, subtle critiques of the incompetence and in-

---

[253] After the marriage, for example, the girl is unable to "settle down" in a new panel building, constantly escaping away, sleeping on the top of a wardrobe instead of in bed, making a campfire from furniture in the middle of the living room, etc.

[254] It does not come as a surprise that the movie *Larks on a String* was immediately forbidden by the communist censorship and could appear in distribution again only after 1989.

[255] *Dikobraz: týdeník humoru a satiry*, (Národní knihovna Karolinum v Praze, *národní konzervační fond NKC.*) Much of folk music was saturated with similar critique, hiding its criticism in lyrics about nature or weekend camping. For published lyrics of most folk

efficiency of the state bureaucracy, lip service to the communist ideology and satire of the "socialist work ethic" were all quite frequent in both cinema and literature, and *Dikobraz* regularly featured politically subversive jokes and satirical columns.[256] Significantly, Gypsy laziness and theft, which were portrayed as challenging the regime's bureaucracy, were used as a subversive strategy to criticize the stupidity of state officials, military personnel and the police.[257]

Jokes involving Gypsies were carefully styled and couched in a way that made it apparent that an overt critique of Romani family and social life was not permissible. For example, while the word "cikánský" (*gypsy* as an adjective) was quite frequent, the word "Cikán" or "Rom" as a noun was not. Other jokes made no reference to the Roma, but use typical Romani names, such as Gejza, Lakatoš or Fero, to indicate the ethnic identity of the characters.[258] Such linguistic usage signified that it was acceptable to make fun of the Gypsy lifestyle, Gypsy behavior, laziness, passion, incompetence, cleverness, and so on, while the regime would censor negative remarks of the

---

bands, see collected volumes *Já, písnička I., II.,* and *III.*, *Táborový zpěvník*, or *Písničky k táboráku*.

[256] For general analyses of East European humor, satire and censorship during the communist period see, for example, a collection of essays *The Administration of Aesthetics: Censorship, Political Criticism and the Public Sphere* (Minneapolis: University of Minnesota Press, 1994); For origins of communist humor and satire mainly in cinema see, Cambridge Studies in Film, *Inside Soviet Film and Satire: Laughter with a Lash* (Cambridge: Cambridge University Press, 1993); For a comparative analysis of communist images and caricatures used in the United States during the Cold War see, for example, Michael Barson, *Red Scared! The Commie Menace in Propaganda and Pop Culture* (San Francisco: Chronicle Books, 2000); For a theoretical treatment of popular culture in the politics of the everyday see, for example, Paulina Bren, "Closely Watched Screens: Ideology and Everyday Life in Czechoslovakia after the Prague Spring, 1968-1989," Ph.D. Dissertation (New York University, 2002); For an early collection of Czech "folk jokes" see, František Hampl and Karel Bradáč, *Žeň českého humoru* (Praha: Práce, 1952).

[257] This practice is, for example, revealed in *Abeceda smíchu* (Praha: Vyšehrad, 1989), a collection of jokes and stories by the most popular Czech and Slovak humorists from the late communist period published a few months before the collapse of the regime.

[258] Collections of anecdotes and satirical stories with such strategies include: Vladimír Jiránek, *Anekdoty o civilizaci* (Praha: Lidové noviny, 1977); Václav Černý, *Aprílové grotesky* (Praha: Lidové noviny, 1983); Jiří Švandrlík and Jiří Neprakta, *106 od Neprakty* (Havlíčkův Brod: krajské nakladatelství, 1961); by the same authors, *Anekdoty s Nepraktou* (Praha: Lidové noviny, 1979) and *Anekdoty a semtamfóry* (Praha: Lidové noviny, 1972).

Roma as a people. More often, however, jokes did not use the word "gypsy" or "Roma" at all, working solely from images and subsequent associations. The fact that those jokes appeared in one of the most widely read weeklies demonstrates that they were considered humorous and that the sentiments, on which these jokes based their humor were present in popular consciousness. Such jokes usually involve typical "gypsy accessories," such as a magic crystal ball, a horse and cart, and bright clothing, and the people portrayed are distinctly darker, with men having thick mustaches and women with huge, shiny jewelry and scarves. One of the jokes, for example, traveling widely by word of mouth in the public, asked whether "you heard about the woman, who had a glass baby? . . . She was raped by a gypsy with a crystal ball..."[259]

Gypsy images were also used in songs that easily made it through the censorship machine, such as in the work of popular folk songwriter and singer Ivo Jahelka, called "the singing lawyer," who rhymed his purportedly true legal cases into songs. Jahelka produced three LP records in the second half of the 1980s, participated in all the major folk festivals, such as Porta, Svojšický slunovrat, and Lochotín, regularly appeared on TV and in radio and was one of the most popular songwriters. His songs humorously narrated the human stupidity, with which individuals tried to circumvent the law and celebrated the ways, in which they got away with it. One of his famous songs, *The Gypsy Ballad*, described an accident in which a group of Gypsy street workers "put down their shovels and went to find a refuge in a nearby pub" because that activity represented "a favorite gypsy understanding of 'employment'."[260]

A popular movie made in 1987 can serve as another case in point when stereotypical images of Gypsies were appropriated for public humor and ridicule. A favorite duet of satirical theater, Zdeněk Svěrák[261] and Ladislav Smoljak, produced in the 1980s several sarcastic screenplays and films that subtly critiqued the regime "between the lines" but were nevertheless approved by

---

[259] How widely this joke apparently circulated is demonstrated by the fact that Hancock cites it as well in his analysis of Gypsy stereotypes in the United States (*Pariah Syndrome*, 57.)

[260] Ivo Jahelka, "Cikánská balada," (Praha, Supraphon, 1988).

[261] In the United States, Svěrák is perhaps best known for his Oscar winning film *Kolya*, a movie about an older Czech man raising a Russian boy during the end of Czechoslovak communism.

the censors. In their movie *Uncertain Season*, two young theater writers are involved in a constant struggle with a cultural censor, who screens their scripts for "proper" ideological content. One of the scenes of the film involves a rehearsal of their new play that is being monitored by the censor. The authors stand nervously backstage as the scene unfolds: A coal magnate, Ptáček, is having his future predicted for him by a local farmer, whose time on Earth ran out and he is supposed to pass away. The figure of Death with a scythe in her hand is waiting in the living room but agrees to wait until the farmer finishes his prophecy. Starring into an open oven, the farmer predicts that the coal magnate would lose his coalmine. "No, that is impossible," the magnate shakes his head in disbelief. "I would never sell it. Who would take over? Who could ever buy me out? Is it Krueger? Is it his crest above the gate?" he asks. The farmer stares even more intensely into the oven. "No, it's a red star," he finally proclaims as the audience bursts out laughing.[262]

However, the fortune telling is taking too long and the figure of Death is getting impatient: "Gentlemen, please, you are really taking way too long. I am not a pedant but my work is calling me. Right now in Tanvald [a Czech town] there is a fight in a pub and a gypsy has been running around the place with a knife in his back for half an hour. Have some respect!" The audience laughs again. When the play ends, the authors meet the censor backstage. "So what did you think?" they ask. "Man, it was so funny that a few times I almost laughed!" says the censor, revealing to the audience of the film that even ideological censors scorn the legitimacy of the regime. Then the dialog continues:

---

[262] The joke rested in the reference to the Communist takeover in 1948 and the abrupt nationalization of all property, especially coal mines, steel plants, banks and other large industries. Clearly, this was a subversive critique of the regime that nonetheless passed the censors and made it into the movie. For an interesting collection of critical essays carefully analyzing communist cinematographic humor still during the communist period see *Humor a satira vo slovenskom hranom filme: zborník referátov a diskuzných príspevkov zo seminára, který usporiadal Slovenský filmový ústav a Zväz slovenských dramatických umielcov dňa 13.11. 1985* (Bratislava: Slovenský filmový ústav, 1986); For a reflective narrative about writing humor and jokes under communist censorship see, Jaroslav Kerles, *Jak vtipy přicházejí na svět* (Praha: Annonce, 1991). For a collection of jokes and anecdotes that traveled in popular discourse unofficially and never made it into the official press see, Václav Budínský, *Anekdoty z trezoru: aneb vtipy o zlatou mříž z období neúspěšného budování socialismu v Československu* (Praha: Svépomoc, 1990).

Censor: "But that gypsy has to go."
Authors: "What gypsy?"
Censor: "That one who is running around with a knife in his back."
Author 1: "Jesus! But that's so beautiful!"
Censor: "I know..."
Author 2: "Come on! Who could mind that?"
Censor: "Well, you know, the director is afraid that it might touch a nerve. So you have to put something else there. How about a horse dealer? There are no horse dealers in our country, it will not insult anybody."
Authors: "Yeah, well, but nobody will laugh either."
The censor leaves and one of the authors says, "Screw it, I'm leaving the gypsy in, a horse dealer is good for nothing."[263]

The dialogue, intended to evoke humorous depictions of gypsies, suggests several things.

First, besides the obvious mockery of the regime personified by the censor, who was supposed to ideologically monitor the production of artwork, the dialogue illuminated the discrepancy between the way the regime approached the Gypsy question and the way people actually understood it. The anxiety the censor expressed about the usage of the Gypsy image revealed that such images were, on the one hand, officially unacceptable, but, on the other hand, were popular sources of laughter. This double meaning unveiled that, officially, the regime tried to espouse a certain image of the Roma but the general population implicitly understood this effort as hypocritical, and went on perceiving and understanding "Gypsies" in its own terms. Ironically, since visual arts, mass media, and popular culture were directly subordinated to centralized planning and the ideological indoctrination of the regime, they have the potential to reveal much of what the system hoped to hide by the application of state censorship.[264]

---

263 Zdeněk Svěrák, Ladislav Smoljak, *Nejistá sezóna* (Divadlo Járy Cimrmanna a Filmové studio Barrandov, Praha, 1987).

264 For a post-communist analysis of the relationship between the government and the official press through a critique of late communist censorship see, Dušan Tomášek, *Pozor, cenzurováno! Aneb ze života soudružky cenzury* (Praha: MV CR, 1994); For a collection of political jokes with commentaries see, C. Banc, *You Call This Living? A Collection of East European Political Jokes* (Athens: University of Georgia Press, 1990) and John Kolasky, *Look Comrade – the People Are Laughing: Underground Wit, Satire and Humor from Behind the Iron Curtain* (Toronto: P. Martin Associates, 1972); For a collection of Czech political jokes and critiques published during communism by the

Interestingly, immediately after the collapse of the communist regime, several novels and movies about the Roma or using the Roma as significant characters appeared, making it clear that the absence of the Roma in literature and cinematography was artificially created. These novels and movies, which are all critiques of the communist regime, present the Roma in unsentimental, harsh, violent and hostile ways, exposing the bottled-up sentiments about interethnic conflict that were not allowed to surface under the communist regime. The characters of these stories are not arbitrary. Once again, they all serve the purpose of denouncing the communist regime, even though this time making a very different argument: they do make people laugh and scorn, but rather, through their violence and hostility erupting outward, represent the desire and ability (of all) to finally openly stand up against the abuse of the communist system. Nonetheless, the "gypsy" act of resistence and speaking up is again presented in socially and morally questionable terms.[265]

III.3 Romani Culture in Academic Writing

Gypsy myths were not only an integral part of Czechoslovak fiction and entertainment, but also proliferated by finding their way into the mass media and academic literature from the beginning of the postwar period. As we have seen already in Chapter two, journalistic accounts perpetuated rather than challenged Czech and Slovak nationalist discourses, disseminating romanticized and demonized images of gypsies as legitimate ways of perceiving the

---

famous Czechoslovak dissident publishing house in Canada see, Pavel Taussig, *Blbé, ale naše = One (Party) Liners* (Toronto: 68 Publishers, 1987).

265 For example, Eva Kantůrková, *Přítelkyně z domu smutku* (Praha: Československý spisovatel, 1991). This novel narrates a story about the year, which the well-known Czech dissident spent in the communist prison, meeting and living there with several Romani women. Her view of the "Gypsy" world is thus told in very unsentimental way, without racist prejudices, but portrayed Romani life within the confines of a criminal existence. Another example is the film *Marián*, based on a true story, which is about the tragic life of a young Romani boy who was raised and abused in a communist foster care institution. Later he was moved into a juvenile correctional facility. After turning 18, he committed street murder and finally committed suicide in a regime-run prison. The movie received several international cinematographic awards. (*Marián*, dir. Petr Václav, Prague: ArtStudio, 1998.)

Roma. These media discourses refused to recognize Roma both as citizens of the state entitled to equal treatment as well as a people who deserved social sympathy as primary victims of the Holocaust. One journalistic account in 1946 went so far as to argue that

> gypsies, who were placed in the concentration camps during the war brought from there the personal papers of gassed people and now are taking advantage of that, creating just more work for our administration. ... The biggest problems are caused by [gypsy] children whose parents did not survive, even though their [the parents'] sharp vision temporarily might have helped them to obtain positions as guards of other prisoners.[266]

Conceptions of the Roma in socialist media continued these myths but in less overt ways. The dissident movement Charter 77, which monitored and criticized the human rights violations of Czechoslovak communism, argued in 1979 that "the regime in power (*společenská moc*) [has done] everything possible to exterminate Romani culture" and that "the mass media have systematically disseminated notions that such a culture does not even exist."[267]

While the media refused to recognize Romani culture as having distinct traditions of its own, academic writing since the 1950s has politicized the strategies, which the socialist regime should use to normalize and reeducate the Roma in order to remove the harmful effects their own culture could have on their social behavior. In 1955, historian Zdeňka Jamnická-Šmerglová sought to dispel the gypsy myth in *History of Our Gypsies* by providing a "factual representation of their character and behavior" set in the context of a historical narrative of their predicament,"[268] although in reality her account mimicked the ideological constructions of the Roma that the regime was trying to disseminate to the population.[269]

---

266 Eva Soukénková, "Co dělat s cikány?," *Lidová demokracie*, September 18, 1946, 3.

267 Charta 77, "Dokumenty: Dokument č. 23," *Listy*, 2:3 (1979): 51.

268 Jamnická-Šmerglová, *Dějiny našich cikánů*, 5.

269 Under the communist regime, all official publishing houses had assigned "political censors," who examined texts proposed for publication for ideological inconsistencies. (Political analyst Milan Šimečka even argued that "censorship [really] did not exist to prevent criticism of the socialist regime from being published: nobody would dare to submit such things to the censor anyway." *The Restoration of Order: The Normalization of Czechoslovakia*, 51.) Since the entire system was as centrally organized as possible, individual publishing houses specialized in distinct types of literature. Orbis, where

The driving motivation behind her work on the Roma was to provide an answer to the "repeatedly asked and so far still unsolved question: 'Will they ever become human'? (*Budou z nich lidé*?)"[270] At the end of her investigation, she answered with optimism that

> today this question is no longer a problem because reality is proving that it is possible, it is happening. Our people's democracy is creating all the [necessary] conditions for that and its [the assimilation's] success depends on us [...] The belief in a person's reeducation has to be our motto and imperative. To our fellow gypsy citizens we have to be good mentors, advisors, helpers, genuine friends and dedicated teachers.[271]

She insisted that the most effective method for re-education of Gypsies is "not coercion and repression, but a deeply convincing, consciously culturally enlightened (*osvětová*) educational work."[272] Pointing out why "the care for gypsy children" is "the most important task ahead of us" she argued that it is "obvious that even our own society cannot achieve the full eradication of the bad habits and qualities of adult generations, but in children we can succeed." On the other hand, she resolutely stood up against "romanticization and bourgeois philanthropy" and reminded her readers that "in our fight against backwardness . . . we have to remember that in front of us we do not have inferior people but gypsies, who are equal members of our state, our fellow citizens."[273] There is a striking irony of denying Romani inferiority on the one hand and asking the question of whether they can ever be human on the other. It indicates the ease with which discourses about the Roma during communism, based on everyday social stereotypes and full of blatant contradictions, managed to create discursive conditions for societal acceptance of these paradoxes as commonsensical assessments of gypsy behavior.

Jamnická-Šmerglová believed that her account was objective, neither romanticizing nor demeaning the Roma. Her account, however, is shot through with rhetoric resemblances of colonial writings of the 18th-19th century

---

Jamnická-Šmerglová's book was published, specialized in "popular-academic" (*populárně-vědecká*) and educational literature.

270 Jamnická-Šmerglová, 5.

271 *Ibid.*

272 *Ibid.*, 105-107.

273 Jamnická-Šmerglová, 108.

imperial observers in African and Asian territories.[274] Jamnická-Šmerglová often belied her claim to objectivity by characterizing the Roma as "these children of *A Thousand and One [Arabian] Nights*" or "our little friends, pupils and good fellow citizens,"[275] unable to perceive how her own descriptions reflected the superiority of her position. Most importantly, her portrayal of the Roma was firmly rooted in the Gypsy myths of the previous decades, romanticizing the Roma in terms of "their light, lively, gracious, irresistible dance," their "rich and colorful imagination," and their "touching storytelling."[276] As with previous writers on the Roma, her romanticized account was inevitably balanced by her sense of their dirtiness and backwardness. She described in disdain the disgust of what "the socialist comrade workers encountered" ... "even in bourgeois Czechoslovakia," during their quest to transform the Roma into "humans" (*lidé*):

> They dwelled in huts made of mud or sun-baked bricks, patched-up together with dry dirt, of which stronger winds and rain frequently blew a part away. There was often no furniture inside, only one or two crooked tiny rooms strewn with dry leaves, rags or hay; moisture and dirt were the perfect seedbed for contagious diseases, mostly scabies. Half-demolished shacks, most of the year submerged in bottomless mud, remnants of food thrown around, swamps of dirty children full of lice, flies and unbearably reeking air, all that made gypsy dwellings truly plague islands that everybody detested and avoided.[277]

Such conditions, of course, were "the historical results of class oppression of the Roma by other regimes." As soon as WWII ended, "thousand of our gypsies trekked back to our country from concentration camps, battlefields and neighboring countries where they hid with such ease as their ancestors did," argued Jamnická-Šmerglová.[278]

Perhaps the most pervasive stereotype she perpetuated was the image of gypsies as children. In her view, many of the Roma "during the war recog-

---

[274] See Ann Stoler, *Race and the Education of Desire*; Timothy Mitchell, *Colonizing Egypt*; Susanne Zantop, *Colonial Fantasies: Conquest, Family, and Nation in Precolonial Germany, 1770-1870* (Durham: Duke University Press, 1997).

[275] Jamnická-Šmerglová, 7 and 18.

[276] *Ibid.*, 37.

[277] Jamnická-Šmerglová, 60-61.

[278] *Ibid.*, 60-61.

nized that the new Czechoslovakia is genuinely counting them in, this time truly as equal citizens," and so they kept "doggedly and totally persistently exclaiming that they were Czechoslovak gypsies."[279] When "our state began to take care of them," the Roma were so bewildered by this assistance, having been "only persecuted for centuries," that they "plundered, looted, destroyed and burned one allotted house [in the borderlands] after another."[280] But according to Jamnická-Šmerglová society should treat gypsies with leniency. They were "childishly excited with an almost unimaginable and dangerous type of freedom," which the resettlement policies of the communist regime provided for them. Social workers and relevant authorities should just make sure that "[the gypsies] are not left at the mercy of their own unconscious gratuitousness."[281]

Despite all its problematic assumptions and suggestions, Jamnická-Šmerglová's description of the "exotic" lifestyles of the Roma, almost incomprehensible to the "civilized" Czechoslovak citizens, sought to instill a sense of the need to treat the Roma as social equals. Yet her tendencies to juxtapose romantic and loathful images of gypsies as noble savages is a classic example of colonial writing fascinated with the Other in both negative and positive terms. Her argument was built on a sense of hope and optimism in the possibility of re-educating gypsies to become modern, rational beings.[282] Despite the many differences between West European colonial missionaries and East European writers, who advocated Stalinist policies toward minority groups, both types of commentators based their thoughts on an enlightened imperialism that naturalized the lifestyle of the Other as both brute and authentic. Since the gypsies were seen as so proximate to nature, socialist re-

---

279 *Ibid.*, 85.

280 In these comments, Jamnická-Šmerglová apparently refers to the settlement of the borderlands in the second half of the 1940s. Yet she provides no evidence either of these events actually taking place or reasons why one should interpret such behavior as "bewilderment at [the state] assistance."

281 *Ibid.*, 89.

282 See for example, Jean and John Comarroff, *On Revelation and Revolution: Christianity, Colonialism, and Consciousness in South Africa*, Vol. I. (Chicago: Chicago University Press, 1991), see especially the essay "Africa Observed."

education was tantamount to transforming them, as Jamnická-Šmerglová put it, into "new human being[s]."[283]

Apparently, some ordinary Czechs and Slovaks passionately felt that this task was their personal struggle as well. Romani poet Anna Koptová, the first Slovak Roma ever to graduate from college with a journalistic degree, told in a postscript to her first post-1989 poetry collection of a childhood memory that stayed with her forever. She was perhaps six or seven, light-heartedly walking with her brother on the street, speaking Romany:

> As we were talking, laughing and excitedly throwing our arms around, one woman stopped in front of us and prevented us from walking. "Why are you talking that gypsy nonsense!? You don't want to ever grow up to be human?" Her angry scream was hammering me to the ground. Neither my brother nor I were capable of saying a word back. We just looked at each other and our throats got tight.[284]

Koptová continues that ever since that day for her, as a small child, the house of the woman was a horror territory to pass by. She had nightmares about the woman and the experience soured her relationship to her own Romani identity. Thirty years later, she wrote that at the time she did not understand "why [her] heart was crying," but the anger and frustration was raising up in her as she more and more frequently "silently asked herself: So our language is just a wolf howling? Is [renouncing our language] really the only way to humanity (*lidství*)?"[285]

Jamnická-Šmerglová's narrative was the only official history of the Roma written in the 1950s. It both presented an ideological critique of prior regimes and recognized (to the limited degree possible) Romani cultural differences. Her analysis of the Roma was gradually supplanted by academic works that more strongly challenged the idea of a Romani ethnic heritage by construing their "cultural" differences as an effect of their historically meager economic conditions. While Jamnická-Šmerglová was still able to recognize that there are differences in "mentality" and "sensibilities" of the Roma, other authors writing after her gradually translated these differences into "social

---

283 Jamnická-Šmerglová, 90.
284 Anna Koptová, *Kale ruži* (Hradec Králové: Romaňi Čhib, 1990), 56-7. (Written in 1988.)
285 *Ibid.*, 57.

characteristics" that were malleable and redeemable. Step by step, the rhetoric of cultural difference transformed into social pathology, which legitimated demands for articulating stricter programs of assimilation.

This shift in official discourse arose in the 1960s, when the presence of the anti-nomadic law boosted the confidence of the state officials in their strategies of dealing with "Gypsies." Two major accounts of Romani history, *Gypsies in Socialist Czechoslovakia*, written by Jaroslav Sus in 1961, and Josef Nováček's *Gypsies Yesterday, Today and Tomorrow*, published in 1968, painted a radically different picture of gypsy life than Jamnická-Šmerglová did in her book.[286] While they both tackled the "Gypsy question" as relating to "gypsy ethnicity" and used the term quite deliberately, their arguments prepared the rhetorical ground for the rejection of Romani distinctiveness. Nováček, titling one of his chapters "Gypsies as a distinct ethnic group of the population," nonetheless came to the conclusion that "while gypsies form a distinct ethnic group," such distinctiveness is a "socially based difference resulting from centuries of isolation."[287] Similarly, Sus proposed a Marxist interpretation of the "material conditions that leave gypsies in debased state" to argue for "the inevitability of assimilation."[288] They both discredited previous attempts to "describe gypsies as distinct culture, or even race"[289] by such authors as Jamnická-Šmerglová or interwar anthropologist František Štampach before her,[290] as "uninformed accounts of a few individuals, who could not let go of [their] romantic notions of gypsies [and perceived] nomadism and other [gypsy] habits as a typical lifestyle."[291]

According to Sus, Romani culture is simply a "result of a 'survival instinct' and an 'animal struggle' that cannot under any circumstances be confused with characteristics of a cultural consciousness or be even taken as a proof of their autonomous existence."[292] Nováček argued that while "the no-

---

[286] Jaroslav Sus, *Cikánská otázka v ČSSR* (Praha: Státní nakladatelství politické literatury, 1961) and Josef Nováček, *Cikáni včera, dnes a zítra* (Praha: Socialistická akademie, 1968).
[287] Nováček, 37.
[288] Sus, 58-60.
[289] *Ibid.*, 21.
[290] František Štampach, *Děti nad propastí* (Košice-Plzeň: M. Labková, 1933).
[291] Nováček, 34.
[292] Sus, 25.

madism of hunters is a phenomenon stemming from a completely different nature [because it is] a means of livelihood in unpopulated areas," the travelling and migrations of the Roma "is conditioned on their parasitism on other societies in fully populated areas, without a concrete working goal [and thus] is a social anachronism that has a deviant character."[293] Both authors focus on Romani nomadism (even though less than one tenth of all Czechoslovak Roma were nomadic) in order to prove that the "gypsy mentality and values stem from the contact between [their] social position and the rest of the society"[294] and that "antagonistic class relations bear the fundamental fault for the uncivilized nature and asocial qualities of gypsies."[295] In summary, "gypsies form a distinctly backward social group . . . whose development was deformed by class inequalities in the society."[296]

Sus admits that "it is necessary to recognize the gypsy language as a feature that quite distinctly characterizes the distinctiveness of gypsy ethnicity," but later dismisses its importance "because [it] has too many mutually incomprehensible dialects and, moreover, gypsies do not fulfill the Stalinist definition of nationality" because they lack territory.[297] He thus conflated culture, ethnicity and nationality together in order to prove that the Roma are in essence no different than Czechs and Slovaks and, therefore, their socialization is only a matter of "bringing them to a higher level" of social conditions.[298] Likewise, Nováček recognized the linguistic differences between Roma and non-Roma, but reiterated that "gypsies from various regions do not understand each other" and that language "is not a tie bonding the gypsies" but merely represents tribal demarcations forced on by isolation.[299]

---

[293] Nováček, 35.
[294] *Ibid.*, 36.
[295] Sus, 47.
[296] Nováček, 21.
[297] For concise treatment of the Stalinist definition of nationality and discussions of the Communist Nationality Question see, for example, Robert Tucker's classis analysis of Stalinism, *The Soviet Political Mind: Stalinism and Post-Stalinist Change* (New York: Norton, 1971), esp. 109 and 260-61, or Stephen Cohen's *Rethinking the Soviet Experience: Politics & History Since 1917* (Oxford: Oxford University Press, 1985), esp. 68-69.
[298] Sus, 73 and 39.
[299] Nováček, 40.

Even though both authors strictly reject idolizing or romanticizing the Roma, they both have their own ways of falling into the trap of talking about Romani characteristics that reflect the traditions of gypsy myths. To them, Roma have sensitivity, an "often impulsive temperament," and "limitless ability to be happy and then immediately break into a fight." According to Nováček, "this trait is not natural only to gypsies, but to all collectivities on low stages of civilization." He argued that educators should also make use of gypsies' "bottomless trust in those who can capture their attention," even though he warns that "because of their historically determined hatred toward 'whites'" it is possible to lose that trust easily. Gypsies can "hate the person they loved with all their gypsy guilelessness." To understand this "mentality" is, according to him, "very important for the reeducation process."[300]

Fortunately, according to Sus, "due to their general, deep backwardness gypsies possess quite a large passive, assimilative and acculturative ability." He argued that this was a very positive finding, but one that created demands and obligations for Czechoslovak – meaning non-Romani – society because "without the help of the higher-standing cultural environment, on their own, [the gypsies] are not able to transfer to a higher level" of social standing.[301] Nováček pointed out that "the work of gypsy educators carries some specific traits resulting from the backwardness of gypsies. They have to bring them in, bathe them, comb them, feed them and clothe them."[302] In other words, they first have to make them into "people" before they can start educating them, a truly colonizing process utterly different from working with "normal" children. Nonetheless, Sus optimistically argued, all these difficulties were created by "long-term racial discrimination," which finally "in our socialist society is over."[303]

Like Jamnická-Šmerglová in the 1950s, Sus and Nováček in the 1960s saw the struggle for Roma assimilation as a pioneering task on the frontiers of civilization that would involve "tackling their backwardness" and "overcoming backwardness as a brake of progress."[304] In the fashion of the 19th century-

[300] *Ibid.*, 38-39.
[301] Sus, 53.
[302] Nováček, 57 and 63.
[303] Sus, 53-54.
[304] *Ibid.*, 47.

tury anthropologists, eager to record extinguishing cultures for their museums, Nováček warned that "we cannot nihilistically reject everything that gypsies produce. With the process of assimilation [gypsy music] will gradually disappear and that is why it is important to write gypsy songs down and preserve them."[305] In other words, ethnographers should work on the frontiers recording the vanishing gypsy culture (which is in actuality a vocalization of social despair), while educators, social workers, medical personnel and the state administration should disseminate civilization through assimilation.

In essence, while rejecting *forceful* assimilation and *coercion*, all three authors argued that assimilation was necessary for improving Romani social conditions. They made it clear that this process had to be carried out with the help of superior cultural and ideological agents. Therefore, even while professing Romani equality, throughout their accounts they openly asserted a civilizational hierarchy between the Roma and Czechoslovak [non-Romani] society. The alleged social backwardness of the Roma resulted in the fact that, as Sus tellingly put it, a rationalist "ideology of will, self-help and autonomy could not resolve the gypsy question."[306] Like imperial colonizers centuries before them, these Czechoslovak ideologues saw their regime as engaging in a fully legitimate, enlightened struggle for the betterment of backward subjects.

As an integral part of this effort, the regime continuously demanded that Gypsies themselves also participate in their own socio-economic and cultural improvement. The official documents repeatedly professed "genuine desire" for the Roma's involvement. But for a variety of reasons, such vision has never materialized. Charges of the Roma's alleged lack of interest in a "dialogue" and "cooperation in the process of integration" were among the most frequently cited reasons for the failure of the communist regime to "solve" the Gypsy question. Likewise, the radicalization of the post-communist interethnic tensions has also been often blamed on Roma's supposed passivity and indifference towards their own situation. However, as the next chapter, discussing the politics of the Union of Gypsies-Roma will show, it would be quite an

[305] Nováček, 55.
[306] Sus, 67.

illusion to think that Romani empowerment and active subjectivity was genuinely welcome.

IV "Amare Nevo Drom"

> The distinct existence of the specificities and differences of Gypsies as a *social group* apart from other *social groups* is unquestionable. We want the state to recognize and in practice adequately respect the significance of the values, customs, interests, attitudes and positions of Gypsies.[307]

These words, boldly proclaimed by Romani intellectuals in the introduction to an early 1968 proposal for a first (and only) Union of the Gypsies-Roma (*Svaz Cikánů-Romů*)[308] in socialist Czechoslovakia, clearly signaled that a new era had arrived. They not only called for the recognition of the Roma as a distinct culture, but also embodied new willingness of Romani elites to mobilize a Romani political identity and create an organized Romani movement. Encouraged by the hopeful spirit of the political and social reformism of the Prague Spring, spearheaded by the country's communist leadership around the Party's First Secretary Alexander Dubček, the Roma intellectuals rode the wave of enthusiasm in order to promote their political cause. It was not the

---

[307] Miroslav Holomek and the preparatory committee of the Union of the Gypsies-Roma for the Czech lands and Moravia, "Návrh programu řešení problematiky cikánů." (December 10, 1968.) MZA Brno, 3. (Emphasis mine.) Note the usage of the term "social group." It is clear here that Holomek is striving for an articulation of Romani cultural distinctiveness but strictly within the parameters of social (not ethnic) categories and rhetoric. The self-designation of the Roma underwent significant changes during the first year of the Union's existence, reflecting both the worsening political circumstances and the Roma's inability to push through their ethnic claims. Please see especially the discussion on pages 147-148.

[308] The title of the Union, unusual for the times in its hyphenated use of the terms "Gypsy" and "Roma" side by side, is significant in two different ways. For one, the Romani leadership wanted to distance itself from the term "Gypsy" and demanded that the title of their organization at least integrally includes the identification "Roma." This can be read, on the one hand, as a clear indication that Romani intellectuals felt the term "Gypsy" is filled with negative and pejorative content. However, there were always at least some Roma, who were proud of the term Gypsy (*Cikán* in Czech; *Cigán* in Slovak), arguing that this name resonates their true identity. And two, from the position of the regime, inclusion of both terms indicated the process of assimilation, which was the fundamental purpose of the association. While "Gypsy" indicated a category of backwardness, "Roma" was a political identity of a socialist citizen of Gypsy origin, who was defined by his or her successful social transformation.

first time they tried to promote a politics of recognition but it certainly was the first time they were winning their battle.

The first attempt by the Roma to call for their own national organization happened in 1957. Roma intellectuals and a few dozen of their supporters, mostly from intellectual and academic circles, met at the spa town of Bardejov in Eastern Slovakia and called for the need to awaken Roma national consciousness. Headed by Dr. Anton Facuna, the later chairman of the Slovak branch of the Roma Union, they drafted a proposal for the organization and sent a request asking for approval to establish a Roma Union to the Board of Trustees of the National Front, the Central Committee of the Communist Party, and the national government. For several months the preparatory committee of the potential Union waited without an answer. The silence of the state administration was, of course, an answer after all, making it clear that the state had no interest in helping the Roma to realize their ambitions. In 1958, the request was unanimously rejected by the Central Committee of the Communist Party and the following decade was marked by the absence of a dialogue between the Party officials and representatives of the Roma.[309] Despite rhetorical calls for Roma's activity, the state placed the entire burden of the "Gypsy question" on its own shoulders and was determined to "solve" it on its own, one-sidedly applying policies without giving the Roma any say in the matters.

In 1968-69, things were different. The Union of Gypsies-Roma in Slovakia (*Zväz Cigánov-Romov*), led by Dr. Anton Facuna, was established about a year after Dubček's rise to power, in January 1969. The Czech counterpart of the Union was founded in August 1969 in Brno, under the leadership of Ing. Miroslav Holomek.[310] Both branches of the Union functioned, as all other

---

[309] Ctibor Nečas, *Historický kalendář*; Hübschmannová, *Šaj pes dovakeras*; Davidová, *Romano Drom*.

[310] The preparatory committees of the Union, both in the Czech Republic and Slovakia, were authorized to begin their preparatory work during the height of Dubček's regime in the spring of 1968. The invasion of the Warsaw Pact armies in August 1968 slowed down and transformed the process, but nonetheless, the work continued, with both branches of the association being formally established in 1969, in January and August respectively. However, informally the Unions functioned already *during* the preparatory period in 1968 and thus it makes sense to talk about the "existence" of the Union from 1968 to 1973, when it was officially abolished.

approved organizations, within the confines of the National Front, which was an umbrella institution that mandatorily associated all organizations in communist Czechoslovakia in order to provide united ideological direction to any expression of civic activities of the population.[311] The cultural and political activity of the Roma, under the spiritual leadership of the Roma Unions in both federal republics of Czechoslovakia, generated conditions for what could be perceived as a brief Romani renaissance. During the following several years, the Roma formed over 200 Romani musical groups, thirty local football [soccer] clubs and membership in both branches of the Union swelled to 20,000 members. Aside from the socio-economic concerns of the sustainability of the Union, it also set for itself the goal of "enhancing the majority population's awareness and understanding of Gypsy culture." It even managed to found a monthly Gypsy journal, called *Romani Lil* in the Czech Republic and *Romani Pajtrin* in Slovakia, with the primary goal of "cementing cultural unity".[312] The Union attracted both Romani and non-Romani members who "ha[d] a genuine interest in working for the Union and in submitting to the organization's charter".[313] However, less than five years after its establishment, the Roma Unions in both republics along with all their sub-organizations were officially expelled from the National Front and in April 1973 were outlawed altogether.

This chapter explores the rise and fall of the Union of Gypsies-Roma and the fatal conclusion drawn by the regime that the Union "failed to fulfill

[311] Anna Jurová, "Riešenie Romskej problematiky na Slovensku po druhej svetovej vojne," in ed. Arne Mann, *Neznámi Romovia: Zo života a kultúry Cigánov-Rómov na Slovensku* (Bratislava, Slovakia: Ister Science Press, 1992), 91-101; and Crowe, *A History of the Gypsies of Eastern Europe and Russia*, 31-67.

[312] It was not explicitly stated exactly what "cultural unity" it should cement but presumably the unity of the Czechoslovak Roma. Miroslav Holomek, "Návrh programu řešení problematiky Cikánů," (Brno, Dec. 10, 1968), 2-3. In Moravský Zemský Archiv (MZA), Brno, G 434, Box 2. Also in Srb, "Ustavující Sjezd Svazu Cikánů - Romů v ČSR v Brně," *Demografie*, 11:4 (1969b): 365. The full text of the program and the goals of the Union as well as all other materials concerning the Union are stored in MZA in Brno and in the adjunct archive in Kunštát na Moravě. The complete archive of the Roma consists of 870 boxes of documents that were gradually moved to Brno between 1975 and 1986. In the early 1990s, all documents were divided by topics and distributed to various archives throughout the Czech Republic. However, all materials concerning the Union, 719 files altogether divided into three cartons, are in the Brno and Kunštát archives.

[313] Anton Facuna, "Zväz Cigánov-Rómov na Slovensku," *Demografie*,11:3 (1969): 214-215. Among the few dozen non-Romani members were primarily academics, such as Davidová or Hübschmannová. (Hübschmannová, *Šaj Pes Dovakeras*, 12-17.)

[its] integrative function."[314] By analyzing the Union's attempts to deal with the "Gypsy question" and the regime's reaction to the Union's policies, the chapter shows that instances of Romani cultural expression were deemed unassimilative and asocial, even though it was the Party organs themselves that most often refused to integrate Roma into their programs. In fact, while calling for Roma integration, "proper citizenship," and civic participation for more than twenty years, the Party was interested in those qualities and activities of the Roma only if they were willing to denounce their "gypsiness" and exercise those rights solely as "socialist citizens." This double standard demonstrates that even though the regime officially claimed its unwavering support for the "advancement of gypsies," the meaning of the term Gypsy (whether with lower or upper "g") was defined in purely negative terms and could not incorporate any aspects of a positive cultural identity that would distinguish its bearers from the rest of the Czechoslovak society in affirmative ways. Therefore, this chapter shows two interrelated things. First, the Union's demand for the recognition of the Romani culture, observation of Roma's civil and human rights and the approval of their nationality status were seen by the regime as too threatening. And second, these ambitions were also the primary causes for the regime's renewed attempts to eliminate such traces of "social deviance" from the Roma population and to make new strides towards "normalizing" Romani social and sexual behavior.

At the same time, the identity formation of Romani intellectuals and the interaction between the Roma Union and state officials reveal that there is no easy target to blame for the failure of the Union. While the regime must be held accountable for exploiting the situation of the Union to achieve its ends through "legitimate" means, the detachment of the Union leadership from Romani communities across the country also had disastrous consequences. It is an irony of history that the very Romani intellectuals who so vigorously fought for Romani interests adopted the system's values, rhetoric, and abused their personal power. The same tools that enabled them to organize the movement were also at the vanguard of its dismantling.

---

314 *Report of the Central Committee of the National Front*, April 1973. MZA, Brno. (G 434, box 18:5, 3).

IV.1 Romani Renaissance in the late 1960s

The decade of the 1960s was marked by the regime's heightened efforts to integrate the Roma with the rest of the society. Guided by the communist ideology, according to which equality of citizenship requires the elimination of markers of cultural or ethnic difference, the regime believed that society would be willing to accept the Roma as equal citizens, but only as Czechs or Slovaks, not as "gypsies." The clash between the assimilatory policies of the state, on the one hand, and the desire of the vulnerable Romani community for recognition, on the other, produced disastrous results. The seeds of mutual mistrust and discontent between the state and the Romani community that were planted during the preceding two decades proved to be too wide a gap to bridge.[315] In the end, the Union's proposal that the state recognize the Roma as a distinctive national ethnic group disputed the very terms of the discourse, which defined and subordinated the Roma as socially inferior; a challenge that ultimately led to the Union's demise.

Like the rest of society, Romani intellectuals enthusiastically welcomed the social and political ideals of the Prague Spring and equally shared in the tragedy and frustration of the Soviet invasion of Czechoslovakia in August 1968. In the midst of the invasion, a group of Romani intellectuals in Western Bohemia declared that

> We, the citizens of Gypsy ancestry, will never forget the years of Hitlerite occupation, when we, just as the citizens of Jewish origin, were persecuted; many members of our families were liquidated in the Nazi concentration camps. Therefore, we strongly condemn the occupation of our lands by the armies of the five states of the Warsaw Pact, among which is also the army of the German Democratic Republic. Since the days of the Munich occupation, this is the second invasion of our lands.[316]

For obvious political reasons, such a manifesto was unacceptable to the new Party leadership, which embarked on the so-called "Normalization" path of restoring hard-line authoritarian control of the country. Not only did the state-

---

[315] Facuna, 214-215.

[316] *Manifesto cikánských občanů v západních Čechách*, *Pravda* (Plzeň), August 27, 1968, 2.

ment adopt a disapproving and denouncing tone, but more importantly, it paralleled the invasion of the "friendly fraternal armies" with the hated Nazi occupation and in doing so suggested a link of continuity between fascist and socialist regimes.[317]

However, what is perhaps even more striking in this statement is the way in which the Roma managed to incorporate their ethnic claims. While sociologist Otto Ulč interprets this manifesto as representing a feeling of "euphoric unity of defiance regardless of one's ethnic background," I argue that it is precisely the articulation of ethnicity, as well as Roma political and historical subjectivity, that serves as the basis and principal message of the community's statement. By referring to themselves in a spontaneous manifesto as "citizens of a certain origin," the writers of the statement reveal the degree to which they have internalized the regime's rhetoric and at the same time identified their historical predicament alongside Jews as a marginalized and persecuted nation.

The statement also reveals the degree to which the Romani struggle for ethnic recognition was bound up with their subjective awareness of being historical victims. Others have pointed out that "the reasons [for Romani hostility toward the Soviet invasion] go deeper . . . having much to do with [their]

---

[317] Along with the Czech/Slovak-German relations, the Prague Spring and the Soviet invasion of 1968 is one of the most researched and studied events in the history of Czechoslovakia. See, for example: the classic and celebrated study by Zdeněk Mlynář, *Nightfrost in Prague: The End of Humane Socialism* (New York: Karz Publishers, 1980. Published in Czech as *Mráz přichází z Kremlu*); also by the same author, *Československý pokus o reformu 1968: Analýza jeho teorie a praxe* (Cologne: Index, 1985). *The Prague Spring 1968: National Security Archive Documents Reader* (New York: Central European University Press, 1998) is an excellent collection of primary sources on the circumstances of the event. It contains top-level documents accessed from previously closed archives in both East and West, thus representing a first look at 1968 from both sides of the Iron Curtain. Besides documents from archives of all members of the Warsaw Pact, the Reader includes previously classified documents selected from the U.S. National Security Council, CIA and other institutions. The documents are accompanied by critical essays introducing them; Will Kieran, *The Prague Spring and Its Aftermath: Czechoslovak Politics, 1968-1970* (New York: Cambridge University Press, 1997); Miklos Kun, *Prague Spring, Prague Fall: Blank Spots of 1968* (Budapest: Akademiai Kiado, 1999); For a comprehensive narrative of the aftermath of the Soviet invasion and the impact of Normalization on civic expression and public life, see, especially, Milan Šimečka, *The Restoration of Order: The Normalization of Czechoslovakia*.

memories of World War II."[318] Ulč's thesis that the Roma's increasingly visible activity, culminating in the formation of the Union, was a mere evidence of the overall rise of popular civic consciousness in the late 1960s not only ignores this historical and ethnic subjectivity, but also comes very close to affirming the regime's discourse of civility, which was a persistent tool in subordinating the Roma as socially inferior and deviant. Although some Roma might have developed a "civic consciousness," Ulč's analysis takes "popular discourse" as a matter of fact, without questioning the forms of power within discourse or the ways Romani groups have attempted to resist it.[319]

Other writers argued that Roma activism in the late 1960s was not so much linked to a general civic consciousness as it was linked to debates about the equal status of Slovaks with Czechs in one common state. Clyde Farnsworth, a *New York Times* correspondent, who was covering the events of the Prague Spring pointed out that the rise of Roma consciousness was linked to growing phenomenon of Slovak exceptionalism, which led to the successful proclamation of the Czechoslovak Federation of two equal nations in 1968. His argument advanced the idea that both the Slovaks and the Roma had much in common in their mutual plea for full recognition of their political and social concerns and in their quest for better conditions to promote their unique cultures. In this sense, both groups could position themselves in opposition to the Czechs, as they both were weary of the centralist policies of integration and discrimination that emanated from Prague. Farnsworth argued that

> with Mr. Dubček came the official recognition that the gypsies represented a nation within a nation. This was a reversal of a policy in effect for twenty years that sought to disperse the gypsies and force them to be assimilated.[320]

[318] Clyde Farnsworth, "Occupation Stirs Czechoslovak Gypsies' Patriotism," *The New York Times*, Nov. 3, 1968, 18.

[319] Ulč, "Integration," 310. See also, Sidney Tarrow, *Power in Movement: Social Movements, Collective Action, and Politics* (New York: Cambridge University Press, 1994); John Mueller, "Minorities and the Democratic Image," *East European Politics and Societies*, 9:3 (Fall 1995): 513-22; Greg Calhoun, ed., *Social Theory and the Politics of Identity* (Cambridge: Blackwell, 1994).

[320] Farnsworth, 18.

Even though Farnworth, as a journalist, is not specific on the ways, in which such recognition came, one can argue that certainly there was an economic dimension to Dubček's policies that also favorably affected the Roma. For example, one Romani blacksmith exclaimed that he liked Dubček's regime because "now I can sell to whichever shops I want to, and not simply to the shops named by the state." Likewise, other Roma enjoyed state grants of 30,000 crowns to buy a house (or 40,000-50,000 crowns to build their own house.)[321] Farnsworth's notion that the Roma's rise of consciousness was linked with the rise of Slovak nationalism merits attention because it is undeniable that the establishment of the Roma Union was partially a consequence of the new regime's effort to remedy problems in ethnic and national organization of the country, resulting in the declaration of the Czechoslovak Federation.[322]

Ulč merits primarily the Czech literary class for bringing the "Gypsy question" into the open.[323] He argues that the Prague Spring of 1968 "thawed" society from the state system of censorship and, for the first time since the Stalinist years of the 1950s, created an environment of openness

---

321 *Ibid.*, also see Kostelancik, 313-314.

322 As was already mentioned in previous chapters, the Czechs did express some grudges against Slovakia in terms of Slovakia getting rid of its gypsies at the expense of the Czechs. (See, Reban, "Czechoslovakia: The New Federation"). Moreover, it also supports the notion of Czech xenophobia, sense of cultural superiority and inability to deal with ethnic difference, all issues extending beyond the Gypsy question. How far these sentiments reach became clear in the context of the separation of Czechoslovakia in 1992. Slovakia was then described as "an aching tooth that must be pulled out" and a respected weekly *Reflex* ran an article entitled "Two Civilizations," demonstrating how deeply the sentiments of cultural homogeneity and difference ran under the surface. (Martin Bútora, "The Dissolution of Czecho-Slovakia: An Unexpected Christmas Present," in *Grappling With Democracy*, ed. Matynia, 218-222.) For essays on Czech-Slovak relations in historical context see, Jiří Musil, ed., *The End of Czechoslovakia* (Budapest: Central European University Press, 1995). However, almost all essays in the Musil collection are written by Czechs (only two are by Slovaks, one of whom is a "pro-Czech" author Milan Kusý.)

323 On the role Czech and Slovak intellectuals, and especially writers, played in the rise of socialism with human face see, Dušan Hamšík, *Writers Against Rulers* (New York: Random House, 1971). For a collection of primary documents that contextualize the events in Czechoslovakia in the atmosphere of reformism and subsequent tightening of the bloc under Brezhnev's rule see Gale Stokes, ed., *From Stalinism to Pluralism: A Documentary History of Eastern Europe Since 1945* (Oxford: Oxford University Press, 1996).

that allowed public and scholarly discourse of sensitive political issues.[324] The "Gypsy question" – more specifically, the integration of the Roma and the denial of their ethnic identity – became a widely debated topic largely due to *Literární Listy*, an influential weekly, which dealt with the question several times and brought it to national attention.[325] While the Czech literary class was certainly influential, Ulč's argument is problematic in that it relegates the Roma to the role of virtual spectators and assigns them a more passive role than they actually had at the time.

The Union was established due to the initiative of Romani intellectuals themselves. In the initial Prague Spring atmosphere of openness and euphoria, the Romani elite, supported by Czech and Slovak intellectuals, rose in a wave of protest, challenging recently issued laws and policies, particularly the 1965 amendments to the anti-nomadic law, which accompanied the creation of the Governmental Committee for the Questions of the Gypsy Population (discussed in Chapter 3). In the new air of relaxed censorship, the future chairman of the Slovak Roma Union Dr. Facuna boldly criticized the regime as discriminatory for its approach to the "Gypsy question." He pointed out the connection between the anti-nomadic law and its abuse, which directly targeted the Roma. Speaking for the Romani representation, he argued that "of course we are against nomadic lifestyle" but pointed out that

> the registry was supposed to contain only nomads, who make up only one tenth of all gypsies . . . but into the registry were taken seven times more gypsies, who properly work and live a decent lifestyle. Every one of them had their ID cards marked, which severely limited their freedom of residence and movement. That is a seriously brutal intervention of civil rights.[326]

He went on to bring his criticism to even a higher level by attacking decree 502/1958 from 1965 on the five percent quota dispersal of the Roma throughout the country:

---

[324] Ulč, 312.

[325] *Literární Listy* published several issues devoted to the "Gypsy question," allowing both Romani and non-Romani scholars to express their views and opinions. After the August invasion the journal kept publishing for another nine months under the name of *Listy* before being finally banned by the state officials. (Hamšík, 24.)

[326] Facuna, "Zväz Ciganov-Romov na Slovensku," 214.

> The entire wording of the decree is in contradiction with the constitution. It is inconceivable that state organs should plan for Gypsies where they should live, in what numbers, and where they should work or find their permanent residence.[327]

Facuna argued that the communist regime's approach – up to now – "profoundly deepened the Roma's mistrust of the state and prevented any possibility of successful cooperation between the Romani community and the government." Immediately, however, he praised the new regime for being sensitive to the need for Roma autonomy and allowing the establishment of the Union.[328] Such proclamations, though critical, reveal that the Romani intelligentsia actively supported Dubček's attempt for "socialism with a human face" and was ready to participate in the newly opened dialogue. It seems to suggest that with the revival of Czech and Slovak national spirit, the Romani intelligentsia, educated at Czech and Slovak universities, found the courage to articulate their own right to claim their ethnic roots. From the very start, the recognition of Romani nationality was one of the pivotal concerns of the Union. The chairman of the Czech Union Miroslav Holomek even suggested that the achievement of other goals depended and derived from the realization of that status when he argued that

> only when Gypsies are designated as a nation, will they be respected for their interests, needs, and opinions, which will make it possible for the society to develop proper acceptance and tolerance.[329]

At the beginning of 1968, the preparatory committees of the future Unions in both parts of the country submitted to the Central Committee a proposal for the recognition of their nation status, as they demonstrated their ethnic awareness in other claims as well. A part of the plans of the Union was also to "create a department of Gypsy Studies affiliated with a school of humanities and social sciences at one of the country's universities." Their ambitions further included the creation of a "gypsy museum and professional rep-

---

[327] Facuna was referring specifically to the article 31 Sb. of the Czechoslovak Constitution from 1960, guaranteeing inviolability of personal housing and the freedom of movement. Facuna, 215.

[328] Facuna, 214-215.

[329] Holomek, "Současné problémy Cikánů," 205.

resentative musical dance ensemble on a high level," all activities implicitly expressing and displaying Roma's belief in their cultural uniqueness.[330]

Like a decade earlier, the Party leadership rejected the claim, supporting its decision by scientific and theoretical research that found the Roma to be an "ethnic group without the potential to reach the level of nationhood, and hence without the right for the legal and political status of a nation."[331] The political circumstances, however, changed considerably. In the spirit of the times, Dubček's regime was more inclined to negotiate with the Roma the establishment of their own organization, and for the first (and last) time the Central Committee of the Party approved the establishment of a Romani organization, not as an ethnic or national representation of the Roma, but specifically as a "cultural" enterprise.[332]

IV.2 The Union of Gypsies-Roma

"Amare Nevo Drom" – These words, meaning in Romany "the beginning of a new road," were the first to fill the room of the Regional Party Committee in Brno, packed with one hundred and eighty five expectant guests. Finally, on August 30, 1969, after almost a year of anxious waiting and busy work of the preparatory committee, the Union of the Gypsies-Roma in the Czech Republic held its first convention. The Slovak Union was already up and running for over a half a year. The atmosphere was both gloomy and hopeful. Just a week before, the country had marked the first anniversary of the tragic invasion of Czechoslovakia by the friendly armies. The time of the convention was cautiously chosen, in the words of the committee, as "not too early and not too late."[333] One can only speculate on what exactly that meant. By setting a September deadline for the Union's formal establishment through a first official convention, the Roma probably wanted to see how the official celebra-

330 Facuna, 214-215.

331 Jurová, 97-99; See also Horváthová, "K otazke etnokulturneho vyvoja," 3-14. (The rejection was based mainly on the arguments articulated by Sus in 1961.)

332 Hübschmannová, "Společenská problematika Romů v ČSSR," 3.

333 "Proposal of the Organizational Aspect of the First Roma Congress," MZA, G 434, box 1:1, 1969, 2.

tions of the Russian intervention would turn out before stepping in front of the microphones with their own proclamations.

The site of the Congress was carefully selected as well. The convention was held in Brno, the second largest city in the Czech Republic and former capital of the Austrain crown land of Moravia, located in the central Moravian plain. It was chosen for alleged best "geographical, financial, and socio-psychological" reasons.[334] Holomek's proposal does not provide further explanation of these qualifiers. But the selection of Brno as the headquarters of the Union and the site of the first Congress reveals more than just the committee's decision. Geographically, Prague was more conveniently located and more accessible than Brno. Demographically, there were four times more Roma in Bohemia than in Moravia.[335] But aside from the unquestionable financial advantages of running the Union from a regional metropolis rather than from the country's capital, Brno's selection could be perceived as a latent critique of Prague's heavy-handed centralization policies after the invasion. Brno's officials and population, never fully satisfied with Moravia's place in the new federation of Czech and Slovak Republics, were more likely to have an understanding for the Union's resentment of Prague's tight grip and its attempt to create the sense of political distance. Last, but certainly not least, Brno had a vibrant intellectual Romani community that had initiated the whole idea. It seemed only fair that their efforts would be crowned by having their hometown assigned as the Union headquarters. An issue, which did not concern anybody at the time, but later came to the forefront of attention, was that the Brno intellectuals founding the Union were not just random colleagues and friends, but rather a few families tightly dominating the highest echelons of the Romani community there.[336]

The establishment of the Union was accompanied by expectations of a better future for the Roma in Czechoslovakia. The excitement and anticipation was apparent from the reports and papers presented during the first two

---

[334] *Ibid.*, 5.

[335] Srb, "Cikáni v Československu," 229. (Statistics from the census of Dec. 31, 1968.)

[336] MZA, G 434, box 1:1, August 1969. The list of the Union leadership and their closest colleagues contains the names of fourteen members of only two families - the Holomeks (Leopold, Evžen, Jaromír, Ladislav, Tomáš, Vincenc, Jaroslav) and the Daniels (Antonín, Bartoloměj, Jiří, Václav, Emil, Robert, Anděla).

days of the convention by both Romani and non-Romani participants. However, as the convention was coming to a close, it was becoming obvious that the historical circumstances had taken their toll in payments of courage and determination. The tone of the presentations changed considerably from the initial proposals and speeches written in the beginning of 1968. In accordance with the development of the Normalization policies, the main focus of the presentations was to demonstrate that the Czech and Moravian Roma support the socialist enterprise and the politics of the Communist party. It was supposed to be abundantly clear that all Romani ambitions were to be realized within the boundaries set up by the National Front.[337]

In his opening contribution to the Congress, the chairman Miroslav Holomek asserted that "only the socialist system, from all existing state regimes in the world, is closest and most natural to the Roma" because of its strongly developed sense of collectivism.[338] His presentation was very positive, almost idealistic in its observations of the current situation of the Roma. However, the previous statement as well as his assertion that the attitude of the population toward the Roma has changed and that the "name gypsy no longer had too negative connotations,"[339] left open many questions. Did he try to simply appease the Party expectations? Or did Holomek and other members of the Union leadership, as intellectuals, truly have different or better experiences than ordinary Roma? Were they treated by the rest of the society with respect and dignity and thus projected that experience onto the Romani community as a whole?

Even though a member of the Communist Party since the early 1950s, Holomek must have been able to see the double-edged sword of his collectivist argument. It is quite clear that should the communist system be completely collective and united, it would have to smooth out all the sharp cleavages and special demands of various groups, the Roma including. Did Holomek truly

337 *Ibid.*, and 3:2, 1968-1969.

338 Paper of Miroslav Holomek, first Congress of the Roma Union in Brno, August 30, 1969, MZA, doc.1:1, 1969.

339 The proposal and goals of the Union were written by Miroslav Holomek at the beginning of 1968, but kept undergoing through changes until the final form, presented at the first congress of the Union, which varied greatly from the original version. Both in MZA, G 434, doc. 1:1, 1968-1969.

believe in the potential of the Romani nation to successfully function within the socialist system or did he just try to duplicate the official line of thinking?

After the welcoming speech, the members of the Congress held a quarter-minute silence for the Roma victims of the *Pořajmos*. However short, it was probably the most emotional part of the Congress, because practically all the Roma in the room had deep personal experiences with the Holocaust and this was the first time they were allowed to acknowledge them publicly. All members of the Union leadership lost some family members in the *Pořajmos* and were able to transpose their compassion on the rest of the Romani community.[340] The very force that was designed to destroy the Roma forever gave the community the determination and interest to preserve their culture and ethnicity. The official recognition of the sufferings of the Roma during WWII and the erection of a national monument to the victims of the *Pořajmos* stood side by side with the claim for national minority status as the pivotal concerns of the preparatory committee of the Union.[341] But even the *Pořajmos*, the unique aspect of the Romani historical identity, had been systematically silenced and leveled with the war memories and experiences of the rest of the country.

There was no effort on the regime's part to teach the Czechoslovak society about or at least formally recognize the *Pořajmos*. This denial, however, did not concern only the Roma but was a part of a larger official tendency not to discuss the Holocaust in any form. Even though the socialist countries, especially the Soviet Union, systematically presented themselves as champions of anti-fascism in Europe, the issue of the Holocaust was equally methodically left out from official rhetoric. The historical question of the complicity of East European interwar and war regimes and societies in the Holocaust was a taboo topic, deemed by the Party too sensitive for public discourse. Recognizing that bringing the *Pořajmos* into the public memory would counter these regime efforts, the Union's request for a monument to commemorate the victims of the *Pořajmos*, so prevalent in the earlier stages of the Union prepara-

---

[340] Nečas, *Našti Bisteras – Nemůžeme zapomenout* and Daniel, *Dějiny Romů*, 102.
[341] The MZA, G 434, doc. 1:1, 1968.

tions, quietly disappeared from the pages of the program.[342] It took nearly thirty more years before the monument was erected and unveiled on a cold rainy day in May 1995, accompanied by a complete lack of interest by the Czech politicians, media and public.[343]

Even though Czech and Moravian Roma did not detract from their political and national aspirations as much as their Slovak counterparts, during the first year of the Union's existence their ambitions shifted away from the demand for the full recognition of their nation status to the call for the recognition of "their specific needs, interests, and attitudes, which are historically determined."[344] In other words, the speakers of the first Congress no longer argued that the Roma were a unique nation or ethnic group, but (though not completely unexpectedly, considering the political circumstances) dully regarded themselves as a "social group." Less than a year earlier, Holomek vehemently asserted that "all Gypsies, the 'official' as well as the 'assimilated' or 'civilized' ones have their own psychological life and feel consciously and subconsciously their origin, values, and uniqueness."[345] He even accused the government that the official reasons for not assigning the Roma the status of a nation were only excuses and fears of the "consequences of the recognition of various rights to the Roma as a nation" and that using arguments such as the absence of "Romani territory" were only "means to prevent the recognition of Romani nationhood."[346]

But less than a year later, the voice of Holomek, echoing throughout the convention hall, declared that

---

342 Interview with Bartolomej Daniel, historian and a member of the Central Committee of the Union, May 14 and 23, 1996, Brno.

343 The then-president Havel was the only member of the top political leadership, who attended the ceremony. None of the leaders of the parliamentary parties or ministers made an appearance. For discussions of the erection of the monument and Czech inability to commemorate the Romani *Pořajmos*, see especially Markus Pape, *A nikdo vám nebude věřit* or Paul Polansky, "Czech Government's Cover–up of a Roma Death Camp," unpublished paper presented to the Human Dimension Seminar on the Roma in the CSCE Region, Warsaw, 1994 (now available on-line) and Dennis Charbonnay, "Let Them Eat Pork!" *Reflex*, 1996.

344 *Romano Lil*, 1970.

345 Holomek, "Program proposal", Dec. 10, 1968, p. 3-4.

346 *Ibid*.

> the voluntary organization of the Roma Union in the Czech Republic ...[is] the equal component (*rovnocenná součást*) of the National Front, [which] recognizes the leadership of the Communist Party and professes its support for proletarian internationalism.[347]

He assured the listeners that the Roma "want to fight for a just social order and for the cultural and social elevation of the Roma in the Czech Republic, and Czechoslovakia as a whole," insisting that "the whole Gypsy movement has a definite socialist and conceptual character." His arguments tried to persuade the audience that the Roma "have learned from the history of our country and our *social group* and along with [their] Slovak brothers [meaning the Slovak Roma] and with the whole society [the Roma] want to attempt to fulfill the progressive program of socialism in our country."[348]

The audience applauded and only Holomek's eyes were silent witnesses to the fact that on his typed speech in front of him the word *nation* had been crossed off with a pen and replaced by a handwritten phrase *social group*. When exactly *nation* was replaced by *social group* and by whom, is impossible to know from the note itself. But this remarkable detail survived in the documents of the Union as a memento, giving one at least some archival ammunition to speculate that perhaps at the last moment Holomek decided not to jeopardize the approval of the organization by making such a blatantly subversive claim. In the end, the Union thus perhaps gave up the "minor" claim for Romani nationhood to secure the support and the blessings of the Communist Party.[349]

A formal confirmation of the state's approval of the Union enterprise at the Brno convention came in the form of a welcoming speech by the Chairman of the Central Committee of the National Front František Klíma, who pledged that the "new organization will have the full support of all leading organs of the Party and the national government." He reminded the guests that

---

347 "Prohlášení Ustavujícího sjezdu SCR v ČSR," (*Declaration of the Constitutive Convention of the Union*), August 30, 1969, MZA G 434, box 1:1, 1.

348 *Ibid.*

349 *Ibid.* This fascinating peek behind the façade of the rhetoric appears on the first page of Holomek's speech. The title of the speech indicates that it was a work of a group of authors, but it is quite likely that it was Holomek himself who reached for the blue pen and changed the words. However, it is also of course possible that Holomek had to turn this speech in to censors for approval and it was the censor(s), who crossed off the nationalist claim.

"the cornerstone of the politics of the Communist Party is to provide equality to all citizens, regardless of differences in their religion, nationality or political belief," and assured the Roma that "through the National Front [the Roma] will [be able to] help to create and control national politics." In the conclusion of his speech, he recommended that the Union take smaller steps rather than to try to achieve too much too quickly. "Believe in the proverb: less is sometimes more," he ended, stepping down from the podium.[350]

How should the Union have interpreted such a statement? As a friendly pat on the back, as a form of sympathy and official recognition of the hard tasks lying ahead of the Union or as a warning not to dare to step outside the demarcated lines of action that would challenge the official ideology? Should it be perceived as an implicit hint to leave the issue of Romani nationality buried in the drawers of the Union and to make sure one proofreads his papers before stepping in front of a microphone so that in the future cross-offs in public speeches were not necessary? To make sure that the visiting Party officials really understood the Roma's loyalty to Gustav Husák's regime, which was placed to power in April 1969, and his process of Normalization, Romani delegate Rudolf Jedla claimed that there was not "a single Roma who would commit any counter-revolutionary or treasonous act against the socialist state." He condemned the year-old Roma denouncement of the Warsaw Pact invasion, blaming it on temporary confusion. He maintained that

> it is clear that the media disoriented us because even there [in the media] the WEST probably had its spies and helpers. The absolute majority of the Roma agrees with the results of the May meeting of the Central Committee of the Communist Party. Consequently it also fully agrees with the measures taken on August 22, 1969 to protect the public safety. Our Communist Party deserves the greatest thanks because only she is the true protector of our peace.[351]

It was the first time some official Roma body assumed itself to be in the position to speak for all Roma in the country. It was also the first time Romani intellectual elite stepped across the imaginary fence to publicly concur with the

[350] Speech of František Klíma, August 1969, MZA, G 434, box 1:1, 7.

[351] Speech of Rudolf Jedla, *Ibid.*, 8-9. (Emphasis in the original). His note to "measures taken on August 22, 1969" refers to the regime's arrests of dissidents protesting against the 1968 Warsaw Pact invasion on its first anniversary.

official ideology and reproach their own community for not being able to see the advantages of socialism. "Even now it is possible to see our [Romani] fellow citizens who do not want or cannot assimilate to their surroundings," complained Jedla.[352]

Was this strategic essentialism in practice? It was no longer clear from these statements whether the Union leadership was still interested in advancing the claims of Romani community and simply out of lack of choice adopted the Normalization rhetoric as a tactical means of survival. But at least through its public rhetoric, the Romani leadership seemed to be another flag-ship of the Communist Party, working from within to assimilate their community. Perhaps inadvertently, by merging its rhetoric and ideology with the official party-line on the "Gypsy question" and dividing the community between "right" (or assimilated) Roma and "wrong" or backward Roma, the Union slowly began to drive a wedge into the community that later backfired. Several years later, this wedge became the Party's main excuse for the dissolution of the Union.

The hope and breathing space of the Prague Spring undoubtedly empowered various groups and individuals to courageously articulate and stand up for their rights. At the same time, one should be careful not to blindly exaggerate the revolutionary potential and defiance of the Romani intellectuals. There is no reason to question their interest in the social and political conditions of the Roma community and their commitment to their improvement. Necessarily, however, to become a trusted member of the Communist system with a degree of executive power even on the lowest local level meant bowing in one way or another to the ideological rhetoric of the Party and an obligation to the reproduction of the officially sanctioned ideas.[353] Paradoxically, their ability to become representatives of the Roma indicates that those intellectuals had already succeeded within the existing system of full-fledged assimilation and by the regime were no longer perceived as "gypsies."[354]

There are some notable parallels between the Romani movement and the national movements in Central and Eastern Europe in the eighteenth and

---

352 *Ibid.*

353 Raymond Pearsons, *The Rise and Fall of the Soviet Empire* (New York: St. Martin's Press, 1998).

354 For a detailed discussion of the "demographic disappearance" of the Roma see the following chapter.

nineteenth centuries. For the most part, the national movements were not organized from within the individual emerging national communities. The realization of national uniqueness and the ambition to form a separate nation state did not come from ordinary people feeling particularly Czech, Greek, Bulgarian, or Romanian. It was a conscious effort of intellectuals, often studying and living abroad, who adopted the fundamentals of Western philosophical thought and applied their newly acquired nationalistic ideas to the context of their homelands. Through their "Western" eyes they were able not only to see their own uniqueness, but also to understand that a nation needs to glorify its past to legitimize its claim to separate existence. The Bulgarians laughed at old Russian legends, while producing allegedly even older Bulgarian myths. The Czechs cried that the Czech language was older and far superior to the harsh German. Digging up art, reviving old legends, or forging manuscripts when necessary, it was a battle of proving that a subordinate nation had a richer history than its ruling entity and thus possessed an authentic claim to national sovereignty.[355]

Like the East European revivalists a century before them, the Czechoslovak Romani elite of the late 1960s adopted the rhetoric and style of thinking of the system that educated them. The leaders of both branches of the Union were graduates of Czech and Slovak high schools and universities. They proudly wore the titles of doctors, lawyers and engineers. And they were

---

[355] See for example, Milan Otáhal, "The Manuscript Controversy in the Czech National Revival," *Cross Currents*, 5 (1986): 247-277; Maria Todorova, "The Balkans: From Discovery to Invention," *Slavic Review*, 53:2 (1994): 453-482; For a literary analysis on nation making of Yugoslavia see Andrew Wachtel, *Making A Nation, Breaking A Nation: Literature and Cultural Politics in Yugoslavia* (Stanford: Stanford University Press, 1988); and Larry Wolff, *Inventing Eastern Europe: The Map of Civilization on the Mind of the Enlightenment* (Stanford: Stanford University Press, 1994). Generally on East European nationalism and comparative nationalism see, Peter Sugar, ed. *Nationalism in Eastern Europe*, (Seattle, London: University of Washington Press, 1994, 3rd ed.), 3-54; Miroslav Hroch, *Social Preconditions of National Revival in Europe: A Comparative Analysis of the Social Composition of Patriotic Groups Among the Smaller European Nations* (New York: Columbia University Press, 2000, 2nd ed.); Liah Greenfeld, *Nationalism: Five Roads to Modernity* (Cambridge: Harvard University Press, 1992); Irina Livizeanu, *Cultural Politics in Greater Romania: Regionalism, Nation Building, and Ethnic Struggle* (Ithaca: Cornell University Press, 1995); Karakasidou, *Fields of Wheat, Hills of Blood*; Rogers Brubaker, *Nationalism Reframed: Nationhood and the National Question in the New Europe* (New York: Cambridge University Press, 1996).

becoming visible. As sociologist Petr Víšek argued, for many people in Czechoslovakia at that time it was shocking to learn and realize that "*they* [the Roma] can also speak in public, that they have names and academic degrees, that they have opinions and needs, about which they are willing to talk."[356] The educational system, however, did not provide these leaders with any Romani role models nor gave them a chance to identify themselves as the Roma.

Quite to the contrary, in order to succeed, they had to denounce their "gypsiness" and embrace "Czechness" or "Slovakness" as their cultural identity. Except for the Daniel family, all the leaders were also members of the Communist Party. Štefan Rigo even became a member of the Central Committee of the Communist Party, the most powerful political organ of the nomenklatura in the country. Other leading members of the small Romani intelligentsia were powerful and well-placed cadres of the Communist Party elite, and held positions in the army, the justice system, or taught Marxist-Leninist philosophy at Charles University.[357] The granddaughter of the first chairman of the Czech Roma Union remembers that

> our family did not socialize with any other Roma. They were absolutely foreign to me, I didn't know anything about their world, and like *all other children* I believed everything negative that was *publicly* said about the Roma [...] Gradually, I came to understand that our family is Romani as well, but at the same time I was constantly indoctrinated [at home] that *we* are *already* different, in the sense of being better. From the point of view of the state administration, a Rom who was not socially problematic was no longer "gypsy." And so it happened that all our family fell out of the registry of the gypsy population.[358]

Where then did the Romani elite acquire their ability to acknowledge their Romani identity, to think and organize *as Roma*? Was it a genuine expression of their ethnic awareness or a simple career move of rising to a position of power?

---

[356] Petr Víšek, "Program integrace – Řešení problematiky romských obyvatel v období 1970 až 1989", in *Romové v České republice* (Praha: Socioklub, 1999), 194-199; 187.

[357] *Kdo je kdo mezi československými Romy?: Příručka Muzea romské kultury v Brně* (Brno, MRK: 1998).

[358] Jana Horváthová, "Jak se žije romským intelektuálům v Čechách," in *Romové v České republice* (Praha: Socioklub, 1999), 311-326; 314-315. (Emphasis mine.)

Their rise to power, apparently, was not a free ride without internal conflicts. According to Karel Holomek, the professed political affinity of the Roma leaders "caused a deep rift between [their sociopolitical identity] and their own ethnic identity, which they inherently felt . . . and which in its consequences could not lead anywhere but to efforts for the recognition of Roma nationality."[359] Whether the Romani intellectuals truly believed or just pretended to believe in the Marxist-Leninist ideals, once "in," the regime would not allow them to divert from the proclaimed official line. Their tendency to bow to the system, as reflected during the first convention, soon fired back at them.

The Union was divided into three departments: political-organizational, educational-cultural, and economical-social. From the Communist Party's perspective, the most important one was, of course, the political-organizational unit. Led by its secretary Zigmund Vagai, it was in charge of political and ideological courses, party meetings, and various training exercises. Of far greater importance to the Union itself was the department of education, culture, propaganda and sport, led by its secretary Antonín Daniel. It was the most active branch of the organization, working most closely with the actual community and gaining both support and new members for the Union among both Roma and non-Roma. Its initiative helped to establish close to one hundred musical groups, over a dozen soccer clubs, and for a short period of time issued a journal called *Romano Lil*. Thanks to the Union, radio stations in Brno, Plzeň, and Ostrava recorded several programs of Romani folk music. The TV and radio were also thinking of creating a few separate programs for the Romani population, but that never happened. It is neither clear whether the programs were supposed to be in Romany or in Czech, nor why they were not realized in the end. But during the first year of its existence, the Union powerfully made the country aware of Romani cultural revival.[360]

359 Karel Holomek, "Vývoj romských reprezentací po roce 1989a minoritní mocenská politika ve vztahu k Romům", in *Romové v České republice*, 290-310; 301.

360 MZA, G 434, box 4:5. It is also important to acknowledge that this was not a one-way street. Due to the residual atmosphere of the Prague Spring and increased Romani visibility, culminating with the establishment of the Union, public opinion was more prone to acceptance of the Roma. Víšek even argues that the founding of the Union in both republics "represents a fundamental turning point in the public perception of the Roma" (187-188).

The activities of the Union seemed to run on two parallel tracks. One was a rather spontaneous course of action that took place at regional and local levels of the Union and was aimed at directly supporting the Romani community. The other was initiated from the top levels of the Union, designed to satisfy the requirements the Party had for all organizations within the National Front. Challenging societal stereotypes that the Roma do not care about education, the Union's department of culture created a school commission consisting of Romani and non-Romani members, who possessed educational training to help at schools with a large number of Roma children. Teachers, such as Miroslav Dědič or middle school principal Rudolf Kratochvil, who led all-Romani elementary schools, tried to show at their institutions that Roma children were not inherently retarded and that there were other paths to try than to routinely send them to "remedial" schools for the mentally handicaped.[361]

Among other activities, the Union, in cooperation with Brno city officials and after an agreement with the Brno steel factory Královopolská, opened a vocational training center (*učiliště*) for Romani students in locksmith and blacksmith design. However, without undermining the significance and importance of such schools, it is also important to see their existence in the full context of the social structure and opportunities in the society. From the documents it is clear that the officials never tried to open Romani gymnasium, which would not produce blue-collar workers but would prepare Roma students for white-collar jobs and entrance to universities and thus would allow the Romani intelligentsia grow. In fact, it is possible to argue that the vocational training centers served two political purposes at once. First, the centers gave the Roma students direction and opportunity, so that the state could visibly show that it was supportive of Romani education. On the other hand, such institutions locked Romani youth within their stereotypical occupations, freezing their access to higher education and possible positions of influence.

---

361 Miroslav Dědič, ***Škola bez kázně*** (České Budějovice: Jihočeské nakladatelství, 1985). Dědič was an elementary school teacher, who for many years taught in a small village in the southern Bohemian bordelands. His school was originally a "remedial school" (for detailed context see the following chapter) but thanks to his compassionate methods of teaching and educating it soon became transformed into a boarding house for Romani youth, who would voluntarily stay and sleep over.

Such division created a false illusion that the Roma were inherently better suited for crafts than for intellectual activities.[362]

The cooperation of the Roma youth and the Socialist Youth Organization (*Socialistický Svaz Mládeže* - SSM) also followed official guidelines. The SSM, by its very definition, was an establishment preparing the country's youth for membership in the Communist party. Even though it was trying to provide "fun" for young people, it was by and large an ossified, artificial organization concerned primarily with ideological training of Czechoslovak youth. It is almost absurd to imagine young Roma, whose opportunities were limited on all fronts, massively marching in the vanguard of this artificial organization.

On May 7, 1971, Antonín and Bartoloměj Daniels wrote to the Central Committee of SSM in Prague that "[their] *social organization*, the Roma Union, has an eminent interest in the ideological political-organizational activity of the SSM and its educational influence on Roma youth." They assured Prague that the majority of Romani youth have "an honest relationship to the SSM and the PO" (*Pioneer Organization*, basically SSM for elementary school children). They concluded that it was important "that we together, hand in hand, create conditions for ideological and political education."[363] Apparently, the SSM either did not share this concern or was not all that impressed by the Romani initiative. Nobody from the SSM committee ever bothered to reply.

A year later, chairman Holomek contacted Jindřich Poledník, the vice-chairman of Czech Central Committee of SSM, stating that he was interested in promoting cooperation between the SSM and the Union. Holomek pointed out that fifty percent of all Roma were adolescents and that he was "convinced that the young generation of Roma will be decisive in the solution of the integration of the Roma." He believed that the cultural-political education of young Roma is a crucial part of the educational process.[364] The silence and passivity of the Central Committee of the Party to these Romani initiatives and their ultimate refusal, especially in the light of the Party's proclaimed ef-

362 MZA, G 434, box 17:129, 1970.

363 MZA, G 434, box 17:122, May 7, 1971.

364 MZA, G 434, box 17:135, June 2, 1972.

fort to integrate the Roma, suggest that the regime had no active interest in educating Romani adolescents to become leaders of their own fate. It wanted "gypsies" to belong to Communist youth organizations, but only as Czechs or Slovaks, without any articulated sense of disctinct Romani identity.

All letters in the Union materials indicate that the Roma were very active in initiating contacts between various groups of Roma and the non-Romani population. The archival documents make it explicit that the Union's main concern and interest was its work with Romani youth but that SSM was ignoring its own goal of recruiting young people with respect to the Roma. After a year of waiting, the Union lost its patience and in a memo to its members strongly criticized the SSM for its lack of effort. The report reminded that the SSM stated as its goal "recruiting young people for the SSM and not the passive awaiting and receiving of applications."[365] A serious critique of the whole system was wrapped in the denouncement of the youth organization's attitude. The report continued that:

> if Roma do not come first, it is perceived as Roma's lack of interest. But the SSM does not take into the account the shyness of young Roma, resulting, for example, from the fact that they [the Roma] are mostly graduates of remedial schools [for the mentally handicapped]. Their self-esteem is also suppressed by the worse social conditions in which they grow up and their feelings of *racial discrimination*![366]

This was the first (and perhaps the only) time when the Union admitted in writing the Roma's feelings of racism from the rest of the population. It also showed that, no matter how much the state tried to pretend that the remedial schools were advantageous and helpful, the Roma themselves were well aware of the stigma the schools left on their children, hindering their opportunities for the rest of their lives.

Only thanks to persistent effort of the Union were Roma finally able to enter the SSM. According to Růžena Kočí, a referent of the culture and education department of the Union, "everywhere, where the SSM is understanding and willing to help the young Roma, we reach good results." Nevertheless, she still complained that in most counties the SSM's bureaucracy and

---

[365] MZA, G 434, box 17:50. (Underlining in the original.)

[366] *Ibid.* (Emphasis mine, exclamation mark in the original).

unwillingness to accept young Roma is the fundamental barrier to their integration. In Hradec Králové, for example, "forty Roma applied to the SSM, but Julius Horváth [who organized the event] encountered an unempathetic SSM."[367] The hostility and indifference on the part of the regional and local branches of the SSM to integrate young Roma into their organizations suggest that the SSM regional leaders were not interested in the membership of and common activities with the Roma. This situation discloses the significant discrepancy between the top level proclamations and local level applications of Romani integration. As this book argues, and this example of local officials' agency shows, even though the party rhetoric and goals might have been noble and ethnically neutral, racial discrimination continued even though few had the courage to label it as such.

The Party staunchly refused to permit the creation of independent Roma youth organizations. One of the reasons given was the "irresponsibility" of Romani youth, largely based on "scientific studies" about Romani children and youth, which pointed out, for example, the "mental inferiority and social non-adaptability of the majority of gypsy children"[368] or which claimed that "hard-to-educate neglected gypsy children are a social problem, which presents acute consequences in the area of education, hygiene, criminality, discipline and other areas of social, cultural and economic life."[369] According to the observation of Party functionaries, "gypsy youth, especially teenagers . . . have very loose morals, are very undisciplined, and frequently visit alcoholic establishments." Paradoxically, Roma youth activists complained in the academic journal *Demografie* that it was the lack of interest from state officials that forced Romani adolescents into such outlets. In 1970 they asserted that

---

[367] MZA, G 434, Box 17:67, no date. Letter to the Central Committee of the Union.

[368] Jan Stuchlík, *O neomorfizaci psychologických testů v československé psychiatrii* (Praha: Státní zdravotnické nakladatelství, 1964). Cited in František Olejár, *Formovanie psychických zvláštností výchovne zanedbaných detí* (Bratislava: Slovenské pedagogické nakladatelstvo, 1972), 21.

[369] Josef Siakel and Štěpán Havlík, "Zpráva o zaškolování detí občanov cigánského povodu a začleňování 15.račného dorastu do učňovského pomeru." Conference paper presented at the *Regional konference for solving questions of the citizens of gypsy origin*, November 11, 1964, 3.

> we want to create an organization of gypsy youth that would find common points of interest among young gypsies so that they can culturally and socially live and meet in clubs. Because we face a tremendous lack of concern and incomprehension on the part of the National Committees and other institutions, our youth, who are determined to at least partially solve their own problems, have to meet in pubs.[370]

Representatives of the Union, from the leadership to youth activists, consistently expressed criticisms of the attitudes of state officials and pushed for their own autonomy. One member pointed out, for example, that in some places, such as Český Krumlov, a small town in southern Bohemia, "attitude of the [local] administration [toward Roma] is very correct," but indicated that in "other regions . . . the attitude of the non-gypsy population [toward the Roma] is far from appropriate."[371] Even though the youth activists adopted official rhetoric by claiming they "want to solve their own problems," thus bowing to the Party by identifying themselves as a "problem," they were still quite firm in insisting that the Party's way of dealing with the situation was not adequate.

IV.3 Economic Problems and Dissolution of the Union

Belonging to the National Front had both its disadvantages and advantages. On the one hand, as the right hand of the Communist Party, the NF held all its subordinate organizations under tight control, making sure the programs of various unions and clubs did not deviate from the course set by the regime.[372] On the other hand, the NF provided funding for all the organizations, according to budget proposals written from the recommendations of national economists. Of course, it was a deceiving charity since all organizations were fully dependent on the logic and mercy of the state funding. Because of centralized planning, the party had a detailed knowledge and control over the ac-

---

370 Rudolf Tancoš, "Problematika cikánské mládeže," *Demografie*, 11:2 (1970): 34-35.

371 Stanislav Kier, "Práce okresní komise pro otázky cikánského obyvatelstva v Českém Krumlově," *Demografie*, 11:1 (1970): 367-369.

372 Even though in most cases organizations of the NF were initiated by the efforts of the party itself and the chances of those organizations going against its maternal guardian were minimal.

tivities and viability of individual organizations. Since the Central Committee of the Party decided the entire process of financial distributions, the survival of any organization laid fully in its hands.

Because the state failed to solve the employment problems of the Roma population, by the end of 1969 the Central Committee of the Union began to negotiate the approval of independent economic units, which would employ Roma not registered at any organizations or firms as permanent workers. Scholars offer different explanations for why the Party allowed, and even initially supported, the creation of semi-private economic units of the Union, which came to be known as *Nevo Droms* (*New Roads*) in the Czech lands and *Bútikers* in Slovakia. Some maintain that it was in the state's genuine interest to let the Roma take care of their own problems: finally, the state would be free from responsibility for Romani unemployment and ensuing social problems.[373] Others speculate that it was obvious to the party from the beginning that the Roma could not succeed in running an economic enterprise within the parameters set out by the NF and that sooner or later this failure could become a good tool to be used against them.[374] There is something to both arguments.

The so-called "gypsy units" (*cikánské jednotky*) officially began their work on March 3, 1970, when the Ministry of Interior at the recommendation of the NF approved their existence and registered them with appropriate labor courts. On March 24, the Central Committee of the Union issued certificates for nine independent Romani economic units and they started their activities.[375] Their primary goal was to address the most pressing needs of the Roma: employment and housing. Using the Union's own resources, the units were supposed to provide members of Romani community with employment opportunities and create housing possibilities. Without appropriate planning, *Nevo Droms* and *Bútikers* spontaneously and hastily began to offer services in their surrounding areas.

---

373 Jurová, 98

374 Daniel, *Dějiny Romů*, 213; and interviews with Dr. Arne Mann, May 10, 1996, Bratislava, and Bartoloměj Daniel, May 14, 1996, Brno.

375 MZA, G 602, box 1:1, 1969-1971; SNA Bratislava, Fond Zvaz Cigánov-Rómov, ZC-R, boxes 1-5. 1969-1973.

The nine independent units in the Czech lands (placed in the cities of Brno, České Budějovice, Hradec Králové, Litvínov, Ústí nad Labem, Olomouc, Ostrava, Plzeň, and Prague) and their counterparts in Slovakia each employed around 100 to 150 workers, in Prague even 500. Even though employment opportunities were not restricted to the Roma, an overwhelming majority of all workers were Roma. With the successful launch of the program, the goal of the units grew from simply providing employment opportunities to actually earning money in order to support more cultural and social activities of the Union than it was able to do by the NF funds. For the first time the Roma, or rather the Romani intelligentsia, found themselves in a position to at least partially decide their own affairs. They were not passive subordinates to the regime, but were in a position to create and produce.[376]

The individual units received contracts from regional and local organizations. Usually, the work consisted of heavy labor requiring no or minimal qualifications, such as digging ditches and gas lines, repairing facades, cleaning roads, improving housing units, driving heavy trucks, etc. In addition to regular work, the units tried to support traditional Roma crafts and arts, such as blacksmithing, metal design, basket weaving, candle making, roof making, etc. Along with the educational department, the units wanted to create apprentice shops for young Roma. Besides regular taxes paid to the state, all profits from the units went to the Union. Gradually, the National Front started to get nervous about its loss of control over how much money the Union makes and for what purposes it spends it.

One of the typical controversies between the Union leadership and the National Front, for example, involved the Union's "reimbursement" of Romani parents, who were financially punished for "not sending their children to school." In accordance with the decree 502/1958 from 1965, the National Committee adopted the strategy of not paying state child support to Romani families if their children did not show up at school for an extended period of time.[377] The Union attempted to protest such a counterproductive punishment by giving small amounts of money to parents, who came to the Union's re-

---

[376] *Ibid.*, and interview with B. Daniel, May 23, 1996.

[377] Nečas, *Historický kalendář*, 82.

gional offices to complain about their insolvency due to this practice.[378] The Union's strategy was spontaneous, uncoordinated and undocumented, which made it quite easy for the National Front to charge the Union with "economic mismanagement" and "counter-socialist practice." While the Union demonstrated by this action its disagreement with such punitive practices and implicitly pointed out their injustice and harmfulness to the Roma community, the Party could reply that these "illegal" incentives of the Union only "legitimized" the criminal behavior so "natural" to the Roma.[379] From the position of non-Romani society, the Union's attempt to defy the party line served to confirm their belief that the Roma were unable to distinguish between right and wrong and follow the socialist moral compass.

On the local level, the Union was succeeding in awakening at least some Roma from the lethargy caused by institutional policies and the attitude of the larger state and society. The journals *Romano Lil* and *Romano Pajtrin* document this sense of revival. The overall character of the journals does not deviate from strict ideological line. They pay homage to the "immense efforts of the state and party organs," and report on political exercises and the "happy and engaged building of the socialist future."[380] Besides such mandatory praises, articles on the gradual "improvement" of the Roma, such as "Lessons on Table Manners" (*Lekce společenského chování*) or "Hygiene and Health Retreat" (*Školení o hygieně a zdraví*) reveal the degree to which the writers of the journals internalized the social and health discourses of the majority population. On the other hand, the journals also discuss the abundance of sport, music, dance, and other activities that were taking place in Romani communities, such as soccer matches, musical get-togethers, or discos, indicating that the journals could have captured the genuine interest of Romani communities.

Encouraged by the smooth running of the Union and *Nevo Droms* and *Bútikers* for well over a year now, Romani communities began to gain self-esteem and identity.[381] Unlike its Slovak counterpart, who did not repeatedly

---

[378] Kostelančik, 315. Interview with B. Daniel, May 21, 1996, Brno.
[379] MZA Brno, G 434, box 2:5.
[380] For example, *Romano Lil*, 12 (November 1971), 3 and 5.
[381] Milena Hübschmannová, "Three Years of Democracy in Czecho-Slovakia and the Roma," *Roma*, 18:38-39 (1993): 30-49.

question the status of the Roma as a social group, the Union in the Czech Republic felt the time had come again to voice their support for the Romani nation status. With the help of several scholars, particularly Hübschmannová, at the end of 1970 the Roma Union drafted a Memorandum concerning the fundamental aspects of the "Gypsy question" and submitted it to the Central Committee of the Party. The memorandum bluntly stated that

> it would be beneficial for the conceptual efforts at solving this [the Gypsy] question if in the constitutional law about national minorities Gypsies were recognized as a nationality with all its constitutional rights . . . and if it would be terminologically defined who Gypsies are . . . so that their social position in our state could be clarified.[382]

After a few years of silence and seeming cooperation between the state and the Roma, the Union's reborn request for the recognition of their nationhood rocked the poor foundations of the state-Roma relationship. This time, at the height of the Normalization effort, the regime was not willing to negotiate with the Roma.

As with many requests and proposals in the past, the Party and the National Front did not hurry to respond to the Memorandum. The Union was functioning but the silence of the Party was like a calm preceding a storm. In 1970, the National Front approved twenty seven full-time workers for the Roma Union in the Czech Republic and a financial subsidy of one and a half million crowns. Along with profits from the *Nevo Droms* the Union was doing quite well financially. The Union's own analysis of its development reported with satisfaction that "the authority of the Union among the Roma is tremendous and the results of its activities are positive." The document informed the National Front that for the next year, the Union would like to increase the number of its full-time workers to forty and expected a financial subsidy of about seven million crowns. The NF approved these numbers.[383]

The Union was preparing new activities, looking for new offices, establishing new business networks, making new connections. When the budget came, everyone at the Union was shocked. The budgetary subsidy for the

---

[382] *Memorandum k základním otázkám cikánské problematiky*, MZA Brno, G 434, MZA, G 434, box 21:6, 1970.

[383] "Analýza vývoje a aktivit SCR v ČSR," MZA, G 434, box 36:186.

Union was not seven million, not five, nor even last year's figure – it was less than four hundred thousand crowns, less than one third of the previous year's allocation. Figures in Slovakia mirrored the Czech financial allocation, receiving one-third of their previous subsidy.[384] The reasoning behind the budgetary cut was simple. Allegedly, the Union was "failing its integrative function," and because of rumors of financial problems in the *Nevo Droms* and *Bútikers*, those units were "failing in their educational functions." As a part of its rationale, the Central Committee of the National Front included as a parenthetical remark its reply to the request for nationality status: it informed the Union that the request was rejected because "the [Czechoslovak] Constitution would have to be reworked."[385] The letter was only half a page long, the Party could not have been more blunt and clear.

Not surprisingly, no document or letter has been found that specifies or elaborates on the process, through which the National Front came to the conclusion that the Union failed its integrative function. It is not clear whether the NF was dissatisfied with the Union's performance or its (in)ability to mobilize the Roma community or if the dismissal was indeed linked to its push for nationality status. However, the sequence of events that transpired can help infer the circumstances that led to the final dissolution of the Union. It is not unsound to speculate that after the Party received the Memorandum, it became clear to the ruling organs of the state that the mere existence of the Union would not satisfy the Roma and that more troubles potentially laid ahead. The stronger the Union became, the more it professed its integration into the National Front and the more it asserted its autonomy in solving the Roma's own "question," the more insubordinate and problematic in the eyes of the Communist Party it got. The Union was more and more visibly demonstrating that "gypsiness" was not a social pathology but a distinct and vibrant identity and thus started to expose the ludicrousness of the Party's rhetoric, arguments and practices.

The NF stood before a difficult task. The Union became a thorn in the Party's side that had to be removed but dissolving the Union solely from the initiative of the Party might be too risky. The Union was, as Karel Holomek

384 SNA Bratislava, ZC-R 1969-1973, box 4:2.

385 MZA, G 601, box 12-4, correspondence between ÚV NF and ÚV SCR.

put it, a "bitter fruit of the Prague Spring."[386] However, its leaders unwaveringly proclaimed that the "Gypsy movement is fully in accord with post-January politics, in support of and interested in the socialist development of our country."[387] The Union was functioning and maintaining the party line, and most of its leaders were Communists, publicly and loudly professing their undying loyalty to and support of the socialist enterprise. Short articles in both daily newspapers and Roma journals of both republics testify to this support, echoing the predictable party lines about "fulfilling the goals of socialism to reach a more just world,"[388] "helping in the process of demonstrating the democratic and humanistic nature of our political system,"[389] or "recognizing the excellent relentless effort and merits of our dear Party."[390]

Moreover, everything pointed to the fact that the Union also had the support of its community, as well as the support of the international community. A Czechoslovak Romani delegation, including the highest placed officials from both branches of the Union, attended the First World Romani Congress in London in 1970, even though the participation of delegations from all East European countries was a mere ideological showcase to demonstrate the regime's understanding of the Roma's plight.[391] The paradox of sending a delegation to the World Romani Congress, which was massive lobbying effort for the international recognition of the Romani nation, while at the same time deafly denying that status to the Roma within Czechoslovakia, did not merit any attention from either press or scholars writing on the Roma.

There was not much the Party could grab onto without being accused of racism and ethnic discrimination from academic circles and international observers, further destroying its "democratic" and "civic" image. The *Nevo Drom* and *Bútiker* units became the easiest targets for the Party to attack and thus the most logical entry point for the destruction of the Union. The state counted on the fact that evidence of financial mismanagement, labeled as "economic crimes against the socialist system," must be considered objective data that

---

386 Karel Holomek, "Vývoj romských reprezentací," 301.
387 Miroslav Holomek, "Stav současného hnutí organizace Cikánů-Romů v ČSR," 215.
388 *Rudé právo*, March 10, 1971.
389 *Romano Lil*, May 5, 1971.
390 *Romano Lil*, April 21, 1971.
391 Davidová, *Romano Drom*, 207.

would take the wind out of the sail of any arguments trying to suggest charges of racism and discrimination. Some scholars argue that the Party knew from the very start that the financial cuts in the third year of the Union's existence would create serious financial problems in the economic department.[392] Others, on the other hand, suggest that it was the complaining, informing, corruption and power struggles in the Union itself that handed the central organs of the Party the best reasons to dissolve the Union.[393] The documents indicate that in the end it was a combination of both causes that finally brought the Union down.

Because of the six-million-crown deficit created by the funding cut, the Union had to use money from the *Nevo Droms* and *Bútikers* to pay for its activities and employees. Regional and local offices, officials, and activities, normally paid from the coffers of the National Front, were now financed from the Central Committee of the Union. Logically, all invoices and receipts were also sent to the Union and the organization assumed the main burden of financing its activities. Even though this shift might suggest at least a partial liberation of the Union from the ever-watchful eye of the Party, the Union's obligation to account for all of the economic activities made this potential freedom illusory. The shift in financing only created a more complicated bureaucracy and confusion. Nonetheless, at the beginning of 1972, immediately after the Party signaled its rejection of the Union through the budgetary cut, the Union leadership sent yet another letter to the Central Committee of the Party, declaring that "socialism is natural and spontaneous to all Roma, even those who are not members of the Communist party" and reporting its intent to continue to "build our socialist society."[394] It seems that the Union leaders wanted to reassure the regime that they, as Party members, were not only committed to the official socialist project but still were in full control over the organization and the Roma community. Was it still true, however?

---

[392] For example Arne Mann, "The Formation of the Ethnic Identity of the Romany in Slovakia", in *Minorities in Politics,* ed. Jana Plichtová (Bratislava: Czechoslovak Committee for the European Cultural Foundation, 1992), 261-5 or Davidová, *Romano Drom*, 208-9.

[393] For example Karel Holomek, "Vývoj romských reprezentací," 188.

[394] MZA, G 601, box 12-4.

A box of letters in the archival files of the Union demonstrates that during the first years of its existence, the Union was perceived by many ordinary Roma in almost mythical terms. Letters of complaints sent to the Union list grievances and document the mistreatment of the Roma by institutions and the majority population; warn other Roma to "avoid certain public places" and restaurants that were thought to openly discriminate against the Roma; protest treatment by state officials and "unprovoked physical attacks by the police"; ask the Union to intervene on their behalf in social and legal cases; plead for compensation for having undergone "scientific tests under Nazism"; and so on.[395] Almost all the letters are written in hand, misspelled, many without dates, addresses, or signatures, in torn, dirty envelopes. Their existence testifies to the fact that the Union did have the trust of the ordinary, in many cases uneducated, Roma. They looked up to "their organization" for help and protection against commonplace administrative and popular discrimination, which they were not equipped to face successfully. The more pleading the letters are the more they reveal that the writers imagined the Union as a form of higher justice that could represent them. In the course of its existence, however, the Union leadership seems to have lost this support.

At the Moravian Regional Archive also sits another box, filled with complaints, bearing witness to this reversal of trust. Even though the senders seem to be the same ordinary Roma from all corners of the country, this time the addressee is not the Union, but the Central Committee of the Communist Party in Prague. In the same misspelled language the letters complain about nepotism and the profiteering of the leading Roma intellectuals. For example, one letter complains that the leaders of the Union "want to employ only their friends and families and do not want to let other Roma in." Another (anonymous) letter informs the Central organs that "the Union functionaries live above standards (*žijou si nad poměry*)" and do not help Roma "outside of the Union."[396]

The Holomeks and Daniels, the most active and dominant families in Romani community in Brno, whose members occupied a substantial number of the important Union positions, were the targets of most of the accusations.

---

395 MZA, G 434, box 130:17,18.

396 MZA, G 434, box 131:1-3.

Bartoloměj Daniel, a historian and one of the members of the Union leadership, admitted that the members of the elite "did not always know where the money went." Because they "considered the Union to be their own," they used the financial resources as they saw fit. According to him, the leadership made lavish banquets for Union guests, organized festivals, conferences, and other cultural events, put money toward education, and helped individual families in cases of need. "Of course, you cannot have receipts for everything," he shrugged his shoulders, "but it was always in the best interest of the Roma. We did not take anything."[397] Obviously, not all Roma shared the view that the leadership acted in the interest of the whole community. Both Karel Holomek and Bartoloměj Daniel admit that many ordinary Roma resented the leadership because of the functionaries' affiliation with the Communist Party.[398] It is rather ironic then, that ordinary Roma turned to the Central Committee of the Party itself in order to vocalize their frustration with their supposed representation.

In turn, there was not much internal trust among the Roma leadership either. Already at the end of 1970, a scandal was forming on the horizon. Supposedly due to "limitations in cadre membership which was unable to coordinate the activity of the *Nevo Droms*," the leadership of the Union established an Economic Committee, which would supervise the financial transactions of the economic units.[399] Since the *Nevo Droms* and *Bútikers* were the Union's enterprises, the National Front did not have free legal access to their files and the leadership of the Union was the only body that knew (or was supposed to know) in detail what was going on in them. This situation changed in late 1971 and 1972, when complaints by ordinary Roma about the leadership provided ammunition for Party investigators and gave the Party a pretext for getting access to the Union files. The Central Committee of the Party got what it believed was "a substantial reason" to investigate the activities of the Union and especially the *Nevo Drom* and *Bútiker* units.[400]

But surprisingly, the Union acted quicker. On the eve of the *Nevo Drom* and *Bútiker* scandal in 1972, the Central Committee of the Union published a

---

397 Interview with Daniel, May 14, 1996, Brno.
398 Holomek, 300 and *Ibid.*
399 MZA, G 602, box 4:1.
400 MZA, G 601, box 12-4, correspondence between ÚV NF and ÚV SCR.

"Political Analysis of the Union."[401] The tone of the document seems to indicate that the leaders of the Union were aware of the gloomy situation and tried to hold the pieces together. The analysis started with a denouncement of discrimination inflicted upon the Roma by previous political systems. "Under socialism, the Roma have for the first time an open road to become real citizens of the state," exclaimed the proclamation, and moved on to assure the party that "the coincidence of the establishment of the Union and the tendencies of 1968-69 should not be alarming, because the Union has had nothing to do with them." To the contrary, the Roma called their initiative and interest in their own matters

> the first expression of their [the Roma's] political and organized beliefs under socialist direction. The actual establishment of the Union was the summit of the efforts of progressive Roma, the majority of whom were Communists. . . In the leadership there are vibrant Roma, who will ensure the Union and its program will walk the road of socialism based on the teachings of Marxism-Leninism.[402]

In this document, the Roma Union took all the blame for the problems on itself. It said it was "aware of complaints" from the ranks of ordinary Roma. But every organization has its "untrustworthy members" who later "cast a bad reflection on the whole organization." The Union strongly distanced itself from several members who "did not conform to its ideological principles" and "brought shame to the Union."[403]

Not sursprisingly, there is not a single hint at the issue of nationality status in the "Political Analysis." Cautiously, the analysis recognized integration as "a process with stages and a goal," which was, predictably, "a full advancement of Gypsies to the level of the rest of the population." In fact, the report is so devoid of any mention of distinct Romani specificity and is so consciously constructed along social lines, that if one would replace the word "Gypsy" it would be hard to tell what interest group might have produced the analysis. Only in the very last sentence, as the last expression of pride and defiance, the analysis ends with an assertion that "the Union fulfills centennial

[401] *Politická analýza Svazu Cikánů-Romů*, MZA, G 434, box 21:7, April 18, 1972.
[402] *Ibid.*, 3.
[403] *Ibid.*, 5.

desires of the Roma and helps to create basic conditions for the fulfillment of current interests and needs of this ethnic group."[404] But throughout the pages, over and over, the words desperately plead the Union's recognition of its own community's backwardness, and pledge loyalty to the Party and the socialist system. Clearly, the Union saw that its existence hung by a thin rope and tried to do everything it could to prevent its end.

After the Union's initial attempt in April 1972 to solve the problems by integrating all independent *Nevo Drom* and *Bútiker* units into one, centrally directed from Brno and Bratislava, the Central Committee of the Union came to the conclusion that the units should be shut down. It is impossible to detect from the documents whether the Committee hoped the investigation would stop there or whether the leaders knew what was coming and tried to hold on to their profits. According to article VI, §2, of the legal code of the Union, "in the case of the abolition of the organization or any of its components, all financial and economic property related to the Union or its abolished enterprises becomes the possession of the state."[405] Had the Union itself dismissed the *Nevo Droms* without the interference of the state and the Union kept existing, the profits would obviously stay in the Union and hence in their own hands. But it seems that the state was aware of this, too. Despite the Union's recommendation to discharge the economic units, it filed its own investigation and on April 21, 1972, based on the findings of the State Civic Control Committee, decided that the *Nevo Droms* and *Bútikers* were to be dissolved by the fiat of the state.[406]

The decision to liquidate the economic units was based on the charge that the Roma mismanaged seven million crowns during the course of their activity. Bartoloměj Daniel confirmed that this was a true assertion but claimed that, on the other hand, the *Nevo Droms* had created property and wealth worth 14.5 million.[407] The valuation of the Union's possessions was not monetary but based mainly on the value of equipment and property – a statewide network of furnished offices with phones, furniture, typewriters, copy machines, cars, etc. As assessed by the liquidation commission, the

[404] *Ibid.*, 41.
[405] MZA, G 434, box 2, *Stanovy Svazu Cikánů-Romů v České republice*, 16-17.
[406] MZA, G 602, box 230:41.
[407] Interview with B. Daniel, May 14, 1996, Brno.

properties of the Union amounted to four million crowns, so if the created surplus were to be true and the assessment accurate, the Union would still be about three and half million crowns ahead in its finances.[408] Unfortunately, the archival documents do not provide evidence to either confirm or reject this assertion. In any case, it seems that economic reasons were only a disguise; the more probable motive behind the Party's decision seems to be the refusal to tolerate a discourse of ethnicity and nationhood, which challenged its own conception of the Roma as a non-ethnic dimension of the population.

The appointed State Liquidation Committee was in charge of a thorough investigation of the economic activities of the Union. Even though it seemed that the investigation would be brief, the various charges, filings, inquiries and legal proceedings took more than four years – longer than the existence of the Union itself. Determining the Union's assets was arduous. The inventory books described what the Union owned, but as it turned out, for example, many of those possessions were in the homes of various members and were oftentimes missing when the inventory was carried out. Lists of musical instruments, used by various groups, on the other hand, were bought with Union money, but not included in the inventories. Further, many goods were broken or damaged but not written off, many Roma were filing late reports of stolen possessions, etc.[409] In short, it was a chaotic process. After the dissolution of the Union the NF claimed in one of its reports in October 1974 that "it would try to make most of the [impounded] properties and instruments available to various Roma groups and cities with large Roma populations."[410] To what extent this promise was realized could not be detected from the files.

Most of the charges against the Union leadership were classified as "abuse of official power" and "larceny of socialist property" (*rozkrádání socialistického majetku*).[411] The Liquidation Commission was elected from both the members of the Union and members of the National Front. Upon the recommendation of the Union, comrade Anna Malá was named the head of the Liquidation Commission. At the end of 1973, the Central Committee of the NF sent a letter to the City Court of Brno, requesting the withdrawal of Malá. The

---

[408] MZA, G 601, box 13, p.2, *Zpráva likvidační komise*. November 17, 1972.
[409] *Ibid.*, 10-11.
[410] *Report about the liquidation process of Nevo Drom*. MZA, G 601, box 13, p.16.
[411] *Ibid.*, 1. October 1974.

court promptly responded to the request and Malá's name was erased from the list of commissioners.[412] Neither the request nor the court compliance provide reasons for Malá's dismissal. But among the letters of complaint from the previous year, there is a letter from Karel Holomek and Antonín Daniel to the Central Committee of the Party in Prague, complaining that "Malá had questioned [Holomek's] loyalty to the party." He considered that assertion to be absurd "because of the affiliation, loyalty and credits of [my] father."[413] Is it possible that Malá was called off because of this incident? If so, it would mean that the leadership of the Union and the Party collaborated much more than it appeared.

About a year into the investigation of the economic units, on April 25, 1973, the Plenary Sessions of both branches of the Union quite unexpectedly announced a "voluntary dissolution" of the Union "for incompetence" to accomplish its set goals. The sessions stripped Miroslav Holomek and Anton Facuna of their chairmanships and the Union ceased its existence on April 30, 1973. It was a surprising move, especially coming from the Union itself. The state commissioner's investigation of the *Nevo Droms* and *Bútikers* was nowhere near being finished.

What prompted the Union leadership not to wait for the results of the investigation or at least for official dismissal but to jump off the cliff voluntarily? The archives do not possess a direct answer, but in the course of several taped interviews, two sources, one in the Czech Republic and one in Slovakia, asserted independently of each other that the dissolution apparently was not that voluntary. The Party had manipulated the Union leadership into a position, from which there was no way out. According to Dr. Arne Mann, the government offered a deal to the Union elite: either they will agree with the abolition of their organization or they will be prosecuted on criminal charges of financial mismanagement.[414] Bartoloměj Daniel echoed Mann's assertion. He alleged that the Union had two options for abolishing the organization. First there was an administrational abolition, which would require the Union to ask the Party to be allowed to abolish itself for incompetence. This solution,

[412] MZA, G 601, box 13, letter from the NF CSR, No. 1268-S/73, Dec.17, 1973. Resolution of the Brno city Court, PN 851/23, Jan.1. 1974.

[413] MZA, G 434, box 130: 17. October 4, 1972.

[414] Interviews with Arne Mann, May 2 and 10, 1996, Bratislava.

which especially outraged the Union leadership, served two purposes at once: the state would not hold any responsibility for the failure of the Union and the Roma intellectuals would be completely humiliated and discredited. The second option did not offer an honorable exit either. If the Union rejected Party's first "offer," it would be abolished anyway by the fiat of the state and all the Committee members would be prosecuted on criminal charges, facing hefty prison sentences. The Union leadership was invited to Prague to the headquarters of the National Front and presented with the two options. To make the decision process easier, the NF secretary Marie Hrušková, allegedly summarized the deal: "If you do not sign [your own dissolution], we will scatter you like cattle!" (*Když nepodepíšete, rozeženeme vás jako dobytek*).[415]

Who would want to voluntarily go to a communist prison? Given the circumstances, Miroslav Holomek signed the deal in the name of the Union and a week later was stripped of his chairmanship. Bartoloměj Daniel and Pavel Šteiner were the only Roma from the leadership, who publicly stood up against the abolition but obviously to no avail. Despite its promises of leniency if the Roma leadership signed the voluntary dissolution, the Liquidation Committee brought up charges against all full-time Union workers and many part-time workers and volunteers, 126 charges altogether. Most of the charges were for illegal use of the organization's cars, illegal use of financial resources, and negligence. The Linquidation Committee complained that "law and respect for the socialist legal code were unknown terms in [the economic units] and the Union itself," which resulted in more work for the commissioners.[416] Most of the Roma leaders were found guilty of the charges, with the members of the Central Committee of the Union (Miroslav Holomek, Zigmund Vagai, Antonín Daniel) receiving the heaviest sentences; "abuse of power of a public official" and "larceny of socialist property" were officially regarded as especially despicable crimes in the socialist system (and highly ironic ones as well, since for many people they were a way of surviving under the commu-

[415] Interviews with B. Daniel, Brno, May 15, 1996.
[416] *Report about the liquidation process of Nevo Drom*. MZA, G 601, box 13, p. 54.

nist regime.)[417] Unfortunately, the Roma's hope for "higher justice" in the form of possible appeals was impossible.[418]

However, Mann argues that this is still not the full story. He asserts that another deal was made between the Party and the Union leadership, giving the most prominent members cushioned state jobs to compensate their humiliation and to retain their party loyalty.[419] It was, of course, impossible to find any archival evidence for this assertion. But on March 23, 1973 (a month before the "voluntary dissolution"), the Central Committee of the Party approved an internal memorandum requiring the prime ministers of Czech Republic and Slovakia to create new "Bureaus for the Questions of the Gypsy Population" that would be staffed with "trusted members" of the *former* Union.[420] This document exposes that the Party had known about the "voluntary dissolution" at least a month before it actually happened and already prepared provisions for the Roma leaders. Despite the deal, however, all Union Committee members received suspended jail sentences, which might be the reason for why there was no interest on either side to start a new dialogue about another Romani association in the following years and why any meaningful communication between the state and the Romani intellectual elite stalemated until the Velvet Revolution.

The enterprise of the Roma Union offers an interesting opportunity to analyze the relationship between the state, Romani intellectuals, and the larger Romani population. It also provides a rare window to Romani cultural and political subjectivity. Though the Union may have not touched the lives of ordinary Romani citizens in a fundamental way, the history of the Union reveals that the attempt to construct and defend a modern Roma identity not only had to struggle against an entrenched political discourse resistant to ethnic distinctiveness, but also faced the more fundamental inability of the high Party leadership and regional institutions to accept Roma as dialogue partners. The experience of the Union exposes that officials at regional and local levels,

---

417 MZA, G 602, box 130:4.

418 *Ibid.*, 65.

419 Interview with Mann, Bratislava, May 10, 1996.

420 *Usnesení o vytvoření komisí národních výborů pro otázky cikánského obyvatelstva, ÚV KSČ*, March 23, 1973.SÚAR Praha. (Emphasis mine).

who were supposed to, according to the Party policy, help the Roma to integrate did much to prevent the actual integration of Roma into society.

Various state administrators were willing and able to engage in the "Gypsy question" from their superior positions as mentors, overseers, guards or controllers, but not from a position of equal partnership. This attitude stemmed from the perpetual treatment of all Roma as an ostracized group understood in the terms of social pathology. The fact that the Roma demonstrated that they were able to produce their own elite did not amount to much because it was taken only as a demonstration that when Roma live "correctly," they simply become Czechs, Slovaks and communists. The nature of the authoritarian regime did not permit a genuine development of a minority elite that would be free to demonstrate its distinctiveness; thus their rise to elite positions was inevitably accompanied by their subordination to the power-holders' values and norms.

The establishment of the Roma Union was the highest point of the struggle of the Romani population to protect their livelihood through collective action. But the circumstances surrounding this development testified to the obstacles and difficulties that the Roma would continue to face. Since the minority did not have their own nation-state to appeal to, the Roma's national and ethnic ambitions had to be realized within the boundaries, both physical and political, of the system they lived in. Even if the Party was initially hospitable to the Union, many local and regional officials, who internalized asocial sterotypes of Roma, were not. Ideologically, the combination of the Roma's cultural values and the ethnic intolerance of the socialist enterprise proved to be incompatible. While Roma intellectuals, many of whom were party members, maintained that the establishment of a Roma Union would be compatible with the building of socialism, they did not comprehend that post-1968 socialism not only meant the imperative of social uniformity, but also the renewed transliteration of expressions of ethnic difference into displays of social deviance. There is neither a simple nor a single answer to the failure of the Union.

Writing in 1991, Jurová argued that "it is possible to establish [that] it was the Roma Union's own fault that it wasted its chances to have a decisive voice, though on a limited scale, in the development of its ethnic group, and that it failed to accomplish its own goals aimed at raising the general level of the Roma."[421] It is puzzling that she reached this conclusion given her own admission that archival sources at the time [of her writing] were "only partially available for study" and their current state "[did] not allow for consideration of all political and social circumstances of [the Union's] existence, and especially its abolishment."[422] Ten years later, the sources concerning both branches of the Union made it quite clear that it would be ludicrous to blame the Roma for a failure of the Union and for not "accomplishing their goals."

The Union documents indicate that, at first, the Romani leaders did have the mass support of their community, which they lost later on. However, it seems clear that the party used various tactics to dismiss the Union when it pushed for Roma nationality status and demanded being an equal partner in the integration process. Ordinary Roma did complain about the leadership of the Union and the *Nevo Droms* and *Bútikers* did have problems in their financial affairs. Was the political participation of the Roma genuinely welcomed and the chain of events an unfortunate result of historical circumstances? It seems that at least the dissolution of the Union was preconceived by the Party as the best way to discredit and eliminate Romani leaders without being accused of racism and discrimination, which was otherwise threatening the regime's badly bruised image during the Normalization period.

---

[421] Jurová, 92.
[422] *Ibid.*, 129.

V Becoming a Gypsy: Social Scientific Discourses

The previous chapter discussed the short life of the Roma Union and argued that in order for the Romani leaders of the Union to become an intellectual elite permitted by the regime to participate in the project of assimilating Gypsy citizens, they had to first transcend the negative conditions of Gypsy "backwardness" or at least not reveal ethnic pride in their Romani heritage. Education, as the site of socialization and the dissemination of ideology, played an instrumental role in this process. A tiny minority of Romani children were lifted from the world of "Gypsiness" into the Czechoslovak world of "normalcy," while the overwhelming majority of them were channeled through special schools for the mentally handicapped into the world of "deviance," contempt and perpetual marginalization.

"Remedial schools" (*zvláštní školy*) were designed by the Czechoslovak communist government to ensure equal educational opportunities for mentally and physically handicapped children.[423] The public school systems in communist regimes have been praised by foreign observers as one of the better consequences of communism, offering wide educational access to all children regardless of their social or economic background. However, few people outside of Czechoslovakia knew until the collapse of the regime that the remedial schools served as dumping grounds for Romani children, stigmatizing them for life.[424]

---

423 Some authors use the term "special schools" to describe these institutions. This book follows the term "remedial," used by contemporary reports and lawsuits of the European Roma Rights Center (ERRC) in Budapest and the Helsinki Human Rights Watch because it more precisely captures the intention and nature of these schools when applied to the Roma. Also, the term "handicapped" has been frequently challenged by the international community of advocates for people with physical and learning disabilities. However, since this work is concerned with examining the ways in which language and discourse operated to discriminate against the Roma and what its usage reveals about the sentiments of the Czechoslovak society, the term "handicapped" is maintained to reflect its usage in the Czechoslovak educational system at the time.

424 See for example, Helena Balabánová, "Romské děti v systému českého základního školství a jejich následná profesionální příprava a uplatnění," in *Romové v České republice*, 333-351.

While boasting that they provided a "head start" or an "extra cushion" to Romani students in need of special attention, for most Romani children the remedial school system effectively closed doors to high schools and universities. The Czechoslovak educational system was a so-called "tracking system," which channeled all students to three distinct educational and professional tracks based on their academic potential. However, while tracking generally started at the end of the seventh grade, Romani tracking was in effect since preschool, as "gypsy" children were subjected to intensive psychological observation and intelligence testing from that time onward. Regardless of the regime's rhetoric that it took "special care for the education of gypsies," once Romani children got into a remedial school, the system made no genuine effort to reintegrate them back into mainstream education.[425] In fact, it was believed by many educators, and the general population alike, that "separate is equal" for the simple reason that Gypsy children "belonged" to remedial schools and their placement there was generally perceived as just and necessary.

During the 1970-75 academic years, eighty percent of all Romani school children attended remedial schools, as opposed to three percent of non-Romani Czech and Slovak children.[426] However, in line with the regime's ideology that the Roma did not constitute a national ethnic group, an official country report about special education in Czechoslovakia in the 1970s written for UNESCO did not mention this striking disproportion at all, treating all students of special schools as "Czechoslovak children."[427] As in other areas and aspects of Romani assimilation, these racist and discriminatory practices went unlabeled and unrecognized, hidden under scientific objectivity and the discourse on the "needs," "reeducation" and "integration" of a backward social group into mainstream society.

Building on the analysis of Chapter three, which illuminated the genealogy of Gypsy myths in Czechoslovakia and their gradual transformation and

---

[425] Laura Conway, *Report on the Status of Romani Education in the Czech Republic* (Prague: HOST, 1996).

[426] Hübschmannová, *Šaj Pes Dovakeras*, 119.

[427] *Economic aspects of special education: reports from Czechoslovakia, New Zealand and the United States of America* (Paris: UNESCO, 1978); the chapter of Czechoslovakia was written by František Kábele, 21-62.

acceptance into communist official discourse, this chapter examines the social scientific discourse on education and family as the most significant sites where the transformation of Romani cultural difference into gypsy social deviance took place. The chapter is divided into three main parts. Section one analyzes the shift in Czechoslovak population policy in the 1970s. It discusses how population policy transformed the scientific discourse on the "Gypsy question" by analyzing anthropological and psychological studies of the "Gypsy population," especially Gypsy children, which aimed to demonstrate Romani mental inferiority and their propensity for sexual promiscuity and asocial behavior.

Section two discusses the inextricable link between the scientific discourse on gypsy pathology and perceptions of the gypsy family. The gypsy family was constructed as an inappropriate environment for raising Romani children and as the greatest obstacle to their education, which in turn threatened the potential success of integrating the Roma into society. An integral aspect of these discussions was, as the chapter demonstrates, the gendered dimension of the discourse on the family, construing the "Gypsy mother" as the cause of the degeneration of the family and blaming her for the failure of gypsies to become "proper" citizens. The final section then discusses how educators perceived the education of gypsies and their own positions in the process, revealing that they often participated in the colonial rhetoric of "otherness" and saw themselves as missionaries working on the threshold of civilization. The chapter ends by examining how these notions were used to discriminate against the Roma in the educational system.

V.1 Anthropology of Deviance

The Normalization period of the early 1970s, following the unsuccessful attempt of political reformers to build a "socialism with a human face" during the Prague Spring, witnessed an abrupt shift in official discourse, and therefore in social policy as well. Czechoslovakia was becoming more concerned with the "proper care" of its children than with their sheer numbers.[428] That is, the state

---

[428] See, David and McIntyre, *Reproductive Behavior*; Heitlinger, *Reproduction*.

became increasingly more interested in the "quality" of the population and its reproductive practices than in the overall "quantity" of the population, a shift that directly targeted the gypsies as contaminating the gene pool through their culture of deviance.

The most significant turning point for this discursive shift came at the National Demographic Conference in May 1970. Here, for the first time, Czechoslovak demographers urged the state to "increase demands for the qualitative makeup of the population" because "current trends indicate that such a development is slowing down."[429] In their documents they listed as the main source of the problem "the population explosion of the gypsy population," and in parentheses added "the growth of inadequately adjustable individuals from gypsy families." At the same time, the demographers cited "the quantitative decrease of the birth rate" in the country as a cause of serious concern, making it explicit that the "Gypsy" birth rate was not considered a part of the general "Czechoslovak" birth rate. The demographers then warned that if this trend would continue it would "result in the impairment (*zhoršení*) of the qualitative composition of the national gene pool (*genofond*) from the point of view of mental abilities (*duševní schopnosti*)" and argued that Czechoslovakia should start "utilizing 'special methods' for regulating fertility in our healthcare," and attempt to "gradually and objectively merge sociological and genetic categories in the population."[430]

Besides the obvious implications of these arguments for the politics of reproduction, which will be discussed in Chapter six, this demographic shift signaled that the official discourse on the "Gypsy question" was becoming increasingly focused on the ability or inability of the Gypsy family environment to produce "adjustable" and assimilable citizens. The policy focus on children and education gained primacy in conjunction with the rise of the rhetoric of social deviance and pathology as the mechanism for articulating Romani difference. Thematically, the greatest majority of studies concerned with the "Gypsy question," which were published in Czechoslovakia in the 1970s, were devoted to education, followed by studies on "social difference and de-

429 Miloš Černý, "Biologické a medicínské apekty populačního vývoje. Perspektivy uplatnění genetiky v populační politice." *Zpráva z II. Demografické konference Československé demografické společnosti, May 20, 1970, Demografie*, 10:2 (1970): 318.

430 *Ibid.*, 318-319.

viance" (physical anthropology, criminality and justice, and pathological psychology), reflecting the changing trend of the regime's approach to the "Gypsy question."[431]

As the previous chapter showed, during the years of functioning of the Roma Union, there was at least some academic interest in acknowledging Romani ethnic and cultural distinctiveness, accompanied by a desire to promote this attitude among the majority population through increased attention to the study of the Roma. However, crippled by the persecutions, blacklisting, intimidation and censorship of the Normalization period, the few academics and activists devoted to the promotion of Romani equal rights were silenced, either by their own fears and conformity or by the systematic pressure of the regime. Two most recognized Czech scholars of the Roma, who reemerged after 1989 to continue their work for Romani emancipation, were linguist Milena Hübschmannová and ethnographer Eva Davidová. During the Normalization, they both paid for their outspoken criticism of the official discourse and policies affecting the Roma by losing their positions in the Czechoslovak Academy of Sciences.[432]

These two scholars were the only prominent voices among social scientists, who insistently and consistently argued for the need to recognize Romani *ethnic* distinctiveness. In 1970, Hübschmannová argued that the fundamental problem of the regime's approach to the "Gypsy question" is that it is "seen as a problem of a group of people who do not want to or cannot adequately perform social roles and common behavioral norms and through their non-integration threaten the functioning of social systems of the society." As perhaps the only officially published critical author at that time she concluded that "there is a tendency to reduce broad social questions concerning the Roma to the question of Roma as a socially deviant class [of society]," which is partly an outcome of the obvious lack of "communication between the majority society and this minority community with a distinct ethnicity."[433]

---

[431] Statistics cited in Jiřina Olmrová, *K osobnosti romského pubescenta a jeho rodinným vztahům* (Praha: Univerzita Karlova, 1973), 17.

[432] *Romové v České republice,* 556.

[433] Series of scholarly articles of Milena Hübschmannová from the early 1970s include: "Co je to tzv. cikánská otázka?," *Sociologický časopis*, 6:2 (1970): 105-120; "What Can Sociology Suggest about the Origins of Roms?," *Archiv Orient*, 40 (1970): 51-64; "Kdo

In 1976, Hübschmannová was in turn accused of "reducing a complex historical-social problem into a one-dimensional question of communication"[434] and was unable to publish any openly critical articles until 1989. Similarly, Davidová criticized the "forceful assimilation enacted from the top down," such as the mandatory dispersal of the Roma after the anti-nomadic law in 1958 as "psychologically and theoretically ill-conceived and doomed to begin with."[435] Like Hübschmannová, Davidová also proposed that the only acceptable and effective way of approaching the "Gypsy question" would be a "process of accommodation, or rather integration – in other words forms of coexistence of this minority with the whole of society – with tolerance and acceptance of the positive aspects of the specificities [of this group]."[436] Their views, calling for the recognition of Romani ethnicity, stood alone among the approaches of the rest of the Czechoslovak intellectual elite and by the mid 1970s their arguments were silenced by a number of studies, which claimed to "objectively" document the alleged pathology of the Roma and proposed "positive" means for grappling with the problem.

Along with the enlightened civilizational efforts of regime ideologues Jamnická-Šmerglová, Sus, and Nováček (discussed in Chapter three), who in the 1950s and 1960s used historical sources to document Gypsy pathology, several new studies appeared in early 1970s addressing the "Gypsy question" from new scientific angles. Anthropological studies began to respond to Hübschmannová's and Davidová's calls for more research into the Romani culture. However, their main focus and objective was an investigation of the physical features and psychological tendencies of the Roma, especially Romani children.

One of the most extensive anthropological studies of Czechoslovak Gypsy men during communism, which took several years to conduct in mid

jsou Romové?," *Nový Orient*, 27:5 (1972): 144-148; "Jazyková politika Sovětského Svazu," *Sociologický časopis* 9:3 (1973): 259-273; and together with Jan Řehák, "Etnikum a komunikace," *Sociologický časopis*, 6:2 (1970): 548-559.

434 *Kontrolní zpráva o plnění usnesení Předsednictva vlády ČSSR č. 21 z 29. ledna 1976 o řešení otázek cikánského obyvatelstva*, FMPSV 1980. In Archiv socioklubu.

435 Eva Davidová-Turčínová, *Cikánské (romské) etnikum v Ostravě: výzkumná zpráva*. (Praha: VÚVA, 1970), 14.

436 Eva Davidová-Turčínová, "K vymezení a specifice současného cikánského problému v Československu," *Sociologický časopis*, 6:2 (1970): 29-41.

1970s, provided an analysis of "seven anthropomotorical features: body height, cranial length and width, facial width, nose height and width, and mouth width" in order to examine the levels of "Gypsy *social* and biological integration" (emphasis mine). The results of the study exposed that "gypsies are of average height;" "their skin is rather dark than light;" "their hair is mostly dark to black;" "their eyes are dark brown;" "their cranial cavity has average length;" "their nose is average height and width;" "their arms and legs are average length;" "their eyebrows are average thickness;" and "their chest hair is average."[437] Besides listing these results, the study provided no interpretations of its findings – perhaps because it indicates and proves nothing distinctive. Likewise, the study did not make any attempts to explain how it might be possible to infer anything about "social integration" by pure measuring of anatomical features. However, "doing science" of and around Gypsies, whether it was actually providing any useful data or not, had crucial impact on the perceived mediocrity and inferiority of the Roma. It is stunning that several decades after WWII such studies were being even conducted, which partly explains the Roma's continuous suspicions of scientific research.[438]

Other physical anthropologists found, for example, that "gypsy children in the Czech lands are significantly smaller and lighter compared to the norm" and pointed out that "their cranial characteristics (*hlavové charakteristiky*) reveal significant pigmentation and a tendency toward distinct or even sharper extension of the head in the face in the course of their ontogenetical development."[439] The conclusion of this particular study claimed that the "anthropological research of gypsy children proves that external factors play a significant role in influencing the development of this segment of children's population."[440]

Such a conclusion provided a double message to policy experts. On the one hand, on the basis of this study Czech anthropologists claimed that Romani children are more prone to socialization and can be more fully shaped

[437] Jan Beneš, *Cikáni v Československu: antropologická studies dospělých mužů* (Brno: Univerzita J. E. Purkyně, 1975), especially pp. 75-78.

[438] For a treatment of this topic, as related mainly to women, see Smith, "Racist Encounters."

[439] Jaroslav Suchý, "Vývoj cikánských dětí v měnících se životních podmínkách," *Čs. Pediatrie*, 27:9 (1972): 430-441.

[440] *Ibid.*, 441.

through education than other children, which was, of course, seen as a positive sign for assimilatory policies. The findings optimistically suggested the potential of educational measures to "reeducate" Romani children to become "proper" socialist citizens. On the other hand, the study pointed to the negative influence "Gypsy" parents and communities exerted over their children, emphasizing the importance of removing those children from potentially "bad" family environments. That Romani children and youth were categorized as endangered by family environment in Czech scientific discourse indicates the degree to which such studies influenced the institutional understanding of Romani difference (discussed further below).

Other studies also linked physical anthropology and the social environment as the causes of Gypsy pathology. Medical research on Romani children conducted in 1973 concluded that "gypsy children's general susceptibility to disease is not higher than that of other children," even though they "often suffer from septic skin disease. In spring and fall as a result of a poor diet their overall physical stamina decreases." The research team also surprisingly found that "puberty starts earlier in gypsy children, and they also have a greater tendency for premature sexual behavior ... and sexually transmitted diseases."[441] Once again, the study did not elaborate on how normative claims about *social behavior* can be based on empirical findings of physical anthropology. Such a mixed conclusion, however, reveals yet again the ways in which physical and social norms were explicitly evoked as evidence to help justify the terms of communist scientific discourse.

Another major research project conducted in 1972-73 by a team of physicians in all Czech regions of the republic was designed to study the health and hygiene of Gypsy schoolchildren. It was titled "The Problems of Health and Hygiene Habits of Gypsy Children" and the research methods consisted of "personal observation of [gypsy] children at school; interviews with school directors, class head teachers (*třídní učitel*) and school physicians; special medical questionnaires handed out to directors, teachers and school physi-

---

441 *Sborník pedagogické fakulty UK, Biologie III. and IV.* (Praha: Univerzita Karlova, 1975); *Cikánské děti v základních devítiletých školách ve školním roce 1969/70 až 1972/73. Zprávy a rozbory.* (Praha: Federální statistický úřad, 1974); Jaroslav Suchý, *Vývojová antropologie obyvatelstva ČSR* (Praha: Univerzita Karlova, 1973).

cians; and school documentation."[442] The used methods indicate that the status of health and hygiene of Gypsy children was primarily determined based on personal opinions of educational personnel and personal observations of the researchers themselves, both of which inextricably subsumed preconceived expectations and attitudes these people held towards the questions asked. Therefore, also the results of the scientific study on the relationship between physical health and behavior reflected the circular nature of such methodology. Often, such research produced little more than popular stereotypes cloaked in the rhetoric of science. The results of such studies were in turn used to place Romani children in remedial schools or to make recommendations to national councils about how to ensure that Gypsy children do not become any more unruly than they already were thought to be. This particular study, published in the scientific journal *Questions of Defectology*, came to the conclusion that

> it is generally impossible to characterize the population of gypsy children as medically or developmentally pathological, because the majority of individuals are healthy. Rather than a product of some hereditary inferiority, most developmental and medical problems [of gypsy children] are consequences of *social and moral causes*.[443]

The authors reasoned that because there was nothing wrong developmentally with Romani children, their problematic performance in school, behavior and integration in society were a product of "external influences". There is no problem with such a conclusion, as long as it would explain external factors in a complex way, bringing together the mutual forces and aspects of Romani and non-Romani interaction. Rather, the study articulated the damaging external factors within the Romani family, particularly its moral values and social adaptability. Therefore, the study supported the prevailing policy stance of the regime that the Romani population could be assimilated as long as the bonds of Romani communities are broken and the state takes primary control over the ways in which Romani children are cared for and educated.

---

[442] Jan Meisner, "Problémy zdravotnické výchovy cikánských dětí," *Otázky defektologie*, 15/1 (1972-73): 9-15.

[443] *Ibid.*, 14. (Emphasis mine.)

The Meisner study, for example, was cited as "theoretical support" in another work that tried to explain the truancy and failure of Romani children in elementary schools in one Czech region. The author cited the "backward values of gypsy family" as one of the main "negative factors" influencing the development of Romani children and recommended the "systematic and rigorous (*důsledný*) dispersal of gypsy families."[444] The racist and eugenic undertones of this study went so far as to argue that

> in some cases it was also [scientifically] proven that when proper hygiene and skin care is applied [to the Roma], it is possible achieve *normal skin color*. As evidence I cite an example: in Rokycany there are two gypsy women who have *beautiful white skin*, achieved by proper attention to personal hygiene.[445]

The author not only linked normalcy and "beauty" with whiteness in a blatanly racist way but also conditioned this type of normalcy on hygienic care. He therefore maintained that not only gypsy behavior, but the perceived inferiority of Gypsy physical make-up, such as "darker skin color," could also be corrected through proper methods. By effectively placing all physical and social properties of individuals within the reach of social manipulation, and by valuating gypsy physical and social characteristics as basically deviant, the author therefore suggested that the Roma themselves were at fault for their inability to be "normal" – no matter how outrageous such notion of "normalcy" was supposed to be.

Studies based on observations of the appearance and/or behavior of Gypsies were not unusual in the scientific discourses of the 1970s. Jiřina Olmrová, in 1973 conducting a "psychological study of gypsy teenagers" listed "observation," as one of her research methods, used in order to "penetrate the power hierarchy of the gypsy family and understand how gypsy children see the world." She came to the conclusion that "gypsy girls make an effort to dress modern, but they don't know how to sew and so they just adjust ready-made clothes amateurishly, sloppily and with only a primitive sense of style."[446] According to Olmrová, "even good clothes look neglectful on

---

444 Josef Buřič, *Škola a život cikánských dětí* (Praha: Pedagogické čtení, 1973), 35.
445 *Ibid.*, 14.
446 Olmrová, *K osobnosti romského pubescenta a jeho rodinným vztahům*, 2 and 14.

gypsy girls. Even though they allegedly spend a great amount of time and care on their hair, their usually long, curly hair looks sloppy."[447] Without explaining what significance such value judgments might have for "Gypsy psychology," Olmrová and others were subsequently cited as support in works on Romani educational pathology and family deviance. Further, such documents, available to local professionals, created the normative framework for interpreting and implementing assimilatory policies.

V.2 Demographic Constructions of the "Gypsy Family"

The "gypsy family" and "gypsy deviance" were inextricably linked together in scientific discourse. Gypsy juvenile delinquency and adult criminality were seen as the result of poor parenting and a deviant family environment, while the deviant family was seen as the result of the Roma's inherent predisposition toward asocial behavior and their "natural" lack of parenting ability and social responsibility. One of the main categories used in the discourses on Gypsy criminality was the "endangerment by the (family) environment," which was a category routinely used in health statistics and records of juvenile delinquency. For example, in 1979, regional pediatricians in the Czech Republic used the category as a definitional term for a separate group of children in a study analyzing the "state of children's health."[448] In 1989, the identical category was used in a National Council study in Ústí nad Labem, analyzing the local educational conditions. The study reported that out of 1976 Gypsy children, 53 were "defective," 120 "chronically ill," 60 "lived in families of chronic alcoholics," and 303 lived in "endangered families." There was no comparable category in the survey for "non-Gypsy" children living in "endangered families" or families of "chronic alcoholics."[449]

---

[447] Olmrová, 29.

[448] *Zpráva Ministerstva zdravotnictví České republiky o zdravotním stavu cikánské populace* (Praha: MZ, 1980). Archiv socioklubu. 75% of children in this category were identified as being subjected to bad "Gypsy environment."

[449] *Studie o současné společenské situaci romského obyvatelstva v ČSFR* (Praha: Skupina nezávislých expertů FMPSV, 1990), Archiv socioklubu.

According to the Ministry of Health, there were no comprehensive statistics compiled or kept about Romani health. However, a 1986 Ministry report submitted to the Governmental Bureau for Questions of the Gypsy Population claims that the health conditions of "gypsy citizens" are worse than those of the rest of the population. The report also asserted that it is caused by "*their way of life*, genetic baggage and health-damaging habits." According to this document, 80 percent of "all gypsy youth live in an endangered environment," leading to the situation in which a "high percentage of gypsy adolescents are not capable of entering into the military draft due to various forms of mental illness, asocial personality types, alcoholism, drug addiction and criminality."[450] The link between unhealthiness, criminality and the deviant "gypsy" family environment is hard to overlook in this report.

The images and scientific studies discussed so far demonstrate the tight conceptual link between the worlds of mythology and social science, which had severe implications for the Czechoslovak population's perceptions and notions of ethnic and cultural difference. In 1976, the Deputy of the Ministry of Health of the Czech Republic even argued that "gypsy cultural and health awareness is influenced by [their] anthropological aspects."[451] He asserted that, from the point of view of "mental hygiene" these aspects, such as Romani "tendency toward romanticism, amusement, temperament expressed in music and dance, their fondness of bright colors, and their modest needs and [absence of] ambition," decrease the chances for Romani successful assimilation. All of these purportedly ingrained characteristics of "Gypsiness," according to him, find their expression in the Roma's bad work ethics, laziness, and low level of responsibility. Even such mundane habits as "disorganization of free time and going to bed late" were considered "typical for them."[452]

Charges of parental incompetence and deviant family environment, repeatedly evoked in relation to the Roma, were not accidental. The notion that

---

450 *Zpráva Ministerstva zdravotnictví České republiky pro vládní komisi pro otázky cikánského obyvatelstva* (Praha: MZ, říjen 1986). Archiv Socioklubu.

451 *Kontrolní zpráva o plnění usnesení Předsednictva vlády ČSSR č. 21 z 29. ledna 1976 o řešení otázek cikánského obyvatelstva; zpráva náměstka Ministerstva zdravotnictví.* (Praha: FMPSV, 1980). Archiv Socioklubu.

452 *Ibid.*, 40.

there is only one proper form of upbringing had deep resonance in a society trained to see itself as homogenous. Such perceptions were built directly into the ways, in which Gypsies were officially defined. Even though demographic data about Gypsies were considered objective, their interpretive, evaluative and methodological frameworks were decidedly subjective.

Demographic data generated its own conclusions about the characteristics of the Gypsy population. In one example already mentioned earlier, demographers analyzing the 1969 census reported that

> if in 1968 the population of Gypsies naturally increased by 5,905, but the absolute difference since the previous study showed an increase by only 2,474 Gypsies, that means that more than 3400 Gypsies were *released* from the new study [...] This fact demonstrates a satisfactory speed of Gypsy integration with the rest of population.[453]

Quantitative conclusions about gypsies were made possible by the peculiar ways, in which one was or was not counted as a "Gypsy." Statistical data about the number and demographic development of "Gypsies" came from two sources – from classic censuses and a so-called "evidence" of the National Councils. The traditional census was quite standard, consisting of a questionnaire form that the entire adult population of the country had to complete. Every individual filled in the relevant nationality from the official list that she or he identified with; Roma, of course, was not an option.[454] The census data about "gypsies" also did not come from the self-identification of the Roma as

---

[453] Srb and Vomáčková, "Cikáni v ČSSR v roce 1968," 221.

[454] Nationality questions were a part of Czecho-Slovak census since 1880, when Austrian-Hungarian censuses of 1880, 1890, 1900 and 1910 asked for one's colloquial tongue (*Umgangsprache*). The first Czechoslovak census of 1921 inquired about nationality through a question about one's maternal language (*mateřská řeč*). In the 1950s and 1960s census asked only for "nationality" by which was meant "affinity with a nation whose cultural heritage one shares and to which one belongs," making German, Rusyn, Jewish or Roma/Gypsy superfluous nationalities that citizens of communist Czechoslovakia could not declare. The census of 1991 was the first one that listed the Romani nationality as an option. *Populační vývoj České republiky* (Praha: PřF UK, 1996).

"gypsies," but through the evaluation of such status by a census commissioner.[455]

The method was shockingly elementary: for all people, whom the commissioner "objectively" considered Gypsy, he or she wrote the letter "c" (*cikán*) with a colored pencil on the front page of the census form. The commissioners were instructed that "skin color" (*barva pleti*) is not a "sufficient objective indication" of gypsiness. They were required to "evaluate the overall way of life" (*celkový způsob života*) of the subjects in question.[456] Clearly, Gypsies were not counted for the purposes of identifying or recording their ethnic subjectivity, but for the purposes of assimilative efforts. Justifying such "philanthropic" methods still in 1999, demographer Květa Kalibová argued that "it is important to stress that the Roma were catalogued [under communism]. . . because they needed help of the society."[457] She is right in that only those "Gypsies" who were considered in need of social attention were identified as such by the commissioners and included into the data as "Gypsy population." Roma who lived in conditions considered normal enough to pass as "Czechs" or "Slovaks," were not included in these numbers. Every year the Ministry of Labor and Social Welfare, which conducted the census evaluations and interpretations, announced whether the number of "gypsies" went down or up, indicating whether or not the "speed of integration" was "satisfactory."

The evidence of the National Councils, which together with the data from the censuses guided official government policies, was also problematic. The number of "Gypsies" counted by National Councils included only those people, who in one way or another came into contact with the administration: for example, when they applied for an apartment, asked for social welfare, looked for employment, were released from jail, committed larceny or other

---

[455] Petr Víšek, "Program integrace – řešení problematiky romských obyvatel v období 1970 až 1989," in *Romové v České republice*, 200.

[456] Sčítání lidu 1968, 1974, 1976-1989. Archiv Ministerstva Práce a Sociálních Věcí (AMPSV). See also, Kalibová, ***Demografické a geodemografické charakteristiky romské populace v České republice***; Alena Šubrtová, ***Z dějin československého sčítání obyvatelstva***. (Praha: Acta Universitatis Carolinae, 1980); and Květa Kalibová, "Romové z pohledu statistiky a demografie" and Petr Víšek, "Evidence cikánských občanů," both in *Romové v České republice*.

[457] Kalibová, "Romové z pohledu statistiky a demografie," 98.

crimes, or had educational problems with their children. In other words, whether ethnically Roma or not, if people did not need the assistance of the national council they would not appear in the Council's "Gypsy" evidence.

Only when people came into contact with local and regional National Councils, the local bureaucracy would evaluate their "social status" and decide whether those people were "gypsies" or not and indicate such status in the proper forms. Roma, who were considered adequately integrated "fell out" of both kinds of statistics. Likewise, non-Romani people with a "low social and cultural level" coud find their way into the definition of "Gypsies."[458] Even more significantly, this practice made it apparent that despite the overwhelming centralization of the regime, such crucial decisions were nonetheless made locally, individually, and subjectively by ordinary social workers and administrators.

The demographic construction of "Gypsies" was also heavily influenced by "social curators," a profession established in 1972. Curators were assigned to oversee the assimilation of individual Gypsies – as long as they were counted as Gypsies. The objective of the curatorial work was the "social ascendance [of a person or a group] ... with the overall goal of totally eliminating them from the [gypsy] demographic evidence."[459] To put it differently, the goal of the work of social curators was to assimilate "gypsies" out of existence. Their role in assimilating the gypsy population was so fundamental that one of the first demands made by representatives of the Romani community after 1990 was the abolishment of the profession of gypsy social curators. Arguing that the curators "did their best to help the Roma," some scholars called this demand a "paradoxical and tragic mistake" of Romani political elites after the collapse of communism.[460] However, for many Roma the social curators clearly represented the personification of a communist regime that denied them their ethnic and human rights by forcing them to live in certain kinds of ways and evaluating their families as deviant and dysfunctional.

---

[458] Sčítání lidu 1968, 1974, 1976-1989. (Archiv AMPSV). And Kalibová, "Romové z pohledu statistiky a demografie," 94.

[459] Vládní usnesení č. 231/1972 a Usnesení vlády ČSSR č. 21/1976, *Zásady celostátních sociálně politických opatření k péči společnosti o cikánské obyvatelstvo*. Archiv Socioklubu.

[460] Víšek, 202.

The allegedly inadequate parenthood of Gypsies was one of the most important issues cited by the regime for the failure of educational measures designed to "reeducate" the Roma into "proper" socialist citizens. The "deviance" of Gypsy children occupied the media spotlight ever since the immediate postwar period. When discussing "Gypsies," journalistic accounts rarely failed to mention the "raggedy clothed children"[461] who were "running around dirty and naked,"[462] and "sleeping in great numbers on one bed or even on rags on the floor,"[463] which was seen as an outcome of gypsy adults' "insistence on their children's early employment and even begging."[464] During the February 3-6, 1959 registry of "all nomadic persons," a survey in Slovakia reported that "there are 46,000 of these wanderers of which 11,000 are children avoiding mandatory school attendance."[465] Gradually, a popular discourse on the gypsy family became the crux of the "gypsy question." In 1976, the education leaders proclaimed that "in the process of integrating the so-far disintegrated group of the gypsy population, the greatest attention should be placed on the upbringing and education of gypsy children."[466] The allegedly poor and lasting influence of the "dysfunctional" family environment on the values and morale of new generations of children was seen as a tremendous threat to the potential success of the assimilation process.

Institutional policies pertaining to the family, childcare and education were interrelated. The 1963 Law No.94/1963 Sb. "On the Family" made it easier for social workers to take away children, who lived in "inappropriate conditions" and whose parents "neglected to take care of them."[467] The 1972 Governmental Decree No.231 turned its attention to mandatory school attendance and made specific provisions for financially punishing parents whose children "failed to regularly attend school." In such cases, social workers at the National Councils were entitled to decide whether or not the family in question should receive its monthly child support. Even though none of these

---

[461] *Hraničářské slovo*, June 26, 1947.

[462] *Národní osvobození*, September 30, 1947.

[463] *Mladá fronta*, October 17, 1951.

[464] *Svobodné slovo*, October 20, 1967.

[465] Cited in: Šrajerová, "K rešeniu romskej otázky na Slovensku po roku 1945," 182.

[466] *Výchova a vzdělávání cikánských dětí: sborník přednášek* (Praha: MŠ, Ústav studií a analýz, 1976), 7.

[467] *Zákon č. 94/1963 Sb.*, "O rodině". Ústava ČSSR. (Národní knihovna v Praze.)

laws or amendments spoke specifically about "gypsies," the language of the provisions was loose enough to accommodate a variety of interpretations of what constituted "regular attendance" and what did not. Needless to say, it was predominantly Romani families that were cited for these "crimes."[468]

These policies and strategies were not abstract proclamations shut in bureaucratic drawers but had deep impact on real lives in the Roma community. From the Romani oral history project it is clear that fear of such practices created real trauma for Romani families. Štefan Mika, for example, remembers that

> at home I always knew exactly what was wanted from me [...] When the teacher yelled at me at school I had no idea why. I hated school and didn't want to go there. I ran away from school, but mom and dad were upset because they [the National Council] took away the child support (*přídavky na děti*) for that.[469]

When he complained about the school, "mom stopped cooking, hugged me to the point that she almost choked me and then said: 'You have to bear it in school! Otherwise they'll send you to a foster house (*do děcáku*) and I'll hang myself.'"[470]

It is clear that educational and social care professionals perceived a fundamental difference between "Gypsy" families on the one hand, and "Czech" and "Slovak" families on the other. However, their reports and discussions indicate that these differences were not perceived as differences in cultural lifestyle, choices or value systems. Such differences were deftly labeled as a matter of deviance or social pathology, an interpretation that was also applied to Romani children's behavior at schools. If "gypsy" children behaved in ways distinct from the required norms or expectations, they were proclaimed mentally retarded and more often than not transferred to remedial schools.[471]

---

468 Michaela Kepková and Petr Víšek, "Romové v systémech sociální ochrany a zdroje sociální distance," in *Romové v České republice*, 378-397; Arne Mann, *Neznámi Romovia*.

469 Memories of Štefan Mika, cited in Hübschmannová, *Šaj Pes Dovakeras*, 90-91.

470 *Ibid.*, 91.

471 David Čaněk, "Roma and Other Ethnic Minorities in Czech and Slovak Schools, 1945-1998" (Budapest: Central European University, Center for Policy Studies, 2001). Čaněk

The communist discourse on family and parenthood was also shot through with gender stereotypes and was squarely understood through the lens of structural functionalism, which statically assigns "appropriate" and "natural" positions, roles and power to women and men based on their presumed biological predispositions.[472] The structural functionalist model fit in nicely with communist family ideology, which, like the sociological concept, also claimed that biologically determined family roles represented a natural order, interpreting the "different" gender roles and positions as "equal" complements. Any individual or family that diverted from this model was classified as "deviant" and "pathological."[473]

Romani mothers often received the blame for the alleged failure of their children in school. One Gypsy social curator asserted that

> it is important to teach gypsy women to better run their households [...] Gypsy children often damage school supplies and parents are not able to correct that. This forces the teachers not to give gypsy children homework, which results in the fact that gypsy children are not graded, fail school and are transferred to remedial schools. The reality that gypsy children finish only low school grades is caused by the small number of gypsy women, who have the greater influence in the family. Because of the large number of children, the [gypsy] woman does not work, is not interested in self-education and thus cannot help her own children. At home children do not have proper care, there is a non-existent daily schedule and the mother does not give enough attention to school preparation.[474]

---

argues that there was a "dramatic increase of Romani children in the remedial schools" especially in the late 1970s and 1980s, due to a major educational reform enacted in 1976. In his paper, he cites statistics, which demonstrate that the increase went from 25% before 1976 to 50% by the mid 1980s (11-12). See also *Zvláštní náprava: Romové a školy pro mentálně postižené děti v České republice* (Budapest: European Roma Rights Center, 1999); Charta 77. "Dokumenty: Charta 77 - Dokument č. 23." *Listy*, 3:2 (1979): 47-52.

472 For an overview of the structural functionalist thesis and its application to East European communist societies see: Heitlinger, *Women and State Socialism*, 9-14; See also the classic study of structural functionalism and sociology of the family: Talcott Parsons and Robert Bales, *Family, Socialisation and Interaction Process* (London: Glencoe Press, 1955).

473 Such differences labeled as pathologies included not only differences related to cultural values, but also sexual preferences or reproductive choices. See, for example, Jiří Fanel, *Gay historie* (Praha: Dauphin, 1999); *Postavení lesbické ženy v České společnosti* (Praha: Alia, 1997); Alena Heitlinger, *Reproduction*.

474 Kier, "Práce okresní komise," 215.

The author aggregated each manifestation of Romani "deviance" as the function of the mother's problems, arguing that the failure of Gypsy children in school is caused by the inadequate care they receive in their homes. Even though at one point he recognizes that it should be *parents* who are responsible for rearing their children, he immediately shifts attention to the inadequacies of the mother: her inability to run the family, her unemployment or poor education, her fault for having too many children, and her indifference to her children and their education once she has them.

The absence of the father in this patriarchal account indicates his faultlessness for the high fertility, bad parenting and educational failure of Roma children. Significantly, the author blames Romani mothers for the state's practice of sending Romani children to remedial schools. According to this view, Romani children are transferred into schools designed for the mentally handicapped not because of biases of the educational system but because gypsy mothers are unable to provide adequate conditions for their children's learning. There are only a few cases where the father is assigned agency in the educational problems of gypsy schoolchildren. But even in these cases, criticism of the father can be seen as a reflection of the mother's failures. For example, in a discussion of the importance of teacher-family relations for the success of a Roma child at school, one pedagogue agued that "it is necessary for [the teacher] to direct his or her attention at the father of the child because mothers are usually less educated and use older siblings for taking care of the younger ones so that they themselves can wander through a village or town."[475] However, it is important to recognize that rhetoric targeting women as the most important element in the educational process was not reserved only for the Roma. Such a patriarchal approach was not different from the sensibilities of the society in general as it reflected gender biases prevalent in communist society.[476]

The Roma themselves held similar gender stereotypes, resulting in Romani women's primary responsibility for the family and children's upbring-

[475] Josef Švarbalík, "Osobitosti pri výchove a vyučování cigánskych žiakov z nevyhovujúceho rodinného prostredia," in *Pedagogické osobitosti vo výchove a vyučování cigánskych žiakov základnej školy* (Bratislava: MŠ, edícia Pedagogické čítanie, 1979), 39.

[476] Heitlinger, *Reproduction*; Einhorn, *Cinderella Goes to Market.*

ing. The Roma Union organized parenting classes and seminars devoted to education, which were designed specifically for women. During its short-lived existence, the Union journals *Romano Lil* and *Romano Pajtrin* contained a section called the "Board of Shame," which exposed issues that the Roma found despicable within their own community. Quite often, it was Romani women who were objects of scorn in these pages, being held solely responsible for family respectability and children's success. In one of the accounts, for example, a member of the leadership of the Prague branch of the Roma Union criticized the attitudes and negligence with which Romani women "enter marriages and take care of their children." He called his contribution "Alcohol and Prostitution on the Pillory!," exclaiming how "appalling" and "common it is to see a 24-year-old mother of four in a bar or at a dance, while her children are surviving at any cost possible," which results in the situation that "every other family has a son or a daughter in a foster care institution." He argued that the Union and "other state institutions" should not be indifferent to these problems and urged the Union "to organize seminars and lectures, led by physicians and psychologists, for single girls and future mothers about how to take care of family and children."[477]

Non-Romani preschool and elementary school teachers, writing for these Romani journals, also contributed to this gendered pressure:

> When we were trying to find out why gypsy children are so unsatisfied, sad and *feel other* than the rest of the children in the school we found out that the main reason is that [gypsy children] are not well prepared by their families [for school life]. ... When his *mom* did not teach him how to button his shirt, tie his shoe, he would immediately be sad and discouraged.[478]

In each issue of the Union's journals there were educational articles about the "proper upbringing" of children in Romani families, detailing how to maintain hygiene, table manners, and the importance of storytelling and discipline. The frequent point of these stories was, of course, to promote the ability of Romani children to succeed in the educational process. But overwhelmingly, and from both Romani and non-Romani ends of the advisory spectrum, it was

---

477 Ladislav Cihy, "Tabule Hany: Na pranýři je alkohol a prostituce!," *Romano Lil*, 2:4 (1970): 26.

478 Marta Milevová, "Aby vaše dítě bylo šťastné!," *Romano Lil*, 16, 1972. (Emphasis mine.)

supposed to be the mothers, who took care of this aspect of Romani integration.

V.3 Education as a Civilizational Frontier

Education, as the pivotal tool of Romani assimilation from the 1970s on, gradually gained importance as the regime transformed its institutional policy toward the Roma. Repressive measures aimed at acquiring physical control over the problematic population were transformed into more tactical forms of power exercised through comprehensive social welfare measures and techniques. Education was never far removed from various institutional strategies enacted on the Roma but changes in the way the regime controlled the Romani population coincided with demographic shifts of the early 1970s. In 1972, the Czechoslovak government issued and approved new "Principles of nationwide social-political measures for the social care of the gypsy population."[479]

For the first time, education was designated as the main tool to combat "Gypsy backwardness." The governmental resolution stated that

> the integration of the entire gypsy population, which is still lagging behind the standards of our society, is a long-term generational process for which it is crucial to create conditions at the earliest age possible. It is necessary to focus society's attention and care first and foremost on the upbringing and education of gypsy children and youth.[480]

At that time, the Roma Union was at the peak of its existence, flourishing and claiming to have taken responsibility "for the future of our community."[481] This situation was arguably one of the reasons why the regime decided to firmly take the indoctrination of the Roma as well as the non-Roma into its own hands.[482] As the circumstances of the existence and dissolution of the Roma

---

479 *Usnesení vlády ČSSR č. 231/1972*, "Zásady celostátních sociálně-politických opatření v péči společnosti o cikánské obyvatelstvo" and amendments to this document from *Usnesení vlády ČSSR č. 21/1976*. (Archiv socioklubu.)

480 *Ibid.*

481 Miroslav Holomek, *Romano Lil*, December 15, 1971.

482 Víšek, "Program integrace," 190.

Union, discussed in the previous chapter suggested, despite its outward rhetoric the regime was not interested in having the Romani elite participate in solving the "Gypsy question."

The most common way government documents defined the process of Romani assimilation was as enlightened coercion requiring the "re-education" or "re-upbringing" (*převýchova*) of the gypsy population. There is no precise translation of this term in English, but the significance of its meaning rests on the fact that "re-upbringing" was not mere reeducation, but entailed redoing the process of Romani socialization or "repeated rearing." The term *převýchova* was used in both Czechoslovak popular and scientific discourses in two different ways: either as describing initial care for infants and the process of family socialization or discussing the correction of the criminal behavior of incarcerated inmates.[483] By using the same term to connote Roma as both infantile subjects in need of guidance and as socially deviant subjects in need of surveillance and correction, official discourse equated Romani behavior with criminality and recirculated the limited ways the media, scientists and educators could interpret Romani difference.

However, educational discourse was not only permeated by rhetoric of deviance and pathology. Educational specialists, teachers and social workers also employed romanticized and exoticized images of gypsies when describing their encounters with Gypsy schoolchildren. Teachers working with or among Gypsy children were celebrated and often saw themselves as missionaries working on the frontiers of civilization. In 1969, Czech sociologist Otto Ulč argued that the "teaching profession considers an assignment with Gypsies as either punishment or a hardship transfer station to a subsequent coveted job in the metropolis."[484]

Popular culture had a considerable influence on the Gypsy question at least until the mid 1970s. Descriptions of "wandering" and "primitive" gypsies that peppered educational literature reveal that pedagogical professionals

---

483 See, for example, Vojtěch Kalibán, Tereza Šišková, and Kazimír Večerka, *Příčiny zvýšené criminality (protispolečenské činnosti) cikánských občanů, zejména mladistvých*. (Archiv vědeckého ústavu kriminologického. Unpublished result report of a research study, 1979); Oldřich Novotný and Jan Zapletal, *Základy kriminologie* (Praha: Karolinum, 1993).

484 Ulč, "Policy," 434.

imagined themselves as encountering a cultural "other," not just socially inferior beings.[485] Articles and letters written by teachers demonstrate that many of the educators shared patronizing attitudes toward the Roma, completely oblivious to the racist and colonial dimensions of their remarks. Such attitudes however, were not incompatible with both the immediate postwar excitement of rebuilding the country from the rubble and the communist ideology that claimed to tackle new horizons of humanity. In a typical discussion, one teacher, whose contribution entitled "Confession" was included in a collection of articles "carefully chosen with the aim of familiarizing the wide pedagogical readership with the social and political significance of our socialist society's coordinated care of gypsy citizens and the difficulties encountered in [their] education process,"[486] started her account by sharing that "work with gypsy children is extremely difficult and those who never tried it cannot even imagine the immense difficulties." She herself had undergone a summer course for "teachers of gypsy children but reality surpassed all expectations."[487]

She then described her encounter with Gypsy children during a class snack break and observed that while other children had "normal snacks," meaning bread and cheese and a piece of fruit, "they [the Roma children] brought 'hearty' snacks to school with them, consisting of cheese, fish, salads, milk, peanuts, soda, candy, meatloaf, sugar, bubble gum, and so on. It was always extremely difficult to force them to wait for a break to eat. After the break, our classroom looked like a monkey cage."[488] The fact that the teacher uses racially charged language referring to monkeys, in order to describe Romani children eating, apparently struck neither her nor any of the editors as inappropriate. The myth of nomadism was also an important part of the cultural construction of gypsy behavior. For example, the teacher claimed that Romani children often got tired during "certain phases of the school

---

485 Hancock argues that in the Western historical discourse the Roma were viewed as colonial subjects and often were compared to black slaves in the Americas. See: Hancock, "Standardization and Ethnic Defence," 10.

486 Úvod," *Výchova a vzdělávání cikánských dětí: sborník přednášek* (Praha: MŠ, Ústav studií a analýz, 1976), 7.

487 Zpověď soudružky učitelky Kopáčkové ze ZŠ Praha 9, Kyje. Cited in Milan Kantor, "Cikánské dítě a škola," in *Výchova a vzdělávání cikánských dětí: sborník přednášek* (Praha: MŠ, Ústav studií a analýz, 1976), 93.

488 *Ibid.*, 96.

year," which, according to her, demonstrated their "longing for freedom, movement and nature," because "nomading is in gypsy blood."[489] On the whole, however, she assured her readers that it was "extremely rewarding to work with gypsies" because one can gain "trust and attachment of the little, at-first deprecated and disdained, children." She ended her "confession" by stressing that "upbringing and educating gypsy children is truly hard work," but "the biggest reward" is the fact that "it is truly pioneering work."[490]

Another teacher shared similar experiences describing that "when we see parents as they snuggle with their beautiful black-haired child we see that they wish that their child is happy and successful in life. They would like to do anything to make that happen, but sadly they don't know how to prepare their child for life."[491] Such a blatantly patronizing attitude put all blame for the failure of the child in the educational system on the parents. In 1979, a director of an elementary school in the Slovakian town Gemerská Hôrka wrote excitedly about the success of his 23-year-long work among the Roma by saying that

> it is almost impossible to compare children today and back then. The progress is undeniable [...] even though the gypsy question is not fully solved yet, many gypsies properly work, build houses, use modern furniture and even have cars. From the example I can see around myself it is clear that this is the right way to change their lifestyle. It is not a short or easy road, but certainly one that is worth the effort.[492]

In another article, a director of a preschool complained about the attitudes Romani children brought with them from their homes and asked the Roma Union for help. She wrote that her school

---

[489] Interestingly, even though he does not cite any of his references, Holy claims that Czechs "vehemently denied the possibility that they [gypsies] could become Czechs: 'A gypsy will remain a gypsy' was a phrase I heard many times. Some argued that national identity was 'in one's blood' and that 'gypsies cannot change their blood.'" (Holy, *The Little Czech and the Great Czech Nation*, 64-65.)

[490] Kopáčková, 97-98.

[491] Milevová, "Aby vaše dítě bylo šťastné!," 16.

[492] Ladislav Jósza, "Cesta k úspechu," in *Na pomoc učitelom cigánských detí zo zanedbaného rodinného prostredia*, ed. Pavol Kuruc (Bratislava: Slovenské pedagogické nakladatelstvo), 1981, 6.

> responsibly fulfills all resolutions of the [Communist] Party concerning the re-education of our *unfortunate fellow citizens and their children*. However this practice is one-sided [...] Often one can hear the racist terms 'black' and 'white' . . . more often from the mouths of our little gypsy children, like a spell which should remedy all lack of discipline and misdemeanors they are doing. We in schools respect the principles of all nations and nationalities in the world, and the Roma Union should help the educational system from its own end.[493]

Quite interestingly, she exposed that there were racial tensions in the school that were vehemently denied by the regime, but argued that these were aspects of reverse racism enacted by the Romani children against their fellow classmates. While she blamed the Roma for those tensions, her argument nevertheless implicitly recognized the Roma as a "nation of the world" or at least a nationality. This revelation signifies that despite the official discourse on social deviance, at least some ordinary professionals understood Romani "difference" as ethnic and cultural distinctiveness, albeit only in a problematic way.

Two other accounts also indicate that Czechoslovak population may have actually perceived the ethnic and racial dimensions of the "gypsy question." As one newspaper article pointed out, "unfortunately, there are still people among us who maintain the old-fashioned views that the Gypsies are lazy and dirty just like the Negroes in the USA." [494] One the one hand, this author suggested that such demeaning views were an exception among the Czechoslovak population but at the same time he effortlessly used racist description of African Americans as a factual comparison, without any further explication. Likewise, another report condemned an incident in the mining town of Sokolov, where "children pulled a Gypsy child in public on a chain, like a trained monkey. On his back he carried the sign – 'Gypsy'." To demonstrate disapproval with such a practice, the author rhetorically asked: "Are we in Dallas or in a country, which considers racism of any sort to be a crime?"[495]

Both articles suggest that racial dimensions of the Gypsy question were present in the sensibilities of Czechoslovak society even though people were

---

[493] Vlasta Kuchařová, "Mateřské školy," *Romano Lil*, 14-15., 1972. (Emphasis mine).
[494] Ondřej Kravec, "Kde rasismus nemá místa," *Tribuna*, 44, October 20, 1974, 2.
[495] Anna Tučková, "Esej," *Kulturní Tvorba*, November 17, 1966, 14.

not allowed to discuss such issues as relating to the "gypsy question."[496] The absence of "race" as a category of difference applicable to social discourses of communist Czechoslovakia produced a lasting effect on the analytical abilities of the society to recognize and deal with questions of ethnic and racial discrimination in an open and complex way. Instead, channeling these differences into discourses on mental deviance and social pathology served as the primary means of addressing these issues, with the remedial schools being a crucial case in point.

Colonial attitudes expressed by Czechoslovak teachers or embedded in the "scientific" studies of gypsy inferiority had profound effects on the educational process. The alleged mental retardation of "Gypsy" children pervaded the documents and materials related to Romani education during the communist period. A director of a remedial school in Northern Bohemia even argued that these schools are "typical by the presence of gypsy children [in them]." However, he also admitted that "a number of mentally retarded gypsy individuals showed themselves to be better than other mentally handicapped pupils." There was a detectable sense of surprise over this situation, which was suggested in the director's assertion that "[we] call them the 'mental elite.'"[497] Such a comment only supports the charges that Romani children were overwhelmingly placed in the remedial schools unwarrantably because were not mentally handicapped in the first place, so of course they formed a "mental elite" in these institutions.

Josef Štěpán, whose works were heralded as "standing out for their scholarly and methodological qualities,"[498] coined in mid 1970s the phrase "asocial sociability" (*asociální sociabilita*), arguing that the main problem in gypsy upbringing and education is the discrepancy between family internal attachments and the Roma's external relationship with society. In other words, he asserted, the problem is that "most of the activities and behavior

---

[496] Once again, Holy in his ethnographic narrative of Czech national identity claims that when talking about gypsies or Jews, "many informants also pointed out their [the gypsy or Jewish] racial difference." (Holy, 65.)

[497] Cited in Josef Štěpán, "Cikánské dítě ve zvláštní škole internátní," in *Výchova a vzdělávání cikánských dětí: sborník přednášek* (Praha: MŠ, Ústav studií a analýz, 1976), 81.

[498] Olmrová, 32.

perceived by the family as acceptable are officially judged as asocial."[499] Even though he attempted to defend the differences in the upbringing of Romani children on other than simply socially pathological grounds, he nonetheless argued that "the upbringing of gypsy children is affected by [parenting] primitivism and spontaneity when the child is both loved, but also brutally punished."[500] According to him, this discrepancy and inconsistency between love and punishment "results in the defective general socialization of the [gypsy] child."[501]

Unlike other authors Štěpán argued that "gypsy parents spend quite large [financial] sums for the well-being of their children . . . so the main problem is not the material inadequacy of care itself." According to him, "the main roots" of both the problems Romani children faced in school and the Roma's participation in society in general was that they are "derailing into moral crisis, absolute meaninglessness and emptiness (*bezobsažnost*) of their lives."[502] That led him to the conclusion that "there is a defective limitation in the interests [of gypsies]."[503] Building on Štěpán's respected studies, other authors found in Romani children "forms of primitive emotive reactions," "higher tendencies to depression," "the increased predominance of fearful experiences," "higher levels of impulsiveness," and "higher levels of *antisocial tendencies*," arguing, for example, that "most often [gypsy adolescents] suffer from a complete absence of life goals."[504] Unable to see or openly admit the correlation between coercive assimilative policies of the state and these findings, the authors concluded in mid 1970s that it is important "to accentuate the necessity of a historical approach" toward the Roma so that their "historically anchored

[499] Josef Štěpán, *Cikánský oligofrenní jedinec v kolektivním zařízení* (Praha: Pedagogické čtení, 1972), 16. See also, Josef Štěpán a Ludmila Ždánská, "Cikánský jedinec v kolektivním zařízení," *Otázky defektologie*, 15:5-6 (1972-72): 173-179.

[500] *Ibid.*, 21.

[501] *Ibid.*, 26.

[502] *Ibid.*, 86.

[503] *Ibid.*, 110.

[504] For example, František Olejár, *Formovanie psychických zvláštností výchovne zanedbaných detí.* (Bratislava: Státní pedagogické nakladatelstvo, 1972), 131-132, 171. Significantly, one of the studies "proving" gypsy children's unadaptability was their "fear of police" which to the psychologists demonstrated "bad conscience [of gypsy children] relating to high incidence of [gypsy] criminality," rather then showing the interconnection between assimilatory practices and children's perception of the world around them.

morality of lumpenproletariat" can be brought to a higher level of socialist consciousness.[505]

The majority of educational studies argued that it is then best for gypsy children to attend remedial schools, citing their poor family environment as the main reason for the inevitability of this measure. It was argued that gypsy children are so handicapped by their family environment that the best strategy for them to "catch up" with the rest of society would be their separation from other, "normal" children. Should this not happen, "in the course of further school grades their retardation will only grow larger and the difference [between gypsy and other Czechoslovak children] will only increase."[506] In a typical recommendation this particular author concluded that "gypsy children achieve better results in remedial schools . . . because the conditions of the [remedial] school better suit the *mentality* and preparedness of gypsy children."[507] While there certainly can be some credence to the author's argument about their level of preparedness, the explicit suggestion that schools designed for the mentally handicapped better serve the "mentality" of Romani children indicates the high degree of obliviousness to the ways in which notions of gypsy inferiority and beliefs about their social welfare went hand in hand under Czechoslovak communism.

Based on the evidence presented so far, it seems plausible to argue that the values and attitudes held by educators and social scientists created a predetermined environment for testing the intelligence, emotional maturity and psychological stability of "gypsy children," which subsequently determined their future educational potential and possibilities. All Romani children were required to undergo expert psychological and pedagogical examinations, created on the basis of "standard intelligence tests for the regular population of preschool children."[508] Since the "experts" devising, administering and evaluating these examinations were the professionals whose implicit and

---

505 Olmrová, 41.

506 Milena Macháčková, *K problémům připravenosti cikánských dětí pro společenské soužití a některé zkušenosti z využití progresivních metod v práci s těmito dětmi.* (Praha: Pedagogické čtení, 1970), 26, 45-46.

507 *Ibid.*, 46. (Emphasis mine).

508 Helena Malá, *Výchova, vzdělávání a biologický vývoj cikánských dětí a mládeže v ČSR* (Praha: Univrezita Karlova, 1984).

explicit notions of Gypsy inferiority have been narrated throughout this chapter, it does not seem all that surprising that "the results of the intelligence tests indicate limited intelligence abilities of the overwhelming majority of examined Romani children."[509]

As the last chapter of the book will discuss, the transformation of social and population policy in Czechoslovakia during the 1970s, which became oriented toward taking "better care of the population" and employed the rhetoric of emphasizing "quality" over "quantity" of children, affected not only the educational policies and system but also had profound consequences on the ways, in which the politics of reproduction and reproductive freedom intersected with the cultural politics of ethnicity.

---

[509] Balabánová, 337.

VI Planned Parenthood behind the Curtain: Sterilization of Romani Women

In 1990, Tibora Vaňková explained why both of her children were in foster-care institutions. She attempted to commit suicide when her partner left her after he learned she had been sterilized four years earlier, in 1986. She got 2,000 crowns for the sterilization, but immediately she gave the money to her social worker as a debt-payment for used children's clothes. Now, she is in therapy. One of Tibora's sisters was sterilized after she had had her first child, when she was nineteen. Her other sister jumped out of a window after she had been sterilized. "She died," states Tibora absent-mindedly.[510] Rumors about sterilization of Roma women in socialist Czechoslovakia were born in the early 1970s. By the end of the decade, the rumors were baptized into a world of legitimate controversy by the ink of dissident writers, criticizing the Czechoslovak "inability to deal with the 'Gypsy question'," and medical experts, explaining the politics of encouragement of sterilization among "women of Gypsy origin."[511] However, vocalized concerns about the issue remained rare.

In 1972, the Health Ministries of both federal republics of socialist Czechoslovakia issued a new Sterilization Law, designed to prevent arbitrary and ill-informed sterilization of all Czechoslovak citizens by outlining specific and strict requirements and indications which a sterilization applicant had to

---

[510] Dana Mazalová, "...a nemnožte se!" (*...and don't multiply!*) *Týden*, 4:51 (1997): 36-42. The personal testimonies used throughout this paper are based on oral interviews with Roma women who underwent sterilization (and who wish to remain anonymous), conducted in summer 1997 by Dana Mazalová. Accordingly, the names of the women used in this chapter were changed. (The interviews are tape-recorded in the personal archive of Dana Mazalová, PDM.)

[511] For example, "Dokumenty: Charta 77 - Dokument č. 23," *Listy*, 3:2 (1979); M. Mohapl and B. Dobešová, "Problematika žen s nežádoucím těhotenstvím," *Československá gynekologie*, 43:8, 1978, 605-7; M. Kubica et al., "Postpartálna sterilizácia," *Československá gynekologie*, 43:8, 1978, 607-8.

fulfill in order to be granted permission to undergo the procedure.[512] However, based on this protective law, between 1972 and 1990, Romani women were sterilized at astonishingly high numbers compared to non-Romani women.[513] Even though there are no decisive statistics available, several estimates claim that anywhere from 21.2 to 36.6 percent of all sterilized women were Romani, while the Roma constituted less than two percent of the overall Czechoslovak population.[514] Since the collapse of the Communist regime in 1989, at least three hundred Romani women came forward to participate in various surveys, studies and interviews.[515] All of them claimed they were ster-

---

512 *Věstník Ministerstva Zdravotnictví České Socialistické republiky* (ČSR), Part 1-2, Volume XX, 1/1972 and *Vestnik Ministerstva Zdravotnictva Slovenskej Socialistickej Republiky* (SSR) 9/1972. (Both in SÚAR.) The specific requirements, discussed later in the chapter, are outlined in the appendix, entitled: "The List of Indications for Sterilization."

513 Given the rhetoric of Czechoslovak socialist population policy, which always emphasized the country's need for more children, it is presumptive that an underlying integral part of the protective content of the law was a desire to *prevent* (or at the very least *discourage*) Czechoslovak, meaning non-Romani, women from obtaining sterilization not only for "arbitrary and ill-informed," but for any reason. In that sense, one could argue that Romani women had, at least theoretically, more rights than non-Romani women, whose access to sterilization was closely monitored and extremely limited. However, given the severe manipulation and abuse of knowledge, will, rights and choices that Romani women were continuously exposed to within the institutions of communist medicine and social work, whether for "enlightened" or racist reasons, such potential analysis seems rather preposterous.

514 Statistics concerning the number of sterilized Roma women vary tremendously. All authors agree that their numbers were "disproportionately high," but there is no consensus on how high. The percentages fluctuate for years as well. See for example statistics in E. Posluchová and J Posluch, "Problémy plánovaného rodičovstva u cigánských spoluobčanov vo Východoslovenskom kraji," in *Zdravotnická pracovnice*, 39:4 (1989): 220-223. Also, Ruben Pellar and Zbyněk Andrš, in "Statistical Evaluation of Romany Women in East Slovakia - Appendix to the report on the Examination in the Problematic of Sexual Sterilization of Romanies in Czechoslovakia," in *Het Afkopen van Vruchtbaarheid: Een onderzoek naar door Paul Ofner en Bert de Rooij in opdracht van de Verenging Lau Mazeril en de Stichting Informatie over Charta 77*, (Amsterdam: Lau Mazeril Foundation, 1990), in ACHC. (The statistics consist of interviews and questionnaires given to 156 Roma women in Slovakia and 123 Roma women in the Czech Republic.)

515 The most articulate and active has been a group of women from Ostrava, organized together under the umbrella NGO Living Together (*Vzájemné soužití*), who have been the driving force behind making forced sterilizations in Czechoslovakia public: putting together photographic exhibitions, submitting official claims, filling lawsuits and complaints and organizing discussions about the issue.

ilized against their will or with ill-informed consent. All of them also claimed that they were offered money for the procedure. Invariably, in their testimonies the women (and Romani advocates by their side) accused the "regime" of explicitly targeting them for sterilization, citing the 1972 sterilization decree as the cornerstone of the practice.

The 1972 law is, however, on paper, strictly ethnicity-neutral. There is no mention of ethnicity anywhere in the text. There is also no mention of financial compensation for the procedure. This seeming paradox raises some important questions. How did it happen that an ethnicity-neutral law resulted in an ethnically inscribed practice? And what does the "regime" signify in the women's testimonies? Some scholars argue that because "the incidence [of sterilization in communist Czechoslovakia] is statistically insignificant," given the total number of procedures, it is not worthy of attention.[516] However, given the involuntary nature of many of the procedures and their ethnic aspect, I believe the sterilizations have considerable importance for exposing the ways in which discrimination against the Roma was carried out, thereby further illuminating another dimension of the way the Gypsy question was transformed from a discourse on ethnicity to a discourse of social deviance and sexuality. Moreover, the circumstances surrounding the sterilizations also hold tremendous significance in their potential for uncovering some of the sites where the tensions between the majority Czechoslovak population and the Romani minority played out in the most striking ways.

Unlike "Czechoslovak" women (meaning ethnically non-Roma) who were never paid for sterilization, Romani women (legally also Czechoslovak citizens) were lured into consent by substantial financial incentives. Beta Kolářová was 27 years old and had two children when she was persuaded by her social worker that a 10,000 crown compensation for the procedure is too good an offer to pass up. The calendar said 1990.[517] The leather-jacketed dissidents from Charter 77, cheered on by excited crowds, had already seized power at the Prague castle and the five-pronged star above the lion's

---

[516] Olga Vidláková, "Law and Fertility in Czechoslovakia," in M. Kirk, M. Livi-Bacci and E. Szabady, eds. *Law and Fertility in Europe* (Dolhain: Ordina, 1976, Vol. 1); See also, David and McIntyre, *Reproductive Behavior*; Heitlinger, *Reproduction*.

[517] Cited in Mazalová, 38 and PDM.

head on the Czech national symbol was replaced by the original royal crown, but the sterilization of Romani women was still going on.

In 2005, 87 victims of forced sterilization submitted a formal complaint to the Czech Ombudsman, who, after a thorough investigation, ruled that "the problem of sexual sterilization carried out in the Czech Republic, either with improper motivation or illegally, exists, and Czech society has to come to terms with this."[518] The Ombudsman's conclusion was the first-ever public and official admission by any state authority that sterilizations in Czechoslovakia (and the Czech Republic) have been indeed a real, and not a made-up or phantom phenomenon. However, despite this revelation, the Ombudsman avoided any discussion of ethnic or racial dimensions of the issue, leaving his statements in general and neutral language. In October 2007, Iveta Červeňáková became the historically first Romani woman awarded a financial compensation by a Czech court for uninformed and involuntary sterilization. She won half a million crowns, to be paid by the Ostrava city hospital where she was sterilized at age 20, while she was giving birth to her second child. Her case happened in 1997, eight years after the collapse of the Communist regime.[519]

One is left wondering, how and why was all this possible. How were the sterilizations conceivable in the first place and why did the practice continue even after the communist regime, supposedly dictating and controlling all aspects of the society and its actions, was gone? If the policies were born in the hands of the "regime" and executed by the "regime," why did not they also die with the "regime"? Some scholars argue that the answer lies in the lag in pol-

---

518 European Roma Rights Centre et al. *Submission to the United Nations Human Rights Committee Concerning Implementation of the International Covenant on Civil and Political Rights (ICCPR) in the Czech Republic*. Budapest, July 2007: 14-15. <http://www.ohchr.org/english/bodies/hrc/docs/ngos/cohre_cz.pdf> [Accessed Dec. 4, 2007].

519 Aleš Honus, "Romka vysoudila za sterilizaci půl miliónu," *Právo*, 12.10. 2007. When the story of the court verdict appeared on Czech internet news *Novinky.cz*, the reader discussion attached to the article was immediately flooded by such severe racist comments that the webmaster had to block the discussion and close it down. (For more detailes, see www.novinky.cz). In a similar court case from November 2005, Helena Ferenčíková was awarded only an apology and no money, because her case was barred by the statue of three-year limitation.

icy change that comes with any transformation of a regime.[520] However, the fact that suspicious cases of sterilization of Romani women have not necessarily stopped within a few years from the end of the communist rule seems to indicate much deeper socio-cultural causes, which are not simply connected to or are a result of the regime type and change. As this last chapter of the book argues and demonstrates, both implicit and explicit racism on a variety of levels has played an important role in the mistreatment of the Roma.

By analyzing the interpretation and implementation of the sterilization policies by ordinary officials sitting in local hospitals and offices, this chapter is further developing the thesis that the commonplace dichotomy between the "regime" versus "people" is not a conceptually meaningful framework for understanding social and political practices. By jettisoning that dualism – itself a heritage of totalitarian conceptions of communist societies – one can better see that the locus of "power" was less embedded in the enunciation of ethnically-neutral Party decrees than it was situated within the discursive arena of local officials who interpreted and implemented laws as they saw fit. In sum, the "invisibility" of the discrimination of Romani women resides in the fact that the ethnic target of the sterilization policy was never fully enunciated from above nor fully institutionalized, but was rather always implicitly understood to refer to Romani women by local practitioners who inhabited a dual world between "official" discourse and unofficial racial bias, and thus who were themselves unable to see the racially-charged nature of their actions.

Ever since 1989, racism and the hostile interaction between the Roma and non-Roma population has been one of the most sensitive, excruciating and talked about social issues in the Czech Republic. In the second half of the 1990s, the issue of the sterilization of Romani women assumed a pivotal place on the pages of the academic and popular press, on TV shows, as well as in public debates, as the symbol of the persecution of the Czechoslovak

[520] An example of this phenomenon can be seen, according to them, for example in the wake of the 1917 Bolshevik Revolution in the Soviet Union (Stephen Cohen, *Rethinking the Soviet Experience*); after the Victorious February 1948 coup in Czechoslovakia (Karel Kaplan, *Short March*); or in other areas of political and social transformations in Eastern Europe after 1989 (Elzbieta Matynia, ed., *Grappling with Democracy*).

Roma.[521] For some, it was and still remains a painful memory and regret. For others, it was an economic necessity at the time. For some, it spells genocide, while for others it is nothing more than a malicious rumor. But for all, it is still an obfuscated and hitherto unexamined area of Czechoslovak history revealing the complicated and dynamic nature of internal social reality that was pulsing behind the seemingly stoic and uniform face of the communist regime. By investigating the circumstances surrounding the sterilization of Romani women during the 1970s and 1980s, the following chapter attempts to untangle the story of the intersection of ethnicity, sexuality and social deviance in socialist Czechoslovakia in order to further expose the transformation of the ethnic discourse concerning the Roma that has been taking place since the 1950s.

The circumstances of the Romani sterilization provide an opportunity to consider the intersection of ethnicity and sexuality under a communist regime, and in doing so offer a new way of looking both at the history of socialist Czechoslovakia and Roma treatment under communism. It is clear from the testimonies of the sterilized women, as well as from interviews with and documents written by local doctors and social workers, that much of the initiative to urge, or even pursue Romani women to undergo sterilization came from these local offices. Despite the official rhetoric of ethnic equality, and contrary to the official assurances that race was a groundless tool for explaining social reality in socialist Czechoslovakia, these regional workers interpreted the 1972 ethnicity-neutral sterilization decree as a mandate to sterilize Roma women and to readily escort them into operating rooms.

Thus, the questions that can help us most to unravel the complexity of this issue have to deal not only with those who issued the decrees and instructions, but equally importantly with those who believed in and implemented the sterilization policies. This chapter is hence interested not only in the decrees themselves but rather in the process of their translation into practice. It investigates the decrees and policies in the hands of local doctors and social workers who translated the ambiguous medical language into an ethni-

521 Popular articles on this issue include for example, Mazalová; Ondrej Giňa, "Dopis na Romské Téma," *Mladý Svět*, 34:3 (1989), 6; Charta 77, "Dokumenty." In other media: Ondrej Giňa on TV Nova, *Aréna*, May 17, 1997; Ruben Pellar and Zbyněk Andrš, Čs. Rozhlas, August 16, 1997.

cally inscribed practice with an astonishing alacrity. The key to unpacking the ethnic dimension of the seemingly impartial social system is, therefore, to explore the intricate relationship between official beliefs, institutional policies and popular consciousness. These relationships informed each other and together created the mechanisms of social control that enabled the discrimination of Czechoslovak Roma to flourish under the guise of social welfare.

The last chapter of this book is organized in four main parts. Building on the discussion in the previous chapter, the first section introduces the genesis of the 1972 Sterilization law by situating it in the context of the transformation of the Czechoslovak population policy in the 1970s. The chapter then goes on to examine the relationship between Czechoslovak perceptions of gypsy parenthood and sexuality. The second part of the chapter focuses on the writings of medical professionals, revealing the presence of "enlightened racism" in their argumentation, hidden under the rhetoric of health and socio-economic welfare not only of the Roma, but the entire country. After that the chapter turns the lens on the inevitably gendered nature of the sterilization practice and discusses its various dimensions, ranging from violation to empowerment. Finally, the fourth part of the chapter takes up the charges that the sterilization practice in communist Czechoslovakia was a premeditated genocide of the Romani population.

VI.1 Czechoslovak Population Policy

Like other countries of the Eastern bloc, during the 1970s and 1980s Czechoslovak officials nervously watched its slowly and steadily declining birth rate, encouraging its population to have more children. During the late 1960s, countries of Eastern Europe experienced some of the lowest fertility rates in the world.[522] By 1968, the total fertility rate in Slovakia, for example,

[522] However, abortions remained legal in all countries of the Eastern bloc, with the exception of Romania where abortion was made illegal in 1966. Nicolae Ceaucescu even ordered a "requirement" for every family to have at least four children. (Gail Kligman, *The Politics of Duplicity: Controlling Reproduction in Ceausescu's Romania* or Mary Ellen Fischer, "Women in Romanian Politics: Elena Ceausescu, Pronatalism, and the Promotion of Women," in Wolchik, *Women, State, and Party in Eastern Europe*, 125.)

reached its lowest-ever recorded level. In the Czech Republic, fertility levels resembled the statistics from the 1930s.[523] Even though these trends were reversed during the 1970s, all countries of the Eastern bloc continued in their effort to promote comprehensive pro-natalist measures. As Alena Heitlinger argues,

> all societies intervene in procreation. The processes of giving birth and raising children are too important for societies to leave uncontrolled, though controls do not always work. Aggregate fertility ultimately determines the survival of a given population ..., the growth and structure of the economy, the structure of the family or kin group ..., and national economic, political, and military power.[524]

The 1972 Sterilization law, as an improved version of the initial sterilization regulation passed in 1966, was a part of this effort to refine the Czechoslovak population policy into what by the mid-1970s became, according to some western demographers, "the best, most comprehensive pro-natalist population policy in the developed world."[525]

Since the establishment of the Czechoslovak Population Commission in 1957 in the wake of the liberalization of abortion in the country, Czechoslovakia engaged in a conscious effort to counter its rapidly falling birth rates. Following the lead of the Soviet Union in 1955, abortion was legalized in Czechoslovakia in 1957 and on the whole was considered "neither sinful nor disgraceful."[526] Despite that, media pamphlets and educational brochures engaged in pro-natalist rhetoric "in the interest of the nation" all throughout the socialist period. Unlike in Romania, for example, where the state involvement in reproduction amounted to a virtual abolition of abortion in 1966, in Czechoslovakia the regime enacted incentive-based, "positive" social and medical pro-natalist measures.[527]

---

[523] Tomáš Frejka, "Fertility trends and policies: Czechoslovakia in the 1970s," *Population and Development Review*, 6:1 (1980): 69.

[524] Heitlinger, *Reproduction, Medicine and the Socialist State*, 15.

[525] J.F. Besemeres, *Socialist Population Politics*, 263.

[526] Heitlinger, "'Management' of Reproduction in Czechoslovakia," in Wolchik and Meyer, eds. *Women, State, and Party in Eastern Europe*, 289.

[527] See Kligman, *Politics of Duplicity: Controlling Reproduction in Ceausescu's Romania*.

In 1964, the regime introduced prolonged maternity leave, increased family allowances for every additional child in a family, gave preferential treatment in housing based on number of children, made reductions in rent, and encouraged early retirement for mothers (they were entitled up to 35 weeks of paid and three years of unpaid maternity leave, and for every child raised, a mother was entitled to one year off of the mandatory retirement age, set at 60 for women and 65 for men).[528] However, it is also important to at least mention that the official recognition of the sexual division of labor within the domestic sphere and parenthood, demonstrated by this entitlement to an early retirement for women, who raised children, points to quite complex relationship between the regime's paternalistic sexism and its commitment to women's emancipation and equality. By the late 1970s, the Czechoslovak government was spending four percent of its annual budget on direct financial benefits awarded to mothers and an additional seven percent on other pro-natalist services and subsidies.[529] The new Sterilization law then was an integral component of this drive to perfect the pro-natalist population policy system.

According to the 1972 Sterilization Decree and a series of subsequent decrees issued by the Czech and Slovak Ministries of Health, being allowed to undergo sterilization was supposed to be extremely difficult. In 1989, an influential study, *Law and Modern Medicine*, summarized the official position on the concept of family and reproduction politics in socialist Czechoslovakia during the socialist period:

> The succession of generations is the only means for the preservation of the human family and is, in its way, the primary task of humanity. Bearing children is thus the unquestionable duty of parents, *regardless of their wishes and plans*. Even children not wanted [initially] often become children loved.[530]

The Czechoslovak Civic Law, anchored in the 1960 Czechoslovak Constitution, considered the "establishment of a family and a *proper* upbringing of

[528] Heitlinger, *Reproduction*, 243; Also Heitlinger, "Management", 289; and Frejka, 69.

[529] David and McIntyre, 222.

[530] Jaromír Štěpán, *Právo a moderní lékařství* (Praha: Avicena, 1989), 153. (Emphasis mine.)

children [to be] the purpose of marriage," and "motherhood the most honorable obligation of a woman."[531]

While the rhetoric of the population policy was consistently both pronatalist and free of any explicit ethnic prejudice, the early 1970s witnessed a marked shift in the concern and emphasis of Czechoslovak population policy. As we have seen in the previous chapter, since the late 1960s, the state became increasingly more concerned with what two leading Czechoslovak demographers at the time called "the qualitative aspect of population development."[532] In 1968, another prominent demographer pointed out the "cultural disadvantages of children raised in very large families" and noted the headaches revolving around constructing "inordinately" large apartments.[533] While the main emphasis of the population policy was a wide range of medical, economic and social measures, a 1974 study argued that "education to proper parenthood must be a an integral part of Czechoslovak state population policy as a whole [as well]."[534]

Concerned about the quality of the family environment, officials gradually modified the population policy to provide only limited encouragement to large families, the majority of whom consisted of the Roma. Since 1970, attention was concentrated on stimulating second and third-order births, which were seen as crucial to a population policy seeking to reverse a declining fertility rate. In the interest of a "healthy" population, the family allowance was adjusted upward for the first three births, but, in contrast to earlier years, reduced for higher numbers.[535] In 1978, demographer Jiří Havelka pointed out that the government's present population policy was less concerned with increasing the birthrate than in maintaining it at its current level, while concen-

---

[531] *Ústava ČSSR*, *Zákon o rodině*, článek I and III, Sb. 1960, (SÚAR Praha). (Emphasis mine.)

[532] Pavel Pavlik and Vaclav Wynnyczuk, "Czechoslovakia," in B. Berelson, ed. *Population Policy in Developed Countries.* (New York: McGraw-Hill, 1974.), 319-354. (320).

[533] M. Kučera, "Population Policy in Czechoslovakia," *Demografie*, 10:1 (1968): 307-317; J. Berent, "Causes of Fertility Decline in Eastern Europe and the Soviet Union II: Economic and Social Factors," *Population Studies*, 24:4 (1970): 247-292.

[534] Pavlik and Wynnyczuk, 320.

[535] Milada Bartošová, et al. *Populační politika v ČSSR, 1945-1975.* Výzkumná práce (Pracoviště Praha), řada B, č. 76. (Bratislava: Československý výzkumný ústav práce a sociálních věcí, 1978); *Demografie*, 1968, 1974.

trating on issues of "the best possible rearing and education of children."[536] Similarly, in 1981 at the International Population Conference in Manila, the Czechoslovak delegate Wynnyczuk argued that the main aim of Czechoslovak population policy was "enhancing the value of children."[537]

While the population policy did not engage in any explicit ethnic bias, there is, of course, an implicit judgment present in its statements about the quality of population, proper parenthood or appropriately sized families. These statements must be read in connection with the officially marketed and popularly reproduced images of a "Gypsy" not as an ethnic and cultural subject, but as a socially, mentally and sexually deviant object. These images, displayed most often in educational and welfare propaganda, drew on exaggerated and caricatured differences in sexual, family, and reproductive patterns between the Roma and Czechs and Slovaks. Moreover, the Roma's higher fertility was rarely mentioned without the context of Roma's bad and "incompetent" parenting.

However, not all citizens were encouraged to reproduce "in the interest of the nation." To the contrary, through a suspiciously similar rhetoric, "in the interest of a healthy population," Roma women were actively discouraged from exercising their reproductive rights. The Governmental Commission for the Gypsy Population even recommended all National Committees to "apply decree No.4/1967-FO issued by the Ministry of Health, which allowed an exemption [from paying for birth control] to those women *whose use of birth control was desirable*, but there was a possibility that its use would fail because of monetary issues."[538] Romani fertility was under a constant attack all throughout the socialist period, but the general focus on the "main problems" of the Roma shifted substantially over time. While immediately after the war it was the "foreign invasion" of the "gypsies" that troubled the country, in the 1950s society made its reluctant peace with the fact that the Roma were a part of the society to stay. However, at that time the main problem was their "nomadic lifestyle" that was in need of violent suppression. In the 1960s and

---

536 Jiří Havelka, "Populační politika," in *Populační politika v Československu* (Prague: Orbis, 1978), 31-35.

537 Quoted in Daniel Wulf, *Family Planning Perspectives*, 1982, p. 66.

538 SNA Bratislava, *Fond Povereníctva SNR pre zdravotníctvo*, 1960-1968, č. kr. 8, č. sp. 52. (Emphasis mine.)

1970s the focus of the "Gypsy question" gradually shifted to considerations of parenthood and sexuality, and with it the Roma's alleged "excessive" fertility rate.

In the late 1960s and throughout the 1970s, academic studies as well as popular magazines were full of worries about the "explosion" of the Romani population. Despite the overall low birthrate in Czechoslovakia, the public seemed to notice that the Roma did not fit into this reproductive pattern.[539] The actual fertility rates vary considerably from source to source. For example, demographic statistics show a 1.1 percent increase in Roma population for 1968.[540] Ulč claims that "between 1972 and 1981, the population [meaning the Czechoslovak population in general] rose by 10.5 percent, while that of the Gypsies increased by 23.8 percent."[541] Mazalova's sources indicate that by 1990, "the average number of children of Czechoslovak citizens was 2.07 and of the Roma 3.5."[542] Given the arbitrariness of the demographic methods by which the Roma were counted, discussed in the previous chapter, there is no way to find the "correct" or "real" statistics. Moreover, given the quite different concept of "family" in Romani culture, with extended kinship living together, it would not be completely surprising if some censuses would have counted the same children several times.

Although Czech and Slovak reproductive patterns also were not synonymous, nonetheless, because the overall family values of Czechs and Slovaks generally coincided, the non-universality of cultural values was not called into question as it was with the Roma. For example, statistical data from the late 1970s indicated important differences between the desired fertility of Czech and Slovak women. "Virtually no Slovak woman desires to be childless," claimed a 1979 sociological study, "and more than one third wishes to have three children." Among Czech women, almost twice as many as their Slovak counterparts wanted only one child.

The Slovak sociologist Mária Schvarcová, who conducted the study, enthusiastically recommended the Slovak model as the ideal family size for the entire country "which would be sufficient to solve the Czechoslovak popula-

539 Heitlinger, *Reproduction*, 139.
540 Srb a Vomáčková, "Cikáni v ČSSR," 193.
541 Ulč, 317.
542 Mazalová, 40.

tion problem."[543] In other words, she suggested that one should have many children, but not too many. Moreover, since the "Czechoslovak population problem" was identified with a low-birthrate of the non-Romani Czechoslovak population, such suggestions reveal the fact that "gypsies" were not considered an equal component of Czechoslovak citizenry. Clearly, models of "ideal" family and parenthood patterns were not universally shared among Czechs and Slovaks, calling into question studies like Schvarcová's that claimed to represent "the" Czech and "the" Slovak culture as stable and fixed entities. Nonetheless, the same "natural" conformity was asked from the Roma and their unwillingness to obey these norms was seen as a sign of social deviance.

Moreover, Romani fertility was rarely mentioned outside of the context of Romani "bad" parenting. Not only did the Roma have a high fertility rate, they were seen as incompetent parents as well. While the Roma themselves considered their family values to be strict and loving, in popular discourse the images of Gypsy parents were transformed and stereotyped into those of negligent and violent drunks and careless prostitutes. For example, a widely read educational weekly, *Učitelské noviny*, reported quite regularly on the problem of Gypsy parenthood, observing that Gypsy "paternal authority is very loose" and claiming on the behalf of the entire society that "[it] is concerned with the lack of [Roma] parental love."[544] Gypsy parenting was criticized also from the perspective of substance abuse; as, for example, one article stated that "it is not uncommon for [Romani] eight-year-olds to smoke and drink alcohol," but what was even worse, they did so "in the presence of their parents."[545]

---

[543] Mária Schvarcová, "Niektoré poznatky o prognózách v oblasti populačnej klimy v ČSSR z hladiska vydatých ekonomicky činných žien s nezaopatrenými detmi (výsledky empirického výzkumu)," *Populační zprávy*, 1:2 (1979), 36-39. Since Schvarcová's study speaks strictly in Czecho-Slovak dichotomy, it would be interesting to know whether, by Czech and Slovak women, she means women living in each respective republic, or women whom she considered to be ethnically Czech and Slovak; and whether she included Roma women in her study as well. It cannot be completely ruled out, but given the ethnic rhetoric of the time, which clearly separated Roma women from "Czechoslovak" women, it is unlikely that Schvarcová steered away from the common pattern.

[544] *Učitelské noviny*, August 24, 1967.

[545] *Svobodné slovo*, October 20, 1971.

Even Miroslav Dědič, by many Roma regarded as one of the most sympathetic educators, argued that

> in their family, gypsy children witness mostly negative phenomena, such as smoking and drinking of alcohol. The child listens to improper conversations and is a witness to unfit scenes from the adult life. In average gypsy family a warm feeling and word are rather exceptions. The preschool must suppress and uproot these inappropriate and premature children's experiences and replace them with positive ones.[546]

Without acknowledging the discriminatory dimension of apartment-distribution practices and coercive settlement of Romani families into small apartments, which effectively encouraged them to have fewer children and live in single-generational households without extensive relatives, the media were also appalled by the housing conditions of the Roma, which were, according to them, "hardly conducive to the preservation of sexual taboos."[547] And while "in the interest of the future citizens" Romani children were forcefully removed from their parents and placed into foster-care institutions to ensure their "proper" upbringing,[548] the general view of the rest of the population of this practice seemed to be that "[Romani] mothers are all too eager to turn their offspring to the care of the state."[549] The chief public health officer of the Czech Socialist Republic complained in a 1970 report that education leading to planned parenthood is still not successful among the Gypsy population" and de-

[546] Miroslav Dědič, *Výchova a vzdělání cikánských dětí a mládeže* (Praha: Státní pedagogické nakladatelství, 1982), 36. Dědič, the first teacher who after WWII systematically engaged in pedagogy for Romani children promoted residential education (*internátní výchova*). He was convinced that the separation of Romani children from their "bad" family conditions will help their faster reeducation and assimilation. (In 2005 and 2006 dr. Dědič donated a vast archive of his educational materials, including seven of his pedagogical diaries from 1950-1955, to the Museum in Roma Culture in Brno. I believe this unique archival collection certainly deserves scholarly attention and thorough academic treatment.)

[547] *Vlasta*, November 9, 1970.

[548] Stewart, *The Time of The Gypsies*, 123. (Also movie "Marián" discussed in Chapter three.)

[549] *Učitelské noviny*, January 12, 1969.

manded that it be "impressed upon Gypsy families that they should have only as many children as they can *properly* take care of."[550]

In a 1975 study about current problems in education, social scientists argued that:

> the explosion of the Gypsy population brings with it a whole number of negative consequences [which] manifest themselves in the decreasing quality of the Gypsy population itself, as well as the population in general, and also in the decreasing social, economic, and cultural level of Gypsy families.[551]

And thirteen years later, in 1988, Slovak physician Kornel Danáš asserted that "in gypsy families in Slovakia there is a rapidly growing rate of mentally retarded children," which he "proved" by pointing to statistics that claimed that ninety percent of all Roma children attended special schools. "And it is terrible," he concluded, "because the mentally retarded grow up and then become fertile ground (*podhoubí*) for delinquency."[552]

While discussing the "problems of difficult-to-raise gypsy children," and arguing for a stricter approach to Romani families, Slovak sociologist František Olejár refers to Soviet scholar Anna Solojevova's observation that "incorrigible children come from bad families" who cannot, "*due to their number of children* and/or lack of competence and interest, take adequate care of their offspring." She offered the following conclusion, praised by Olejár as a great model to confront the problems of Romani parenting in Czechoslovakia:

> We all have to take care of the evil (*zlo*) in the family. Not only teachers, who already have their heads full of problems, but the state, all our organizations. It is inevitable to start with the families, not with the children.[553]

---

550 *Report of the Governmental Commission for the Questions of Gypsy Population*, CKC-4509/1970. In USAP. (Emphasis mine.)

551 Ministerstvo školství ČSR, *Předškolní a školní výchova cikánských dětí: aktuální problémy speciální pedagogiky* (Praha: Státní Pedagogické Nakladatelství (SPN), 1975); 7. Other studies, arguing in a similar manner include: Ferdinand Smrčka, *Hovoříme s rodiči* (Praha: SPN, 1974); F. Výborný, *O výchově dětí ke kázni* (Praha: SPN, 1958); Eva Syřišťová a kol., Normalita osobnosti (Praha: Avicenum, 1972); L. Podmele, *Komunistická morálka a výchova nového člověka* (Praha: SPN, 1971); Ladislav Podmele, *Učení o společnosti a státu* (Praha: SPN, 1972).

552 Kornel Danáš, "Bolavý problém," *Nedelná Pravda*, Poprad, August 5, 1988.

553 Anna Solojevova, "Zlé deti a čo s tým súvisí", originally published in *Moskevskaja Literaturnaja Gazeta*, (1965), cited in Olejár, 21. (Emphasis mine.)

As these examples demonstrate, not only Romani reproduction but the Romani family as an institution were seen as damaging to the socialist enterprise, harmful to the assimilation process and detrimental to the Roma themselves. The Roma were seen as the locus of evil of future generations and the society as a whole was asked to participate in the civilizational process of eradicating this menace through greater surveillance of Roma's private lives and choices and subsequent streamlining of these with the "normal" values of socialist society.

Of course, the conditions of this judgment were determined by those who were in the position to define what constituted *proper* parenthood – scientists, psychologists, educators, and others, on whose expertise and labor the invisible machinery of social control relied. Insignificant officials operating within the hierarchical channel of command approved the wording with a nod, changed a sentence here and there, and with a rubber stamp magically increased the scientific value of the material. By the time the scientific data reached the official press machine, anonymous and stripped of all individuality, it had acquired an aura of unquestionable truth filled with an authoritarian, yet paternalistic tone. A correct way to be a parent was born.

VI.2 "Enlightened Racism" in Medical Discourse

The 1972 law introduced additional measures for increasing the protection of applicants' rights and for ensuring the safety of the procedure. Among other rules, it specifically stated that women could not be sterilized without their explicit written consent and a full medical examination prior to the procedure.[554] However, these regulations did not stop some doctors from by-passing the requirement of patients' personal consent in the interest of, what they believed was, "general" health. Discussing her experience with the procedure in an interview twenty years later, Ida Horváthová recalled that she saw the doctor write into a form that she was "of Gypsy origin" and that she had "many children." Barbora Boganová said she first signed "something" only moments

[554] *Věstník MZ č.1/1972*, § 4 (on the necessity of the internal exam) and § 5 (on the written consent), 2.

before going under the anesthesia. And Regina Mňačková disclosed that she was threatened by her social worker that if she did not undergo sterilization all her children would be sent to a foster-care institution.[555] The ethnic dimension, though not perceived as such, is the most startling aspect of the local deliberate adjustments of the required procedure. Despite the ethnic neutrality of the sterilization law itself, it was unequivocally Romani women who were identified by regional practitioners as the threat to the "healthy population."

The text of the Sterilization law at least partially explains why it was possible for local doctors and social workers to view the issue strictly as a medical one. The law includes a "List of Medical Indications" that an applicant had to qualify for in order to be granted permission to undergo the procedure. Categories such as "psychopathy with asocial behavior and recurrent criminality;" "severe sexual deviations;" "idiocy and imbecility;" "chronic alcoholism;" "a specific parental pair already having a genetically defective child," etc [...] all address legitimate medical conditions. Even a condition stipulating, for example, that a woman is eligible for sterilization if she is "medically fit and did not give birth to a genetically defective child yet, if expert tests show that she is most likely predisposed to give birth to a genetically defective child in the future," cannot be attacked on medical grounds. However, the ultimate power to precisely define the behavior and condition corresponding to these categories as well as to diagnose a patient with a particular condition or provide the "expert tests," rested in the hands of local medical and social practitioners.[556]

Moreover, the casual wording of several suspicious categories, such as "unfit parenthood" and "multiple children" points to the apparent confusion over the distinctions between medical and social discourses in socialist Czechoslovakia. Clearly social workers did not often need to labor too hard to find the appropriate column to check to satisfy the bureaucratic illusion of competent social health practices. As, for example, Uršula Hečková revealed: "After my mother's death, my father remarried a Czech woman who had five children, like me. When she saw that I got 4,000 [crowns] for sterilization, she

[555] Interviews in PDM, August-September 1997.

[556] *Věstník MZ ČSR and SSR*, 1972, § 15, especially Article IX (Mental Diseases) and Article XV (Genetic Indications.)

went too. But she didn't get a dime."[557] Her testimony implies that the application of designed categories and indications for sterilization were left at the discretion of the local staff to determine who qualified as having "many children" and who did not. While these categories seemed to address social and medical differences, they were inseparable from ethnic associations. The crucial question then is what prompted and enabled the doctors and social workers to make the conceptual leap to use the ethnicity-neutral *protective* law as an ethnically inscribed *punitive* law? Or to put the question differently, why was "Gypsy" almost universally translated as "unhealthy" in Czechoslovak social speech?

In 1972, the same year the Sterilization law was issued, the Ministry of Labor and Social Work issued a "Methodical Handbook for Social Workers of the National Committees" entitled "Care for the Socially Unadjusted (*nepřizpůsobené*) Citizens."[558] The handbook was a compilation of eight theoretical and five empirical articles written by psychologists, sociologists, sexologists, criminologists, lawyers and physicians, all addressing the problems of "socially abnormal, pathological and deviant persons." The introduction to the volume asserted that the "socialist [effort] to prevent criminality, alcoholism, prostitution, sexual deviance, parasitism and other negative phenomena cannot consist only of punitive and repressive measures."[559] It argued that to date, care for "socially unadjusted citizens has not been a component of general social politics" and praised the Ministry of Labor and Social Work in that it "filled the gap [in social work] by instituting comprehensive care for the socially unadjusted citizens serviced by special social workers – social curators."[560]

In the course of four hundred pages, the articles thoroughly define and explain the "unadjustable" (*nepřizpůsobitelní*) citizens, the underlying cause of their non-adaptability, their behavior, the circumstances in which they live,

---

[557] Interviews in PDM. Also, see interviews and statistics concerning sterilization in Pellar and Andrš, in "Statistical Evaluation of Romany Women in East Slovakia - Apendix to the report on the Examination in the Problematic of Sexual Sterilization of Romanies in Czechoslovakia."

[558] *Péče o společensky nepřizpůsobené občany: metodická příručka pro pracovníky národních výborů* (Praha: MPSV, 1972).

[559] *Ibid.*, 1.

[560] *Ibid.*, 2.

and the consequences of their presence for the entire society. It states that there is an "acute interrelationship among the diverse pathological phenomena, such as criminality-alcohol, criminality-parasitism, parasitism-alcohol, alcohol-prostitution, prostitution-parasitism, and so on" and points out that the most important "common denominator of such diverse phenomena of social pathology is precisely their negative social evaluation and their undesirability." According to these studies, "the subjects of these negative phenomena usually constitute a rather small body of deviant, socially not-adapted persons, problem families and conflict groups."[561]

It further argues that the reason why "such phenomena still exist in socialist society, which has succeeded in eradicating material inequalities," is that they are the "residue of the previous capitalist regime." Allegedly, "pathological conditions" and such behavior, travel from generation to generation:

> An individual usually prefers the subculture, norms and values that are closest to him. If a child is raised in a pathological subculture, which is in contradiction with the prevailing culture, he [or she] will become delinquent in a similar process, in which an Eskimo becomes an Eskimo.[562]

The document explains that if "deviant behavior is passed within problem families from generation to generation," it then becomes a "social inheritance" that is hard to eradicate from the society.[563] While Czechoslovak society is considered more advanced in fighting pathology than other countries because "Czechoslovak population is homogenous, socially only mildly stratified, sharing the same culture, which varies only in few insignificant details," it still has to "firmly battle social deviancy."[564] The book explains to the social curators that

> most carriers of socially pathological phenomena come from seriously deficient families. Many criminals, recidivists, alcoholics, prostitutes, citizens avoiding work and other not-adjusted citizens grew up in conditions of broken

---

561 *Péče o společensky nepřizpůsobené občany*, 4-5.
562 *Ibid.*, 9.
563 *Ibid.*, 11.
564 *Ibid.*, 19.

> families, families of alcoholics and otherwise not-adjusted persons, as well as from families with substandard cultural levels.[565]

After the introduction, the handbook discusses various definitions, diagnoses of diseases and pathological conditions, often making recourses to theories of psychology, pathological psychology, toxicology and criminal justice. Not a single time there is any mention of "Gypsies" anywhere in the four-hundred-page-long text. Should there be since it was about "general delinquency and pathology"? Or was it about "Gypsies" after all? Since the book makes a specific claim to present "general informational material about the fundamental problems of socialization and social non-adaptability designed especially for orientation of social workers and curators,"[566] whose work description often dealt with "citizens of gypsy origin," the question about the interchangeability and translatability of these terms in various contexts is crucial to understanding the ways in which discrimination of the Roma functioned in the Czechoslovak social care system.

The rhetoric of this document is a typical example of an obfuscated language that can be understood, interpreted and implemented in a variety of ways. The comparison of definitions and terms used in this handbook and definitions and terms used by various physicians, social workers and state administrators to address the Gypsy question in a number of other contexts reveals that they are strikingly similar and often indistinguishable. Indeed, the terminology used in the Sterilization Decree is in many cases identical. The scientific medical and social discourse was so profusely intertwined with rhetoric used in describing the "actual" problems and conditions of the Roma that the interpretation of these theories and their subsequent translation to practice was left completely open. And as is evident from the plethora of exact quotes, citations and examples shared on the pages of all previous chapters, in which journalistic accounts, cultural production and ordinary people described and spoke about the "Gypsies," society was indeed making the unspoken connection, creating a deep abyss between the "normality" of Czechoslovak world and "pathology" of the Romani one.

---

565 *Péče o společensky nepřizpůsobené občany*, 26.

566 *Ibid.*, 27.

Indeed, very different standards were evoked when discussing sexuality and reproduction of the Roma on the one hand and of Czechs and Slovaks on the other. Demographers in the early 1970s even pointed to "an unnatural sex-ratio among Gypsies," which might result in problematic sexuality of the Roma in general.[567] "Gypsy" reproduction and sexuality were defined explicitly in terms of primitiveness, unhealthiness, and ignorance, while "Czechoslovak" sexuality was defined in terms of civilization, health, rationality, and progress. For example, one weekly exclaimed that "unabashed promiscuity among [gypsy] teenagers and condoned prostitution of gypsy girls with whites are also a norm," while expressing distaste over the "fact" that "13-year-old [gypsies] have more than a theoretical knowledge of procreative acts."[568]

But it was not only the alleged young age of first sexual encounters of the Roma that consternated the "Czechoslovak" society. The most appalling and alarming to proper Czech and Slovak citizens seemed to be the notion of "gypsy inbreeding," which was immediately linked to the horror vision of an increasing mental debility of the whole society. Even the usually sober and pro-Romani weekly *Literární noviny*, reported that the practice of inbreeding among the Roma leads to "crowds of thousands who are illiterate . . . crowds of inferior individuals, parasites and thieves, prostitutes and children running around naked."[569]

This juxtaposition combated the Gypsy question on two fronts: First, it allowed the society to measure the Roma against the Czechs and Slovaks in categories that were defined by Czech and Slovak cultural models, with *Czech* and *proper* functioning as synonyms. Second, relegating the difference between Czechs and Slovaks on the one hand and the Roma on the other hand into the realm of sexuality and reproduction, equipped the society with means to articulate its concerns with Romani ethnicity without being accused of racism. It is not difficult to read between the lines of the decrees in order to

---

[567] Srb, "Cikáni v Československu v roce 1971," *Demografie*, 13:3 (1971.) The "natural" ratio was that of non-Roma Czechoslovak population, which consisted of 51.2% women, while the Roma had "only" 49.96% women. The author also hinted that "lately there are many mixed marriages [...] and a substantial part of the Gypsy female population thus *disappears from the Gypsy population*," demonstrating once again the arbitrariness of the definition of a "Gypsy." (Emphasis mine.)

[568] *Učitelské noviny*, October 5, 1972.

[569] *Literární noviny*, March 5, 1966.

see what interpretations were possible when a suggestive wording met with implicit attitudes toward the Roma smoldering in popular consciousness. Since the Roma were (in official reports, popular jokes, and media images) routinely associated with mentally and socially deviant behavior, even though in theory these categories were free of any mention of ethnic or cultural difference, they were flexible enough to hide social and ethnic concerns under a veil of medical science.

In fact, the Health report of the Slovak government explicitly urges local establishments to make use of such an option:

> The unhealthy population of *gypsy* children is not adequately monitored by the appropriate sectors of Regional Municipal Committees (*ONV*) or by the Ministry of Health of the SSR and that is the reason why *there is no effort being made to find new ways to suppress further unhealthy populations* in these families. *Not even health indications, which could be used as justification for sterilization, are being used.*[570]

The following example reveals how short the distance between official rhetoric and practice on local levels actually was. The Secretary of the Municipal Committee in Jarovnice, a town in Eastern Slovakia where, between 1971 and 1989, 127 Gypsy women out of 2024 were sterilized, complained about the mental retardation of parents and the debility or imbecility (*oligophreny*) of

570 "Selected Problems Associated with the Negative Situation of Health Standards and Health Education of the Gypsy Population," *Sekretariát Komisie vlády SSR pre otázky cigánských obyvatelov*, SKC - 6406/77, Bratislava, July 1977, Ministry of Labor and Welfare of SSR, in PRP, 5. (Emphasis mine.) The existence of this document – even though it is *the only* official governmental document with such rhetoric found during the course of the research for this book – which targets directly and clearly *Gypsies*, identifying them as unhealthy, deficient, and problematic, and urging their sterilization and discrimination, might seem to contradict my main argument that the state rhetoric was ethnically neutral and that the regime did not use the category of ethnicity as a salient way to address the "Gypsy question." However, even in this document "Gypsy" arguably does not refer to Romani ethnicity, but functions precisely as a category of mental and social deviance. The document does, of course, challenge my argument that involuntary sterilization of Romani women was not a direct policy of the regime but a result of complex web of interpretive agency on the part of local practitioners. However, what is key in this context is still the fact that "Gypsy" was not a category of ethnicity, but a label of backwardness and that it was local demographers, physicians and social workers who filled the category with concrete individuals and thus chose *who* the "Gypsies" in the need of sterilization were.

their children. According to her, the "obvious retardation does not have to be measured by any special tests," but is "readily apparent to anybody who sees the way the Gypsies live," as well as by the fact that the "children are unable to succeed in regular elementary school." The chairman of the town argued that "Gypsy women should be sterilized after the second child, without regard to age." The town council also recommended gynecological check-ups of "retarded" Romani girls from fourteen years of age. "Women who give birth to several mentally retarded or otherwise damaged children should be compulsorily sterilized, regardless of age."[571] Neither the town's representatives nor the medical establishment of the town even attempted to deny the history of the sterilization practice. They believed they did a good and necessary deed for the future of *their* nation and they did not seem to question at all the legitimacy of *their* standards of "mental retardation" as a license to sterilize the Roma. Even though the article covering this issue was written in 1990, its author did not bring up the question of potential racism of the town's attitudes towards its Roma a single time. Quite to the contrary, the article is written in an approving manner and entitled "Heaven Must Be Earned."

The Jarovnice town council's sentiments (and its media coverage) blatantly demonstrate how deeply racism was ingrained at least in some regions in the social fabric of Czechoslovak society during the communist regime and how easily it got disseminated as a scientific discourse. Under its auspices, "good intentions in the interest of a healthy population" and scientific racism merged in the highway of discrimination and abuse of human rights.

It is impossible to investigate and find the "correct route" of travel of racist sentiments between institutional orders and popular consciousness, most of which did not use any predictable or recognizable racist rhetoric and instead were ciphered in the rhetoric of social pathology and backwardness. As previous chapters demonstrate, no literature, institutional, academic or popular, allowed for the identification of the Roma as a distinct and sovereign ethnic identity, ascribing any cultural difference to social residue of past neglect. Under the shield of the communist ideology of universal humanity and homogenous social progress, "Gypsy" became a social category curable only

---

571 Pavol Komanický, "Nebo si treba zaslúžiť: O Rómoch a ich svojskej životnej filozófii," *Východ*, April 13-14, 1990, 1-2. Statistics cited in Pelar and Andrš, 20, in ACHC.

through assimilation. Official integrative policies disciplining the Roma found a fertile ground among the otherwise ethnically homogenous population. Prevented from traveling abroad and from engaging with a diverse range of other cultures, the average Czechoslovak citizen formed his or her opinions in relation to the "scientific knowledge" of the "objective inferiority" of the Roma that people were exposed to in media, social institutions and scientific discourse. Conversely, the people who filled the offices of state and Party administration and who issued and implemented these policies were the same people who were acculturated with these norms and expectations about health and sexuality.

One of the most astonishing things about the majority of the assimilation decrees and regulations is how extremely vague and ambiguous they were. And yet, there seemed to be a latent, unspoken consensus by local doctors and social workers all across the country to decode the ambiguity of the decrees in similar ways. Quite remarkably, in the context of the sterilization practice, many local offices translated ethnicity-neutral instructions as a mandate to sterilize Romani women in a belief they were acting in the interest of both the nation and the Roma women themselves. Such a high level of agreement on an ordinary level demonstrates that, contrary to the official rhetoric, racism was a pervasive and vital phenomenon manifesting itself in the everyday life of the society. "Gypsy" was almost *universally* translated into a "Czechoslovak" social speech as "unhealthy," complying with the officially marketed image of a "Gypsy" not as an ethnic/cultural subject, but as a socially/mentally/sexually deviant object. For example, Heitlinger argues that seeking medical care during pregnancy became such a common norm among non-Romani women that the non-attendance of Romani women at prenatal clinics, stemming from their mistrust of non-Romani services, was viewed as synonymous with deviance, indicating an inherent negative predisposition towards the child.[572]

Tracy Smith points out, however, that besides Romani cultural values and their traditional mistrust toward *Gaje* (non-Romani) medicine, the traumatic experience of the Holocaust, when along with the mentally and physically handicapped the Roma were a prime target of Nazi sterilization prac-

[572] Heitlinger, *Reproduction*, 179.

tices and medical tests, is a major factor behind Romani women's apprehension toward hospital care. She asserts that "the Holocaust has had a major impact on the way Romani people in Europe today perceive government-run welfare and health care services" due to the memories of genocidal practices and enforced sterilization associated with these institutions, which have survived in and have formed the Romani collective consciousness.[573]

Given the anti-Roma sentiments, discussed in both popular and scientific literature, it does not seem so surprising that many Czechoslovak doctors did not see ethical problems with executing sterilization procedures on Romani women. To the contrary, they often took the cause up as their own, seeing themselves as saviors of the nation. A gynecologist from Slovakia explained: "Here [in Slovakia] they multiply like rabbits," adding that when he performed cesarean sections on Romani women, he automatically tied their tubes.[574] Similarly, a pediatrician from Northern Bohemia reasoned: "When you see how these Gypsies multiply and you see that it is a population of an inferior quality, and when you look at the huge sums that ha[ve] to be paid for the care of these children, it [the sterilization] is understandable."[575]

In 1975, doctor Jiří Vacek, a chief gynecologist at a hospital in Ústí nad Orlicí, sterilized 29 Romani women for "socio-economic reasons." He published the results of this practice in a professional medical journal *Československá gynekologie*, where he emphasized the financial advantages of sterilization over governmental spending for the institutional upbringing of Romani children. The compensation of 38,800 crowns that the women were together paid for the sterilization[576] was "absolutely insignificant in comparison to the price of 250,000 crowns the state would have to pay for one asylum child, often genetically damaged," Vacek explained, implicitly assuming most Roma children simply would be born mentally handicapped and inevitably end up in

---

573 Smith, "Racist Encounters," 189.

574 Interviews conducted by Pelar and Andrš between 1986 and 1991 and Helsinki Human Rights Watch between 1990 and 1991. In *Struggling for Ethnic Identity: Czechoslovakia's Endangered Gypsies* (New York, L. A., London: Helsinki Human Rights Watch, 1992), 19-35.

575 *Ibid.*

576 This figure came to 1,338 crowns per person, which equaled with a little over one-third of an average monthly salary.

a foster-care institution. "Evidently, from those families, there were a ton of kids in the homes. We more or less knew that," he added.[577]

Once Romani women were identified as eligible and desirable for sterilization, all that was needed for the legality of the procedure was their consent. Libuše Balážová wrote in her application as a reason for sterilization "problems with varicose veins;" before the surgery nobody checked if it was true. Other women either did not know what they signed or were threatened by their social workers. Only Eva Lilová did not try to camouflage her true reason for undergoing the procedure. Without hiding behind a medical condition, she blatantly wrote in: "money." Nobody found that suspicious or alarming. Even so, just before the surgery she ran away with her sister, who was only eighteen at the time. The next day, the social worker brought both of them back for the procedure and, as a punishment, deducted 2,000 crowns from the promised 10,000.[578]

One wonders what ever happened to the 1972 Sterilization Decree that was allegedly designed to increase the protection of applicants' rights. In Slovakia, the rigor of the decree's conditions even prompted the Governmental Bureau for the Questions of the Gypsy Population to complain about it as too limiting for their effort to protect the "healthy population":

> In practice, Gypsy citizens are still being encouraged *too little* to use the possibility of sterilization, in accordance with the 1972 Decree published by the Ministry of Health SSR, in cases *where further pregnancy threatens the healthy population*. In many cases, especially when the parents are mentally retarded, they are not able to realize that for their own health, as well as for the child that would be born psychologically defective, sterilization is necessary. But even such parents [meaning mentally retarded ones] cannot be sterilized without their consent. The only legal way *to circumvent this problem* right now, allowed by §10 of the Civil Code, is to constitute such a citizen legally incapacitated and [officially] assign her a social guardian.[579]

---

[577] Jiří Vacek, "Nové metody v moderní gynekologii," *Československá gynekologie*, 8:8 (1976): 622. And interview with him, in PDM.

[578] Mazalová, 36-42, and in PDM.

[579] Sekretariát Komísie vlády SSR, "Selected Problems…," 6. Paragraphs 7 (ČSR) and 10 (SSR) of the 1972 Sterilization Decree state that: "Applications for sterilization submitted by minors and persons with limited mental capacity have to be accompanied by consent of their legal guardian (i.e. a state-assigned social worker.) For a person who is *fully legally incapacitated*, the entire application is submitted by the legal guardian. In cases when sterilization should be carried out because of mental disease, but the per-

Such circumvention, however, provided enough space for Dr. Vacek. He willingly explained the "simplification" of the consent procedures in his hospital and district. Executing the procedure according to the decree was "for these women, habitually with low IQ, impossible," he explained. That was why he created a special form, where the application was filled by a social worker from the regional welfare office instead of by the woman herself. Vacek boasted that his form served as an example for the entire region.[580] This process made Romani women not only sterile, but also mute.

Like other doctors and social workers, Vacek, too, felt that he understood enough about the inherent inferiority of the Roma to take the decision into his own hands. He is still proud of his method of sterilizing women within 48 hours of giving a birth. "Otherwise, nobody would be able to chase those women back to the hospital," he explained. "Before a woman would sweat out an application, she would be pregnant again," he nonchalantly remarked, justifying his simplification of the procedures by sterilizing Romani women with forced or ill-informed consent. Efficiency, usually used as a unit of measurement, was in the hands of doctors like Vacek "magically" transformed into a powerful instrument of control. For doctors like Vacek, the issue of sterilization was a strictly medical issue, free of any ethnic dimension. The association of the Roma with social and mental deviance became so ingrained in official reports and popular consciousness that even a decade after the collapse of the communist regime (not to mention during the 1970s and 1980s) the allegation that these procedures might have been racist, seems absurd to many. "We did not force anybody . . . we did it decently," insisted Vacek indignantly.[581]

---

son in question is not fully legally incapacitated, the law requires consent of a *guardian assigned for this specific reason by a court*, according to § 29 of the Civil Code." (p.2, all emphases mine.)

[580] Vacek, p. 625. And interview with him, in PDM.

[581] *Ibid.*

VI.3 The Gendered Nature of Romani Sterilization

Romani men are simply missing from the story as told by the documents. They have no voices. They have no bodies. They are not subjected to the pressure to get sterilized "in the interest of the health of the population." They are not being visited by social workers and offered thousands of crowns "in order to help to overcome the adverse living conditions of their families." They are not consulted as husbands, lovers, or fathers. None of the studies, investigations, statistics or doctors mentioned in the literature is concerned with either men's voices in the story or with men as objects of sterilization procedures. And yet, their absence is significant as well, inviting a completely new set of questions, concerns, and sites for historical analysis and interpretation. Dr. Vacek has already foreshadowed one aspect of the sex-specific sterilization policy: convenience. Romani women were simply already there, in the medical establishments, giving births, getting abortions. Many of them got sterilized without their knowledge, while undergoing a different medical procedure. A Romani woman from Slovakia disclosed that she

> went to get an abortion, and they told me, "Be so kind as to sign here before you go in for the abortion." So I signed and went in for the abortion. They just gave me a paper to sign, folded it, and put it into an envelope. I didn't know anything. After the procedure, they told me that something went wrong, that they had to repeat the procedure. I was afraid that part of the fetus would stay in me, so they gave me an injection and brought me upstairs to the operating room. After the operation, when I went downstairs [...] [the other women] told me that I had been sterilized. [...] I was shocked. [...] Now I have a new boyfriend and we want to get married, but I'm shocked because I can't give him any children.[582]

Even if it might have been more medically and economically "efficient" and less painful to sterilize men,[583] it seems that socially and politically it was much more convenient to sterilize women. In modern societies, hospitals

---

[582] A.D. from Krompachy, cited among the interviews conducted by the Helsinki Human Rights Watch, 23.

[583] M. Púchala, "Nepriaznive následky podvazu vajcovodov na ženský organismus," *Praktický lekár*, 69:4 (1989): 138-140. Púchala argues that male vasectomy is faster, more economic and has fewer medical repercussions for the male body than ovarian sterilization has for the female body.

have been recognized as means of tremendous social control, and the situation in the communist societies was not different in this respect. Women's bodies became the canvas on which to paint social deviance. In 1989, doctors Posluch and Posluchová published an academic article in which they argued, based on "legitimate, scientific" studies, that

> the regulation of their [Gypsy] reproduction is necessary even in our advanced society, because it concerns citizens who have overwhelmingly negative attitudes toward work ethics and education. They have a high level of criminality, alcoholism and *women have a tendency toward promiscuity*. Significant is also their cultural and social retardation behind the rest of the population. All this leads to the fact that *their sexual life starts very early*. Young gypsy girls give birth without biological and social readiness for maternity. Another negative aspect is their high fertility, [...] but many gypsy women don't want to use birth control.[584]

These authors define sexuality and reproduction solely as a female problem. While their (meaning *all* Roma's) sexual life allegedly starts earlier, it is the woman on whose body this concern is being played out. Of course, the authors are concerned with health, hygiene and social education when they call for "planned parenthood" among the Roma. Vacek, too, stated that "we particularly place great hopes on expanding the number of sterilizations. [...] Into the future, we expect this form of regulation to increase especially among younger women with fewer children."[585] While one could argue that such statements constitute a "propagation of genocide" and thus could be prosecuted under the §259 of the Czech Penal Code,[586] the authors of such statements have been routinely convinced that sterilization is a social and medical, and not an ethnic or racial, issue. High Romani fertility was, according to these authors, the result of the sexual deviance of Romani women. Thus if one wanted to control Romani reproduction, one had to control the female body.

Active sexual behavior in socialist Czechoslovakia was confined to the realm of heterosexual marriage. Even a woman who deliberately and independently decided to be a single mother officially carried an "illegitimate

---

584 Posluchová and Posluch, 220-223. (Emphasis mine.)

585 Vacek, p. 625. And interview with him, in PDM.

586 *Trestní právo České republiky*. (Praha: Fakulta právní Univerzity Karlovy, 1995), § 259.

child."[587] Proper womanhood was defined by woman's reproductive ability and her motherhood. However, while a proper woman could not have been defined without being associated with a man, a sexually deviant woman was vested with agency of her own. Not only was the concept of monogamy among Romani couples implicitly called into question when evoking promiscuity and prostitution of Romani women, female sexual deviance clearly could not have been solved through male sterilization. Moreover, because of the traditional cultural bond between masculinity, sexuality, and natural parenthood in Czechoslovakia, the interference with men's ability to naturally procreate would have resulted in their public emasculation, and hence in a threat to the patriarchal order of the society as a whole.

The Romani woman was singled out and overwhelmingly blamed for the high Romani fertility rate and her body was targeted as the key to Gypsy planned parenthood. However, the number of children in the family was, besides mutual desire for them, often a logical result of existing gender power relations rather than a consequence of ignorance, irrationality or irresponsibility. In Romani culture, as in most East European societies in general, traditional patriarchal gender norms were the prevailing pattern of family and sexual life.[588] Women were still in subordinate positions in the relationship: the man "took care of the sexual act" and the woman was expected to bear the consequences of his irresponsibility or failure in case of pregnancy.[589] Thus, ironically, by becoming pregnant, the Romani woman was seen as the locus of the "fertility problem," which in turn could be addressed only through the control and regulation of her body. "It is important to teach gypsy *women* to [...] better plan *their* population," claimed a member of a Regional Commission for the Questions of the Gypsy Population in the late 1960s.[590]

The Ministry of Health proclaimed its immense attention to the "care for gypsy woman, mother and child" and reported that it succeeded in getting

---

587 Heitlinger, *Reproduction*, 243.

588 *Ibid.*, 144.

589 Mirjana Morokvasic, "Sexuality and Control of Procreation," in *Of Marriage and the Market: Women's Subordination in International Perspective,* eds. K. Young, C. Wolkowitz and R. McCullagh (London: CSE Books, 1981), 139.

590 Kier, "Práce okresní komise pro otázky cikánského obyvatelstva v Českém Krumlově," 215. (Emphasis mine.)

gypsy women to give birth in institutions "even though many agreed only under the threat of their child support money being withdrawn."[591] Such logic and argumentation made it also potentially easy for Roma men not to fully comprehend the discriminatory nature of these measures and instead to perceive a potential loss of financial child support as the woman's fault and blame her for it, opening the door to domestic violence or other subordination and abuse. The Ministry also complained that "gypsy women refused to take birth control and only in exceptional cases [doctors] succeeded in implanting intrauterine birth control."[592] While it was quite difficult for non-Romani Czechoslovak women to obtain birth control unless they were married, already had children and the health practitioners decided it was "good for them,"[593] the Commission for Gypsy Population recommended since 1967 to all National Councils that their social and health care workers should "guarantee the widespread extension of birth control use among gypsy women by any means of urging and health education."[594] Since many Romani women refused birth control based on their cultural beliefs and values (which nobody else seemed to care about), often the only means of "urging" and "educating," which social and health care workers felt were left, was the Romani women's sterilization.

Many articles and studies concerned with the Romani sterilization indicate that many Romani women allegedly underwent sterilization voluntarily, attracted to the high financial incentives connected to the procedure.[595] The question is, of course, whether consent based on financial incentives offered to a person belonging to the economically weakest segment of the population and living in substandard social conditions can be considered truly voluntary. Applying the concept of free choice and agency in this particular way comes close to blaming the victims themselves. However, surprisingly, none of these

---

[591] SNA Bratislava, Fond Povereníctva SNR pre zdravotníctvo 1960-1968, č. kr. 8, č. sp. 52.

[592] *Ibid.*

[593] Heitlinger, *Women and State Socialism*, 186.

[594] SNA Bratislava, Fond Povereníctva SNR pre zdravotníctvo 1960-1968, č. kr. 8, č. sp. 52.

[595] See especially statistics published by Pelar and Andrš in Lau Mazeril Foundation, in ACHC.

articles or studies attempts to investigate the potential of the reversal of these policies to empower or even protect Romani women.

Czech psychiatrist Radkin Honzák argues that while "some psychiatrists consider a woman after a uterus removal to be healthy, as a psychiatrist I do not consider this a healthy condition. In a psychological self-evaluation, a woman after sterilization is different than before."[596] While such essentialist interpretations of gender might generally coincide with traditional Romani perception of a healthy woman, which is based on assumptions of female fertility as the necessary precondition for "normal" womanhood, not all Romani women felt bound by that tradition. At least some of them preferred having a control over their own bodies, sexuality and life choices to considerations of proper womanhood, whether prescribed by medical authorities or Romani cultural values.[597]

One of the very first books published by the first independent Romani publishing house *Romaňi Čhib*, established in 1990, was a novel based on a true story by a well-known Romani writer Ilona Ferková called *She Destroyed Her Life For Money* (*Mosarďa peske o dživipen anglo love*). Next to other books published by this press, which narrated gypsy fairy tales, legends, magic stories, wisdom of the elders, and other oral-based fiction, this was the only story that dealt with realities of Romani survival under the Communist regime. Significantly, it was a story about the trauma of sterilization, whose main character, a young Romani woman "succumbed to the high financial seduction [of sterilization] and secretly got rid of her womanhood."[598] Her husband soon gets to know about it and is never able to forgive his wife for undergoing the procedure, which destroys their marriage and life. Even worse is that the young heroine herself realizes what indiscretion she got lured into

---

596 Radkin Honzák, cited in Štěpán, *Moderní lékařství*, 42.

597 See also Marilyn Strathern, *The Gender of the Gift: Problems with Women and Problems with Society in Melanesia* (Berkeley: University of California Press, 1988). Strathern warns against assumptions that women everywhere are the same, that women's speech reveals "a woman's point of view," and that women always speak from the gender identity of "woman." She urges the necessity of investigating the forms of power and discourse that constitute the frames and contexts in which women enact their choices.

598 Ilona Ferková, *Zničila si život pro peníze – Mosarďa peske o dřivipen anglo love*. (Praha: Romani Čhib, 1990). Description cited from the introduction to the book.

– her womanhood and entire meaning of her existence is indeed vested in her reproductive capability and thus her barrenness makes her completely unworthy, in the eyes of herself, her husband and the whole community and her life is over.

The story is remarkable for its lack of any moralizing or accusing the regime of forcing the financial incentives on Romani women. There is not a single word of criticism of "the inhuman and implicitly genocidal practices of the assimilatory regime," as Hübschmannová calls the communist sterilization.[599] Yet its absence is a very powerful tool for considering the personal dilemmas and intricacies of exercising individual agency and power in the face of the double oppression of regime discrimination and strict cultural values. This story, as well as the story of Eva Lilová mentioned above, who also decided "voluntarily" and "for money" to undergo sterilization, demonstrates the complexities of decision making Romani women faced and made.

Being often squeezed between economic difficulties and gender subordination, undergoing sterilization might have been for at least some of them one of few ways of exercising control over their bodies and lives. Margita Lakatošová, for example, confided that despite her husband's disapproval, she decided to undergo sterilization because "[she] couldn't defend herself against him." She complained that "he just doesn't care [if we have more children] but it's impossible, we can't feed them. We already have three."[600] These experiences challenge the interpretation that Romani women have been only silent victims of sterilization practices. This reality does not negate the violation of the many Romani women who did not have any control over their bodies or were misinformed about the procedure. But it does suggest that the Romani women who have been sterilized (and who constitute the existing statistics), especially those who underwent the procedure in the late 1980s and early 1990s, might not all belong demographically to the same segment of the population and their experiences should not be universalized. Moreover, it points to Romani women's ability to transform the practices

599 Hübschmannová, introduction to Ferková's second collection of essays *Čorde Čhave – Ukradené děti* (Brno: Společenství Romů na Moravě, 1996), 5.

600 Oral interviews with Margita Lakatošová, Prague, August 13, 16, and 24, 1997.

meant to control them to their advantage and to take charge over their own bodies.[601]

VI.4 The Thin Ice of Genocide

In the mid 1990s, when the discussion about Romani sterilization was at its peak, many Romani advocates, as well as the sterilized women themselves, called the sterilization practices in Czechoslovakia during the 1970s and 1980s "Romani genocide," or even "a new Holocaust."[602] There is, undoubtedly, convincing evidence that at least several hundred Romani women across the country were sterilized. However, because of the specific set of implications tied to concepts such as "ethnic cleansing" or "Holocaust," it is dangerous and detrimental to historical analysis to use such terms in carefree way. Many of the current inquiries into the issue of Roma sterilization ambiguously cry out that there was "a conspiracy" to annihilate the entire Romani population in Czechoslovakia, often starting out with and/or heavily drawing on comparisons of Czechoslovak and Nazi sterilization practices. "They wanted to exterminate us," insisted several interviewed Roma women on the pages of a serious Czech contemporary magazine.[603]

Without ridiculing or deprecating these real feelings of victimization, it is important to investigate the circumstances of the laws, policies, reports and internal memos, as well as the personal involvement and responsibility of individual legislators, doctors and social workers before supporting the sweeping charges of government-directed genocide. Moreover, such vague accusations often tend to view problems in black and white terms, drawing on a simple dichotomy of an omnipresent party apparatus on the one hand and an in-

---

[601] In terms of Roma women's empowerment it is also remarkable, as mentioned earlier, that in the Ostrava region, involuntarily sterilized Romani women recently founded their own organization where they meet, discuss their experiences, offer each other support and plan together legal actions to be taken against their violation. Honus, *Právo*, 12.10. 2007.

[602] For example, Charta 77; Giňa, "Dopis na romské téma"; Helsinki Human Rights Watch, *Struggling For Ethnic Identity*, and a variety of articles in contemporary Czech magazines and newspapers.

[603] Mazalová, *Týden*. (And interviews in PDM).

nocent population on the other – a concept that the post-Cold War East European historiography has been successfully challenging. This chapter has attempted to demonstrate the complexity of the practice and the crucial role of lower-level professionals in the process of translation of official ethnically neutral policy into ethnically inscribed practice.

Nonetheless, it is neither surprising nor ridiculous that comparisons of sterilization under the communist regime with the Holocaust experience preoccupy the minds of many Roma and their advocates. The Holocaust became, in a sense, the cornerstone of the modern Roma identity. The collective memory of the tragedy in which ninety-six percent of the Czech and Moravian Roma perished has served as the unifying force for both the survivors and the new generations of the Czechoslovak Roma. Moreover, comparative approaches toward communism and Nazism are at the core of many popular debates and academic studies.[604] As discussed earlier, the Romani Holocaust experience of "scientific testing" left a deep scar in Roma's ability to trust medical and social institutions in any subsequent regime. Given this context, it would be problematic to simply dismiss the tendency and urge to collapse the circumstances of the two sterilization practices into one as acts of imagination or melodrama.

Moreover, even without recourse to Romani collective memory and using the Holocaust as a referent for comparison, there is at least partial evidence from the socialist period itself for taking the charges of potential genocide seriously. Since 1995, The Bureau of the Documentation and Investigation of the Crimes of Communism (*Úřad dokumentace a vyšetřování zločinů komunismu* – ÚDV) has been investigating the charges of alleged Romani genocide connected to the sterilization practices in socialist Czechoslovakia. Paragraph 259 of the Czech Penal Code states specifically that a policy (or a set of policies) restricting a biological reproduction of any ethnic, racial, or religious group, adopted with the objective to exterminate that group is considered a genocide.[605] However, "I cannot believe only the victims," says Pavel Bret, the deputy director of ÚDV. Bret argues that in order for the ÚDV to be

[604] See for example Ian Kershaw and Moshe Lewin, eds., *Dictators Unleashed: Historical Approaches to Nazism and Stalinism* (Cambridge University Press, 1996).
[605] *Trestní právo ČR*, § 259.

able to accuse the former Czechoslovak Communist government of genocidal practices against the Roma, the organization would have to demonstrate that *the government's objective* was to suppress the Romani population.[606]

For example, a Special Decree of the Ministry of Health of CSSR from 1988 states that

> [c]itizens who, according to the special regulations, undergo a medical procedure *in the interest of the healthy population* and *in order to overcome adverse living conditions of their family*, are entitled a one-time financial or material compensation from the Regional Municipal Committees (*ONV*).[607]

The question is, of course, how a procedure that helps to heal the population can lead to overcoming personal adverse living conditions. The answer lies in the connection between the mysterious procedure (sterilization) and the financial incentives offered to Romani women in an attempt to decrease Romani fertility. One would have to be purposefully blind not to at least consider this connection and to argue for the innocence of these statements. But Bret explains that

> if the legal language [of the health decrees] demonstrates that the motivation for sterilization was the *healthy development of the individual* and not a suppression of population, I cannot prove [...] that it was genocide.[608]

Bret's ÚDV, of course, investigates the *institutional* crimes of Communism. It is not concerned with personal crimes of individuals involved in the process, unless those individuals directly followed documented official orders. Moreover, after the split of Czechoslovakia into two separate countries on January 1, 1993, the ÚDV investigates the role of either federal institutions of the CSSR or the state institutions of the Czech Republic, but not the institutions of the Slovak Republic during the time of the Czechoslovak Federation. Czechoslovakia had only one federal body dealing with the Gypsy question, the National Council for Questions of the Gypsy Population, created in 1966, which dealt primarily with the issues of housing relocation and migration of

---

606 Interview with Pavel Bret, August 1997, in PDM. (Emphasis mine.)

607 *Vyhláška MPSV CSR* No. 152/1988 Sb, in USAP. (Sbírka zákonů ČSSR, Částka 33, § 35, 965.) (Emphasis mine.)

608 Interview with Pavel Bret, August 1997, in PDM. (Emphasis mine.)

the Roma.[609] Issues of education, labor, crime, health and reproduction were relegated to the appropriate ministries of both federal republics. Hence when dealing with policies concerning sterilization, delinquency, reproduction and mental health, one has to deal with two sets of largely analogous, but not entirely synonymous, policies and documents issued individually in each republic.

The language of the 1972 Sterilization Decree, issued in identical wording by the Health Ministries of both republics, is strictly ethnicity-neutral. While virtually all Roma could have been deliberately defined into (at least one) of the medical categories in the "List of Indications for Sterilization," (which is, in other words, suggesting that these categories opened a window for ethnically motivated abuses) such an allegation is based on an interpretation of the policies in their historical and cultural context. However, the official report of the Slovak Governmental Bureau for the Questions of the Gypsy Population, written for the Slovak Ministry of Labor and Welfare in 1977, is surprisingly candid. It states that

> even a backward Gypsy woman can calculate that it is more economically advantageous for her to give birth every year, because for her fifth child, and every one following that, she will get from the Welfare office much more money than is the current compensation rate for sterilization. For that reason health experts recommend to increase this [the sterilization] financial contribution to 5,000 crowns. With Gypsy population, it is not unusual to see families with too many members where there are a lot of chronic alcoholics, freeloaders (*příživníci*) and habitual offenders (*recidivisti*) who do not know how to raise children properly. From a social point of view, *further population is not desirable for such people*. For this reason it seems necessary to expand the decree of the Ministry of Health SSR about the practice of sterilization to include an approval for the procedure not only on medical grounds, but on *social* grounds as well.[610]

The unambiguous rhetoric of this document, explicitly urging sterilization of Romani women as the means of solving the "social problem" connected to the Gypsy question, is stunning. Even though it is likely that the majority of people concerned with the Romani sterilization would not be familiar with this document because the archives were not open to the general public,

---

[609] Kostelancik, 312.

[610] Sekretariát Komísie vlády SSR, "Selected Problems…," 7. (Emphasis mine.)

suspicion about the existence of such reports and recommendations laying on dusty archive shelves or locked in the drawers of the then-responsible officials is what fuels the public, mostly international, outcry about this issue. It suddenly becomes more understandable why charges of genocide dominate these discussions and that such documents could constitute proof for these allegations. At the moment, there are several of the Czechoslovak sterilization cases, compiled together as one joint lawsuit, being processed at the European Court of Human Rights in Strasbourg. The court's ultimate verdict will be, of course, of tremendous importance in regard to the charges of genocide and might prompt more comprehensive legal investigations and historical research into this issue. However, based on the evidence found in the course of the research for this book, it is impossible and would be both analytically flawed and historically inaccurate to argue that the Czechoslovak communist government engaged in a premeditated and concerted genocide against the Romani population.

The circumstances surrounding the practice of sterilization show how important the regulation of sexuality was in reaffirming lines of ethnic difference between the Roma and non-Roma in socialist Czechoslovakia. Sterilization among Romani women was encouraged because cultural means (i.e. education or labor ethic) were seen as ineffective to remedy the problem of "Gypsy" deviance. Social deviance was allegedly so ingrained in the "Gypsy" character that it was essential to cure it through biological means. Before the Roma could even start to be civilized, they first had to catch up with the "Czechoslovak" model of parenthood and sexuality. It does not seem accidental that Roma's alleged derelict parenting and careless reproduction were at the core of the concerns with the "Gypsy question." Only after the Roma fit into these generally accepted norms of social behavior, there was hope for them to become "civilized." At the same time, this tendency also demonstrates that normative sexuality, parenthood and reproduction served not only as a way for the non-Roma to control the Roma, but also as a self-disciplinary tool for the regulation of the non-Roma Czechoslovak population's behavior as well.

However, because the Roma were seen as unable to conform to the normative model of social and sexual behavior on their own, they had to be helped through sterilization. Since the discourse on parenthood and sexuality in general was essentially gendered, this aspect logically extended to the issue of sterilization. While sterilization was seen as a possible solution to the Gypsy question as such, in reality it was strictly a female issue. In order to regulate the reproduction of the Roma, the Czechoslovak society had to regulate the bodies of Romani women. This conceptual link resulted in a gendered notion of Romani deviance, since Romani fertility became a problem of allegedly sexually irresponsible and promiscuous Romani women, and since other forms of social deviance, such as mental retardation, were born within the woman's body.

While those involved in the sterilization process did not see any connection between the politics of ethnicity and ideology of normative sexuality and reproduction, this chapter demonstrates that such a connection deserves to be seriously considered. The latent consensus of the majority of local social workers and local doctors to translate the ambiguity of the official medical lingo into a "discourse on ethnicity," suggests that, contrary to the official rhetoric, racism remained a salient and pervasive feature at the everyday social level of the society. Clearly, the country practiced a double standard of citizenship based on ethnic grounds. The meaning of "Gypsiness" kept shifting to fit various individual and collective senses of identity, permeating both gender/sexual and racial/ethnic matrixes. It seems feasible to argue that the construction of ethnicity in socialist Czechoslovakia was heavily informed and inextricably linked with the discourse on social deviance and sexuality.

Moreover, the circumstances of the sterilization practice in socialist Czechoslovakia show that the communist regime was far from exercising a total control over all aspects of the society. In fact, this chapter demonstrated that there was no such clear division between the "regime" and the "people." Power could be found at all levels of the society, as "obvious" intentions and objectives of various laws and policies were transformed and acquired radically different meaning in the hands of those who interpreted and implemented them. Equally importantly, this chapter argued that the story of sterilization cannot be written as a simple study in victimology or identity politics. Even though the evidence and current lawsuits suggest that the story will get only increasingly more complex and difficult to untangle, further research needs to be conducted in order to better understand the social mechanisms that informed the construction of ethnicity and sexuality in Czechoslovakia under the communist regime.

Conclusions

Xenophobia and Racism in the Past and Present

On October 13, 1999, little after 4 a.m., a construction crew with the assistance of the city police secretly erected a large wall, soon to be heralded as the city's "most famous structure of the century," in the North Bohemian city of Ústí nad Labem. The sixty-meter-long and two-meter-high wall was hastily built in a mere five hours, dividing a residential street into two opposing rows of houses and segregating the residents of each side from the other. On one side of the street stood the neatly tended houses of the city old-timers, who initially demanded a wall be built to protect their quaint and orderly homes from those across from them. On the other side crouched "bareflats" (*holobyty*), town-owned apartment houses for "non-payers" (*neplatiči*), residents who failed to pay regular rent, mostly members of the Romani ethnic minority.

The issue that prompted the old-timers to construct the wall, and which shot the sleepy city into the international media spotlight, was not so much the financial irresponsibility of these "careless" residents, as it was charges of their "unbearable noise, mess and smell"[611] brought up against them by the respectable citizens from across the street.[612] Though the concrete structure, officially called the "anti-noise" wall (*protihluková zeď*), has come to represent in Western eyes the recurring problem of racism in post-communist politics, the Wall was also one of the latest episodes of another, and perhaps more fundamental, story: how Czech and Slovak society has historically managed ethnic relations through discourses on hygiene, normality, and deviance.

"The Wall on Matiční," as the case began to be known, immediately monopolized national media attention. Between mid October, when the wall

---

611 "Soud: Romka za zeď v Matiční nedostane 100 tisíc ani omluvu", *Lidové noviny*, December 19, 2001, 2.

612 Already at the end of May 1998, when the building of the wall on Matiční street was only a subject of an emerging debate, one of the most prominent international journals *The Economist* ran an article on the controversy, revealing critical attitudes of the international community and condemning the racism of the potential wall. See, "Ghettoes for Czech Gypsies," *The Economist* (May 30, 1998), 50.

went up and the end of November, when it finally went down, the country's three top daily newspapers (*Mladá Fronta DNES*, *Lidové Noviny* and *Právo*) ran a total of 143 articles related to the issue.[613] All top political officials of the Czech Republic, including the then-president Václav Havel, repeatedly voiced out their positions and many visited the street in order to learn "what was really going on." In his typical straightforward fashion, Havel called the wall a "symbol of Czech racism and discrimination against the Roma."[614] Roma politicians, activists and sympathizers protested on the spot, building a tent city in front of the wall. Seminars, conferences, TV debates and radio talk shows about "The Wall" were organized almost every week. The questions asked and debated were always the same: Is the wall racist or not? Does a city (or citizens) have the right to build such a wall? What does the construction of such a wall mean?

Attitudes and answers to these questions were sharply divided. Those who defended it argued that it had nothing to do with racism, but was a reasonable outcome of the failure of those across the street to respect the needs of the elderly residents for a peaceful living environment. Indeed, the supporters of the wall often pointed out that among those fenced off were not only Roma but also a few "Czechs" who failed to pay rent and acted in similarly inconsiderate manner. They also repeatedly argued that the wall was needed because of social differences, not ethnic ones, even though the asocial behavior, noise, and smell of the problematic residents were unmistakably identified as "gypsy." The mayor of the town, Pavel Tošovský, even flew with pictures of the wall to a Roma seminar in Helsinki in an attempt "to explain again why the wall is not racist."[615]

By contrast, the opponents of the wall (who included the entire political leadership of the country) argued that it was a "Great Chinese Wall separating the Czech Republic from the rest of Europe" and unanimously wanted to

---

613 Newton archival press agency.

614 Václav Havel, "Hovory z Lán" (*Conversations from Lány*), a regular live weekly Sunday one-hour radio talkshow broadcasted from the presidental chateau of Lány, in which the president critically commented on domestic and international political issues. (November 8, 1999).

615 Pavel Tošovský, *Mladá Fronta DNES*, November 11, 1999.

see it down.[616] They all agreed that it affirmed negative sentiments that *could lead* to racism and heightened animosities between the Romani minority and the non-Romani majority. On the whole, the political leadership was worried much more about the country's international image as a prospective member of the European Union committed to human and civic rights than it was interested in considering the underlying motivations for building the wall in the first place. Only Havel and the Government Human Rights Representative Petr Uhl consistently acknowledged that the Czech Republic continues to grapple with implicit and occasionally even explicit racism. Havel openly criticized the mayor of the town for building the wall by saying that "[the mayor] probably thinks that part of his obligation as an elected official is also to share all racist prejudices of his constituents."[617] Other politicians and public figures reassured the public that Czech society is not, nor has ever been, racist.[618]

At the end of November, after six weeks of constant controversy, protest, confrontations, bickering, stand-offs, and heavy political pressure from Prague, the wall went down, in the very same manner as it went up: at night, quickly, with police assistance and, as the mayor explained the following day, "secretly in order not to cause a commotion."[619] The city, unable to reconcile the pressure from angry residents demanding the wall on the one side and the government and Roma activists insisting on its removal on the other, bought out the private houses of the residents who complained about the unruliness of the Roma, giving them a chance to move out. Rather than recognizing the ethnic segregation the wall physically and symbolically entailed, many non-Romani residents of the city considered the disappearance of the wall as their defeat. "The ceramic fence gives a nice esthetic impression. To

---

616 Petr Uhl, talkshow "*Aréna*", TV Nova, October 8, 1998.

617 Václav Havel, *Mladá Fronta DNES*, October 18, 1998.

618 On the contrary, the mayor of Ústí nad Labem criticized the concerns, asserting that it is "pseudo-protectors of human rights like the president or Mr. Uhl [who] do not come with any constructive solutions and only heighten tensions and emotions." (Hruška about Havel, *MFD* Oct. 10, 1998) In a rather absurd statement reacting to protests about the city's brutal reaction to the Romani activists protest camping in front of the wall, the press secretary of the town council announced that "if the Roma-by-profession on Matiční street had their foreign cars parked properly . . . and did not disturb local respectable residents by the loud ringing of their cellular phones, then it might be possible to tolerate their tent potlatch." (Milan Knotek, *MFD*, November 8, 1999).

619 Pavel Tošovský, *MFD*, November 26, 1999.

remove it is just reverse racism," exclaimed a businessman from a nearby town. Another resident explained:

> We are conceding too much to various protectors of human rights and to the Roma themselves. I fear that soon it will be us, who will have to emmigrate abroad, not them. Everything, whether it is criminality, drugs, whatever comes to your mind, everything was first started by the Roma. And the wall? I would love to have such a pretty fence around my house.[620]

Others echoed similar sentiments about the lack of ethnic problems in the city:

> I don't understand why the government sticks its nose into our affairs. The Roma in Ústí nad Labem are in no way discriminated against. I would like to see the wall standing and the houses not bought out. Why can't the Roma behave as decently as we do?[621]

A hairdresser from the town's neighborhood of Březno wrote that

> I visited London and even there Englishmen build around their luxurious houses tall walls so I don't understand who minds the Matiční wall. On the other hand, I know several Roma who are decent and so clean that you can eat in their houses off of the floor. I don't understand why other Roma can't be like that, too.[622]

Many, if not most, Czechs, who sympathized with the old-timers repeatedly denied the significance of ethnicity as a salient category for interpreting differences between residents. Yet ethnicity was everywhere present in public debate and opinion polls on the matter, though it was rarely mentioned explicitly or even recognized as the point of controversy. The preoccupation of public opinion with differences in hygiene, health, noise and behavior between the residents on Matiční street underscores how perceived "social" differences stood for and were easily translated into a silent but unmistakable ethnic hierarchy between the Roma and the larger non-Romani society.

---

620 *Mladá fronta DNES*, "Hotline", November 25, 1999.

621 *Ibid.*

622 *Ibid.* Another caller to the *MFD* hotline shared her view that "I disagree with removing the wall, but if it were possible, I would take the material from the wall to my country house." (November 26, 1999).

Complaints about "noise" or "uncleanliness" were ethnically-neutral and purportedly unbiased terms that described problems in social behavior; at the same time, these terms acted as codes that took on ethnically relevant valuations within the minds and imagination of those engaged in public discourse. Charges of impropriety or uncleanliness appeared to have nothing to do with ethnic discrimination if one took language at face value, yet ideas like "impropriety" or "uncleanliness" were culturally meaningful precisely because they signified Romani behavior. In turn, such ethnicity-free language can be an invaluable tool for justifying and designing social policies and projects that intentionally, but never explicitly, discriminate against the Roma, as the Matiční case has shown. This ability of Czech society to manage ethnic tensions by translating ethnically-neutral language into ethnically discriminatory judgments did not merely emerge as a problem of post-communism but, as this book has demonstrated, slowly and systematically developed during the communist period as a way for Czechoslovak society to deal with the "Gypsy question" in line with Party ideology.

In an article entitled "What is Racism?" a well-known and widely-respected social critic and columnist of the major daily *Mladá fronta DNES*, Martin Komárek, whose commentaries "represent the official position of the newspaper," attempted to sort out confusions and controversies on the nature of racism.[623] Komárek presented several controversial issues, such as the wall on Matiční Street; the "G" that Prague airport workers wrote into travel documents of "those Czech travelers to Britain, who were brown"; the "R" that Czech state employment agencies wrote in the personal files of Romani applicants for work; and the newest questionnaires for physicians asking them to answer questions about the "health of the Roma." After elaborating on the substance of what is and is not racism, Komárek came to the conclusion that from these examples, only the wall was a racist endeavor, because it "objectively cut across racial lines." He was one of only very few public figures who directly pointed out the discrepancy between the official interpretation of the wall as a "technical barrier" against the noise and mess of the "non-respectable" residents to "protect" the "decent ones" on the other side, and,

---

[623] Martin Komárek, "Co je rasismus?," in *Mladá fronta DNES*, November 22, 1999, 8.

on the other hand, the racial claim that "everyone respectable is white and all the hooligans are Roma!"[624]

However, Komárek failed to see that racism has discursive and symbolic properties, not only "objectively" real ones. To him, "there is nothing wrong or deviant about the fact that physicians research the health of the Roma as long as they observe the standards of professional ethics." There is also nothing wrong with providing employment programs that appear to some as "reverse racism, because it is true that among the unemployed there are more Roma than whites and [the Roma] really did not have equal starting conditions." In such a case, according to Komárek, "it is always better to help than not to help." Similarly, while the "G" which the British embassy in Prague asked the Czech airport personnel to write into the passports of their "brown" customers "might be perceived as racist," he argues, "it was rather [Czech] inherent subservience and lack of diplomacy" than racism because behind these requests was "nothing more" than a "reasonable desire to simplify the hectic traffic at Heathrow." Komárek concluded the article by stating that the wall on Matiční street was not just racist but that it produced an "unwanted side effect, for now the Roma feel threatened even by perfectly rational scientific research and virtuous employment programs."[625]

Komárek's commentary represents a widely-shared contemporary attitude toward the nature of racism in the Czech Republic and the deeply-seated belief that racial discrimination, as a phenomenon, is alien to Czech society. Such a view ignores that, time and again in Czechoslovak history, linguistic practices subjected the Roma to disciplinary institutions and forms of control on the basis of dubious ideological presuppositions about what those linguistic practices intended. With an armory of linguistic weapons appropriated from popular gypsy myths to define and subordinate their object, communist official discourse generated a myriad of normative evaluations about the Roma that were so resonating that they still have the power to convince almost two decades after the fall of communism. These evaluations deprived the Roma of public recognition of their ethnicity, naturalized cultural forms of life into sociologically analyzable data points, exaggerated, reconfig-

---

[624] Komárek, 8.
[625] *Ibid.*

ured and constructed those data into ideologically consistent myths of Romani behavior, and then attached demeaning and denigrating beliefs to them. Although "objectively real" practices, such as sterilization, were certainly racist and had long lasting effects on the relations between Roma and non-Romani society, such racist acts were made possible through discursive frameworks that gave "objective reality" to the forms of deviance the regime wanted to eliminate.

Since the communist regime was ideologically restricted in dealing with the "Gypsy question" by having to appear egalitarian and as a bulwark of social justice, the strategy most commonly used by the regime was to appropriate popular discourse about gypsy lifestyles, construct sciences, policies and discourses around those myths, and then use the rhetoric of deviance and asociality produced by those institutions to legitimate subjugating, ethnically targeted practices. Because the politics of the "Gypsy question" deployed such resonating forms of discursive power, their effects do not simply die off with ideology or political institutions. Since Romani discrimination is embedded in language, it defies historical periodization that understands political power as merely institutional. As contemporary forms of racism in the Czech Republic indicate, there is a great deal of continuity rather than discontinuity with the politics of the "Gypsy question" under communism.

"Free to Hate"

The title of Eric Hockenos' book on the explosion of racial violence in Eastern Europe after the collapse of communism connotes the view that contemporary racism and ethnic violence reflect a resurgence of attitudes and beliefs towards others that were pent up during communism but can now be freely expressed. The "pent up" thesis evokes imagery of severe acts of physical violence and abuse, such as the Romanian pogroms of 1996, to argue that skinheads, militants and other "new" radicals have led the right-wing movements in Eastern European countries. The Czech Republic has had its own acts of violence of this kind. One of the most horrifying cases happened in a mid-sized town of Klatovy on February 21-23, 1991. In the course of two days, a group of thirty town residents, not members of the skinhead movement, attacked a Romani family, which was causing allegedly "objective trouble" in the local neighborhood. The attack culminated by rabid rampage assault, ending in a murder of the 21-year-old son of the family. A partial group of the assailants was found guilty of ten criminal charges, including murder. However, the charge of racially motivated attack was not among them.[626]

In another incident, in May 1995, a couple of skinheads broke into a house of a long-term Romani resident in the small town of Žďár nad Sázavou and beat him to death with a baseball bat. This time, nobody dared to even question the racist motivation of this horrid act. Arguably, it was also the first case to truly shake Czech collective consciousness and challenge the popular and state attitudes toward racial violence. The most controversial case happened in September 1993, when a young Romani boy jumped into a river out of fear from a group of skinheads, who demonstrated and loudly marched through the town of Písek and started to chase the boy. The group of skinheads prevented the boy from getting out of the river, even though he was clearly struggling in the cold water and calling for help, thus causing him to drown. It took the regional court four years to start prosecuting the offenders, even though their identity was known the whole time. In the end, four defendants were found guilty of indirect manslaughter and sentenced to two and half years in jail. Once again, charges of racial motivation were not listed among the crimes committed.[627] In 2006, the Ministry of Interior of the Czech Republic officially reported 248 extremist and hate-related crimes and the International Helsinki Federation for Human Rights (IHF) recorded in the country 25 cases of explicit racial violence, most of them directed against the Roma. In the small town of Svitavy, local Roma even evacuated the town when 90 skinheads demonstratively marched through the streets.[628]

---

[626] Hana Frištenská, "Interetnický konflikt po roce 1989 s ohledem na soužití s Romy", in *Romové v České republice*, 244-266.

[627] *Ibid.* Instances of physical racial violence against members of other races and citizens of other countries include a stabbing to death of a Sudanese university student in 2000, the beating of an Indian diplomat in 1999, and stabbing to death of several Vietnamese and Chinese merchants in the late 1990s.

[628] European Union (EU): European Union Agency for Fundamental Rights, *Report on Racism and Xenophobia in the Member States of the EU* (2007).

On the whole, however, the most troubling dimensions of "Czech hate" are not such reactionary, cathartic acts, but involve normative frameworks that give credence and acceptability to the importance of controlling socially dangerous and deviant elements of society.[629] Based on regularly conducted surveys and studies since the early 1990s, contemporary Czech society can perhaps be best defined as deeply latently xenophobic. The results of these inquiries indicate that "Czech society," as a collective body represented by the respondents, disapproves of racism, its expressions and outcomes. However, the causes of racism are not seen as originating in the lack of tolerance of the majority, but rather in allegedly "unacceptable behavior" of the racially and ethnically different. Consequently, these surveys reveal that Czech society does not see the solution for racial and ethnic tensions in the transformation of the attitudes of the population at large but in the stricter enforcement of "others" to assimilate to the norms and values held by the majority. Finally, most respondents have not considered racism as their own problem or problem of their environment but instead asserted that racism is either a "theoretical issue" or a far removed problem.[630]

<http://fra.europa.eu/fra/material/pub/racism/report_racism_0807_en.pdf> [Accessed Nov. 16, 2007].

629 See, for example, Helsinki Human Rights Watch, *Destroying Ethnic Identity: The Roma in Romania*; Fonseca, *Bury Me Standing*; Eric Hockenos, *Free to Hate*; Jan Chmelík, *Extremismus* (Praha: SLON, 1997).

630 Hana Frištenská, 244-266; *Zvláštní zpráva o projevech rasové a národnostní nesnášenlivosti* (Praha a Brno: Nejvyšší státní zastupitelství, 1994, 1995, 1996, 1997); *Zpráva o bezpečnostní situaci na území ČR v letech 1994, 1995, 1996, 1997, 1994* (Praha: Ministerstvo vnitra.) *Výzkumy Institutu pro výzkum veřejného mínění z let 1990-1997* (Praha: IVVM); *Výzkumy Střediska empirických výzkumů z let 1990-1997* (Praha: STEM). All in Archiv socioklubu. For example, in 1991, 33% of STEM respondents, mostly young people under 29, supported the skinhead movement. In 1993, 77% of IVVM respondents answered that they have "hostile relationship" toward the Roma and 31,2% of people surveyed by STEM even indicated that they would desire "stricter laws" for this minority. In 1994, however, the desire for "special laws for the Roma" was expressed by 51,1% of STEM respondents. In 1995, 76% of IVVM respondents claimed they were "aware of incidents of racial violence," however the same year over 90% of respondents in a sociological study conducted by Ivan Gabal indicated that they "consider Roma parasites," "do not trust them," and "would prefer their separation from the everyday life of the society." And finally, in a curiously phrased 1999 survey IVVM found out that most respondents "mind Roma more than homosexuals."

One of the most recent research studies of the attitudes of Czech population towards national and ethnic minorities, especially towards the Roma minority, in April 2006 revealed that two thirds of the Czech adult population – 67 percent out of 1690 respondents in a representative survery of the prestigious sociological agency STEM – have "negative relationship" to the Roma. Out of these, a whole 10 percent even indicated that they "feel repugnance toward them." Only one quarter of all respondends felt that "greater attention should be paid to the rights of Romani fellow citizens." The research survey concluded that overall, "the Czechs have steadily rather hostile relationship towards the Roma."[631]

However, xenophobia is not confined to the level of popular sentiments but permeates legislation and policy making, which has reinforced popular attitudes and perpetuated ethnic and racial intolerance in the country. The most obvious example of this phenomenon is the Czech citizenship law, enacted after the division of Czechoslovakia in 1993. The new law No. 40/1993 Sb., issued on the eve of the country's separation, closely followed the prior communist citizenship law No. 165/1968 Sb. (created for the purposes of legal adjustments for the new Czechoslovak federation in 1968) and strictly and precisely defined who will and will not automatically receive Czech citizenship and how others can apply for it in the future. According to the Czech Helsinki Human Rights Committee, this law left over 15,000 Roma, permanently residing in the Czech Republic and having no ties to Slovakia, without Czech citizenship, making them literally stateless and forcing on them the status of foreigners, who live in the Czech Republic without legal title.[632]

Many of these Roma moved or were forced to move to the Czech part of the country from Slovakia during the communist coercive resettlement policies of the 1950s and 1960s. Now, because of Czechoslovakia's "velvet di-

---

631 "The relationship of Czech population towards the Roma." STEM, *Trendy* 2006/4. The research survey was conducted in April 1-8, 2006. Its details, including questions, charts, and analysis are publicly available in the STEM archive on the STEM website: www.stem.cz.

632 *Zpráva o stavu lidských práv v České republice* (Praha: Český helsinský výbor, 1994, 1995, 1996). The estimates of various non-governmental organization at the time of the split of the federation dramatically differed and ranged anywhere from a few hundreds to 100,000. See, Marta Miklušáková, "Stručný nástin důsledků zákona č. 40/1993 Sb., "O nabývání a pozbývání státního občanství ČR", in *Romové v České republice*, 522.

vorce" and since most of these Roma were born in Slovakia, they were required to formally apply for Czech citizenship despite their long-term residence in the Czech Republic. However, many other Roma were born in the Czech Republic, lived there their entire lives and had no kin or formal ties to Slovakia at all, and they, too, found themselves in the same situation. Their problem rested in their "inability" to exercise in the proper time frame their "citizenship option," a strict and confusing procedure of residence declaration, which channeled them into the pool of all other applicants for Czech citizenship, including thousands of war refugees pouring into the country at the time from various parts of South East Europe.

The ministry of interior created a vicious circle of requirements, including the demand that applicants have permanent residence, active employment, and a clean criminal record, which were virtually impossible requirements for many Roma to fulfill due to their prior criminalization during communism and/or contemporary high unemployment rates. As a result of the law many Roma found themselves in the circular predicament that without a clean criminal record they could not find a job, without a job they could not rent an apartment, without permanent address they could not find employment, and without work they were prone to petty criminal activity.[633]

The most controversial, and internationally criticized, condition of the law was the requirement of a five-year clean criminal record for anyone applying for Czech citizenship, including all the Czechoslovak Roma. The Roma, as a marginalized minority, have had notoriously high criminality, given the way the justice system defined, recognized and treated criminal activity differently for the Romani and non-Romani population, a phenomenon observed and analyzed in other societies and countries as well.[634] There are only two possible explanations for the way this law was written and enacted. Either the legal problems that this legislation would cause for the Romani minority were anticipated and incorporated into the law intentionally, or the wording, condi-

---

633 For a comprehensive treatment of the Czech citizenship law with regard to the Roma minority, see, Marta Miklušáková, "Romové a zákon o občanství," M.A. thesis (Praha: Filozofická fakulta University Karlovy, 1998) and in English, Jiřina Šiklová and Marta Miklušáková, "Denying Citizenship to the Czech Roma," *East European Constitutional Review*, 7:2 (1998): 58-64.

634 Markéta Štěchová, "Etnicita a kriminalita," in Oldřich Novotný and Jiří Zapletal, *Základy kriminologie* (Praha: PF UK, 1993), 105-135.

tions and implications of the law indicate the government's lack of consideration and comprehension of the ethnic dimensions of policy making. In either or both cases, the implications are worrying.

These examples indicate that the most significant instances of interethnic tensions in the contemporary Czech Republic occur at hard-to-define and complex sites, involving structural inequalities and asymmetrical access to power. More importantly, because Czech society and its institutions are largely unwilling to identify ethnic discrimination and recognize it as a product of racism and ethnic hostility, the state does not consider this issue a priority and government organs do not systematically deal with it. The fact that the Roma themselves have not been so far questioned as respondents in any of the major surveys and studies signifies the case in point. As this book has attempted to show, these attitudes, both popular and institutional, are a direct result of the sensibilities produced during the communist period.

While it is doubtful that similar attitudes would not have developed in a "free" political system, the research conducted for this study indicates that the crucial element in the development of these sentiments was the suppression of an open discourse about the ethnic and racial dimensions of Roma-Czechoslovak relations during the communist regime. While the laws and policies produced in communist Czechoslovakia were in line with the ideological rhetoric of the regime and espoused beliefs in universal equality, democracy, and human rights, the interpretation and implementation of these policies were carried out by local actors who inherited popular gypsy myths and translated those myths into coercive and legitimated forms of control.

The "Gypsy Question" Reframed

In closing, the politics of the "Gypsy question" in communist Czechoslovakia had compelled this study to reframe the traditional ways power, racism and state-society relations are characterized in the historical literature on communist Europe. This book has contributed to this literature by reframing four different and fundamental areas of historical analysis: the politics of cultural definition, discourse as a medium of social control and legitimation, the location of power and agency in authoritarian regimes, and the use of gender as evidence of social deviance.

First, the literature on Romani history has used the concept of "culture" in several contentious ways. Some historians of the Roma have affirmed their cultural distinctiveness and "otherness" from the societies in which they live, treating them as a homogeneous group whose history can be recorded independently from the history of the majority society. Other historians have interpreted Romani culture as having been formed by centuries of violence and control, once again treating the Roma as a homogeneous group whose identity is defined by their status as pariahs. Lastly, more recent scholars, particularly anthropologists, have sought to narrate Romani struggles for cultural subjectivity, thereby affirming their cultural difference as something to be cherished and celebrated. While each of these approaches have problems and merits, few of them deal adequately with the ways, in which ideas about Romani "culture" have been used (for example by Czechoslovak society) in order to discriminate. Rather than construing "culture" as an attribute of groups in need of recognition or celebration, this study has reframed culture as a collection of value claims societies use to create hierarchies of order. In the Czechoslovak context, the communist regime, as well as its local officials, used notions of Romani culture to "prove" Roma's social backwardness or deviance, and therefore to impose regulations and policies to "correct" or erase those abnormalities out of existence. Rather than a latent phenomenon, "culture" primarily inhabits a linguistic space that those in power use to articulate their visions of social order. By defining those "cultural' characteristics that defy such visions of social order as "deviant," the Czechoslovak communist regime was able to effectively control its Romani population even in the name of social tranquility and justice. When these beliefs about social normalcy and deviance inhabit popular consciousness, citizens then identify cultural differences between the Roma and (non-Romani) Czechoslovak society as fundamental differences in socialization, even fueling popular demands for Romani assimilation in the post-communist period.

Second, scholarship on the Roma has naturally sought to identify the "objective" sources of Romani discrimination: racist laws, policies, legal categories, the educational system, etc. Barany, for example, measures Romani social and ethnic marginality primarily on the basis of the presence or absence of such objective conditions, the exclusion of the Roma from positions of power, and their various forms of "peripherality." This study has challenged this objectivist stance for not taking into account the fact that state policies and other "exogenous" sources of marginality become operative only through the medium of official *and* popular discourses. In communist Czechoslovakia, social policies were not *themselves* discriminatory; objectively speaking, the policies that affected the Romani population the most do not even mention the Roma at all. As I have argued, such policies became discriminatory within the space of discourse, precisely because the ways the Roma were depicted and talked about in public entered into the way policies were interpreted and implemented. While official discourses of the regime had the legitimating function of defining ideologically correct conceptions of the Roma, popular discourses made practical sense of how local bureaucrats were to apply policies in ethnically punitive ways. Further, such practices do not change with regime transitions as Barany would suggest. Rather, the power to discriminate, precisely because it inhabits a discursive and not an institutional space, can continue to shape political power long after regimes themselves disappear.

Third, my emphasis on discourse does not mean that agency does not matter, for it was local officials who, by using their authority to interpret the ethnically-neutral policies, were the conduits for translating the terms of popular discourses into racially discriminatory practices. The role of local officials in this study reveals the degree to which political power resides less in a mythological "totalitarian system" than in the hands of officials who made private sense of public laws. However, this study has not merely challenged the "totalitarian thesis," the image of authoritarian regimes as monoliths ruling masses of relatively passive people. It has also attempted to identify important similarities in the ways agents of the state discriminate, whether in a democratic or authoritarian society. Unless the decisions of local political actors are strongly monitored from above, such actors retain a discursive freedom to interpret and apply laws according to popular prejudices and stereotypes. Therefore, if Czech society were to be committed to eradicating discrimination against the Roma, not only must it reexamine the ethnic dimensions of what counts as "normal" or "proper" in society but also how such norms influence the way state actors interact and view Romani behavior.

Lastly, this study has shown that Romani discrimination took on significantly gendered terms. This does not mean that Romani women were more discriminated against than men but rather that the categories used to define Romani deviance were injunctions intended to express the failure of Roma to adhere to proper gendered and sexual norms. Value judgments about how Romani women raised their children also served the inadverted purpose of disciplining Czechoslovak women to maintain their proper gender roles. Gender norms, as one of the most important organizing principle of running and controlling the society in general, did not simply enter into prejudices against the Roma when only sexual or reproductive behavior was at stake, but were intrinsic to virtually all the forms of "deviance" Roma were guilty of: their parenting, their domestic lifestyles, their work habits as well as their sexual life. Scholarship that analytically distills gender out from the history of Romani discrimination, therefore, does not merely omit one dimension of Romani marginalization but fundamentally misconstrues the nature of that discrimination.

This book has taken a critical stance toward scholarship on the Roma that either optimistically hopes for Romani emancipation through cultural recognition or believes social justice can be achieved by simply changing policies or regimes. It is not to say that emancipation and social justice are not immensely important goals worth striving for. They are. But the message provided by this book is that changes in policy or regime may only alleviate some forms of discrimination at the surface, while leaving the underlying prejudices and social regulation of normalcy intact. Romani discrimination can be reduced in the long run only by a deeper transformation of the way Czech society views itself, defines others, and interacts with the Roma. That requires a long and ongoing process of dialogue but mainly it calls for reframing the categories through which the Roma have for so long been understood.

Bibliography

Secondary Literature refers to academic scholarship related to the Roma, Romani Studies and relevant theoretical and historiographical literature and research studies. Since the book is focused primarily on the analysis of popular, academic and political discourses on the Roma under communism, for better lucidity the ***Primary Materials*** are broken down into different categories of works and documents analyzed in the book. Lastly, the ***Sources*** identify archival and documentary collections, newspapers, magazines and Romani journals utilized in the course of the research.

SECONDARY LITERATURE

Abrams, Bradley. *The Struggle for the Soul of the Nation: Czech Culture and the Rise of Communism* (Lanham, MD: Rowman & Littlefield Publishers, Inc., 2005).

Abu-Lughod, Lila. *Remaking Woman: Feminism and Modernity in the Middle East* (Princeton: Princeton University Press, 1998).

________. *Veiled Sentiments: Honor and Poetry in Bedouin Society* (Berkeley: University of California Press, 1986).

________. "Writing Against Culture," in Richard Fox, ed., *Recapturing Anthropology* (Santa Fe: School of American Research Press, 1991).

Acton, Thomas. "Ethnic Stereotypes: who are the true Gypsies?," in Thomas Acton, ed., *Current Changes amongst British Gypsies and their Place in international Patterns of development* (Oxford: Oxford University Press, 1971).

________. *Gypsy Politics and Social Change: The Development of Ethnic Ideology and Pressure Politics Among British Gypsies from Victorian Reformism to Romani Nationalism* (London and Boston: Routledge, 1974).

Acton, Thomas and Gary Mundy, eds. *Romani Culture and Gypsy Identity* (Hatfield: University of Hertfordshire Press, 1997).

The Administration of Aesthetics: Censorship, Political Criticism and the Public Sphere (Minneapolis: University of Minnesota Press, 1994).

Altheer, David. "Roma Suffer as Eastern Europe Explodes." *Roma*, 18:38-39 (1993): 1-4.

Andersen, Ruth. "Women of Kalderas," in Matt Salo, ed., *The American Kalderas: Gypsies in the New World* (Centenary College: Gypsy Lore Society, North American Chapter Publications, No. 1, 1981).

Anderson, Benedict. *Imagined Communities: Reflections on the Origin and Spread of Nationalism* (New York: Verso, 2006).

Appadurai, Arjun. "Global Ethnoscapes," in Richard Fox, ed., *Recapturing Anthropology* (Santa Fe: School of American Research Press, 1991).

Argent, Angie. "Post-Communism and 'Women's Experience'?," in Robin Teske and Mary Ann Tetreault, eds., *Feminist Approaches to Social Movements, Communism and Power* (Columbus: University of South Carolina Press, 2000).

Auletta, Ken. *The Underclass* (New York: Random House, 1982).

Balabánová, Helena. "Romské děti v systému českého základního školství a jejich následná profesionální příprava a uplatnění," in *Romové v České republice, 1945-1998: sešity pro sociální politiku* (Praha: Socioklub, 1999), 333-351.

Banc, C. *You Call This Living? A Collection of East European Political Jokes* (Athens: University of Georgia Press, 1990).

Bancroft, Angus. *Roma and Gypsy - Travellers in Europe: Modernity, Race, Space and Exclusion* (Aldershot and Burlington, VT: Ashgate Publishing, 2005).

Barany, Zoltan D. *The East European Gypsies: Regime Change, Marginality, and Ethnopolitics* (Cambridge: Cambridge University Press, 2002).

________. "Living on the Edge: The East European Roma in Postcommunist Politics and Societies." *Slavic Review*, 53:2 (1994): 321-344.

________. "Roma: Grim Realities in Eastern Europe." *Transitions,* 1:4 (March 1995): 3-8.

Barany, Zoltan and Robert G. Moser, eds. *Ethnic Politics after Communism* (Ithaca: Cornell University Press, 2005).

Barson, Michael. *Red Scared! The Commie Menace in Propaganda and Pop Culture* (San Francisco: Chronicle Books, 2000).

Bartošek, Luboš. *Náš film: kapitoly z dějin, 1896-1945* (Praha: Mladá fronta, 1985).

Belton, Brian. *Gypsy and Traveller Ethnicity: The Social Generation of an Ethnic Phenomenon* (New York: Routledge, 2005).

________. *Questioning Gypsy Identity: Ethnic Narratives in Britain and America* (Lanham, MD: AltaMira Press, 2005).

Benedict, Ruth. *Patterns of Culture* (New York: Houghton Mifflin Co., 1934).

Berent, J. "Causes of Fertility Decline in Eastern Europe and the Soviet Union II: Economic and Social Factors." *Population Studies*, 24:4 (1970): 247-292.

Besemeres, John. *Socialist Population Policy: The Political Implications of Demographic Trends in the USSR and Eastern Europe* (New York: M.E. Sharpe, 1980).

Bhopal, Kalwant and Martin Myers. *Insiders, Outsiders and Others: Gypsies and Identity* (Hatfield: University of Hertfordshire Press, 2008).

Block, Martin. *Gypsies, their life and their customs* (New York: AMS Press, 1987).

Boas, Franz. *Anthropology and Modern Life* (New York: Norton, 1928).

Bourdieu, Pierre. *Language & Symbolic Power* (Cambridge, MA: Harvard University Press, 1991).

Boym, Svetlana. *Common Places: Mythologies of Everyday Life In Russia* (Cambridge, MA: Harvard University Press, 1994).

Bren, Paulina. "Closely Watched Screens: Ideology and Everyday Life in Czechoslovakia after the Prague Spring, 1968-1989." Ph.D. Dissertation. (New York University, 2002).

Brown, Kate. *A Biography of No Place: From Ethnic Borderland to Soviet Heartland* (Cambridge, MA: Harvard University Press, 2005).

Brown, Kathleen. *Good Wives, Nasty Wenches & Anxious Patriarchs: Gender, Race, and Power in Colonial Virginia* (Chapel Hill: University of North Carolina Press, 1996).

Brož, Aleš. "Minority Rights in the Czechoslovak State." *Foreign Affairs*, Oct. 1927: 160.

Brubaker, Rogers. *Nationalism Reframed: Nationhood and the National Question in the New Europe* (New York: Cambridge University Press, 1996).

Bryant, Chad. "Either German or Czech: Fixing Nationality in Bohemia and Moravia, 1939-1946." *Slavic Review*, 61:4 (2002): 683-706.

Burleigh, Michael and Wolfgang Wippermann. *The Racial State: Germany 1933-1945* (Cambridge: University Press, 1991).

Butcher, Timothy. *The Sudeten German Question and Czechoslovak-German Relations since 1989* (London: Royal United Services Institute for Defense Studies, 1996).

Bútora, Martin. "The Dissolution of Czecho-Slovakia: An Unexpected Christmas Present," in Elzbieta Matynia, ed., *Grappling With Democracy: Deliberations on Post-Communist Societies, 1990-1995* (Praha: SLON, 1996), 218-222.

Calhoun, Greg, ed. *Social Theory and the Politics of Identity* (Cambridge: Blackwell, 1994).

Campbell, F.G. *Confrontation in Central Europe: Weimar Germany and Czechoslovakia* (Chicago: Chicago University Press, 1975).

Čaněk, David. "Roma and Other Ethnic Minorities in Czech and Slovak Schools, 1945-1998." (Budapest: Central European University, Center for Policy Studies, 2001).

Caulfield, Sueann. "Getting into Trouble: Dishonest Women, Modern Girls, and Women-Men in the Conceptual Language of Vida Policial, 1925-27." *Signs*, 19:1 (Fall, 1993): 147-175.

Český národní filmový archív. *Umlčený film: kapitoly z bojů o lidskou tvář československého filmu* (Praha: Národní filmový archív, 1993).

Chaman, Lal. *Gypsies: forgotten children of India* (Delhi: Ministry of Information and Broadcasting, 1962).

Charbonneau, Louis. "Let Them Eat Pork!" *Pozor: News From Around the Bloc*, 6 (June 1996): 2-6.

Chase, Allan. *The Legacy of Malthus: The Social Costs of the New Scientific Racism* (Urbana: University of Illinois Press, 1980).

Chatwin, Bruce. *Anatomy of Restlessness: Uncollected Writings, 1969-1989* (New York: Viking Press, 1996).

Chmelík, Jan. *Extremismus* (Praha: SLON, 1997).

Clebért, Jean-Paul. *The Gypsies* (Baltimore: Penguin Books, 1963).

Clifford, James. *The Predicament of Culture* (Cambridge: Harvard University Press, 1988).

Cohen, Stephen. *Rethinking the Soviet Experience: Politics & History Since 1917* (Oxford: Oxford University Press, 1985).

Cohn, Werner. *The Gypsies* (Reading, MA: Addison-Wesley Pub. Co., 1973).

Collins, Patricia Hill. *Fighting Words: Black Women and the Search for Justice* (Minneapolis: University of Minnesota Press, 1998).

________. *Black Feminist Thought: Knowledge, Consciousness, and the Politics of Empowerment* (Boston: Unwin Hyman, 1990).

Connelly, John. *Captive University: The Sovietization of East German, Czechoslovak and Polish Higher Education, 1945-1956* (Chapel Hill: University of North Carolina Press, 2000).

Conway, Laura. *Report on the Status of Romani Education in the Czech Republic* (Prague: HOST, 1996).

Comarroff, Jean and John Comarroff. *On Revelation and Revolution: Christianity, Colonialism, and Consciousness in South Africa*. Vol. I. (Chicago: Chicago University Press, 1991).

Crenshaw, Kimberlé. "Demarginalizing the Intersection of Race and Sex: A Black Feminist Critique of Antidiscrimination Doctrine, Feminist Theory and Antiracist Politics." *The University of Chicago Legal Forum*, (1989): 139-67.

Crowe, David. *A History of the Gypsies of Eastern Europe and Russia* (New York: St. Martin's Press, 1995).

Crowe, David and John Kolsti, eds. *The Gypsies of Eastern Europe* (Armonk, New York: M. E. Sharpe, 1991).

Csepeli, Gyorgy. "The Role of Fear in Ethnic and National Conflicts in Eastern Europe," in Elzbieta Matynia, ed., in *Grappling with Democracy: Deliberations on Post-Communist Societies, 1990-1995* (Prague: SLON, 1996), 287-296.

Cultures and Nations of Central East Europe: Essays in Honor of Roman Szporluk (Cambridge, ME: Harvard University Press, 2000).

Dallin, Alexander. "Bias and Blunders in American Studies on the USSR." *Slavic Review*, 32:3 (September 1973): 560-576.

Daniel, Bartoloměj. *Dějiny Romů* (Olomouc: Univerzita Palackého Press, 1991).

David, Henry and Robert McIntyre. *Reproductive Behavior: Central and Eastern European Experience* (New York: Springer Publ. Co., 1981).

Davidová, Eva. *Romano Drom: Cesty Romů, 1945-1990* (Olomouc: Univerzita Palackého Press, 1995).

________. *Social Change and Stratification in Postwar Czechoslovakia* (New York: Columbia University Press, 1972).

Davis, Mike. *City of Quartz: Excavating the Future in Los Angeles* (New York: Vintage, 1992).

Dawson, Michael. "A Black Counterpublic?: Economic Earthquakes, Racial Agenda(s), and Black Politics." *Public Culture*, 7 (1994): 195-223.

Deleuze, Gilles and Felix Guartari. "1227: Treatise On Nomadology – The War Machine," in *A Thousand Plateau: Capitalism and Schizophrenia* (Minneapolis: University of Minnesota Press, 1987), 351-423.

Dijk van, Teun A. "Multidisciplinary CDA: a plea for diversity," in Ruth Wodak and Michael Meyer, eds., *Methods of Critical Discourse Analysis* (London: Sage Publications, 2001): 95-120.

Douglas, Mary. *Purity and Danger: An Analysis of the Concepts of Pollution and Taboo* (London and New York: Ark Paperbacks, 1984).

Dumont, Jean-Paul. *The Headman and I: Ambiguity and Ambivalence in the Fieldwork Exeprience* (Austin: University of Texas Press, 1978).

Early, Gerald, ed. *Lure and Loathing: Essays on Race, Identity, and the Ambivalence of Assimilation* (New York: Penguin, 1993).

Einhorn, Barbara. *Cinderella Goes to Market: Citizenship, Gender and Women's Movements in East Central Europe* (London and New York: Verso, 1993).

European Roma Rights Centre et al. *Submission to the United Nations Human Rights Committee Concerning Implementation of the International*

Covenant on Civil and Political Rights (ICCPR) in the Czech Republic. Budapest, July 2007. <http://www.ohchr.org/english/bodies/hrc/docs/ngos/cohre_cz.pdf> [Accessed Dec. 4, 2007].

European Union (EU). European Union Agency for Fundamental Rights. *Report on Racism and Xenophobia in the Member States of the EU.* 2007. <http://fra.europa.eu/fra/material/pub/racism/report_racism_0807_en.pdf> [Accessed Nov. 16, 2007].

Fabian, Johannes. *Time and The Other: How Anthropology Makes Its Object* (New York: Columbia University Press, 1983).

Fairclough, Norman. "Critical discourse analysis as a method in social scientific research," in Ruth Wodak and Michael Meyer, eds., *Methods of Critical Discourse Analysis* (London: Sage Publications, 2001): 121-138.

Fanel, Jiří. *Gay historie* (Praha: Dauphin, 1999).

Farnsworth, Clyde. "Occupation Stirs Czechoslovak Gypsies' Patriotism." *The New York Times*, Nov. 3, 1968, 18.

Fawn, Rick. "Czech Attitudes Towards the Roma: 'Expecting More of Havel's Country'?" *Europe-Asia Studies*, 53:8 (2001): 1193-1219.

Felak, James. *At the Price of the Republic Hlinka's Slovak People's Party, 1929-1938* (Pittsburgh: University of Pittsburgh Press, 1994).

________. "Slovak Considerations of the Slovak Question: the Ludak, Agrarian, Socialist and Communist views in interwar Czechoslovakia," in J. Morison, ed., *The Czech and Slovak Experience* (New York: St. Martin's Press, 1992).

Fischer, Mary Ellen. "Women in Romanian Politics: Elena Ceausescu, Pronatalism, and the Promotion of Women," in Sharon Wolchik and Alfred Meyer, eds., *Women, State, and Party in Eastern Europe* (Durham: Duke University Press, 1985), 121-137.

Fonseca, Isabel. "Among Gypsies." *The New Yorker*, 71:29 (1995): 92.

________. *Bury Me Standing* (New York: Vintage Books, 1995).

Foucault, Michel. *Birth of the Clinic: An Archeology of Medical Perception* (New York: Vintage, 1973).

Foucault, Michel. *Discipline and Punish: The Birth of the Prison* (New York: Vintage Books, 1979).

________. *History of Sexuality: An Introduction* (New York: Vintage, 1980).

________. *The Order of Things: An Archeology of the Human Sciences* (London: Tavistock, 1970).

________. "The Subject and Power," in Hubert Dreyfus and Paul Rabinow, *Michel Foucault: Beyond Structuralism and Hermeneutics* (Chicago: University of Chicago Press, 1983).

Fraser, Angus. *The Gypsies* (Oxford: Blackwell Press, 1995).

Frejka, Tomáš. "Fertility trends and policies: Czechoslovakia in the 1970s." *Population and Development Review*, 6:1 (1980): 65-93.

Friedlander, Henry. *The Origins of Nazi Genocide: From Euthanasia to the Final Solution* (Chapell Hill: University of North Carolina Press, 1995).

Frištenská, Hana. "Interetnický konflikt po roce 1989 s ohledem na soužití s Romy," in *Romové v České republice* (Praha: Socioklub, 1999), 244-266.

Frommer, Benjamin. *National Cleansing: Retribution against Nazi Collaborators in Postwar Czechoslovakia* (Cambridge: Cambridge University Press, 2005).

Fulbrook, Mary. *The Anatomy of a Dictatorship: Inside the GDR, 1949-1989* (New York: Oxford University Press, 1995).

________. *Citizenship, Nationalism and Migration in Europe* (New York: Routledge, 1996).

Funk, Nannette and Magda Mueller, eds. *Gender Politics and Post-Communism: Reflections from Eastern Europe and the Former Soviet Union* (New York: Routledge, 1993).

Gal, Susan and Gail Kligman. *The Politics of Gender after Socialism: a comparative-historical essay* (Princeton: Princeton University Press, 2000).

Gal, Susan and Gail Kligman, eds. *Reproducing Gender: Politics, Publics, and the Everyday Life after Socialism* (Princeton: Princeton University Press, 2000).

Garton Ash, Timothy. *History of the Present: essays, sketches and dispatches from Europe in the 1990s* (London: Penguin, 1999).

Garton Ash, Timothy. *Magic Lantern: the Revolution of 1989 witnessed in Warsaw, Budapest, Berlin and Prague* (New York: Vintage, 1993).

_______. *The Uses of Adversity* (Cambridge: Penguin, 1989).

Gecelovský, Vladimír. "Perzekúcia Cigánov v období tzv. Slovenského štátu." *Obzor Gemera*, 3 (1986).

_______. "Právne normy týkajúce sa Rómov a ich aplikácia v Gemeri (1918-1938)," in Arne Mann, ed., *Neznámi Rómovia: Zo života a kultúry Cigánov-Rómov na Slovensku* (Bratislava: Ister Science Press, 1992), 79-90.

Geertz, Clifford. *Interpretation of Cultures* (New York: Basic Books, 1973).

_______. *Local Knowledge: Further Essays in Interpretive Anthropology* (New York: Basic Books, 1983).

Gellner, Ernst. *Nations and Nationalism* (Ithaca: Cornell University Press, 1983).

Gheorghe, Nicolae. "Ethnic Minorities in Romania under Socialism." *East European Quarterly*, 7:4 (January 1974): 435-58.

_______. "The Roma-Gypsy Ethnicity in Eastern Europe." *Social Research*, 58:4 (Winter 1991): 829-44.

Gilman, Sander. *Difference and Pathology: Stereotypes of Sexuality, Race, and Madness* (Ithaca and London: Cornell University Press, 1985).

Glassheim, Eagle. "National Mythologies and Ethnic Cleansing: The Expulsion of Czechoslovak Germans in 1945." *Central European History*, 33:4 (2000): 463-486.

Gramsci, Antonio. *Selections from the Prison Notebooks of Antonio Gramsci* (New York: International Publishers, 1972).

Greenfeld, Liah. *Nationalism: Five Roads to Modernity* (Cambridge: Harvard University Press, 1992).

Gronemeyer, Reimer. *Zigeuner in Osteuropa: eine Bibliographie zu den Landern Polen, Tschechoslowakei und Ungarn: mit einem Aunang uber altere Sowjetische Literatur* (Munchen, New York: Saur, 1983).

Grulich, Tomáš and Tomáš Haišman. "Institucionální zájem o cikánské obyvatelstvo v Československu v letech 1945-1958." *Český lid*, 73:2 (1986): 72-85.

Guy, Will, ed. *Between Past and Future: The Roma of Central and Eastem Europe* (Hatfield: University of Hertfordshire Press, 2002).

Guy, Willy. "Attempt of Socialist Czechoslovakia to assimilate its Gypsy Population." Ph.D. Thesis. (Bristol University, 1977).

________. "Ways of Looking at Roms: The Case of Czechoslovakia," in Farnham Rehfisch, ed., *Gypsies, Tinkers, and Other Travellers* (London: Academic Press, 1975).

Haišman, Tomáš. "Romové v Československu v letech 1945-1967: vývoj institucionálního zájmu a jeho dopady," in *Romové v České republice, 1945-1998: sešity pro sociální politiku* (Praha: Socioklub, 1999), 137-183.

________. "Snahy centrálních orgánů státní správy o řešení tzv. cikánské otázky v českých zemích v letech 1945 až 1947 ve světle tisku." *Český lid*, 76:1 (1989): 4-11.

Hall, Timothy McCajor and Rosie Read, eds. *Changes in the Heart of Europe: Recent Ethnographies of Czechs, Slovaks, Roma and Sorbs* (Stuttgart: *ibidem*-Verlag, 2006).

Hamšík, Dušan. *Writers Against Rulers* (New York: Random House, 1971).

Hancock, Ian. "Anti-Gypsyism in the New Europe." *Roma*, 18: 38-39 (1993): 5-29.

________. "The Function of the Gypsy Myth." *Roma*, 12:3 (1987): 35-44.

________. "Gypsy History in Germany and Neighboring Lands: A chronology of the Holocaust and beyond." *Nationalities Papers*, (1991).

________. Non-Gypsy Attitudes toward Rom: The Gypsy Stereotype." *Roma*, 9:1 (1985): 50-65.

________. *The Pariah Syndrome: An Account of Gypsy Slavery and Persecution* (Ann Harbor: Karoma Publishers, 1987).

________. "Some Contemporary Aspects of Gypsies and Gypsy Nationalism." *Roma*, 1:2 (1975): 46-55.

________. "Standardization and Ethnic Defence in Emergent Non-Literate Societies: The Gypsy and Caribbean Cases," in Thomas Acton and Morgan Dalphinis, eds., *Language, Blacks and Gypsies: Languages Without a Written Tradition and Their Role in Education* (London: Whiting & Birch, 2000), 9-23.

Hancock, Ian. *We Are the Romani People* (Hatfield: University of Hertfordshire Press, 2002).

Haney, Lynne. *Inventing the Needy: Gender and the Politics of Welfare in Hungary* (Berkeley: University of California Press, 2002).

Harding, Sandra. *The Science Question in Feminism* (Ithaca: Cornell University Press, 1986).

________. *Is Science Multicultural? Postcolonialisms, Feminisms, and Epistemologies* (Bloomington: Indiana University Press, 1998).

Harris, Marvin. *Cultural Materialism: the Struggle for a Science of Culture* (New York: Random House, 1979).

Hartman, Betsy. *Reproductive Rights and Wrongs: The Global Politics of Population Control* (Boston: South End Press, 1995).

Havel, Václav. "The Power of the Powerless," in *Open Letters* (London: Faber and Faber, 1991).

Havelková, Hana. "Abstract Citizenship? Women and Power in the Czech Republic," *Social Politics: International Studies in Gender, State and Society*, 3:2-3 (Summer/Fall 1996): 243-260.

________. "Women in and after a 'classless' society," in Christine Zmroczek and Pat Mahony, eds., *Women and Social Class – International Feminist Perspectives* (London: Taylor and Francis Group, 1999), 69-84.

Havelková, Hana, ed. *Existuje středoevropský model manželství a rodiny? Sborník z mezinárodního sympozia* (Praha: Divadelní ústav, 1995).

Heitlinger, Alena. "Passage to Motherhood: Personal and Social 'Management' of Reproduction in Czechoslovakia in the 1980s," in Sharon Wolchik and Alfred Meyer, eds., *Women, State, and Party in Eastern Europe* (Durham: Duke University Press, 1985), 286-302.

________. *Reproduction, Medicine and the Socialist State* (London: The Macmillan Press, 1987).

________. *Women and State Socialism: Sex Inequality in the Soviet Union and Czechoslovakia* (Montreal: McGill-Queen's University Press, 1979).

Hobbes, Thomas. *Leviathan* (Cambridge: Hackett Publishing Company, Inc., 1994).

Hockenos, Eric. *Free to Hate: the Rise of the Right in Post-Communist Eastern Europe* (New York: Routledge, 1993).

Holomek, Karel. "Vývoj romských reprezentací po roce 1989 a minoritní mocenská politika ve vztahu k Romům," in *Romové v České republice* (Praha: Socioklub, 1999), 290-310.

Holý, Dušan and Ctibor Nečas. *Žalující píseň* (Olomouc: Univerzita Palackého, 1995).

Holý, Ladislav. *The Little Czech and the Great Czech Nation: national identity and the post-communist social transformation* (Cambridge: Cambridge University Press, 1996).

Honneth, Axel. *The Critique of Power* (Cambridge, MIT Press, 1991).

Horváthová, Jana. "Jak se žije romským intelektuálům v Čechách," in *Romové v České republice* (Praha: Socioklub, 1999), 311-326.

Hroch, Miroslav. *Social Preconditions for National Revival in Europe: A Comparative Analysis of the Social Composition of Patriotic Groups Among Smaller European Nations* (New York: Columbia University Press, 2000, 2nd ed.).

Hübschmannová, Milena. *Šaj Pes Dovakeras: Můžeme se domluvit* (Olomouc: Univerzita Palackého, 1993).

________. "Three Years of Democracy in Czecho-Slovakia and the Roma." *Roma*, 18:38-39 (1993): 30-49.

Hübschmannová, Milena, ed. *Po Židoch cigáni – svědectví Romů ze Slovenska, 1939-1945* (Praha: Triáda, 2005).

Hübschmannová, Milena, Hana Šebková and Anna Žigová. "Bori." *Roma*, 11:24 (1986): 19-25.

Humor a satira vo slovenskom hranom filme: zborník referátov a diskuzných príspevkov zo seminára, ktorý usporiadal Slovenský filmový ústav a Zväz slovenských dramatických umielcov dňa 13.11. 1985 (Bratislava: Slovenský filmový ústav, 1986).

Huntington, Samuel. *Clash of Civilizations and the Making of World Order* (New York: Simon and Schuster, 1996).

Huttenbach, Henry. "The Romani Porajmos: The Nazi Genocide of Europe's Gypsies." *Nationalities Papers*, 19:3 (1991): 373-94.

Inside Soviet Film and Satire: Laughter with a Lash. Cambridge Studies in Film. (Cambridge: Cambridge University Press, 1993).

Ioviță, Radu P. and Theodore G. Schurr. "Reconstructing the Origins and Migrations of Diasporic Populations: The Case of the European Gypsies." *American Anthropologist*, New Series 106:2 (2004): 267-281.

Jäger, Siegfried. "Discourse and knowledge: theoretical and methodological aspects of a critical discourse and dispositive analysis," in Ruth Wodak and Michael Meyer, eds., *Methods of Critical Discourse Analysis* (London: Sage Publications, 2001): 31-62.

Jancar, Barbara. *Czechoslovakia and the Absolute Monopoly of Power: A Study of Political Power in a Communist System* (New York: Praeger Publishers, 1971).

Johnson, Lonnie. *Central Europe: Enemies, Neighbors, Friends* (Oxford: Oxford University Press, 1997).

Joshi, Anirudh. "The Etymology of the Word 'Gajo'." *Roma*, 1:1 (1974): 47-49.

Jurová, Anna. "Riešenie Romskej problematiky na Slovensku po druhej svetovej vojne," in Arne Mann, ed. *Neznámi Rómovia: Zo života a kultúry Cigánov-Rómov na Slovensku* (Bratislava: Ister Science Press, 1992), 91-101.

________. *Vývoj romskej problematiky na Slovensku po roku 1945* (Bratislava: Goldpress Publishers, 1993).

Kalibová, Květa. *Demografické a geodemografické charakteristiky romské populace v České republice* (Praha: Univerzita Karlova, 1995).

________. "Romové z pohledu statistiky a demografie," in *Romové v České republice, 1945-1998: sešity pro sociální politiku* (Praha: Socioklub, 1999), 91-114.

________. *Sources on Information on the demographic situation of the Roma/Gypsies in Europe* (The European Council, Feasibility Study, 1997).

Kamenická, Veronika. "Obraz Romů v české literatuře." M.A. Thesis. (Praha: Pedagogická fakulta Univerzity Karlovy, 1999).

Kann, Robert and Zdenek David. *The Peoples of the Eastern Habsburg Lands, 1526-1918* (Seattle: University of Washington Press, 1984).

Kaplan, Karel. *The Communist Party in Power: A Profile of Party Politics in Czechoslovakia* (Boulder and London: Westview Press, 1987).

Kaplan, Karel. *O cenzuře v Československu v letech 1945-1956* (Praha: Ústav soudobých dějin, 1994).

________. *The Short March: The Communist Takeover in Czechoslovakia, 1945-1948* (New York: St. Martin's Press, 1987).

Karakasidou, Anastazia. *Fields of Wheat, Hills of Blood: Passages to Nationhood in Greek Macedonia, 1870-1990* (Chicago: University of Chicago Press, 1997).

Kaushal, Hari Har. "Legal Status of Roma in Europe and America." *Roma*, 5:1 (1980): 20-31.

Kdo je kdo mezi československými Romy?: Příručka Muzea romské kultury v Brně (Brno, MRK: 1998).

Kenedi, James. "Why Is the Gypsy the Scapegoat and Not the Jew?" *East European Reporter*, 2:1 (1986): 11-14.

Kenrick, Donald. *The Destiny of Europe's Gypsies* (New York: Basic Books, 1973).

Kenrick, Donald and Grattan Puxon. *Gypsies Under the Swastika* (Hatfield: Gypsy Research Centre, University of Hertfordshire Press, 1995).

________. *Destiny of Europe's Gypsies* (New York: Basic Books, 1972).

Kepková, Michaela and Petr Víšek. "Romové v systémech sociální ochrany a zdroje sociální distance," in *Romové v České republice, 1945-1998: sešity pro sociální politiku* (Praha: Socioklub, 1999): 378-394.

Kershaw, Ian. "Totalitarianism Revisited: Nazism and Stalinism in Comparative Perspective," in Ian Kershaw, ed., *The Nazi Dictatorship: Problems and Perspectives of Interpretation* (London, Baltimore: Edward Arnold, 1985 and 2000).

Kershaw, Ian and Moshe Lewin, eds. *Dictators Unleashed: Historical Approaches to Nazism and Stalinism* (Cambridge University Press, 1996).

Kevles, Daniel. *In the Name of Eugenics: Genetics and the Uses of Human Heredity* (New York: Alfred Knopf, 1985).

Kieran, Will. *The Prague Spring and Its Aftermath: Czechoslovak Politics, 1968-1970* (New York: Cambridge University Press, 1997).

Kladivová, Vlasta. *Konečná stanice Auschwitz-Birkenau* (Olomouc: Univerzita Palackého, 1994).

Klein, George and Milan Reban, eds. *The Politics of Ethnicity in Eastern Europe* (Boulder, Colorado: Eastern European Monographs No. 93, 1981).

Kligman, Gail. *The Politics of Duplicity: Controlling Reproduction in Ceaucescu's Romania* (Berkeley: University of California Press, 1998).

Kochanowski, Jan. "The Origins of the Gypsies." *Roma*, 1:1 (1974): 25-28.

Kolasky, John. *Look Comrade – the People are Laughing: Underground Wit, Satire and Humor from Behind the Iron Curtain* (Toronto: P. Martin Associates, 1972).

Konrad, Geörgy. *Antipolitics: An Essay* (Longon: Quartet, 1984).

Kostelancik, David. "The Gypsies of Czechoslovakia: Political and Ideological Considerations in the Development of Policy." *Studies in Comparative Communism*, 22:4 (1989): 307-321.

Kramářová, Jana a kol. *(Ne)bolí: Vzpomínky Romů na válku a život po válce* (Praha: Člověk v tísni, 2005).

Krejčí, Jaroslav and Vítězslav Velimski. *Ethnic and Political Nations in Europe* (New York: St. Martin's Press, 1984).

Kubik, Jan. *The Power of Symbols Against The Symbols of Power* (University Park: Pennsylvania State University Press, 1994).

Kuhar, Roman. *Media Representations of Homosexuality: An Analysis of the Print Media in Slovenia, 1970-2000* (Ljublana: Mirovni inštitut, 2003).

Kun, Miklos. *Prague Spring, Prague Fall: Blank Spots of 1968* (Budapest: Akademiai Kiado, 1999).

Leff, Caroll S. *National Conflict in Czechoslovakia: the making and remaking of a state, 1918-1987* (Princeton: Princeton University Press, 1988).

Lewy, Guenter. *The Nazi Persecution of the Gypsies* (Oxford: Oxford University Press, 2000).

Liegeois, Jean Pierre. *Gypsies: An Illustrated History* (London: Al Saqi Books, 1985).

________. *Roma, Gypsies, Travellers* (Strasbourg: Council of Europe Press, 1994).

Lisický, Karel. *Problém česko-slovenský a problém česko-německý* (London: Blackwell, 1954).

Livizeanu, Irina. *Cultural Politics in Greater Romania: Regionalism, Nation Building, and Ethnic Struggle* (Ithaca: Cornell University Press, 1995).

Lombroso, Cesare. *Crime: Its Causes and Remedies* (Boston: Little, Brown &Co., The Modern Criminal Science Series, 1918).

Luža, Radomír. *The Transfer of the Sudeten Germans: A Study of Czech-German Relations, 1933-1962* (New York: New York University Press, 1964).

Machačová, Jana. "K výzkumu romského etnika." *Slezský Sborník*, 91:3 (1993): 170-177.

Macura, Vladimír. *Znamení zrodu: České obrození jako kulturní typ* (Praha: Československý spisovatel, 1983).

Mann, Arne, ed. *Neznámi Rómovia: Zo života a kultúry Cigánov-Rómov na Slovensku* (Bratislava, Slovakia: Ister Science Press, 1992).

________. "The Formation of the Ethnic Identity of the Romany in Slovakia," in Jana Plichtová, ed., *Minorities in Politics* (Bratislava: Czechoslovak Committee for the European Cultural Foundation, 1992), 261-5.

Marsh, Adrian and Elin Strand, eds. *Gypsies and the Problem of Identities: Contextual, Constructed and Contested* (Istanbul: Swedish Research Institute and I. B. Tauris, 2006).

Mauss, Marcel. *The Gift: Forms and Functions of Exchange in Archaic Societies* (New York: Norton, 1967).

Mayall, David. *History of Gypsy Identities, 1500-2000: From Egipcyans and Moon-Men to the Ethnic Romany* (New York: Routledge, 2004).

Mazalová, Dana. "...a nemnožte se!" *Týden*, 4:51 (1997): 36-42.

McCagg, William. "Gypsy Policy in Socialist Hungary and Czechoslovakia, 1945-1989." *Nationalities Papers*, 3 (1991): 313-336.

Mead, Margaret. *Coming of Age in Samoa: A Psychological Study of Primitive Youth for Western Civilization* (New York: Morrow Quill Paperbacks, 1973).

Měchýř, Jan. *Slovensko v Československu: Slovensko-české vztahy 1918-1991* (Praha: Práce, 1991).

Michnik, Adam. *Letters from Prison and Other Essays* (Palo Alto: University of California Press, 1986).

Miklušáková, Marta. "Romové a zákon o občanství." M.A. Thesis. (Praha: Filozofická fakulta University Karlovy, 1998).

________. "Stručný nástin důsledků zákona č. 40/1993 Sb., O nabývání a pozbývání státního občanství ČR," in *Romové v České republice, 1945-1998: sešity pro sociální politiku* (Praha: Socioklub, 1999), 267-271.

Miklušáková, Marta and Jiřina Šiklová. "Denying Citizenship to the Czech Roma." *East European Constitutional Review*, 7:2 (1998): 58-64.

Mitchell, Timothy. *Colonizing Egypt* (Berkeley: University of California Press, 1988).

Mlynář, Zdeněk. *Nightfrost in Prague: The End of Humane Socialism* (New York: Karz Publishers, 1980).

________. *Československý pokus o reformu 1968: Analýza jeho teorie a praxe* (Cologne: Index, 1985).

________. *The Prague Spring 1968: National Security Archive Documents Reader* (New York: Central European University Press, 1998).

Moon, Michael and Cathy Davidson, eds. *Subjects and Citizens: Nation, Race, and Gender from Oroonoko to Anita Hill* (Durham: Duke University Press, 1995).

Morokvasic, Mirjana. "Sexuality and Control of Procreation," in K. Young, C. Wolkowitz and R. McCullagh, eds., *Of Marriage and the Market: women's subordination in international perspective* (London: CSE Books, 1981): 127-143.

Mossa. *La Gitane et son destin: Temoignages d'une jeune Gitane sur la condition feminine at l'evolution du monde gitan.* With comments by Bernard Leblon. (Paris: L'Harmattan, 1992).

Mróz, Lech. *Geneza Cygánow a ich kultúry* (Oswiecim: Biblioteczka Cyganologii Polskiej, 1993).

Mueller, John. "Minorities and the Democratic Image." *East European Politics and Societies*, 9:3 (Fall 1995): 513-22.

Mulcahy, Francis David. "Gitano Sex Role Symbolism and Behavior." *Anthropological Quarterly*, 49:2 (April 1976): 135-151.

Musil, Jiří, ed. *The End of Czechoslovakia* (Budapest: Central European University Press, 1995).

Naimark, Norman. *Fires of Hatred: Ethnic Cleansing in Twentieth-Century Europe* (Cambridge, MA: Harvard University Press, 2002).

Nečas, Ctibor. *Českoslovenští Romové v letech 1938-1945* (Brno: Masarykova Univerzita, 1994).

_______. *Historický kalendář: Dějiny českých Romů v datech* (Olomouc: Univerzita Palackého, 1997).

_______. *Nad osudem českých a slovenských cikánů* (Brno: ÚJEP Press, 1981).

_______. *Nemůžeme zapomenout – Našti Bisteras* (Olomouc: Univerzita Palackého Press, 1994).

Noakes, Jeremy. "Life in the Third Reich: Social Outcasts in Nazi Germany." *History Today*, 17:35 (1985): 15-19.

Nosková, Helena. "Češi, Slováci a Romové po II. světové válce." *Romano Džaniben*, VII:3 (2000): 58-63.

Nosková, Helena et al. *Vývoj národnostní a etnické struktury československé společnosti v letech 1945-1950* (Praha: Ústav soudobých dějin, edice Studijní materiály, 1999).

Novotný, Oldřich and Jan Zapletal. *Základy kriminologie* (Praha: Karolinum, 1993).

O'Hanlon, Rosalind. "*Recovering the Subject:* Subaltern Studies *and Histories of Resistance in Colonial South Asia.*" *Modern Asian Studies*, 22:1 (1988): 189-224.

Okely, Judith. "Gypsy Women: Models in Conflict," in Shirley Ardener, ed. *Perceiving Women* (New York: John Wiley & Sons, 1975).

_______. *The Traveller-Gypsies* (Cambridge University Press, 1983).

Otáhal, Milan. "The Manuscript Controversy in the Czech National Revival." *Cross Currents*, 5 (1986): 247-277.

Palley, Claire. et. al. *Coexistence in Some Plural European Societies* (London: Minority Rights Group Report, 1972, 1986).

Pape, Marcus. *A nikdo vám nebude věřit: Dokument o koncentračním táboře Lety u Písku* (Praha: G+G, 1997).

Parsons, Talcott and Robert Bales. *Family, Socialisation and Interaction Process* (London: Glencoe Press, 1955).

Pavelčíková, Nina. *Romové v českých zemích v letech 1945-1989.* SEŠITY Úřadu dokumentace a vyšetřování zločinů komunismu č. 12 (Praha: ÚDV, 2004).

Pavlík, Pavel and Václav Wynnyczuk. "Czechoslovakia," in B. Berelson, ed., *Population Policy in Developed Countries* (New York: McGraw-Hill, 1974), 319-354.

Pearson, Roger. *Shockley on Eugenics and Race: The Application of Science to the Solution of Human Problems* (Washington, D.C.: Scott-Townsend Publishers, 1992).

Pearsons, Raymond. *The Rise and Fall of the Soviet Empire* (New York: St. Martin's Press, 1998).

Pellar, Ruben and Zbyněk Andrš. "Statistical Evaluation of Romany Women in East Slovakia - Appendix to the report on the Examination in the Problematic of Sexual Sterilization of Romanies in Czechoslovakia," in *Het Afkopen van Vruchtbaarheid: Een onderzoek naar door Paul Ofner en Bert de Rooij in opdracht van de Verenging Lau Mazeril en de Stichting Informatie over Charta 77* (Amsterdam: Lau Mazeril Foundation, 1990).

Phillips, Nelson and Cynthia Hardy. *Discourse Analysis: Investigating Processes of Social Construction* (London: Sage Publications, 2002).

Pittaway, Mark. "Language, Identity and Nation," in Christina Chimisso, ed. *Exploring European Identities* (Walton Hall: Open University Press, 2003): 149-183.

Plichtová, Jana, ed. *Minorities in Politics* (Bratislava: Czechoslovak Committee for the European Cultural Foundation, 1992).

Polansky, Paul. "Czech Government's Cover-up of a Roma Death Camp." Paper presented to the Human Dimension Seminar on Roma in the CSCE Region, Warsaw, 1994 (unpublished.)

Populační vývoj České republiky (Praha: PřF UK, 1996).

Port, Mattijs, van de. *Gypsies, Wars and Other Instances of the Wild* (Amsterdam: Amsterdam University Press, 1998).

Postavení lesbické ženy v České společnosti (Praha: Alia, 1997).

Průcha, Jan. *Multikulturní výchova: Teorie, praxe, výzkum.* (Praha: nakladatelství ISV, 2001).

Przeworski, Adam. *Democracy and the Market: Political and Economic Reforms in Eastern Europe and Latin America* (Cambridge: Cambridge University Press, 1991).

Puxon, Grattan. *ROM: Europe's Gypsies* (London: Minority Rights Group, 1975).

________. "Toward Nationality Recognition." *Roma*, 3:1 (1977): 15-21.

Ragsdale, Hugh. *The Soviets, the Munich Crisis, and the Coming of World War II* (Cambridge: Cambridge University Press, 2004).

Reban, Milan. "Czechoslovakia: The New Federation," in George Klein and Milan Reban, eds. *The Politics of Ethnicity in Eastern Europe* (Boulder: East European Monographs, Columbia University Press, 1981): 234-235.

Reed Jr., Adolph. "The 'Underclass' as Myth and Symbol: The Poverty of Discourse about Poverty," in Adolph Reed Jr., *Stirrings in the Jug: Black Politics in the Post-Segregation Era* (Minneapolis: University of Minnesota Press, 1999), 179-196.

Reilly, Phillip. *The Surgical Solution: A History of Involuntary Sterilization in the United States* (Baltimore: Johns Hopkins University Press, 1991).

Reyniers, Alain. *Gypsy Population and their Movements within Central and Eastern Europe* (Paris: OECD, 1995).

Říčan, Pavel. *S Romy žít budeme – jde o to jak* (Praha: Portál, 1998).

Richardson, Joanna. *The Gypsy Debate: Can Discourse Control?* (Exeter and Charlottesville, VA: Imprint Academic, 2006).

Rishi, W. R. *Roma: The Panjabi Emigrants in Europe, Central and Middle Asia, the USSR, and the Americas* (Patiala: Punjabi University, 1976).

Roberts, Dorothy. *Killing the Black Body: Race, Reproduction and the Meaning of Liberty* (New York: Vintage, 1999).

Rousseau, Jean-Jacques. *A Discourse on Inequality* (New York: Penguin Classics, 1984).

Salecl, Renata. "How to Identify with the Suffering Other," in Elzbieta Matynia, ed., *Grappling with Democracy: Deliberations on Post-Communist Societies, 1990-1995* (Prague: SLON, 1996): 250-256.

Sandford, Jeremy. *Gypsies* (London: Secker & Warburg, 1973).

Sapir, Edward. *Culture: Genuine and Spurious* (Berlin, New York: Mouton de Gruyter, 1999; first published in 1924).

Scott, Hilda. *Does Socialism Liberate Women? Experiences from Eastern Europe* (Boston: Bacon Press, 1974).

Scott, James. *Domination and the Arts of Resistance: Hidden Transcripts* (New Haven: Yale University Press, 1990).

Scott, Joan Wallach. *Gender and the Politics of History* (New York: Columbia University Press, 1988).

Sharma, A. P. "Distinct Identity of ROMA." *Roma*, 2:2 (1976): 5-7.

Silverman, Carol. "Pollution and Power: Gypsy Women in America," in Matt Salo, ed., *The American Kalderas: Gypsies in the New World* (Centenary College: Gypsy Lore Society, North American Chapter Publications, No. 1, 1981).

Šimečka, Milan. *The Restoration of Order: The Normalization of Czechoslovakia, 1969-1976* (New York: Verso, 1984).

Slezkine, Yuri. *Arctic Mirrors: Russia and the Small Peoples of the North* (Ithaca: Cornell University Pres, 1993).

________."The USSR as a Communal Apartment, or How a Socialist State Promoted Ethnic Particularism." *Slavic Review*, 53:2 (Summer 1994): 414-52.

Šmejkalová, Jiřina. "Gender as an Analytical Category of Post-Communist Studies," in G. Jahnert, J. Gohrisch, D. Hahn, H. M. Nickel, I. Peinl a K. Schafgen, eds., *Gender in Transition in Eastern and Central Europe Proceedings* (Berlin: Trafo Verlag, 2001).

Smith, Tracy. "Racist Encounters: Romani 'Gypsy' Women and Mainstream Health Services." *The European Journal of Women's Studies*, 4 (1997): 183-196.

Smith, Valerie. *Not Just Race, Not Just Gender: Black Feminist Readings* (New York and London: Routledge, 1998).

Sokolová, Gabriela, et al. *Soudobé tendence vývoje národnosti v ČSSR* (Praha: Akademia, 1987).

Sokolova, Vera. "Representations of Homosexuality and the Separation of Gender and Sexuality in the Czech Republic before and after 1989," in

Katherine Isaacs, ed., *Political Systems and Definitions of Gender Roles* (Pisa, Italy: Edizione Plus, Universita di Pisa, 2001): 273-290.

Sokolova, Vera. "'Don't Get Pricked!': Representation and the Politics of Sexuality in the Czech Republic," in Sibelan Forrester, Elena Gapova and Magdalena Zaborowska, eds., *Over the Wall/After the Fall: Post-Communist Cultures Through an East-West Gaze* (Bloomington: Indiana University Press, 2004): 251-267.

________. "Černý trojúhelník: Vratký terén historiografie Holocaustu a romská perspektiva," in Jaroslav Balvín a kol., eds., *Romové a Majorita* (Kladno: Hnutí R, 1999): 48-76.

Solinger, Rickie. *Wake Up Little Susie: Single Pregnancy and Race Before Roe v. Wade* (New York: Routledge, 1992).

Sonneman, Toby, F. "Old Hatreds in the New Europe: Roma After the Revolutions." *Tikkun*, 7:11 (1992): 51.

Šrajerová, Olga. "K rešeniu romskej otázky na Slovensku po roku 1945." *Slezský sborník*, 91:3 (1993): 178-189.

Stavenhagen, Rodolfo. *Old and New Racism in Europe. New Expressions of Racism: Growing Areas of Conflict in Europe*, International Alert, ed., SIM Special No. 7. (Utrecht: Netherlands, Institute of Human Rights, 1987).

Štěchová, Markéta. "Etnicita a kriminalita," in Oldřich Novotný and Jiří Zapletal, *Základy kriminologie* (Praha: PF UK, 1993): 105-135.

STEM. "The Relationship of Czech Population towards the Roma." In *Trendy* 2006/4.

Štěpán, Jaromír. *Právo a moderní lékařstí* (Praha: Avicena, 1989).

Stepan, Nancy. *The Hour of Eugenics: Race, Gender, and Nation in Latin America* (Ithaca: Cornell University Press, 1991).

Stewart, Kathleen. *A Space on the Side of the Road: Cultural Poetics in an "Other" America* (Princeton: University of Princeton Press, 1996).

Stewart, Kevin. *The Deep Dark Heart of Asia: Mongols in Western Consciousness* (Lewiston, NY: The Edwin Mellen Press, 1997).

Stewart, Michael. *The Time of the Gypsies* (Boulder: Westview Press, 1997).

Stokes, Gale, ed. *From Stalinism to Pluralism: A Documentary History of Eastern Europe from 1945* (Oxford: Oxford University Press, 1996, 2nd Ed.).

Stoler, Laura Ann. *Race and the Education of Desire* (Durham: Duke University Press, 1995).

Strathern, Marilyn. *The Gender of the Gift: Problems with Women and Problems with Society in Melanesia* (Berkeley: University of California Press, 1988).

Strayer, Robert. *Why Did the Soviet Union Collapse?: Understanding Historical Change* (New York: M.E. Sharpe, 1998).

Struggling For Ethnic Identity: Czechoslovakia's Endangered Gypsies. Helsinki Watch. (New York, L.A., London: Helsinki Human Right Watch, 1992).

Studie o současné společenské situaci romského obyvatelstva v ČSFR (Praha: Skupina nezávislých expertů FMPSV, 1990).

Šubrtová, Alena. *Z dějin československého sčítání obyvatelstva* (Prague: Acta Universitas Carolinae, 1980).

Sugar, Peter, ed. *Nationalism in Eastern Europe* (Seattle, London: University of Washington Press, 1994, 3rd Ed.).

Sugrue, Thomas. *The Origins of the Urban Crisis: Race and Inequality in Postwar Detroit* (Princeton: Princeton University Press, 1996).

Sutherland, Anne. *Gypsies: The Hidden Americans* (London: Tavistock Publishers, 1975).

Sway, Marlene. *Familiar Strangers: Gypsy Life in America* (Urbana and Chicago: University of Illinois Press, 1988).

Szporluk, Roman. *National Identity and Ethnicity in Russia and the New States of Eurasia* (Armonk: M.E. Sharpe Press, 1994).

Tarrow, Sidney. *Power in Movement: Social Movements, Collective Action, and Politics* (New York: Cambridge University Press, 1994).

Taussig, Michael. *Mimesis and Alterity: A Particular History of the Senses* (New York: Routledge, 1993).

________. *Shamanism, Colonialism, and the Wild Man: a Study in Terror and Healing* (Chicago: University of Chicago Press, 1987).

Taylor, Charles. *Sources of the Self: the Making of the Modern Identity* (Cambridge, MA: Harvard University Press, 1989).

Todorova, Maria. "The Balkans: From Discovery to Invention." *Slavic Review*, 53:2 (1994): 453-482.

Tomášek, Dušan. *Pozor, cenzurováno! Aneb ze života soudružky cenzury* (Praha: MV CR, 1994).

Tomova, Ilona. *The Gypsies in the Transition Period* (Sofia: International Center for Minority Studies and Intercultural Relations, 1995).

Trestní právo České republiky (Praha: Fakulta Právní Univerzity Karlovy, 1995).

Trumpener, Katie. "The Time of the Gypsies: A 'Peoples Without History' in the Naratives of the West," *Critical Inquiry*, 18:4 (1992): 843-884.

Tsing, Anna Lowenhaupt. *In the Realm of the Diamond Queen: Marginality in an out-of-the-way Place* (Princeton: Princeton University Press, 1993).

Tucker, Robert. *The Soviet Political Mind: Stalinism and Post-Stalinist Change* (New York: Norton, 1971).

Tylor, Edward Burnett Sir. *Primitive Culture* (New York: Harper, 1958).

Tyrnauer, Gabrielle. *The Fate of the Gypsies during the Holocaust: Special Report for the U.S. Holocaust Memorial Council* (Washington: U.S. Holocaust Memorial Council, 1985).

Ulč, Otto. "Gypsies in Czechoslovakia: A Case of Unfinished Integration." *East European Politics and Societies*, 2:2 (1988): 306-332.

________. "Integration of the Gypsies in Czechoslovakia." *Ethnic Groups*, 9:2 (1991).

________. "Communist National Minority Policy: The Case of the Gypsies in Czechoslovakia." *Soviet Studies*, 20:4 (1969): 421-443.

Usborne, Cornelie. *The Politics of the Body in Weimar Germany: Women's Reproductive Tights and Duties* (Ann Arbor: The University of Michigan Press, 1992).

Vagačová, Ingrid and Martin Fotta, eds. *Rómovia a druhá svetová vojna – čítanka* (Bratislava: Nadácia Milana Šimečku, 2006).

Vermeersch, Peter. *The Romani Movement: Minority Politics And Ethnic Mobilization in Contemporary Central Europe* (Oxford and New York: Berghahn Books, 2006).

Vidláková, Olga. "Law and Fertility in Czechoslovakia," in M. Kirk, M. Livi-Bacci and E. Szabady, eds., *Law and Fertility in Europe* (Dolhain: Ordina, 1976, Vol. 1).

Víšek, Petr. "Program integrace – Řešení problematiky romských obyvatel v období 1970 až 1989," in *Romové v České republice: Sešity pro sociální politiku, 1945-1998* (Praha: Socioklub, 1999): 194-199.

Výsledky sčítání osob, bytů a domácností za rok 2001: zpráva českého statistického úřadu (Praha: ČSÚ, 2002).

Výzkumy Institutu pro výzkum veřejného mínění z let 1990-1997 (Praha: IVVM).

Výzkumy Střediska empirických výzkumů z let 1990-1997 (Praha: STEM).

Wachtel, Andrew. *Making a Nation, Breaking a Nation: Literature and Cultural Politics in Yugoslavia* (Stanford: Stanford University Press, 1988).

Wagner, Roy. *The invention of Culture* (Chicago: University of Chicago Press, 1981).

Ware, Vron. "Moments of Danger: Race, Gender, and Memories of Empire." *History and Theory*, 31:41 (1992): 110-122.

Weinerman, Richard. *Social Medicine in Eastern Europe: The Organization of Health Services and the Education of Medical Personnel in Czechoslovakia, Hungary and Poland* (Cambridge, MA: Harvard University Press, 1969).

Weinerová, Renata. "Romanies - In Search of Lost Security: An Ethnological Probe in Prague 5." *Ethnology: Occasional Papers*, No. 3 (1994): 137-49.

Weisbord, Robert. *Genocide? Birth Control and the Black American* (Westport: Greenwood and Two Continents, 1975).

Weitz, Eric. "Racial Politics without the Concept of Race: Reevaluating Soviet Ethnic and National Purges." *Slavic Review*, 61:1 (2002): 1-29.

White, Stephen. "Political Science as Ideology: The Study of Soviet Politics," in B. Chapman and A. Potter, eds., *Political Questions* (Manchester, 1975).

Williams, Patricia. *The Alchemy of Race and Rights* (Cambridge, MA: Harvard University Press, 1992).

Williams, Patricia. *Seeing a Color-Blind Future: The Paradox of Race* (New York: Noonday Press, 1998).

________. *The Rooster's Egg* (Cambridge, MA: Harvard University Press, 1995).

Wolchik, Sharon and Alfred Meyer, eds. *Women, State and Party in Eastern Europe* (Durham: Duke University Press, 1985).

Wolchik, Sharon and J. Jaquette, eds. *Women and Democracy in Latin America and Central and Eastern Europe* (Baltimore: Johns Hopkins University Press, 1998).

Wolff, Larry. *Inventing Eastern Europe: The Map of Civilization on the Mind of the Enlightenment* (Stanford: Stanford University Press, 1994).

Zantop, Susanne. *Colonial Fantasies: Conquest, Family, and Nation in Precolonial Germany, 1770-1870* (Durham: Duke University Press, 1997).

Zimmermann, Michael. *Verfolgt, vertrieben, vernichtet: Die Nationalsozialistische Vernichtungspolitik gegen Sinti und Roma* (Essen: Klartext Verlag, 1989).

PRIMARY MATERIALS

Policy and Legislative Documents:

Charta 77. "Dokumenty: Charta 77 - Dokument č. 23." *Listy*, 3:2 (1979): 47-52.

Dekret prezidenta republiky ze dne 21. června 1945 "O konfiskaci a urychleném rozdělení zemědělského majetku Němců, Maďarů, jakož i zrádců a nepřátel českého a slovenského národa." (SÚAR, Praha).

Dekret prezidenta republiky ze dne 20. července 1945 "O osídlení zemědělské půdy Němců, Maďarů ajiných nepřátel státu českými, slovenskými a jinými slovanskými zemědelci." (SÚAR, Praha).

Kontrolní zpráva o plnění usnesení Předsednictva vlády ČSSR č. 21 z 29. ledna 1976 o řešení otázek cikánského obyvatelstva. FMPSV 1980. (ARSOC, Praha).

Košický vládní program. April 5, 1945 (SÚAR, Praha).

Manifesto of the Romani Community of Western Bohemia. Pravda (Plzeň), August 27, 1968, 2.

Memorandum k základním otázkám cikánské problematiky. 1970. (MZA, Brno).

Modrý bulletin ÚV KSČ. April 30, 1958. (SÚAR, Praha).

Návrh programu řešení problematiky cikánů. December 10, 1968. (MZA, Brno).

Niektoré problémy súvisajúce s nepriaznivým stavom zdravotnej úrovne a zdravotnej výchovy cigánskych obyvatelov. Sekretariát Komísie vlády SSR pre otázky cigánskych obyvatelov. SKC - 6406/77. Bratislava, July 1977 (ŠNA, Bratislava).

Péče o společensky nepřizpůsobené občany: metodická příručka pro pracovníky národních výborů (Praha: MPSV, 1972).

Politická analýza Svazu Cikánů-Romů. April 18, 1972 (MZA, Brno).

Prohlášení Ustavujícího sjezdu SCR v ČSR. August 30, 1969. (MZA, Brno).

Sbírka oběžníků pro Krajské národní výbory (KNV), roč. IV, 1952, č. 13, poř. č. 140, March 5, 1952. (SÚAR, Praha).

Stanovy Svazu Cikánů-Romů v České republice. (MZA, Brno).

Usnesení ÚV KSČ o vytvoření komisí národních výborů pro otázky cikánského obyvatelstva. March 23, 1973 (SÚAR, Praha).

Usnesení vlády ČSSR č. 231/1972. "Zásady celostátních sociálně-politických opatření v péči společnosti o cikánské obyvatelstvo" and amendments to this document from *Usnesení vlády ČSSR č. 21/1976* (ARSOC, Praha).

Usnesení vlády ČSSR č. 502/1958 Sb, June 15, and October 13, 1965. (SÚAR, Praha).

Věstník Ministerstva zdravotnictví České socialistické republiky, Part 1-2, Vol. XX, 1/1972.

Vestník Ministerstva zdravotnictva Slovenskej socialistickej republiky, 9/1972.

Vyhláška Ministerstva práce a sociálních věcí ČSR č. 152/1988 Sb, Částka 33, § 35, 965. (SÚAR, Praha).

Výpis ze zprávy předložené a schválené sekretariátem ÚV KSČ. September 15, 1954. (SÚAR, Praha).

Zákon č. 74/1958 Sb., "O trvalém usídlení kočujících osob." November 11, 1958. (Ústava ČSSR).

Zákon č. 94/1963 Sb. "O rodině." (Ústava ČSSR).

Zákon "O potulných cikánech." July 14, 1927. (SÚAR, Praha).

Zpráva kriminální ústředny z r. 1948, E/2 III/6 (SÚAR, Praha).

Zpráva likvidační komise. November 17, 1972. (MZA, Brno).

Zpráva Ministerstva zdravotnictví České republiky o zdravotním stavu cikánské populace (Praha: MZ, 1980).

Zpráva Ministerstva zdravotnictví České republiky pro vládní komisi pro otázky cikánského obyvatelstva (Praha: MZ, October 1986).

Zpráva o bezpečnostní situaci na území ČR v letech 1994, 1995, 1996, 1997, 1994 (Praha: Ministerstvo vnitra).

Zpráva o plnění usnesení ÚRO. June 5, 1958. (SÚAR, Praha).

Zpráva o stavu lidských práv v České republice (Praha: Český helsinský výbor, 1994, 1995, 1996).

Zpráva o životě cikánů v ČSR. MPS, 1950. (SÚAR, Praha).

Zpráva Ústředního výboru Národní fronty. April 1973. (MZA, Brno).

Zpráva vládní komise pro otázky cikánského obyvatelstva, CKC-4509/1970. (SÚAR, Praha).

Zvláštní zpráva o projevech rasové a národnostní nesnášenlivosti (Praha a Brno: Nejvyšší státní zastupitelství, 1994, 1995, 1996, 1997).

Demographic and Population Studies:

Bartošová, Milada, et al. *Populační politika v ČSSR, 1945-1975*. Výzkumná práce (Pracoviště Praha), řada B, č. 76. (Bratislava: Československý výzkumný ústav práce a sociálních věcí, 1978).

Charvát, František. *Sociální Struktura socialistické společnosti a její vývoj v Československu - srovnávací analýza, reprodukce, perspektivy* (Praha: Academia, 1980).

Černý, Miloš. "Biologické a medicínské apekty populačního vývoje. Perspektivy uplatnění genetiky v populační politice." *Zpráva z II. Demografické konference Československé demografické společnosti, May 20, 1970. Demografie*, 10:2 (1970): 318-319.

Havelka, Jiří. *Populační politika v Československu* (Praha: Orbis, 1978).

Kábele, František. "Czechoslovakia," in *Economic aspects of special education: reports from Czechoslovakia, New Zealand and the United States of America* (Paris: UNESCO, 1978), 21-62.

Kalibán, Vojtěch, Tereza Šišková, and Kazimír Večerka. *Příčiny zvýšené kriminality (protispolečenské činnosti) cikánských občanů, zejména mladistvých.* (Archív vědeckého ústavu kriminologického. Unpublished result report of a research study, 1979).

Kučera, M. "Population Policy in Czechoslovakia." *Demografie*, 10:1 (1968): 307-317.

Schvarcová, Mária. "Niektoré poznatky o prognózách v oblasti populačnej klímy v ČSSR z hladiska vydatých ekonomicky činných žien s nezaopatrenými detmi (výsledky empirického výzkumu)." *Populační zprávy*, 1:2 (1979): 36-39.

Sčítání lidu 1968, 1974, 1976-1989. (AMPSV, Praha).

Srb, Vladimír. "Cikáni v Československu." *Demografie*, 11:3 (1969): 191-200.

Srb, Vladimír, and Olga Vomáčková. "Cikáni v ČSSR v roce 1968." *Demografie*, 11:3 (1969): 221-239.

Anthropological and Medical Studies:

Beneš, Jan. *Cikáni v Československu: antropologická studie dospělých mužů* (Brno: Univerzita J. E. Purkyně, 1975).

Kubica, M. et al., "Postpartálna sterilizácia." *Československá gynekologie*, 43:8 (1978): 607-8.

Meisner, Jan. "Problémy zdravotnické výchovy cikánských dětí." *Otázky defektologie*, 15:1 (1972-73): 9-15.

Mohapl, M. and B. Dobešová. "Problematika žen s nežádoucím těhotenstvím." *Československá gynekologie*, 43:8 (1978): 605-7.

Púchala, M. "Nepriaznivé následky podvazu vājcovodov na ženský organismus." *Praktický lékař*, 69:4 (1989): 138-140.

Posluch, J., and E. Posluchová. "Problémy plánovaného rodičovstva u cigánských spoluobčanov vo východoslovenskom kraji." *Zdravotnická pracovnice*, 39:4 (1989): 220-223.

Stuchlík, Jan. *O neomorfizaci psychologických testů v československé psychiatrii* (Praha: Státní zdravotnické nakladatelství, 1964).

Suchý, Jaroslav. "Vývoj cikánských dětí v měnících se životních podmínkách." *Čs. Pediatrie*, 27:9 (1972): 430-441.

________. *Vývojová antropologie obyvatelstva ČSR* (Praha: Univerzita Karlova, 1973).

Vacek, Jiří. "Nové metody v moderní gynekologii." *Československá gynekologie*, 8:8 (1976): 620-625.

Ethnographic and Sociological Studies, History of the Roma:

Davidová, Eva. *Cikánské (romské) etnikum v Ostravě: výzkumná zpráva* (Praha: VÚVA, 1970).

________. "K vymezení a specifice současného cikánského problému v Československu." *Sociologický časopis*, 6:1 (1970): 29-41.

Facuna, Anton. "Zväz Cigánov-Romov na Slovensku." *Demografie*, 11:3 (1969): 214-215.

Holomek, Miroslav. "Současné problémy Cikánů v ČSSR a jejich řešení." *Demografie*, 11:3 (1969): 205-221.

Horváthová, Emília. *Cigáni na Slovensku* (Bratislava: Vydavatelstvo Slovenskej akademie vied, 1964).

________. "K otázke etnokulturného vývoja a etnickej klasifikácie Cigánov." *Slovenský Národopis*, 22:1 (1974): 3-14.

Hübschmannová, Milena. "Co je tzv. cikánská otázka." *Sociologický časopis*, 6:2 (1970): 105-20.

________. "Jazyková politika Sovětského Svazu." *Sociologický časopis*, 9:3 (1973): 259-273.

________. "Kdo jsou Romové?" *Nový Orient*, 27:5 (1972):144-148.

________. "K jazykové situaci Romů v ČSSR." *Slovo a Slovesnost*, 37 (1976).

________. "Some Proverbs of Slovak Roms." *Roma*, 3:2 (1977): 18-22.

________. "Společenská problematika Romů v ČSSR." *Demografie*, 12:1 (1970): 16-21.

________. "What Can Sociology Suggest about the Origins of Roms?" *Archív Orient*, 40 (1970): 51-64.

Hübschmannová, Milena and Jan Řehák. "Etnikum a komunikace." *Sociologický časopis*, 6:2 (1970): 548-559.

Jamnická-Šmerglová, Zdeňka. *Dějiny našich cikánů* (Praha: Orbis, 1955).

Kára, Karel. "Cikáni v ČSSR a jejich společenská integrace," *Sociologický časopis*, 12:2 (1977): 366-375.

Kier, Stanislav. "Práce okresní komise pro otázky cikánského obyvatelstva v Českém Krumlově." *Demografie*, 12:2 (1970): 367-369.

Nováček, Josef. *Cikáni včera, dnes a zítra* (Praha: Socialistická akademie, 1968).

Srb, Vladimír. "Ustavující sjezd Svazu Cikánů-Romů v ČSSR v Brně." *Demografie*, 11:4 (1969): 360-367.

Sus, Jaroslav. *Cikánská otázka v ČSSR* (Praha: Nakladatelsví politické literatury, 1961).

Pedagogical and Psychological Studies, Educational Sources:

Buřič, Josef. *Škola a život cikánských dětí* (Praha: Pedagogické čtení, 1973).

Čítanka pro 7. třídu (Praha: Státní pedagogické nakladatelství, 1978).

Cikánské děti v základních devítiletých školách ve školním roce 1969/70 až 1972/73. Zprávy a rozbory (Praha: Federální statistický úřad, 1974).

Dědič, Miroslav. *Škola bez kázně* (České Budějovice: Jihočeské nakladatelství, 1985).

________. *Výchova a vzdělání cikánských dětí a mládeže* (Praha: Státní pedagogické nakladatelství, 1982).

Jósza, Ladislav. "Cesta k úspechu," in Pavol Kuruc, ed., *Na pomoc učitelom cigánských detí zo zanedbaného rodinného prostredia* (Bratislava: Slovenské pedagogické nakladatelstvo, 1981), 6.

Macháčková, Milena. *K problémům připravenosti cikánských dětí pro společenské soužití a některé zkušenosti z využití progresivních metod v práci s těmito dětmi* (Praha: Pedagogické čtení, 1970).

Malá, Helena. *Výchova, vzdělávání a biologický vývoj cikánských dětí a mládeže v ČSR* (Praha: Univrezita Karlova, 1984).

Ministerstvo školství ČSR. *Předškolní a školní výchova cikánských dětí: aktuální problémy speciální pedagogiky* (Praha: Státní pedagogické nakladatelství, 1975).

Olejár, František. *Formovanie psychických zvláštností výchovne zanedbaných detí* (Bratislava: Slovenské pedagogické nakladatelstvo, 1972).

Olmrová, Jiřina. *K osobnosti romského pubescenta a jeho rodinným vztahům* (Praha: Univerzita Karlova, 1973).

Podmele, Ladislav. *Komunistická morálka a výchova nového člověka* (Praha: SPN, 1971).

________. *Učení o společnosti a státu* (Praha: SPN, 1972).

Sborník pedagogické fakulty UK, Biologie III. and IV. (Praha: Univerzita Karlova, 1975).

Siakel, Josef and Štěpán Havlík. "Zpráva o zaškolování detí občanov cigánského povodu a začleňování 15.račného dorastu do učňovského pomeru." (Conference paper presented at the Regional konference for solving questions of the citizens of gypsy origin, November 11, 1964).

Smrčka, Ferdinand. *Hovoříme s rodiči* (Praha: SPN, 1974).

Solojevova, Anna. "Zlé deti a čo s tým súvisí." *Moskevskaja Literaturnaja Gazeta*, (1965).

Štěpán, Josef. "Cikánské dítě ve zvláštní škole internátní," in *Výchova a vzdělávání cikánských dětí: sborník přednášek* (Praha: MŠ, Ústav studií a analýz, 1976).

________. *Cikánský oligofrenní jedinec v kolektivním zařízení* (Praha: Pedagogické čtení, 1972).

Štěpán, Josef and Ludmila Ždánská. "Cikánský jedinec v kolektivním zařízení." *Otázky defektologie*, 15:5-6 (1972): 173-179.

Švarbalík, Josef. "Osobitosti pri výchove a vyučování cigánskych žiakov z nevyhovujúceho rodinného prostredia," in *Pedagogické osobitosti vo výchove a vyučování cigánskych žiakov základnej školy* (Bratislava: MŠ, edícia Pedagogické čítanie, 1979).

Syřišťová, Eva a kol. *Normalita osobnosti* (Praha: Avicenum, 1972).

Tancoš, Rudolf. "Problematika cikánské mládeže." *Demografie*, 12:1 (1970): 34-35.

Výborný, František. *O výchově dětí ke kázni* (Praha: SPN, 1958).

Výchova a vzdělávání cikánských dětí: sborník přednášek (Praha: MŠ, Ústav studií a analýz, 1976).

"Zpověď soudružky učitelky Kopáčkové ze ZŠ Praha 9, Kyje," cited in Milan Kantor, "Cikánské dítě a škola," in *Výchova a vzdělávání cikánských dětí: sborník přednášek* (Praha: MŠ, Ústav studií a analýz, 1976): 92-96.

Romani Autobiographies, Memoirs and Fiction:

Adler, Marta. *My Life with the Gypsies* (London: Souvenir Press, 1960).

Berkovici, Konrad. *The Story of the Gypsies* (London: Jonathan Cape, 1929).

Boswell, Silvester. *The Book of Boswell: an Autobiography of a Gypsy* (London: Gollancz, 1970).

Fabiánová, Tera and Milena Hübschmannová. *Čavargoš: Romaňi paramisi / Tulák: Romská pohádka* (Praha: Apeiron, 1991).

Ferková, Ilona. *Čorde Čhave – Ukradené děti* (Brno: Společenství Romů na Moravě, 1996).

________. *Zničila si život pro peníze – Mosarďa peske o dřivipen anglo love* (Praha: Romani Čhib, 1990).

Koptová, Anna. *Kale ruži* (Hradec Králové: Romaňi Čhib, 1990).

Patočková, Katarina. *Som Cigánka* (Bratislava, Slovakia: Mikromex, 1992).

Petulengro, Gipsy. *A Romany Life* (New York: Funk & Wagnalls company, 1936).

Whyte, Betsy. *The Yellow on the Broom* (Edinburgh: Chambers Press, 1979).

Yates, Dora. *My Gypsy Days: Recollections of a Romany Rawnie* (London: Phoenix House, 1953).

Yoors, Jan. *The Gypsies* (New York: Touchstone Book, 1983).

Popular Literature and Fiction:

Abeceda smíchu (Praha: Vyšehrad, 1989).

Aškenazy, Ludvík. *Etudy dětské a nedětské* (Praha: Československý spisovatel, 1963).

Baar, Jindřich Šimon. *Český lid* (Praha: J. Otto, 1886).

Benešová, Božena. *Don Pablo, Don Pedro a Věra Lukášová* (Praha: SNKLU, 1962).

Budínský, Václav. *Anekdoty z trezoru: aneb vtipy o zlatou mříž z období neúspěšného budování socialismu v Československu* (Praha: Svépomoc, 1990).

Čapek, Karel. *Obyčejný život* (Praha: Fr. Borový, 1935).

Čelakovský, František Ladislav. *Ohlasy písní českých* (Praha: 1839).

Černý, Václav. *Aprílové grotesky* (Praha: Lidové noviny, 1983).

Hálek, Vítězslav. *Pohádky z naší vesnice* (Praha: Mladá fronta, 1956).

Hampl, František and Karel Bradáč. *Žeň českého humoru* (Praha: Práce, 1952).

Hašek, Jaroslav. *Črty, povídky a humoresky z cest* (Praha: SNKHLU, 1955).

Heyduk, Adolf. *Cikánské melodie a jiné písně* (Praha: SNKHLU, 1955).

Hugo, Victor. *The Hunchback of Notre Dame* (New York: The Modern Library, 1941).

Janáček, Leoš. *Zápisník zmizelého* (Praha: Hudební matice Umělecké besedy, 1949).

Jiránek, Vladimír. *Anekdoty o civilizaci* (Praha: Lidové noviny, 1977).

Kantůrková, Eva. *Přítelkyně z domu smutku* (Praha: Československý spisovatel, 1991).

Kerles, Jaroslav. *Jak vtipy přicházejí na svět* (Praha: Annonce, 1991).

Lawrence, D.H. *The Virgin and the Gipsy* (New York: A.A. Knopf, 1930).

Mácha, Karel Hynek. *Básně KHM* (Praha: J. Otto, 1897).

Meriméé, Prosper. *Carmen* (London: George Routledge & sons, 1877).

Němcová, Božena. *Listy II*, "Dopis Sofii Podlipské, 24. června, 1853" (Praha: Československý spisovatel, 1952), 30-31.

________. *Sebrané spisy B.N., svazek X.* (Praha: J. Laichter, 1911).

Neruda, Jan. *Knihy básní* (Praha: Orbis, 1951).

Puchmajer, Antonín Jaroslav. *Mluvnice cikánského jazyka a zlodějské hantýrky* (Praha: 1821).

Pushkin, Alexander. *Tsygany* (Moskva: Gosudartvenoe izdavatelstvo detskoi literatury, 1949).

Sekera, Jan. *Děti z hliněné vesnice* (Praha: Československý spisovatel, 1952).

Štampach, František. *Děti nad propastí* (Košice-Plzeň: M. Labková, 1933).

Švandrlík, Jiří, and Jiří Neprakta. *106 od Neprakty* (Havlíčkův Brod: krajské nakladatelství, 1961).

________. *Anekdoty s Nepraktou* (Praha: Lidové noviny, 1979).

________. *Anekdoty a semtamfóry* (Praha: Lidové noviny, 1972).

Taussig, Pavel. *Blbé, ale naše = One (Party) Liners* (Toronto: 68 Publishers, 1987).

Newspaper Articles and Essays:

Cihy, Ladislav. "Tabule Hany: Na pranýři je alkohol a prostituce!" *Romano Lil*, 2:4 (1970): 26.

Giňa, Ondřej. "Dopis na Romské Téma." *Mladý Svět*, 34:3 (1989): 6.

Tučková, Anna. "Esej." *Kulturní Tvorba*, November 17 (1966): 14.

Danáš, Kornel. "Bolavý problém." *Nedelná Pravda*, (Poprad), August 5, 1988.

Honus, Aleš. "Romka vysoudila za sterilizaci půl miliónu," *Právo*, 12.10. 2007.

Komanický, Pavol. "Nebo si treba zaslúžiť. O Rómoch a ich svojskej životnej filozófii." *Východ*, April 13-14 (1990): 1-2.

Komárek, Martin. "Co je rasismus?" *Mladá fronta DNES*, November 22, 1999, 8.

Kravec, Ondřej. "Kde rasismus nemá místa." *Tribuna*, 44 (October 20, 1974): 2.

Kuchařová, Vlasta. "Mateřské školy." *Romano Lil*, (1970): 14-15.

Milevová, Marta. "Aby vaše dítě bylo šťastné!" *Romano Lil*, (1970): 16.

Films and Plays:

Larks on a String. Directed by Jiří Menzel (Praha: Bontonfilm, 1969).

Latcho Drom. Directed by Tony Gatlif (New York: New York Video, 1996).

Marián. Directed by Petr Václav (Prague: ArtStudio, 1998).

Nejistá sezóna. Written and Directed by Zdeněk Svěrák and Ladislav Smoljak (Divadlo Járy Cimrmanna a Filmové studio Barrandov, Praha, 1987).

Trobriand Cricket: an Ingenious Response to Colonialism. Directed by Jerry W. Leach (Berkeley: University of California Media Center, 1975).

SOURCES

Archives and Private Collections:

ACHC – Archiv Českého helsinského výboru, Praha

AMRK – Archiv Muzea romské kultury, Brno

AMPSV – Archiv Ministerstva práce a sociálních věcí, Praha

ARSOC – Archiv Socioklubu, Praha

MZA – Moravský zemský archiv, Brno:

- Fond Svazu Cikánů-Romů v ČSR, G 434, box 1:1; G 434, box 21:7; G 434, box 2; G 434, box 21:6; G 434, box 36; G 601, box 13;

NFA – Národní filmový archiv, Praha

PDM – Private Collection of Dana Mazalová. (Oral interviews with sterilized Romani women; Pavel Bret, ÚDV deputy; and Dr. Jiří Vacek, chief gynecologist from Ústí nad Orlicí.)

PRP – Private Collection of Rubben Pellar. (Statistics of sterilized 123 Slovak and 156 Czech Romani women.)

ŠNA – Štátny národní archiv, Bratislava

- Fond Úradu predsednictva sboru poverenikov 1945-1960, č. kr. 4, č. sp. II-1.
- Fond Policajného riaditelstva, Bratislava 1920-1945 (1950), č. kr. 31, č. sp. 8/133.
- Fond Povereníctva informácií a osvety, 1945-1952, č. sp. 8500/46, č. kr. 43.
- Fond Povereníctva vnútra – Obežníky (PV-O), č. kr. 230/71-1-BK/6, č. sp. 51.

SPA – Státní pedagogický archiv, knihovna Jana Ámose Komenského, Praha

SÚAR – Státní ústřední archiv, Praha (since 2005 renamed as Národní archiv):

- Fond Generálního velitelství četnictva, i.č. 117, čj. 850 k. 63.
- Fond Ministerstva vnitra – Dodatky (MV-D) 1918-1961, č.kr. 1282, č.sp. I/1-882/1, I/1-4521/17, I/1-4521/15, I/1-4521/4, I/1-4521/21, I/1-4521/19.
- Fond Ministerstva pracovních sil (MPS), č. kr. 47, č. sp. 100-1950.
- Fond MPS, č. kr. 400, č. sp. 212.
- Fond Ministerstva sociální péče (MSP), č. kr. 01-0053-0076/1956.

- Fond Předstednictva vlády (UPV), č. kr. 1163, č. sp. 1424/b/2, 1946-1951.
- Fond Zemského úřadu (ZÚ), č. kr. 855, č. sp. III-8, 1946-1948.

ÚVA – Ústřední všeodborový archiv, Praha:
- Fond předsednictva Ústřední rady odborů (ÚRO), č. sp. 46/292, 1958.
- Fond předsednictva (ÚRO), č. sp. 46/323.

Newspapers and Magazines:

Dikobraz: týdeník satiry a humoru
Lidová demokracie
Lidové noviny
Hraničářské slovo
Magazín Dikobrazu
Mladá fronta
Mladá fronta DNES
Národní osvobození
Nedelná Pravda
The New York Times
Práca
Práce
Právo
Právo lidu
Pravda (Plzeň, Bratislava)
Rudé právo
Smena
Svobodné noviny
Svobodné slovo
Tvorba
Týden
Večerník
Východ
Zemědělské noviny

Romani Journals and Magazines:

Amaro Gendalos
Journal of the Gypsy Lore Society (Romani Studies)
Roma
Romano Džaniben
Romano Lil
Romani Pajtrin

SOVIET AND POST-SOVIET POLITICS AND SOCIETY

Edited by Dr. Andreas Umland

ISSN 1614-3515

1 *Андреас Умланд (ред.)*
Воплощение Европейской конвенции по правам человека в России
Философские, юридические и эмпирические исследования
ISBN 3-89821-387-0

2 *Christian Wipperfürth*
Russland – ein vertrauenswürdiger Partner?
Grundlagen, Hintergründe und Praxis gegenwärtiger russischer Außenpolitik
Mit einem Vorwort von Heinz Timmermann
ISBN 3-89821-401-X

3 *Manja Hussner*
Die Übernahme internationalen Rechts in die russische und deutsche Rechtsordnung
Eine vergleichende Analyse zur Völkerrechtsfreundlichkeit der Verfassungen der Russländischen Föderation und der Bundesrepublik Deutschland
Mit einem Vorwort von Rainer Arnold
ISBN 3-89821-438-9

4 *Matthew Tejada*
Bulgaria's Democratic Consolidation and the Kozloduy Nuclear Power Plant (KNPP)
The Unattainability of Closure
With a foreword by Richard J. Crampton
ISBN 3-89821-439-7

5 *Марк Григорьевич Меерович*
Квадратные метры, определяющие сознание
Государственная жилищная политика в СССР. 1921 – 1941 гг
ISBN 3-89821-474-5

6 *Andrei P. Tsygankov, Pavel A.Tsygankov (Eds.)*
New Directions in Russian International Studies
ISBN 3-89821-422-2

7 *Марк Григорьевич Меерович*
Как власть народ к труду приучала
Жилище в СССР – средство управления людьми. 1917 – 1941 гг.
С предисловием Елены Осокиной
ISBN 3-89821-495-8

8 *David J. Galbreath*
Nation-Building and Minority Politics in Post-Socialist States
Interests, Influence and Identities in Estonia and Latvia
With a foreword by David J. Smith
ISBN 3-89821-467-2

9 *Алексей Юрьевич Безугольный*
Народы Кавказа в Вооруженных силах СССР в годы Великой Отечественной войны 1941-1945 гг.
С предисловием Николая Бугая
ISBN 3-89821-475-3

10 *Вячеслав Лихачев и Владимир Прибыловский (ред.)*
Русское Национальное Единство, 1990-2000. В 2-х томах
ISBN 3-89821-523-7

11 *Николай Бугай (ред.)*
Народы стран Балтии в условиях сталинизма (1940-е – 1950-е годы)
Документированная история
ISBN 3-89821-525-3

12 *Ingmar Bredies (Hrsg.)*
Zur Anatomie der Orange Revolution in der Ukraine
Wechsel des Elitenregimes oder Triumph des Parlamentarismus?
ISBN 3-89821-524-5

13 *Anastasia V. Mitrofanova*
The Politicization of Russian Orthodoxy
Actors and Ideas
With a foreword by William C. Gay
ISBN 3-89821-481-8

14 *Nathan D. Larson*
Alexander Solzhenitsyn and the Russo-Jewish Question
ISBN 3-89821-483-4

15 *Guido Houben*
Kulturpolitik und Ethnizität
Staatliche Kunstförderung im Russland der neunziger Jahre
Mit einem Vorwort von Gert Weisskirchen
ISBN 3-89821-542-3

16 *Leonid Luks*
Der russische „Sonderweg"?
Aufsätze zur neuesten Geschichte Russlands im europäischen Kontext
ISBN 3-89821-496-6

17 *Евгений Мороз*
История «Мёртвой воды» – от страшной сказки к большой политике
Политическое неоязычество в постсоветской России
ISBN 3-89821-551-2

18 *Александр Верховский и Галина Кожевникова (ред.)*
Этническая и религиозная интолерантность в российских СМИ
Результаты мониторинга 2001-2004 гг.
ISBN 3-89821-569-5

19 *Christian Ganzer*
Sowjetisches Erbe und ukrainische Nation
Das Museum der Geschichte des Zaporoger Kosakentums auf der Insel Chortycja
Mit einem Vorwort von Frank Golczewski
ISBN 3-89821-504-0

20 *Эльза-Баир Гучинова*
Помнить нельзя забыть
Антропология депортационной травмы калмыков
С предисловием Кэролайн Хамфри
ISBN 3-89821-506-7

21 *Юлия Лидерман*
Мотивы «проверки» и «испытания» в постсоветской культуре
Советское прошлое в российском кинематографе 1990-х годов
С предисловием Евгения Марголита
ISBN 3-89821-511-3

22 *Tanya Lokshina, Ray Thomas, Mary Mayer (Eds.)*
The Imposition of a Fake Political Settlement in the Northern Caucasus
The 2003 Chechen Presidential Election
ISBN 3-89821-436-2

23 *Timothy McCajor Hall, Rosie Read (Eds.)*
Changes in the Heart of Europe
Recent Ethnographies of Czechs, Slovaks, Roma, and Sorbs
With an afterword by Zdeněk Salzmann
ISBN 3-89821-606-3

24 *Christian Autengruber*
Die politischen Parteien in Bulgarien und Rumänien
Eine vergleichende Analyse seit Beginn der 90er Jahre
Mit einem Vorwort von Dorothée de Nève
ISBN 3-89821-476-1

25 *Annette Freyberg-Inan with Radu Cristescu*
The Ghosts in Our Classrooms, or: John Dewey Meets Ceauşescu
The Promise and the Failures of Civic Education in Romania
ISBN 3-89821-416-8

26 *John B. Dunlop*
The 2002 Dubrovka and 2004 Beslan Hostage Crises
A Critique of Russian Counter-Terrorism
With a foreword by Donald N. Jensen
ISBN 3-89821-608-X

27 *Peter Koller*
Das touristische Potenzial von Kam''janec'–Podil's'kyj
Eine fremdenverkehrsgeographische Untersuchung der Zukunftsperspektiven und Maßnahmenplanung zur Destinationsentwicklung des „ukrainischen Rothenburg"
Mit einem Vorwort von Kristiane Klemm
ISBN 3-89821-640-3

28 *Françoise Daucé, Elisabeth Sieca-Kozlowski (Eds.)*
Dedovshchina in the Post-Soviet Military
Hazing of Russian Army Conscripts in a Comparative Perspective
With a foreword by Dale Herspring
ISBN 3-89821-616-0

29 *Florian Strasser*
Zivilgesellschaftliche Einflüsse auf die Orange Revolution
Die gewaltlose Massenbewegung und die ukrainische Wahlkrise 2004
Mit einem Vorwort von Egbert Jahn
ISBN 3-89821-648-9

30 *Rebecca S. Katz*
The Georgian Regime Crisis of 2003-2004
A Case Study in Post-Soviet Media Representation of Politics, Crime and Corruption
ISBN 3-89821-413-3

31 *Vladimir Kantor*
Willkür oder Freiheit
Beiträge zur russischen Geschichtsphilosophie
Ediert von Dagmar Herrmann sowie mit einem Vorwort versehen von Leonid Luks
ISBN 3-89821-589-X

32 *Laura A. Victoir*
The Russian Land Estate Today
A Case Study of Cultural Politics in Post-Soviet Russia
With a foreword by Priscilla Roosevelt
ISBN 3-89821-426-5

33 *Ivan Katchanovski*
Cleft Countries
Regional Political Divisions and Cultures in Post-Soviet Ukraine and Moldova
With a foreword by Francis Fukuyama
ISBN 3-89821-558-X

34 *Florian Mühlfried*
Postsowjetische Feiern
Das Georgische Bankett im Wandel
Mit einem Vorwort von Kevin Tuite
ISBN 3-89821-601-2

35 *Roger Griffin, Werner Loh, Andreas Umland (Eds.)*
Fascism Past and Present, West and East
An International Debate on Concepts and Cases in the Comparative Study of the Extreme Right
With an afterword by Walter Laqueur
ISBN 3-89821-674-8

36 *Sebastian Schlegel*
Der „Weiße Archipel“
Sowjetische Atomstädte 1945-1991
Mit einem Geleitwort von Thomas Bohn
ISBN 3-89821-679-9

37 *Vyacheslav Likhachev*
Political Anti-Semitism in Post-Soviet Russia
Actors and Ideas in 1991-2003
Edited and translated from Russian by Eugene Veklerov
ISBN 3-89821-529-6

38 *Josette Baer (Ed.)*
Preparing Liberty in Central Europe
Political Texts from the Spring of Nations 1848 to the Spring of Prague 1968
With a foreword by Zdeněk V. David
ISBN 3-89821-546-6

39 *Михаил Лукьянов*
Российский консерватизм и реформа, 1907-1914
С предисловием Марка Д. Стейнберга
ISBN 3-89821-503-2

40 *Nicola Melloni*
Market Without Economy
The 1998 Russian Financial Crisis
With a foreword by Eiji Furukawa
ISBN 3-89821-407-9

41 *Dmitrij Chmelnizki*
Die Architektur Stalins
Bd. 1: Studien zu Ideologie und Stil
Bd. 2: Bilddokumentation
Mit einem Vorwort von Bruno Flierl
ISBN 3-89821-515-6

42 *Katja Yafimava*
Post-Soviet Russian-Belarussian Relationships
The Role of Gas Transit Pipelines
With a foreword by Jonathan P. Stern
ISBN 3-89821-655-1

43 *Boris Chavkin*
Verflechtungen der deutschen und russischen Zeitgeschichte
Aufsätze und Archivfunde zu den Beziehungen Deutschlands und der Sowjetunion von 1917 bis 1991
Ediert von Markus Edlinger sowie mit einem Vorwort versehen von Leonid Luks
ISBN 3-89821-756-6

44 *Anastasija Grynenko in Zusammenarbeit mit Claudia Dathe*
Die Terminologie des Gerichtswesens der Ukraine und Deutschlands im Vergleich
Eine übersetzungswissenschaftliche Analyse juristischer Fachbegriffe im Deutschen, Ukrainischen und Russischen
Mit einem Vorwort von Ulrich Hartmann
ISBN 3-89821-691-8

45 *Anton Burkov*
The Impact of the European Convention on Human Rights on Russian Law
Legislation and Application in 1996-2006
With a foreword by Françoise Hampson
ISBN 978-3-89821-639-5

46 *Stina Torjesen, Indra Overland (Eds.)*
International Election Observers in Post-Soviet Azerbaijan
Geopolitical Pawns or Agents of Change?
ISBN 978-3-89821-743-9

47 *Taras Kuzio*
Ukraine – Crimea – Russia
Triangle of Conflict
ISBN 978-3-89821-761-3

48 *Claudia Šabić*
"Ich erinnere mich nicht, aber L'viv!"
Zur Funktion kultureller Faktoren für die Institutionalisierung und Entwicklung einer ukrainischen Region
Mit einem Vorwort von Melanie Tatur
ISBN 978-3-89821-752-1

49 *Marlies Bilz*
Tatarstan in der Transformation
Nationaler Diskurs und Politische Praxis 1988-1994
Mit einem Vorwort von Frank Golczewski
ISBN 978-3-89821-722-4

50 *Марлен Ларюэль (ред.)*
Современные интерпретации русского национализма
ISBN 978-3-89821-795-8

51 *Sonja Schüler*
Die ethnische Dimension der Armut
Roma im postsozialistischen Rumänien
Mit einem Vorwort von Anton Sterbling
ISBN 978-3-89821-776-7

52 *Галина Кожевникова*
Радикальный национализм в России и противодействие ему
Сборник докладов Центра «Сова» за 2004-2007 гг.
С предисловием Александра Верховского
ISBN 978-3-89821-721-7

53 *Галина Кожевникова и Владимир Прибыловский*
Российская власть в биографиях I
Высшие должностные лица РФ в 2004 г.
ISBN 978-3-89821-796-5

54 *Галина Кожевникова и Владимир Прибыловский*
Российская власть в биографиях II
Члены Правительства РФ в 2004 г.
ISBN 978-3-89821-797-2

55 *Галина Кожевникова и Владимир Прибыловский*
Российская власть в биографиях III
Руководители федеральных служб и агентств РФ в 2004 г.
ISBN 978-3-89821-798-9

56 *Ileana Petroniu*
Privatisierung in Transformationsökonomien
Determinanten der Restrukturierungs-Bereitschaft am Beispiel Polens, Rumäniens und der Ukraine
Mit einem Vorwort von Rainer W. Schäfer
ISBN 978-3-89821-790-3

57 *Christian Wipperfürth*
Russland und seine GUS-Nachbarn
Hintergründe, aktuelle Entwicklungen und Konflikte in einer ressourcenreichen Region
ISBN 978-3-89821-801-6

58 *Togzhan Kassenova*
From Antagonism to Partnership
The Uneasy Path of the U.S.-Russian Cooperative Threat Reduction
With a foreword by Christoph Bluth
ISBN 978-3-89821-707-1

59 *Alexander Höllwerth*
Das sakrale eurasische Imperium des Aleksandr Dugin
Eine Diskursanalyse zum postsowjetischen russischen Rechtsextremismus
Mit einem Vorwort von Dirk Uffelmann
ISBN 978-3-89821-813-9

60 *Олег Рябов*
«Россия-Матушка»
Национализм, гендер и война в России XX века
С предисловием Елены Гощило
ISBN 978-3-89821-487-2

61 *Ivan Maistrenko*
Borot'bism
A Chapter in the History of the Ukrainian Revolution
With a new introduction by Chris Ford
Translated by George S. N. Luckyj with the assistance of Ivan L. Rudnytsky
ISBN 978-3-89821-697-5

62 *Maryna Romanets*
Anamorphosic Texts and Reconfigured Visions
Improvised Traditions in Contemporary Ukrainian and Irish Literature
ISBN 978-3-89821-576-3

63 *Paul D'Anieri and Taras Kuzio (Eds.)*
Aspects of the Orange Revolution I
Democratization and Elections in Post-Communist Ukraine
ISBN 978-3-89821-698-2

64 *Bohdan Harasymiw in collaboration with Oleh S. Ilnytzkyj (Eds.)*
Aspects of the Orange Revolution II
Information and Manipulation Strategies in the 2004 Ukrainian Presidential Elections
ISBN 978-3-89821-699-9

65 *Ingmar Bredies, Andreas Umland and Valentin Yakushik (Eds.)*
Aspects of the Orange Revolution III
The Context and Dynamics of the 2004 Ukrainian Presidential Elections
ISBN 978-3-89821-803-0

66 *Ingmar Bredies, Andreas Umland and Valentin Yakushik (Eds.)*
Aspects of the Orange Revolution IV
Foreign Assistance and Civic Action in the 2004 Ukrainian Presidential Elections
ISBN 978-3-89821-808-5

67 *Ingmar Bredies, Andreas Umland and Valentin Yakushik (Eds.)*
Aspects of the Orange Revolution V
Institutional Observation Reports on the 2004 Ukrainian Presidential Elections
ISBN 978-3-89821-809-2

68 *Taras Kuzio (Ed.)*
Aspects of the Orange Revolution VI
Post-Communist Democratic Revolutions in Comparative Perspective
ISBN 978-3-89821-820-7

69 *Tim Bohse*
Autoritarismus statt Selbstverwaltung
Die Transformation der kommunalen Politik in der Stadt Kaliningrad 1990-2005
Mit einem Geleitwort von Stefan Troebst
ISBN 978-3-89821-782-8

70 *David Rupp*
Die Rußländische Föderation und die russischsprachige Minderheit in Lettland
Eine Fallstudie zur Anwaltspolitik Moskaus gegenüber den russophonen Minderheiten im „Nahen Ausland" von 1991 bis 2002
Mit einem Vorwort von Helmut Wagner
ISBN 978-3-89821-778-1

71 *Taras Kuzio*
Theoretical and Comparative Perspectives on Nationalism
New Directions in Cross-Cultural and Post-Communist Studies
With a foreword by Paul Robert Magocsi
ISBN 978-3-89821-815-3

72 *Christine Teichmann*
Die Hochschultransformation im heutigen Osteuropa
Kontinuität und Wandel bei der Entwicklung des postkommunistischen Universitätswesens
Mit einem Vorwort von Oskar Anweiler
ISBN 978-3-89821-842-9

73 *Julia Kusznir*
Der politische Einfluss von Wirtschaftseliten in russischen Regionen
Eine Analyse am Beispiel der Erdöl- und Erdgasindustrie, 1992-2005
Mit einem Vorwort von Wolfgang Eichwede
ISBN 978-3-89821-821-4

74 *Alena Vysotskaya*
Russland, Belarus und die EU-Osterweiterung
Zur Minderheitenfrage und zum Problem der Freizügigkeit des Personenverkehrs
Mit einem Vorwort von Katlijn Malfliet
ISBN 978-3-89821-822-1

75 *Heiko Pleines (Hrsg.)*
Corporate Governance in post-sozialistischen Volkswirtschaften
ISBN 978-3-89821-766-8

76 *Stefan Ihrig*
Wer sind die Moldawier?
Rumänismus versus Moldowanismus in Historiographie und Schulbüchern der Republik Moldova, 1991-2006
Mit einem Vorwort von Holm Sundhaussen
ISBN 978-3-89821-466-7

77 *Galina Kozhevnikova in collaboration with Alexander Verkhovsky and Eugene Veklerov*
Ultra-Nationalism and Hate Crimes in Contemporary Russia
The 2004-2006 Annual Reports of Moscow's SOVA Center
With a foreword by Stephen D. Shenfield
ISBN 978-3-89821-868-9

78 *Florian Küchler*
The Role of the European Union in Moldova's Transnistria Conflict
With a foreword by Christopher Hill
ISBN 978-3-89821-850-4

79 *Bernd Rechel*
The Long Way Back to Europe
Minority Protection in Bulgaria
With a foreword by Richard Crampton
ISBN 978-3-89821-863-4

80 *Peter W. Rodgers*
Nation, Region and History in Post-Communist Transitions
Identity Politics in Ukraine, 1991-2006
With a foreword by Vera Tolz
ISBN 978-3-89821-903-7

81 *Stephanie Solywoda*
The Life and Work of Semen L. Frank
A Study of Russian Religious Philosophy
With a foreword by Philip Walters
ISBN 978-3-89821-457-5

82 *Vera Sokolova*
Cultural Politics of Ethnicity
Discourses on Roma in Communist Czechoslovakia
ISBN 978-3-89821-822-1

FORTHCOMING (MANUSCRIPT WORKING TITLES)

Margaret Dikovitskaya
Arguing with the Photographs
Russian Imperial Colonial Attitudes in Visual Culture
ISBN 3-89821-462-1

Sergei M. Plekhanov
Russian Nationalism in the Age of Globalization
ISBN 3-89821-484-2

Robert Pyrah
Cultural Memory and Identity
Literature, Criticism and the Theatre in Lviv - Lwow - Lemberg, 1918-1939 and in post-Soviet Ukraine
ISBN 3-89821-505-9

Andrei Rogatchevski
The National-Bolshevik Party
ISBN 3-89821-532-6

Zenon Victor Wasyliw
Soviet Culture in the Ukrainian Village
The Transformation of Everyday Life and Values, 1921-1928
ISBN 3-89821-536-9

Nele Sass
Das gegenkulturelle Milieu im postsowjetischen Russland
ISBN 3-89821-543-1

Julie Elkner
Maternalism versus Militarism
The Russian Soldiers' Mothers Committee
ISBN 3-89821-575-X

Alexandra Kamarowsky
Russia's Post-crisis Growth
ISBN 3-89821-580-6

Martin Friessnegg
Das Problem der Medienfreiheit in Russland seit dem Ende der Sowjetunion
ISBN 3-89821-588-1

Nikolaj Nikiforowitsch Borobow
Führende Persönlichkeiten in Russland vom 12. bis 20. Jhd.: Ein Lexikon
Aus dem Russischen übersetzt und herausgegeben von Eberhard Schneider
ISBN 3-89821-638-1

Martin Malek, Anna Schor-Tschudnowskaja
Tschetschenien und die Gleichgültigkeit Europas
Russlands Kriege und die Agonie der Idee der Menschenrechte
ISBN 3-89821-676-4

Andreas Langenohl
Political Culture and Criticism of Society
Intellectual Articulations in Post-Soviet Russia
ISBN 3-89821-709-4

Thomas Borén
Meeting Places in Transformation
ISBN 3-89821-739-6

Lars Löckner
Sowjetrussland in der Beurteilung der Emigrantenzeitung 'Rul', 1920-1924
ISBN 3-89821-741-8

Ekaterina Taratuta
The Red Line of Construction
Semantics and Mythology of a Siberian Heliopolis
ISBN 3-89821-742-6

Bernd Kappenberg
Zeichen setzen für Europa
Der Gebrauch europäischer lateinischer Sonderzeichen in der deutschen Öffentlichkeit
ISBN 3-89821-749-3

Siegbert Klee, Martin Sandhop, Oxana Schwajka, Andreas Umland
Elitenbildung in der Postsowjetischen Ukraine
ISBN 978-389821-829-0

Natalya Ketenci
The effect of location on the performance of Kazakhstani industrial enterprises in the transition period
ISBN 978-389821-831-3

Quotes from reviews of SPPS volumes:

On vol. 1 – *The Implementation of the ECHR in Russia*: "Full of examples, experiences and valuable observations which could provide the basis for new strategies."

Diana Schmidt, *Неприкосновенный запас*, 2005

On vol. 2 – *Putins Russland*: "Wipperfürth draws attention to little known facts. For instance, the Russians have still more positive feelings towards Germany than to any other non-Slavic country."

Oldag Kaspar, *Süddeutsche Zeitung, 2005*

On vol. 3 – *Die Übernahme internationalen Rechts in die russische Rechtsordnung*: "Hussner's is an interesting, detailed and, at the same time, focused study which deals with all relevant aspects and contains insights into contemporary Russian legal thought."

Herbert Küpper, *Jahrbuch für Ostrecht, 2005*

On vol. 5 – *Квадратные метры, определяющие сознание*: „Meerovich provides a study that will be of considerable value to housing specialists and policy analysts."

Christina Varga-Harris, *Slavic Review*, 2006

On vol. 6 – *New Directions in Russian International Studies*: "A helpful step in the direction of an overdue dialogue between Western and Russian IR scholarly communities."

Diana Schmidt, *Europe-Asia Studies*, 2006

On vol. 8 – *Nation-Building and Minority Politics in Post-Socialist States:* "Galbreath's book is an admirable and craftsmanlike piece of work, and should be read by all specialists interested in the Baltic area."

Andrejs Plakans, *Slavic Review*, 2007

On vol. 9 – *Народы Кавказа в Вооружённых силах СССР:* "In this superb new book, Bezugolnyi skillfully fashions an accurate and candid record of how and why the Soviet Union mobilized and employed the various ethnic groups in the Caucasus region in the Red Army's World War II effort."

David J. Glantz, *Journal of Slavic Military Studies*, 2006

On vol. 10 – *Русское Национальное Единство*: "Pribylovskii's and Likhachev's work is likely to remain the definitive study of the Russian National Unity for a very long time."

Mischa Gabowitsch, *e-Extreme*, 2006

On vol. 13 – *The Politicization of Russian Orthodoxy*: "Mitrofanova's book is a fascinating study which raises important questions about the type of national ideology that will come to predominate in the new Russia."

Zoe Knox, *Europe-Asia Studies, 2006*

On vol. 14 – *Aleksandr Solzhenitsyn and the Modern Russo-Jewish Question*: "Larson has written a well-balanced survey of Solzhenitsyn's writings on Russian-Jewish relations."

Nikolai Butkevich, *e-Extreme*, 2006

On vol. 16 – *Der russische Sonderweg?:* "Luks's remarkable knowledge of the history of this wide territory from the Elbe to the Pacific Ocean and his life experience give his observations a particular sharpness and his judgements an exceptional weight."

Peter Krupnikow, *Mitteilungen aus dem baltischen Leben*, 2006

On vol. 17 – *История «Мёртвой воды»*: "Moroz provides one of the best available surveys of Russian neo-paganism."

Mischa Gabowitsch, *e-Extreme*, 2006

On vol. 18 – *Этническая и религиозная интолерантность в российских СМИ*: "A constructive contribution to a crucial debate about media-endorsed intolerance which has once again flared up in Russia."

Mischa Gabowitsch, *e-Extreme*, 2006

On vol. 25 – *The Ghosts in Our Classroom*: "Freyberg-Inan's well-researched and incisive monograph, balanced and informed about Romanian education in general, should be required reading for those Eurocrats who have shaped Romanian spending priorities since 2000."

Tom Gallagher, *Slavic Review*, 2006

On vol. 26 – *The 2002 Dubrovka and 2004 Beslan Hostage Crises:* "Dunlop's analysis will help to draw Western attention to the plight of those who have suffered by these terrorist acts, and the importance, for all Russians, of uncovering the truth of about what happened."

Amy Knight, *Times Literary Supplement*, 2006

On vol. 29 – *Zivilgesellschaftliche Einflüsse auf die Orange Revolution*: „Strasser's study constitutes an outstanding empirical analysis and well-grounded location of the subject within theory."

Heiko Pleines, *Osteuropa*, 2006

On vol. 34 – *Postsowjetische Feiern*: "Mühlfried's book contains not only a solid ethnographic study, but also points at some problems emerging from Georgia's prevalent understanding of culture."

Godula Kosack, *Anthropos*, 2007

On vol. 35 – *Fascism Past and Present, West and East*: "Committed students will find much of interest in these sometimes barbed exchanges."

Robert Paxton, *Journal of Global History*, 2007

On vol. 37 – *Political Anti-Semitism in Post-Soviet Russia*: "Likhachev's book serves as a reliable compendium and a good starting point for future research on post-Soviet xenophobia and ultra-nationalist politics, with their accompanying anti-Semitism."

Kathleen Mikkelson, *Demokratizatsiya*, 2007

Series Subscription

Please enter my subscription to the series *Soviet and Post-Soviet Politics and Society*, ISSN 1614-3515, as follows:

❒ complete series OR ❒ English-language titles
❒ German-language titles
❒ Russian-language titles

starting with

❒ volume # 1

❒ volume # ___

❒ please also include the following volumes: #___, ___, ___, ___, ___, ___, ___

❒ the next volume being published

❒ please also include the following volumes: #___, ___, ___, ___, ___, ___, ___

❒ 1 copy per volume OR ❒ ___ copies per volume

Subscription within Germany:

You will receive every volume at 1st publication at the regular bookseller's price – incl. s & h and VAT.

Payment:

❒ Please bill me for every volume.

❒ Lastschriftverfahren: Ich/wir ermächtige(n) Sie hiermit widerruflich, den Rechnungsbetrag je Band von meinem/unserem folgendem Konto einzuziehen.

Kontoinhaber: ______________________ Kreditinstitut: ______________________

Kontonummer: ______________________ Bankleitzahl: ______________________

International Subscription:

Payment (incl. s & h and VAT) in advance for

❒ 10 volumes/copies (€ 319.80) ❒ 20 volumes/copies (€ 599.80)

❒ 40 volumes/copies (€ 1,099.80)

Please send my books to:

NAME ______________________ DEPARTMENT ______________________

ADDRESS ____

POST/ZIP CODE ______________________ COUNTRY ______________________

TELEPHONE ______________________ EMAIL ______________________

date/signature ____

A hint for librarians in the former Soviet Union: Your academic library might be eligible to receive free-of-cost scholarly literature from Germany via the German Research Foundation. For Russian-language information on this program, see http://www.dfg.de/forschungsfoerderung/formulare/download/12_54.pdf.

Please fax to: **0511 / 262 2201 (+49 511 262 2201)**
or mail to: *ibidem*-Verlag, Julius-Leber-Weg 11, D-30457 Hannover,Germany
or send an e-mail: ibidem@ibidem-verlag.de

***ibidem*-Verlag**
Melchiorstr. 15
D-70439 Stuttgart

info@ibidem-verlag.de

www.ibidem-verlag.de
www.edition-noema.de
www.autorenbetreuung.de

www.ingramcontent.com/pod-product-compliance
Lightning Source LLC
Chambersburg PA
CBHW060147280326
41932CB00012B/1674